Administrative Law

by

MICHAEL ASIMOW

Visiting Professor of Law, Stanford Law School
Professor of Law Emeritus
University of California, Los Angeles

RICHARD MURPHY

Professor of Law
Texas Tech University

Fifteenth Edition

The publisher is not engaged in rendering legal or other professional advice, and this publication is not a substitute for the advice of an attorney. If you require legal or other expert advice, you should seek the services of a competent attorney or other professional.

Gilbert Law Summaries is a trademark registered in the U.S. Patent and Trademark Office

© 2008 Thomson/West
© 2014 LEG, Inc. d/b/a West Academic
  444 Cedar Street, Suite 700
  St. Paul, MN 55101
  1-877-888-1330

West, West Academic Publishing, and West Academic are trademarks of West Publishing Corporation, used under license.

Printed in the United States of America

ISBN: 978-1-62810-109-6

Summary of Contents

TEXT CORRELATION CHART V

GILBERT EXAM STRATEGIES XXIX

Chapter One. Separation of Powers and Control of Agencies 1
    A.   Separation of Powers 3
    B.   Nondelegation Doctrine (Legislative Power) 4
    C.   Nondelegation Doctrine (Judicial Power) 11
    D.   Executive Controls Over Administrative Action 15
    E.   Legislative Controls Over Administrative Action 21

Chapter Two. The Due Process Right to a Hearing 25
    A.   Interests Protected by Due Process—"Liberty" and "Property" 26
    B.   Timing of the Hearing 33
    C.   Elements of the Hearing 36
    D.   Issues That Do Not Require a Hearing for Resolution 39
    E.   The State Action Requirement for Triggering Due Process 42

Chapter Three. Adjudicative Procedures 45
    A.   Overview of the APA's Procedural Template 46
    B.   A Summary of APA Requirements for Formal Adjudication 50
    C.   Triggering Formal Adjudication Under the APA 50
    D.   Agency Adjudicators 53
    E.   Prehearing Process for Formal Adjudication 53
    F.   The Process of Proof at the Hearing for a Formal Adjudication 56
    G.   Agency Decisions and Explanations 62
    H.   Procedures for Informal Adjudication 66
    I.   Declaratory Orders 67
    J.   Agency Adjudication and Retroactivity 68
    K.   Choosing Between Adjudication and Rulemaking to Develop Policy 70

Chapter Four. Adjudicative Integrity 73
    A.   Constitutional Combination and Statutory Separation of Functions 74
    B.   Controlling Other Forms of Bias 78
    C.   Legislative Pressure on Agency Adjudicators 81
    D.   Ex Parte Communications 82
    E.   Decisionmaker Familiarity with the Case 84
    F.   Consistency Across Cases 86

Chapter Five. Rulemaking Procedures 91
    A.   Introduction 93
    B.   Legal Effect of Rules—The Legislative/Nonlegislative Distinction 99
    C.   The Notice-and-Comment Rulemaking Process 102
    D.   Exceptions to Notice-and-Comment Rulemaking Requirements 109
    E.   Impartiality of Rulemakers 116
    F.   The Rulemaking Record 118

Chapter Six. Obtaining Information and Attorney's Fees 121
    A. Agency Acquisition of Information 123
    B. Constitutional Protection from Agency Information Gathering 126
    C. Freedom of Information Act 129
    D. Government in the Sunshine Act 140
    E. Attorney's Fees 141

Chapter Seven. Scope of Judicial Review 143
    A. Introduction 145
    B. Scope of Review of Questions of Fact 146
    C. Scope of Review of Legal Interpretations 150
    D. Scope of Review of Application of Law to Fact (a/k/a "Mixed Questions") 160
    E. Scope of Review of Exercises of Discretion 162

Chapter Eight. Access to the Courts: Types of Review, Immunities, Tort Liability, Reviewability 169
    A. Types of "Review" Available 171
    B. Sovereign Immunity 176
    C. Tort Liability of Government 178
    D. Tort Liability of Government Officials 181
    E. Statutory Preclusion of Judicial Review 185
    F. Commitment to Agency Discretion 187
    G. Threshold Requirements of "Agency Action" by an "Agency" 189

Chapter Nine. Access to the Courts: Standing and Timing 193
    A. Standing to Seek Judicial Review in Federal Court 195
    B. The Timing of Judicial Review 208

REVIEW QUESTIONS AND ANSWERS 225

EXAM QUESTIONS AND ANSWERS 267

TABLE OF CASES 289

TABLE OF STATUTES 295

INDEX 297

Text Correlation Chart

Gilbert Law Summary ADMINISTRATIVE LAW	Asimow, Levin *State and Federal Administrative Law* 2014 (4th ed.)	Hickman, Pierce *Federal Administrative Law* (2010)	Funk, Shapiro, Weaver *Administrative Law & Procedure* 2014 (5th ed.)	Lawson *Federal Administrative Law* 2013 (6th ed.)	Strauss, Rakoff, Farina, Metzger *Gellhorn and Byse's Administrative Law* 2011 (11th ed.)
I. SEPARATION OF POWERS AND CONTROLS OVER AGENCIES					
A. Separation of Powers	429–430	13–14	543–546	41–59	548–761
B. Nondelegation Doctrine (Legislative Power)	430–459	24–74	546–559	59–114, 131–140	580–630
C. Nondelegation Doctrine (Judicial Power)	460–469	74–106	560–575	217–243	631–650
D. Executive Controls Over Administrative Action	496–552	141–224	585–633	140–215	685–761
E. Legislative Controls Over Administrative Action	469–496	106–139	576–584	114–131	651–685
II. THE DUE PROCESS RIGHT TO A HEARING					
A. Interests Protected by Due Process—Liberty and Property	26–44	234–262	244–257	805–806, 818–894	766–826
B. Timing of the Hearing	44–54	275–276	258–273	810–818, 900–935	826–899
C. Elements of the Hearing	54–65	262–292	258–273	895-935	826-881

D. Issues Requiring a Hearing—The Rulemaking-Adjudication Distinction	65–72	225–234	240–244	14–22, 895	35–50, 765
E. The State Action Requirement				805	900–924
III. ADJUDICATIVE PROCEDURES					
A. Overview of the APA's Procedural Template	3–5		26–36	256–263	50–65
B. Summary of APA Requirements for Formal Adjudication			196–207	250–253, 259–263	267–278, 278–286
C. Triggering Formal Adjudication Under the APA	74–93	293–300	192–196	288–306	269–278
D. Agency Adjudicators	144–157	293, 316–323	199–201	250–253	308–332
E. Prehearing Process for Formal Adjudication	159–179		196–199	259–260, 288–306	261–269, 382–384, 297–307
F. The Process of Proof at the Hearing for a Formal Adjudication	179–195		202-206	259–260, 288–306	60–61, 280–97
G. Agency Decisions and Explanations	195–203		204		283–286, 377–378, 394–395
H. Procedures for Informal Adjudication	74, 80, 145	300–307	191	261–262, 413–426	372–382
I. Declaratory Orders	226				
J. Agency Adjudication and Retroactivity	218–220, 405	387	319–327	453–456	406–420
K. Choosing Between Adjudication and Rulemaking to Develop Policy	229–236, 398–409	370–386	313–339	426–456	385–434

IV. ADJUDICATIVE INTEGRITY					
A. Constitutional Combination and Statutory Separation of Functions	124–137	307–316	30–31, 201–202, 274–278	243–253	312–314, 330–331, 338–340, 354–358
B. Controlling Other Forms of Bias	137–144	313–315, 444–450	274–278	253–255	314–317, 333–342
C. Legislative Pressure on Agency Adjudicators	119–124	114–120			362–365, 676
D. Ex Parte Communications	108–119		204–205, 220–239		342–371
E. Decisionmaker Familiarity with the Case	100–108	430			320–332
F. Consistency Across Cases	203–228	343–344			928–938
V. RULEMAKING PROCEDURES					
A. Introduction	229–250	345–355, 381–389	23–24, 27–30, 51–54, 62–63, 67–68, 73–76, 90–91, 97–99, 111–113, 128–133	259–263, 306–308	110–119
B. Legal Effect of Rules—Legislative/Nonlegislative Distinction	241–242, 378–380	345–346, 462–480	328–329, 339–342	375–378	119, 132, 178–190, 197–199
C. The Notice-and-Comment Process	246–331	394–444	62–73, 97–128	306–365	119–165
D. Exceptions to Notice-and-Comment Rulemaking Requirements	363–398	455–480	73–90, 313, 339–84	365–413	165–202
E. Impartiality of Rulemakers	288–314	444–455		255, 315	242–258, 342–371
F. The Rulemaking Record	322, 661–662		164–166	759–763	158

VI. OBTAINING INFORMATION AND ATTORNEY'S FEES					
A. Agency Acquisition of Information	8		647–738		77–108
B. Constitutional Protection from Agency Information Gathering			649–698, 706–728		81–108
C. Freedom of Information Act	553–572		740–783	2	456–517
D. Government in the Sunshine Act	572–581		803–808		518–525
E. Attorney's Fees			809–853		870–871
VII. SCOPE OF JUDICIAL REVIEW					
A. Introduction		323–324, 337, 343–344, 480–482, 518–519	26–27, 145–146, 278	457–464	926–927
B. Scope of Review of Questions of Fact	581–600, 681–691	323–343	162–187, 278–304	464–501	938–964
C. Scope of Review of Agency Legal Interpretations	600–655	518–662	146–162, 294–304, 384–406	501–696	964–976, 1014–1159
D. Scope of Review of Application of Law to Fact	605	519–531	294–304	508–527	964–971
E. Scope of Review of Agency Exercises of Discretion	655–689	343–344, 480–512	162–187, 304–311	697–801	976–1013, 1132–89
VIII. ACCESS TO THE COURTS: TYPES OF REVIEW, IMMUNIITES, TORT LIABILITY, REVIEWABILITY					
A. "Types" of Review Available	692–698	663–664	32–33, 408, 489–490	936–954	1192–1203
B. Sovereign Immunity	694, 698–702	663–664		936–954	1192–1205
C. Tort Liability of Government	698–705			936–954	1198, 1202–1205

D. Tort Liability of Government Officials	702–705	803–811		936–954	1199–1203
E. Statutory Preclusion of Judicial Review	710–717	664–679	454–462	955–972	1308–1327
F. Commitment to Agency Discretion	717–729	679–720	463–479	972–989	978–980, 1327–1347
G. Threshold Requirements of "Agency Action" by an "Agency"	729–736	779	479–489	1–5	
IX. ACCESS TO THE COURTS: STANDING AND TIMING					
A. Standing to Seek Judicial Review	737–761	781–844	411–454, 489–503	989–1053	1207–1302
B. Timing of Judicial Review	761–801	727–781	503–542	1053–1117	1347–1381

Capsule Summary

TEXT CORRELATION CHART V

GILBERT EXAM STRATEGIES XXIX

Chapter One. Separation of Powers and Control of Agencies 1
- **A. Separation of Powers** 3
  1. In General 3
  2. Judicial Enforcement of Separation of Powers 3
  3. Formalism vs. Functionalism 3
  4. Checks and Balances 4
- **B. Nondelegation Doctrine (Legislative Power)** 4
  1. Introduction to the Nondelegation Doctrine 4
  2. Nondelegation Doctrine—Evolution of the Case Law 4
     - a. Early Cases—Formulas to Legitimate Delegation 4
       - (1) Ascertainment of Facts 4
       - (2) Filling in Details 5
       - (3) Finding an "Intelligible Principle" 5
     - b. The National Industrial Recovery Act Cases—The 1935 Anomaly 5
       - (1) Background 5
         - (a) Comment 5
       - (2) *Panama Refining:* The "Hot Oil" Case 5
         - (a) Dissenting Argument 5
       - (3) The *Schechter Poultry* Case 6
         - (a) Rationale 6
     - c. Post-NIRA Cases from the Twentieth Century 6
       - (1) Public Interest 6
       - (2) Fair Prices 6
       - (3) No Standards 6
       - (4) Economic Stabilization 7
         - (a) The *Meat Cutters* Case 7
     - d. The Nondelegation Doctrine Today—*Whitman v. American Trucking Associations* 7
       - (1) The D.C. Circuit Tries the *Meat Cutters* Suggestion 7
       - (2) The Supreme Court Rejects That Suggestion 8
         - (a) Rationale for Refusing to Find a Violation 8
     - e. Dissents Advocating Revival of the Nondelegation Doctrine 8
     - f. Delegations to Federal Judges 8
     - g. Delegations to Private Parties 9
       - (1) State Cases 9
       - (2) Federal Cases 9
  3. **Nondelegation and the Canon of Constitutional Avoidance** 9
     - a. Constitutional Avoidance and OSHA 9
     - b. An Example from the States 10
     - c. Deploying the Canon to Avoid Other Constitutional Issues 10
- **C. Nondelegation Doctrine (Judicial Power)** 11
  1. Introduction 11
  2. **The *Schor* Framework for Determining Article III Violations** 11
     - a. Essential Attributes of Judicial Power 11
     - b. Origins and Importance of the Right—The Public/Private Rights Distinction 12
       - (1) Private Disputes over Public Rights 12
       - (2) Significance of the Public/Private Distinction 12
       - (3) Two Paths Through the Thicket 13

			(4) State Courts and the Public/Private Right Distinction 13
		c.	Concerns That Drove Congress 13
		d.	Consent of the Parties 13
		e.	Questions About *Schor* Raised by Stern 13
	3.	**An Older, Overlapping Framework—Non-Article III "Adjuncts"** **14**
	4.	**Administrative Authority to Adjudicate Penalties** **14**
		a.	Criminal Sanctions 14
			(1) Agency May Not Imprison 14
			(a) Exceptions 14
		b.	Civil Penalties 14
			(1) Importance of "Civil" vs. "Criminal" Penalty Distinction 14
			(a) Double Jeopardy 15
			(b) Jury Trial 15
			(2) Punitive Damages 15
D.	**Executive Controls Over Administrative Action** **15**
	1.	**Appointment Power** **15**
		a.	"Officers of the United States" 15
			(1) There are also Officers of Congress 15
			(2) Employees 16
		b.	Appointment of "Inferior" Officers 16
			(1) Who Are You Calling "Inferior"? 16
			(2) Court Martial Judges 16
			(3) Independent Counsel 16
			(4) Public Company Accounting Oversight Board Members 16
		c.	Recess Appointments 17
			(1) The D.C. Circuit on Recess Appointments in 2013 17
	2.	**Removal Power** **18**
		a.	Clash of Titans: Unitary Executive vs. Independent Agencies 18
		b.	Evolution of the Constitutional Law of Independent Agencies 18
			(1) 1926: The President Must Have Plenary Removal Power over Executive Officials 18
			(2) 1935: Quasi-Legislative/Quasi-Judicial Independent Agencies 18
			(3) 1988: Don't Interfere with the President Too Much 18
			(4) 2010: Double For-Cause Limits Interfere Too Much 19
			(5) Sidebar on Legislative Courts 19
		c.	No Congressional Removal (Other than by Impeachment) 19
	3.	**Fiscal Power** **19**
	4.	**Organizational Power** **19**
	5.	**Centralized Review of Rulemaking** **20**
	6.	**Direction of Agency Heads** **20**
	7.	**Inspectors General** **20**
	8.	**Ombudsman** **20**
	9.	**Gubernatorial Veto of Rules** **20**
E.	**Legislative Controls Over Administrative Action** **21**
	1.	**Introduction** **21**
	2.	**Standing Committees** **21**
	3.	**Review Committees** **21**
	4.	**Investigations** **21**
	5.	**Appropriations** **21**
	6.	**Appointments** **21**
	7.	**Legislative Veto—A Power Congress Used to Have** **21**
		a.	Congressional Vetoes 21
		b.	State Legislative Vetoes 22
		c.	Congressional Review Act 22
	8.	**Presidential Line Item Vetoes** **22**
	9.	**Miscellaneous Controls** **22**

Chapter Two. The Due Process Right to a Hearing 25
    A.   **Interests Protected by Due Process—"Liberty" and "Property"** 26
        1.   **Procedural Due Process** 26
            a.   Purposes of Procedural Due Process 27
            b.   Distinguish—Substantive Due Process 27
        2.   **"Liberty"** 27
            a.   Imposition of "Stigma-Plus" 27
                (1)   Public and Allegedly False Information 27
                (2)   The "Plus" Part of "Stigma-Plus" 27
            b.   Deprivation of Constitutional Rights 28
            c.   Deportation of Aliens 28
            d.   The Liberty Interest in Prison After Criminal Conviction 28
                (1)   Liberty Interests Protected in Prison Independent of State Regulation 29
                (2)   Liberty Interests in Prison Created by State Laws or Policies 29
                      (a)   Early Release Cases and the "Entitlement" Approach to Finding a Liberty Interest 29
                      (b)   *Sandin*'s Stricter Approach to the Liberty Interest 29
            e.   Expulsion or Suspension from School 30
                (1)   Expulsion from College 30
                (2)   Academic Dismissals 30
                (3)   High School Suspensions 30
        3.   **"Property"—Old and New** 30
            a.   Welfare 30
                (1)   Post-*Goldberg* Approach 31
            b.   Government Employment 31
                (1)   Constrained Discretion Creates "New Property" 31
                (2)   De Facto Tenure 31
                (3)   State Law 31
                (4)   Limited Power of State to Prescribe Procedure 32
            c.   Utility Service 32
            d.   Licenses 32
            e.   Domestic Violence Restraining Orders 33
            f.   Applications for Benefits 33
        4.   **Deprivation** 33
            a.   Indirect Deprivations 33
    B.   **Timing of the Hearing** 33
        1.   **General Rule** 33
        2.   **Emergency Exception** 34
        3.   **Balancing Test** 34
            a.   Factors 34
        4.   **Application of the Balancing Test of *Mathews*** 34
            a.   The Pre-*Mathews* Regime: Welfare Benefits in *Goldberg* 34
            b.   Social Security Disability Benefits in *Mathews* 34
                (1)   Private Interest 34
                (2)   Risk of Error 34
                (3)   Government Interest 34
            c.   Employment Discharge 35
                (1)   Probable Cause Procedure 35
                (2)   Suspension Without Pay in Emergency 35
            d.   Licenses 35
                (1)   Unsafe Driver 35
                (2)   Professional License 35
            e.   Creditors' Remedies 35
                (1)   Absolute Rule 35
                (2)   Judicial Determination 36
                (3)   Exigent Circumstances 36
    C.   **Elements of the Hearing** 36
        1.   **Same *Mathews* Balancing Test** 36

		2.	**Elements of Due Process** **36**
			a. Notice 36
			(1) *Mathews* Not Applied to Notice for Civil Actions 37
			(2) Fair Warning of What the Law Requires 37
			b. Oral Testimony and Confrontation of Witnesses 37
			c. Impartial Decisionmaker 37
			d. Findings and Reasons 38
			e. Right to Counsel 38
			(1) Counsel at the Party's Expense 38
			(2) Appointed Counsel 38
			f. State Law Judicial Remedies as Sufficient Due Process 39
	D.	**Issues That Do Not Require a Hearing for Resolution** **39**
		1.	**Procedural Due Process Does Not Apply to "Rulemaking"** **39**
			a. The *Due Process* Distinction Between Rulemaking and Adjudication 39
			b. Due Process Does Not Require a Hearing to Resolve Legislative Facts 40
			c. Due Process May Require a Hearing to Resolve Adjudicative Facts 40
			d. Application of Rulemaking—Adjudication Distinction 40
			(1) Traditional Leading Cases—*Londoner*/*Bi-Metallic* 40
			(a) An Adjudication—*Londoner* 40
			(b) A Rulemaking—*Bi-Metallic* 40
			(2) Modern Applications 40
		2.	**Immaterial Issues** **41**
		3.	**Issues Conclusively Determined by Agency Rule** **41**
			a. A Few Examples 41
			b. Waivers 42
		4.	**Administrative "Summary Judgment"** **42**
	E.	**The State Action Requirement for Triggering Due Process** **42**
		1.	**Due Process and the State Action Requirement** **42**
		2.	**Distinguishing State and Non-State Action—Fair Attribution Test** **42**

Chapter Three. Adjudicative Procedures **45**
	A.	**Overview of the APA's Procedural Template** **46**
		1.	**The APA's Four Basic Procedural Types** **46**
			a. Formal Adjudication 47
			b. Informal Adjudication 47
			c. Formal Rulemaking 47
			d. Informal Rulemaking 47
		2.	**The APA's Clumsy Rulemaking/Adjudication Distinction** **47**
			a. "Adjudication" 48
			b. The Oddest Part of the APA's Definition of "Rulemaking" 48
			c. Distinguish the *Constitutional* Dichotomy Between Rulemaking and Adjudication from the APA's 48
			(1) Due Process Can Apply to a Statutory Rulemaking 48
		3.	**Other Sources of Law That Might Alter or Supplement APA Procedures** **49**
			a. Due Process 49
			b. Agency Enabling Acts 49
			c. Agency Rules 49
	B.	**A Summary of APA Requirements for Formal Adjudication** **50**
	C.	**Triggering Formal Adjudication Under the APA** **50**
		1.	**Agency Enabling Acts Pull the Trigger** **50**
		2.	**Courts Do Not Take a "Magic Words" Approach to the Trigger** **51**
			a. But Courts Do Take Something Close to a "Magic Words" Approach to Triggering Formal *Rulemaking* 51
		3.	**Three Circuit Court Approaches to the Formal Adjudication Trigger** **51**
			a. *Chevron* Deference to the Agency's Interpretation 51
			(1) Did "After Public Hearing" Pull the Trigger? 51
			(2) Application of *Chevron* Deference 51

		b.	Presumption of Formality for Statutory Hearings Subject to Judicial Review 52
			(1) The *Seacoast* Presumption That the First Circuit Abandoned 52
			(2) But That Some Courts Still Follow 52
		c.	Presumption of Informality Absent the "Magic Words" 52
			(1) The *City of West Chicago* Approach 52
			(2) Facts from *City of West Chicago* 52
	4.	**Two State Approaches to the Trigger Problem** 52	
D.	**Agency Adjudicators** 53		
	1.	**Formal Adjudication: ALJ or Agency Head** 53	
	2.	**Non-APA Cases** 53	
E.	**Prehearing Process for Formal Adjudication** 53		
	1.	**Notice** 53	
	2.	**Parties and Intervention** 54	
		a.	Purpose of Intervention 54
		b.	Discretion 54
		c.	Relation Between Intervention and Standing 54
	3.	**Discovery** 54	
		a.	Subpoena Power 55
		b.	Freedom of Information Act 55
	4.	**Settlement and Alternative Dispute Resolution** 55	
		a.	APA Amendments 55
		b.	ADR Techniques 55
		c.	When ADR Is Used 55
F.	**The Process of Proof at the Hearing for a Formal Adjudication** 56		
	1.	**Burden of Proof** 56	
		a.	Placement of Burden 56
			(1) Burden of Persuasion 56
			(2) Proving an Exception 56
		b.	Standard of Proof 56
	2.	**Evidentiary Rules for Administrative Proceedings** 57	
		a.	Admissibility of Evidence 57
		b.	Reliance on Hearsay Alone 57
			(1) State Courts—Conflict over the "Residuum Rule" 57
			(a) Illustration 57
			(2) Federal Rejection of Residuum Rule 57
			(a) Potential Weakness of *Perales* 57
			(3) Unreliable Hearsay Doesn't Constitute Substantial Evidence with or Without a Residuum Rule 58
			(4) Reliance on Hearsay Alone Can Violate Due Process 58
	3.	**Exclusive Record Principle** 58	
		a.	Physical Inspections 58
		b.	Assistance to Adjudicators 58
		c.	Official Notice 59
			(1) Opportunity to Contradict 59
			(a) Criteria for Rebuttal 59
			(b) Timing of the Opportunity to Rebut 59
		d.	Use of Expertise in Evaluating Evidence 60
			(1) Matters of Prediction 60
			(2) Limitation—Conjecture 60
			(3) Limitation—Lack of Reasons 60
			(4) Case-by-Case Review of Agency Invocation of "Expertise" 60
	4.	**Right of Cross-Examination** 61	
		a.	The APA's General Provision 61
		b.	An APA Carve-Out 61
G.	**Agency Decisions and Explanations** 62		
	1.	**Types of Decisions for Formal Adjudication** 62	
		a.	Initial Decision 62
			(1) Note—Agency Control over ALJ Initial Decisions 62

| | | b. | Recommended Decision ....62 |
| | | c. | Tentative Decision ....62 |

    2. Statutory Duty to Explain Decisions in Formal Adjudication 62
        a. Party Must Have Opportunity to Submit Own Findings 63
        b. Adoption of ALJ Decisions by Agency Heads 63
    3. Other Sources of a Duty to Explain Adjudicatory Decisions 63
        a. Section 555 of the APA 63
        b. Agency Enabling Acts or Procedural Rules 63
        c. Due Process..63
    4. Purposes for Explaining 63
    5. Courts Will Not Supply Explanations 64

H. Procedures for Informal Adjudication 66
    1. Gap in APA Coverage 66
        a. APA Provisions..66
            (1) Right to Counsel; Right to Appear 66
            (2) Timely Conclusion 66
            (3) Explanation of Denial...66
            (4) Enforcement of Subpoenas...66
            (5) Licensing Provisions 66
    2. Filling the Gap with Due Process 67
    3. Filling the Gap with Another Statute 67
    4. Filling the Gap with Procedural Regulations 67
    5. Courts Don't Get to Fill the Gap 67

I. Declaratory Orders 67
    1. Introduction 67
    2. APA Provisions 67
    3. Broad Power...67
        a. Implied Power 67
    4. Judicial Review 68

J. Agency Adjudication and Retroactivity 68
    1. Overview of the Problem...68
    2. *Wyman-Gordon* Sort of Bars Prospective Adjudication 68
        a. One Majority Rejected Prospective Adjudication..68
        b. A Different Majority Upheld the Agency's Order Anyway..68
        c. Dissenting Opinion 69
    3. Retroactive Application of Agency Adjudications 69
        a. The (Very) General Rule from *Chenery II*..69
        b. More Factors to Apply 69

K. Choosing Between Adjudication and Rulemaking to Develop Policy 70
    1. The Basic Rule—Broad Agency Discretion 70
    2. Factors That Favor Use of Adjudication 70
    3. Judicial Review for Abuse of Discretion 70
        a. Application—*Chenery II*..71
        b. Application—*Bell Aerospace*...71
        c. Application—*Ford Motor Co.*—A Rare Agency Loss 71
    4. Another Approach—Required Rulemaking 71
        a. Duty to Adopt Rules—*Oregon* 71
        b. 1981 Model Act Approach...72
            (1) Preference for Rulemaking over Adjudication 72
            (2) Replacement of Adjudicatory Law with Rules...72

Chapter Four. Adjudicative Integrity..73
A. Constitutional Combination and Statutory Separation of Functions 74
    1. Overview of the Problem...74
    2. Agencies Can Combine Functions Consistent with Due Process..75
        a. But Combination at Lower Levels Might Violate Due Process 75
        b. The Split-Enforcement Model..75

			(1) Judicial Deference Where the Split Agencies Disagree 75

- 3. **Statutory Separation of Functions for Formal Adjudication 76**
  - a. Adjudicators May Not Work for Prosecutors..76
  - b. Adversaries May Not Adjudicate 76
  - c. APA Exceptions Allowing Combination of Functions 76
  - d. More on the "Agency Heads" Exception 77
    - (1) Scope of Exception for Agency Heads...77
    - (2) Advisers and Agency Heads...77
- 4. **Additional Statutory Protections for ALJ Independence 77**
  - a. In-House ALJs in the Federal System..77
    - (1) Agency Power to Guide ALJs via General Policies 78
  - b. Central Panel Alternative for Protecting ALJ Independence 78

B. **Controlling Other Forms of Bias..78**
  1. **Proscribed Forms of Bias..78**
  2. **Prejudgment of the Facts..78**
      - a. Public Statements Concerning Adjudicative Facts 78
      - b. Legislative Facts, Law, or Policy 79
      - c. Contacts with Facts Arising While Decisionmaker Is in Role 79
  3. **Financial Bias...79**
      - a. Institutional Interest 79
        - (1) Prosecutors Distinguished 80
      - b. Professional Interest—Licenses 80
        - (1) Optometry Cases 80
  4. **Animus Toward a Party..80**
      - a. Conduct at Hearing 80
  5. **The Rule of Necessity 80**
  6. **APA Provision on Bias 81**
      - a. Timing...81

C. **Legislative Pressure on Agency Adjudicators 81**
  1. **Illustration—*Pillsbury* Case 81**
  2. **Narrow Application of *Pillsbury*...81**
  3. **Causing Consideration of Irrelevant Factors 81**

D. **Ex Parte Communications 82**
  1. **Limits on Ex Parte Contacts in Formal Proceedings, APA § 557(d)................82**
      - a. "Interested Person" 82
      - b. Outside the Agency but Inside the Government 82
        - (1) Distinguish—Informal Rulemaking 82
      - c. "Ex Parte Communication"...82
      - d. Relevant to the Merits 83
      - e. Effect of Ex Parte Contact 83
      - f. Judicial Review...83
      - g. Reciprocal Prohibition for Agency Employees 83
  2. **Additional Limits on Ex Parte Contacts in Formal Adjudication, APA § 554(d) 83**
  3. **Due Process and Ex Parte Contacts 84**

E. **Decisionmaker Familiarity with the Case 84**
  1. **Overview of the Problem..84**
  2. **Theoretical Obligation—"The One Who Decides Must Hear" 84**
      - a. Delegation of Decisionmaking..85
      - b. Failure to Hear Oral Argument 85
      - c. A *Morgan I*-style Problem for ALJs 85
  3. **Practical Reality...85**
      - a. Effect of *Morgan IV* 85
      - b. A Threatened Exception for Lack of Findings...85
      - c. Exception for "Bad Faith or Improper Behavior" 86

F. **Consistency Across Cases..86**
  1. **Introduction 86**
  2. **Res Judicata 86**
      - a. General Rule 86

		b.	Preclusion Against the Government...86
		c.	Nonmutual Collateral Estoppel 86
			(1) Exception for the Government 87
		d.	Exceptions to Administrative Res Judicata..87
			(1) Statutory Policy 87
			(2) Other Factors 87
	3.	**Stare Decicis**..**88**
		a.	The Very Weak "Stare Decisis" Force of Agency Decisions 88
		b.	Judicial Stare Decisis and the Problem of Agency Nonacquiesence...............88
	4.	**Equitable Estoppel**..**88**
		a.	Estoppel and Apparent Authority in the Private Sector 88
		b.	Estopping the Government Under State Law..89
		c.	Estopping the Government Under Federal Law..89
			(1) Supreme Court Cases 89
			(a) Money Judgment Cases 89
			1) *Richmond* Case..89
			2) *Community Health* Case..89
			3) *Merrill* Case 90
			(b) Immigration Cases 90
			1) *Hibi* Case 90
			2) *Moser* Case 90
			(c) Civil or Criminal Sanctions 90

Chapter Five. Rulemaking Procedures..**91**
   A. **Introduction** **93**
      1. **What We Mean by a "Rule"**..**93**
          a. Definitions..93
              (1) "Rule"...93
              (2) "Rulemaking"..93
              (3) "Regulation"..93
          b. Characteristics of a "Rule"..93
          c. Sometimes, a "Rule" Can Affect a Class of One 93
          d. Classifying Agency Action Under the APA 94
              (1) Legal Consequences of Classification as Rulemaking or Adjudication 94
              (2) Distinguishing Rulemaking and Adjudication in APA Terms 94
      2. **Sources of Rulemaking Procedure** **95**
          a. Due Process (Is Mostly Inapplicable) 95
              (1) A Narrow, Quasi-Exception 95
          b. The APA (!) 96
              (1) Informal Rulemaking..96
              (2) Formal Rulemaking 96
          c. Agency Enabling Acts/Hybrid Rulemaking..96
          d. Generally Applicable Statutes (Other Than the APA) 96
              (1) National Environmental Policy Act 96
              (2) Regulatory Flexibility Act..96
              (3) Paperwork Reduction Act...97
              (4) Unfunded Mandates Reform Act..97
              (5) Information Quality Act 97
              (6) E-Government Act of 2002 97
              (7) Congressional Review Act 97
          e. Agency Procedural Rules...97
          f. Executive Orders...97
              (1) Question of Authority...97
              (2) E.O. 12,866 and Cost-Benefit Analysis..98
          g. Judicially-Imposed Procedures—*Vermont Yankee* Principle 98
      3. **Advantages of Rulemaking as Technique for Policy Making** **98**
      4. **Retroactive Rules**..**98**

			a.	Application 98
				(1) Justice Scalia's Alternative Approach 99
				(2) The Primary/Secondary Distinction 99
B.	Legal Effect of Rules—The Legislative/Nonlegislative Distinction 99
	1.	Some Rules Have the "Force of Law," and Some Don't 99
	2.	Legislative Rules 100
		a.	Legislative Rules Bind the Agency 100
		b.	Broad Construction of Legislative Rulemaking Authority 100
		c.	Special Considerations for "Procedural" Rules 100
	3.	Nonlegislative Rules 100
		a.	Types of Nonlegislative Rules Include 100
		b.	Nonlegislative Rules Do Not "Bind" the "Agency" (*i.e.*, the Agency Heads) 100
			(1) But Interpretive Rules Can Bind Agency Staff 101
		c.	An Example 101
C.	The Notice-and-Comment Rulemaking Process 102
	1.	Notice-and-Comment as the Default Procedure for Rulemaking 102
	2.	Notice of Proposed Rulemaking 102
	3.	Disclosure of Data in the Notice (and Later) 102
		a.	Limitation 102
		b.	After Comment Period Closes 102
		c.	Impact of *Vermont Yankee* Case 102
	4.	Public Participation 103
		a.	Time for Comments 103
			(1) Caution 103
		b.	Oral Presentation 103
		c.	Electronic Rulemaking 103
	5.	Revisions to Proposed Rules—Logical Outgrowth Limit 103
	6.	Statement of Basis and Purpose 104
		a.	"Concise and General" 104
		b.	Response Requirement 104
		c.	Post Hoc Rationalizations 104
	7.	Publication 104
	8.	Delayed Effective Date 105
		a.	Exceptions 105
	9.	Right to Petition 105
	10.	Judicial Remedies 105
		a.	In General—To Vacate or Not to Vacate 105
		b.	Particular Issues Relating to Petitions for Rulemaking 105
			(1) Denial of Rulemaking Petition Is Reviewable 105
			(2) Petition as a Prerequisite for Seeking an "Update" 106
			(3) Scope of Review 106
	11.	Courts Don't Get to Add Procedures—*Vermont Yankee* Again 106
		a.	Core Rationales 106
		b.	Two Narrow Exceptions 106
	12.	Negotiated Rulemaking 106
		a.	Negotiated Rulemaking Act 107
			(1) When Negotiated Rulemaking Used 107
			(2) Procedure 107
			(3) Agency Participation 107
			(4) Agency Discretion to Reject the Negotiated Outcome 107
			(5) Judicial Review 107
D.	Exceptions to Notice-and-Comment Rulemaking Requirements 109
	1.	Introduction 109
	2.	Formal Rulemaking 109
	3.	Categorical Exceptions to Notice-and-Comment 109
	4.	Procedure Exception 109
	5.	Good Cause Exception 110
		a.	APA Provisions 110

    b. Unnecessary Exception 110
      (1) Definition of "Unnecessary" 110
      (2) Direct Final Rules 110
    c. Impracticable or Contrary to the Public Interest 110
      (1) Emergencies 111
      (2) Public Interest 111
      (3) Statutory Deadlines 111
      (4) Interim-Final Rules 111
  6. **Interpretive Rules** 111
    a. Definition 111
      (1) Procedures 112
    b. Distinguishing Interpretive from Legislative Rules 112
      (1) Agency Intent 112
      (2) Does It Look Like Something Is Being "Interpreted"? 112
      (3) Did the Rule Make "New Law"? 112
      (4) Ouch! Some Amendments to Interpretive Rules Are Legislative—*Alaska Prof. Hunters* Problem 113
  7. **Policy Statements** 114
    a. Definition 114
    b. Procedures 114
    c. Distinguishing Policy Statements from Legislative Rules 114
      (1) Both Language and Practice Are Relevant 114
      (2) Enforcement Guidelines 115
E. **Impartiality of Rulemakers** 116
  1. **Overview: "Unbiased" Rulemaking Is Problematic** 116
  2. **Ex Parte Contacts and Formal Rulemaking** 116
  3. **Ex Parte Contacts and Informal Rulemaking** 116
    a. *Sangamon* Rule 116
    b. *Home Box Office* Rule 116
    c. *Home Box Office* Narrowed Almost Out of Existence 116
  4. **Legislative or Executive Interference** 117
    a. Presidential Communications 117
    b. Congressional Pressure and "Relevant Factors" 117
  5. **Bias** 117
  6. **Separation of Functions** 118
F. **The Rulemaking Record** 118
  1. **Introduction** 118
  2. **Rules on Scientific Evidence and Contemporaneous Rationales** 118
  3. **Closed Record Approach** 119
  4. **Exceptions** 119
  5. **State Law** 119

Chapter Six. Obtaining Information and Attorney's Fees 121
A. **Agency Acquisition of Information** 123
  1. **Methods of Obtaining Information** 123
    a. APA Provisions on Gathering of Information 123
  2. **Agency Power to Subpoena** 123
    a. Fourth Amendment Limitations 123
      (1) Subpoena Must Be "Reasonable" 123
      (2) Legal Issues 124
      (3) Burdensomeness of Subpoena 124
      (4) Review for Improper Purpose 124
    b. Third Party Subpoenas 124
  3. **Agency Power to Make Physical Inspections** 124
    a. Home Inspections 124
      (1) Probable Cause 125
    b. Warrants Required for Some Business Inspections 125

			(1)	General Rule	125
			(2)	OSHA Inspection	125
		c.	Exceptions		125
			(1)	Requirements for Warrantless Inspection	125
			(2)	Application	125
				(a) Auto Junkyards	125
				(b) Gun and Liquor Dealers	126
				(c) Mines	126
B.	**Constitutional Protection from Agency Information Gathering**				**126**
	1.	**Introduction**			**126**
	2.	**Privilege to Refuse to Furnish Information**			**126**
		a.	When Privilege Arises		126
			(1)	Immunity	126
			(2)	Privilege Limited to Natural Persons	126
		b.	Scope of Fifth Amendment Privilege		127
			(1)	Private Papers	127
			(2)	Search Warrant	127
			(3)	Required Records	127
				(a) Distinguish—Records of Criminal Activity	127
		c.	Availability of Other Privileges		127
	3.	**Rights to Procedural Due Process in Investigations**			**127**
		a.	Notice and Hearing		127
			(1)	Illustration	128
			(2)	Distinguish—Proceedings Accusatory in Nature	128
	4.	**Right to Counsel**			**128**
	5.	**Use of Information from Unlawful Searches**			**128**
C.	**Freedom of Information Act**				**129**
	1.	**In General**			**129**
		a.	"Agencies" Covered		129
		b.	Entities Not Subject to the Act		129
			(1)	Entities Not in Executive Branch of the Federal Gov't	129
			(2)	The President	129
	2.	**Three Levels of Disclosure—Publication, Inspection, Production on Request**			**129**
		a.	Publication of Procedures and Rules		129
		b.	Records Available for Public Inspection		130
			(1)	Definition of Terms	130
				(a) "Opinion" vs. "Memorandum"	130
				(b) "Interpretations"	130
			(2)	Invasion of Privacy	130
		c.	Agency Records to Be Produced on Request		130
			(1)	FOIA on "Records"	130
			(2)	Definition of "Agency Records"	131
				(a) Factors Relating to "Agency Control"	131
				(b) No Obligation to Obtain Records Not in Agency Control	131
				(c) A Partial Exception for Records in Possession of Grantees	131
				(d) "Agency Records" Need Not Be Stored by the Agency	131
				(e) Storage Format Doesn't Matter	131
				(f) Congressional Records Aren't Covered	132
				(g) Personal Records Aren't Covered	132
			(3)	Procedures	132
				(a) "[A]ny Person" Can Make a Request	132
				(b) Reasonable Requests That Follow Regulations	132
				(c) Agency Denials—Reasons and Right to Appeal	132
				(d) The *Glomar* Response	132
				(e) De Novo Judicial Review	133
				(f) *Vaughn* Index	133
				(g) In Camera Review	133
				(h) Attorney's Fees	133

3. Exemptions to the Act 133
   a. Exemption 1: National Security 133
   b. Exemption 2: Internal Matters 133
      (1) Recent Narrowing... 133
   c. Exemption 3: Matters Exempted by Other Statutes 133
   d. Exemption 4: Trade Secrets and Confidential/Financial Information 134
      (1) Trade Secrets 134
      (2) Commercial or Financial Information 134
      (3) Confidential 134
         (a) Information Voluntarily Shared with the Government 134
         (b) Compelled Information 134
      (4) Exemption 4 Doesn't Require Agencies to Keep Secrets, but the Trade Secrets Act Does 135
         (a) Relation of TSA to Exemption 4.. 135
   e. Exemption 5: Inter- or Intra-Agency Memoranda 135
      (1) Criteria—Discovery Standards 135
      (2) Deliberative Process Privilege... 135
         (a) Pre- and Post-Decisional Memoranda at NLRB 135
         (b) Factual Material Not Exempt 136
      (3) Attorney Work-Product Privilege.. 136
      (4) Presidential Privilege... 136
   f. Exemption 6: Invasion of Personal Privacy 136
      (1) Personnel and Medical Files and Similar Files... 136
      (2) Privacy Interest 136
      (3) Balancing Private and Public Interest 137
      (4) Illustration 137
   g. Exemption 7: Law Enforcement Records 137
      (1) Exemption 7(C)'s Protection of Privacy... 137
         (a) Illustration of Exemption 7(C) 138
   h. Exemption 8: Bank Regulations.. 138
   i. Exemption 9: Natural Resources 138
4. Exclusions—Which Are Very Different from Exemptions 140
D. Government in the Sunshine Act.. 140
  1. General Rule 140
     a. Definition of Agency 140
     b. Definition of Meeting.. 140
     c. Consultations... 140
  2. Exceptions 140
E. Attorney's Fees 141
  1. General Rule 141
  2. Specific Statutory Provisions 141
     a. Prevailing Parties 141
        (1) Voluntary Change Will Not Warrant Fee Award 141
        (2) The FOIA Exception to *Buckhannon* 141
     b. Awarding Fees "If Appropriate"... 141
  3. General Authorization—Equal Access to Justice Act 142
  4. Amount 142
     a. Setting the Rate 142
     b. Adjustment of Lodestar... 142

Chapter Seven. Scope of Judicial Review..143
A. Introduction 145
  1. Scope of Review—In General..145
  2. The APA's Scope-of-Review Provision, § 706(2) 145
  3. Other Statutory Instructions 146
B. Scope of Review of Questions of Fact..146
  1. Deferential Review by Various Names..146

- a. "Substantial Evidence" 146
- b. "Arbitrary and Capricious" 146
  - (1) Distinction with a Difference? 146
- c. "Clearly Erroneous" 147
- d. "Preponderance of the Evidence" 147
- e. Variations in Standards Maybe Not So Significant in Practice 147

2. **More About "Substantial Evidence"** 147
   - a. APA Provision 147
     - (1) "Substantial Evidence" as Rationality Review 147
     - (2) "Whole Record" 147
     - (3) Inferences of Fact 148
   - b. Disagreement Between Agency and ALJ on Credibility 148
     - (1) The Classic Illustration—*Universal Camera* 148
     - (2) Findings Based on a Mix of Demeanor and Other Evidence 148
     - (3) Reminder: Limited Scope of the *Universal Camera* Principle 149
     - (4) Duty to Explain Disagreement on Credibility 149
   - c. General Duty to Explain Disagreement with ALJ 149

3. **Constitutional Facts** 149
   - a. "*Ben Avon* Rule" 149
   - b. Its Demise 149

4. **Jurisdictional Facts** 150

C. **Scope of Review of Legal Interpretations** 150
   1. **Agency Interpretations of Law and Judicial Deference Doctrines** 150
   2. ***Chevron*'s Strong Deference** 150
      - a. Overview of *Chevron*'s Two (or Three) Steps 150
      - b. Very Short Summary of Facts of *Chevron* 151
      - c. *Chevron* Step One—Did Congress Speak Directly to the Precise Issue? 151
        - (1) Criteria for Identifying Clear Intent 151
        - (2) Contrasting Judicial Approaches to the Toolkit 152
      - d. *Chevron* Step Two—Was the Agency's Choice Reasonable? 153
        - (1) Wait a Second—What Is Step Two For? 153
        - (2) One Possibility: Step Two Doesn't Do Much 153
        - (3) Another Possibility: Step Two as Arbitrariness Review 153
      - e. *Chevron* Step 0—What Is *Chevron*'s "Domain"? 153
        - (1) The *Mead* Framework for *Chevron* Step 0 154
        - (2) *Mead*'s Safe Harbors 154
        - (3) Application of the *Mead* Framework to *Mead* 154
        - (4) Justice Scalia Wrote a Heckuva Dissent 154
        - (5) Reaching *Chevron* from Outside a *Mead* Safe Harbor—The *Barnhart* Approach 155
      - f. *Chevron* and the Problem of Agency "Jurisdiction"—*City of Arlington* 155
      - g. *Chevron*'s Interaction with Stare Decisis—*Brand X* 155
      - h. *Chevron* and Agency Flip-Flops 156
   3. ***Skidmore*'s Weak Deference** 158
      - a. Details from *Skidmore* 158
      - b. Factors Bearing on the "Power to Persuade" 158
        - (1) Consistency 158
        - (2) Contemporaneousness 158
        - (3) Thoroughness of Consideration 158
        - (4) Agency Expertise 158
   4. ***Auer* Deference to Agency Interpretations of Its Own Regulations** 159
      - a. No Step 0 159
      - b. *Auer* Applies Only to "Fair and Considered Judgment" 159
      - c. *Auer* Doesn't Apply to Parroting Rules 159
      - d. *Auer* Doesn't Apply to Unfair Surprises 159

D. **Scope of Review of Application of Law to Fact (a/k/a "Mixed Questions")** 160
   1. **Overview** 160
   2. **Reasonableness Test—The *Hearst* Framework** 161

    a. *Hearst*'s Contrast Between Pure Issues of Law and Mixed Questions 161
    b. *Hearst*'s Rationales for Deferential Review 161
  3. **Judicial Inconsistency on Application Questions** 162
 E. **Scope of Review of Exercises of Discretion** 162
  1. **Overview of the Problem** 162
  2. **APA Standard—Arbitrariness Review** 162
  3. **The Meaning of Arbitrariness Review** 162
    a. Threshold Legal Questions 163
    b. Review for Reasoned Decisionmaking 163
     (1) The *State Farm* Gloss 163
     (2) "Hard Look" Review 163
    c. Relevant Factors 164
     (1) Agencies Don't Have to Consider Other Agencies' Relevant Factors 164
    d. Reasonableness of Agency Action 164
    e. Mixed Messages on the Duty to Explain Policy Changes 165
  4. **Review of Facts Underlying Rules** 166
    a. Old Fashioned Arbitrariness Review of Facts 166
    b. Modern Arbitrariness Review of Facts 166
     (1) Duty to Respond to Criticism 166
     (2) Scientific Frontiers 166
     (3) Substantial Evidence Standard 166
     (4) Actual Mileage Varies 166
  5. **Limited Review of Administrative Remedy** 167
    a. Abuse of Discretion 167
    b. Scope of Remedy Within Agency Discretion 167

Chapter Eight. Access to the Courts: Types of Review, Immunities, Tort Liability, Reviewability 169
 A. **Types of "Review" Available** 171
  1. **Special Statutory Review** 171
  2. **Introduction to General Statutory Review Under the APA** 171
    a. Section 704—Review Available for "Final Agency Action" 171
     (1) State Analogues 171
    b. Section 703—Available "Forms" of Review 172
    c. Section 702—Statutory Standing 172
    d. More from § 702—Partial Waiver of Sovereign Immunity 172
     (1) Note: "Money Damages" as Compensatory Relief 172
    e. Jurisdiction for General Statutory Review 172
     (1) Some Additional Jurisdictional Statutes 173
  3. **"Nonstatutory" Review** 173
    a. Injunctive and Declaratory Relief 173
    b. Mandamus 173
    c. Certiorari 173
    d. Habeas Corpus 174
    e. Damages Actions 174
  4. **Review During Enforcement Actions** 174
    a. Preclusion of Review by a Statutory Deadline 174
     (1) Challenge Precluded by Deadline—*Yakus* 174
     (2) Substantive Challenges Allowed After Deadline 175
    b. Right to Jury Trial 175
     (1) No Jury Trial in Agency Enforcement 175
 B. **Sovereign Immunity** 176
  1. **In General** 176
    a. Waivers to Be "Strictly Construed" 176
  2. **Waivers by the Federal Government** 176
    a. Waiver for Actions That Do Not Seek Money Damages 176
    b. Cross-Cutting Statutes That Waive as to Money Damages 176

		c.	Agency-Specific Statutes 177
	3.	**Overview of the Eleventh Amendment and Related Law** **177**
		a.	Citizens Can't Sue Their Own States 177
		b.	Bar on Private Actions Against States in State Courts 177
		c.	Bar on Private Actions in Administrative Courts 177
		d.	Congressional Abrogation Through the Fourteenth Amendment 177
		e.	Congress Cannot Use Article I Powers to Abrogate 178
		f.	Federal Government as Plaintiff 178
		g.	Suing a State Official for Injunctive Relief as a Work Around 178
		h.	Limits on Suing State Officials for Damages 178

C. **Tort Liability of Government** **178**
  1. **In General** **178**
  2. **Introduction to the Federal Tort Claims Act** **178**
     a. Federal Government Liability for Negligent Torts 178
     b. Strict Liability Torts 179
     c. Intentional Torts 179
     d. Discretionary Functions 179
        (1) High-Level Decisions 179
        (2) Lower Level Implementation Decisions 179
     e. FTCA Excludes Constitutional Torts 180
     f. FTCA Expands *Official* Immunity 180
  3. **Liability of State Government** **180**
     a. Traditional Rule and Its "Proprietary" Exception 180
     b. Modern Trend—Immunity Limited or Abolished 180
     c. Governmental Liability Under § 1983—Local vs. State 180

D. **Tort Liability of Government Officials** **181**
  1. **In General** **181**
  2. **Modern Law—Immunities for Officials** **181**
     a. Absolute Immunity Based on Official Position 181
        (1) The President 181
        (2) Presidential Aides 181
        (3) Judges 181
            (a) Injunctive Relief and Attorneys' Fees 182
        (4) Others Engaged in Adjudicative Process 182
        (5) Legislators 182
            (a) Congress 182
            (b) State Legislators 182
     b. Absolute Immunity Under the Westfall Act/FTCA 182
        (1) Common Law Immunity 183
     c. Qualified Immunity 183
        (1) An Objective Test That Is Fact Sensitive 183
  3. **Legal Basis for Damage Actions** **183**
     a. Federal Officials—Common Law Torts 183
     b. Federal Officials—*Bivens* Actions for Constitutional Violations 183
        (1) Three Decades of Refusing to Expand *Bivens*' Reach 184
        (2) The Two-Step Inquiry 184
        (3) *Bivens* Limited to Actions Against Officials 184
     c. State Officials—Liability Under § 1983 for Violations of Federal Law 184
        (1) Official Immunities Apply 184
        (2) Section 1983 Extends to Some Statutory Violations 185

E. **Statutory Preclusion of Judicial Review** **185**
  1. **In General** **185**
  2. **Background Presumption of Reviewability** **185**
  3. **Interpretation to Avoid Preclusion** **185**
     a. Illustration—Preclusion of Review of Factual Determinations 186
     b. Illustration—Avoiding Preclusion of Review of Rules 186
     c. Illustration—Construing to Avoid Preclusion of a Constitutional Issue 186
  4. **Implied Preclusion** **186**

		F.	Commitment to Agency Discretion 187
		1.	The Apparent Contradiction 187
		2.	"No Law to Apply"..187
			a. Illustration: Finding Some Law to Apply in *Overton Park*............................187
			b. Illustration: "High Quality and Cost-Effective" Is Law................................187
		3.	What Is "Committed to Agency Discretion" 188
			a. Decisions Not to Enforce or Prosecute 188
			b. Dismissal of Intelligence Officers..188
			c. Agency Allocations of Lump-Sum Appropriations 188
	G.	Threshold Requirements of "Agency Action" by an "Agency".......................................189
		1.	"Agency"—A Broad Definition That Excludes the President 189
			a. APA Definition of "Agency" 189
			b. The President Is Not an "Agency" 189
		2.	"Agency Action" Under the APA 189
			a. APA Definition of "Agency Action..189
			b. "Programmatic" Attacks 190
			c. Limiting Judicial Power to Fix "Failure[s] to Act"...190
			(1) The Court's Narrow Construction of "Failure to Act" 190
			(2) Remedy Extends to Compelling Actions "Unlawfully Withheld or Unreasonably Delayed"..191
			(3) The Combined Force of These Requirements 191

Chapter Nine. Access to the Courts: Standing and Timing...193
	A.	Standing to Seek Judicial Review in Federal Court 195
		1. Introduction—One Word; Three Doctrines..195
		a. Flexibility on Order of Decision 195
		2. Constitutional Standing 196
		a. The Injury/Causation/Redressability Test...196
		(1) A Test That Is Easy to Memorize but Hard to Apply 196
		(2) Disagreement over Purpose 196
		b. Injury-in-Fact—Principles, Dichotomies, Pressure Points.........................197
		(1) Injury Need Not Be Economic 197
		(2) But the Injury Can't Be Solely "Ideological" 197
		(3) The Injury Must Be "Concrete" Rather than "Abstract" 197
		(4) The Injury Must Be "Particularized" Rather than a "Generalized Grievance"....198
		(5) The Injury, If Not "Actual," Must Be "Imminent" Rather than "Conjectural" or "Speculative" 199
		(a) Probabilistic Injury at the Supreme Court................................199
		(b) Probabilistic Injury at the D.C. Circuit 199
		(6) Procedural Injuries 200
		(7) Associational Standing 200
		(8) Do States Sometimes Get "Special Solicitude" on Standing? 200
		(9) Taxpayer Standing..201
		(a) General Rule 201
		(b) The *Flast v. Cohen* Exception..201
		(c) Distinguishing *Flast* Nearly Out of Existence 201
		c. Causation and Redressability 202
		(1) Vagueness and, ahem, Room for Judgment..202
		(2) Tough Applications of Causation/Redressability 202
		(a) Tax Exemptions and Hospitals 202
		(b) Tax Exemptions and Desegregation 202
		(c) Endangered Species 203
		(d) Violation of Reporting Rules for Past Conduct 203
		(3) More Relaxed Applications of Causation/Redressability 203
		(a) Civil Penalties to Deter Future Misconduct 203
		(b) Regulating One Source of Greenhouse Gas Emissions 203
		(4) Relaxed Redressability for Procedural Claims 204

		3.	Statutory Standing...204
			a. Historical Development 204
			(1) The Old "Legal Interest" Test 204
			(2) Congress Expands Standing to "Aggrieved Persons"............................205
			b. Section 702 and the Zone of Interests Test...205
		4.	**Prudential Standing**..207
			a. Third Party Standing (or Jus Tertii) 207
			b. The Zone-of-Interests in Non-APA Cases 208
			c. Congress Can Trump Prudential Standing 208
B.	**The Timing of Judicial Review**..208
	1.	**In General**...208
	2.	**Final Order Rule**..208
		a. Statutory Requirements 209
		b. Some Leading Cases 209
		(1) Decision to Issue a Complaint Was Not Final 209
		(2) Biological Opinion with Legal Consequences Was Final 209
		(3) Administrative Compliance Order Held Final...210
		c. Finality and the Problem of Guidance Documents 210
		d. Exception—Violation of Clear Right..211
		e. Exception—Unreasonable Delay 211
		(1) APA Provisions 211
		(2) *TRAC* Factors 211
		(3) Violation of Statutory Deadlines and Claims of Delay 212
	3.	**Ripeness**...212
		a. Purposes of Requirement 212
		b. Ripeness as Constitutional and Prudential Limitation......................................213
		c. Test for Ripeness...213
		(1) Fitness for Review..213
		(2) Hardship to the Parties...213
		(a) Benefit-Creating Programs 214
		d. Review of Informal Administrative Action 214
		e. Statutory Time Limits for Review 215
		f. Statutory Preclusion of Pre-Enforcement Review...215
	4.	**Exhaustion of Administrative Remedies**..216
		a. Purposes of Exhaustion Rule 216
		(1) Agency Autonomy 216
		(2) Judicial Efficiency 216
		b. Common Law Exhaustion Doctrine 216
		(1) Undue Prejudice 217
		(2) Inadequate Agency Authority to Remediate...217
		(a) More on Constitutional Claims 217
		(3) Bias or Otherwise Predetermined Result 218
		c. Exhaustion Under the APA 218
		d. Exhaustion as Preclusion of Judicial Review..219
		(1) Review in Criminal Case 219
		e. Civil Rights Statute 219
		f. Issue Exhaustion 219
		(1) Application—Social Security Cases 220
		(2) Application to Rulemaking...220
	5.	**Primary Jurisdiction** 221
		a. Factors Favoring Application of Primary Jurisdiction 221
		b. Factors Weighing Against Application of Primary Jurisdiction 221
		c. Judicial Disposition of Matters Subject to Primary Jurisdiction 222
	6.	**Stays Pending Judicial Review** 222
		a. APA Provisions..222
		b. Factors Considered in Granting Stay 222
		(1) Likelihood of Prevailing on the Merits...223
		(2) Irreparable Injury..223

		(3) Effect of Stay on Other Interested Parties	223
		(4) Public Interest	223
	c.	Illustration—Stay Denied	223
	d.	Illustration—Stay Granted	223

REVIEW QUESTIONS AND ANSWERS 225

EXAM QUESTIONS AND ANSWERS 267

TABLE OF CASES 289

TABLE OF STATUTES 295

INDEX 297

Gilbert Exam Strategies

A. GENERAL CONSIDERATIONS

1. **Nature of Administrative Law**

   Administrative law is basically *procedural* law. Each administrative agency is responsible for a particular body of substantive law (*e.g.,* the National Labor Relations Board administers federal labor statutes), but certain procedural principles apply to all agencies.

2. **Function of Agencies**

   Administrative agencies are entities formed by the legislature to implement desired changes in policy. The legislature creates an agency if it determines that certain functions—investigation, law enforcement, rulemaking, or adjudication—are best performed by a separate body. The impact of such rulemaking and adjudication on the general public is vast, far exceeding the impact of the judicial process.

3. **Organization of Summary**

   This Summary, like leading casebooks and treatises, deals with the following matters:

   a. The *position of the agency* in government, including the *legislative* and *executive* controls over the agency.

   b. The *administrative process*—*i.e.,* the complexities of government activity that include the formulation of rules (other than by the legislature) and the investigation and adjudication of cases (other than by the courts). The statutory and constitutional requirements for *rulemaking* and for *adjudication* are discussed.

   c. *Judicial review* of agency decisions.

4. **Statutes and Due Process**

   In analyzing a particular administrative law problem (or exam question), you must always consider:

   a. **The statute creating the particular agency**

   That statute sets forth the *law* the agency is expected to implement and often contains the *procedural requirements* for the agency to follow in its investigation, rulemaking, and adjudication. Often the statute will contain specific provisions about how to seek judicial review.

   b. **Agency regulations**

   In many cases, the agency promulgates regulations that provide procedures that may go beyond what the statute or the Constitution would require. Your client is entitled to the benefit of the protections set forth in the regulations.

   c. **Administrative Procedure Act**

   In addition to analyzing the agency's own statute and regulations, it is always necessary to apply the federal or state Administrative Procedure Act ("APA") to the agency function in question. The APA's provisions for rulemaking and adjudication usually provide the applicable ground rules.

d. **Constitution**

Finally, constitutional due process requirements often provide greater protection than any applicable statute or regulation; thus, constitutional law should always be considered.

5. **Judicial Review**

Administrative law questions usually focus on whether a court will judicially review a particular agency action and, if so, what the court will decide. Almost all agency action is reviewable (it is seldom precluded by statute or by commitment to agency discretion), but there are severe limitations: The plaintiff must have *standing* and seek review *at the appropriate time.* In addition, the court's power to substitute its judgment for that of the agency is usually quite limited.

B. APPROACH

Administrative law exam questions generally focus on the legality and procedural validity of agency action and on various doctrines that limit the judicial review that courts will provide. For a general approach to exam questions, consider the following; for more detailed approaches, review the chapter approaches found at the beginning of each chapter as well as the exam tips and charts found throughout each chapter.

1. **Delegation of Authority**

Many exam questions focus on the delegation of legislative or judicial authority to an agency. While it is *unlikely that a delegation will be struck down* by a modern court, the *issue must still be addressed*. Recall that even if the delegation is valid, the agency's action may be beyond its delegated powers (*ultra vires*). Also, there are numerous executive and legislative controls over agency action that frequently come into play in administrative law exams.

2. **Procedural Validity**

Many issues relating to agency procedure ask whether a *hearing is required* by due process, the agency statute, the APA, or agency regulations.

a. If a hearing is required, *consider what type of hearing*—trial-type or legislative—must be provided. Also, *when* must it be provided?

b. Note that it is critical to observe the *distinction between rulemaking and adjudication* since the entire subject is based on that distinction. Wholly different procedures are required for the two modes of agency action.

c. In many cases, an agency can *choose* one mode of action over the other. A series of issues arise when the agency so chooses—*e.g.*, can rulemaking resolve a broad issue so that no future adjudications are needed? Can an agency choose to make policy through adjudication rather than rulemaking even though adjudication has a retroactive effect?

d. Remember that a series of doctrines *constrain agency choices in adjudication*: equitable estoppel, res judicata, the duty of consistency, and the duty to follow procedural regulations.

e. A series of doctrines help to assure the *impartiality of agency decisionmakers*, both at the hearing level (hearings usually are conducted by hearing officers who are sometimes administrative law judges ("ALJs")) and at the agency head level. Pay attention to facts implicating bias, ex parte contact, separation of functions, command influence, and *Morgan I*. In addition, watch for rules relating to evidence (including the residuum rule) and official notice and rules requiring explanation and findings.

3. **Judicial Review**

   Analyze a judicial review question as follows:

   a. ***Is the action reviewable?*** Consider the doctrines of ***preclusion of review*** and ***commitment to agency discretion.*** If the plaintiff seeks a tort-type recovery, you must consider the obstacles to recovery of damages both from individual wrongdoers and from government.

   b. ***What is the scope of review?*** Here you must decide what type of ***issue*** is under challenge (basic facts, law, application of law to facts, discretion, procedure) and then apply the applicable rules concerning scope of review. In most cases, a court must ***uphold a reasonable decision*** by the agency even though the court might prefer a different outcome.

   c. ***Is plaintiff limited by the doctrines of standing or timing?*** For standing, check constitutional, statutory, and prudential limits; as for timing, look for facts indicating applicability of the final order rule, ripeness, exhaustion of remedies, and primary jurisdiction doctrines.

Administrative Law

Fifteenth Edition

Chapter One

Separation of Powers and Control of Agencies

CONTENTS	PAGE
Key Exam Issues	2
A. Separation of Powers	3
B. Nondelegation Doctrine (Legislative Power)	4
C. Nondelegation Doctrine (Judicial Power)	11
D. Executive Controls Over Administrative Action	15
E. Legislative Controls Over Administrative Action	21

Key Exam Issues

This chapter discusses constitutional limits on the powers of agencies as well as legislative and executive controls over those powers. Key issues include:

1. The Nondelegation Doctrine (Legislative Power). The Supreme Court has construed the Constitution as barring Congress from delegating its legislative power to agencies. This is obviously problematic insofar as Congress commonly delegates to agencies the power to promulgate "rules" with the force of law. The Supreme Court has addressed this tension by holding that a delegation of rulemaking power does not violate the Nondelegation Doctrine so long as Congress includes some "intelligible principle" limiting the scope of the delegation.

    a. As discussed below, the Court's approach to finding the needed "intelligible principle" is extraordinarily forgiving. Indeed, since adopting this approach about a century ago, the Court has struck a statute for delegating legislative power on only two occasions—both in 1935. Some state courts are somewhat stricter.

    b. The Nondelegation Doctrine has a bit more bite than one might expect from the preceding paragraph thanks to the canon of constitutional avoidance. Courts applying this doctrine will favor (reasonable) statutory constructions that avoid serious constitutional questions. The Supreme Court has deployed this canon to adopt narrow statutory constructions of agency authority that avoid the nondelegation problem.

2. The Nondelegation Doctrine (Judicial Power). Article III of the Constitution vests the "judicial power" of the United States in federal courts staffed by judges with life tenure and salary protection. Nonetheless, Congress commonly grants agencies power to issue adjudicatory orders. The law governing the scope of congressional power to delegate adjudicative authority to agencies without running afoul of Article III is difficult. That said, courts use two basic, overlapping approaches:

    a. The *Schor* multi-factor test. This framework turns on: [a] the extent to which the agency has assumed the "range of jurisdiction and powers normally vested only in Article III courts"; [b] "the origin and importance of the right to be adjudicated"; and [c] the congressional purpose underlying the delegation. In applying this test, you should be especially sensitive to whether Congress has delegated to an agency the power to determine a matter of "private right." The outer boundaries of this concept are not clear, but it includes liability of one private person to another under common law (e.g., for breach of contract or a tort).

    b. The "adjunct" theory. This approach concedes the validity of adjudication by non-Article III decisionmakers (agencies, bankruptcy judges, magistrate judges, etc.) so long as their decisions are subject to sufficient control by Article III judges.

3. Appointments. The Constitution provides as a default rule that "officers of the United States" are appointed by the President, subject to the advice and consent of the Senate. Congress may by law, however, vest appointment of "inferior officers" in the President alone, the heads of departments, or the courts of law. Issues you may encounter related to appointments include:

    a. Congress cannot arrogate to itself power to appoint "officers of the United States." Just to keep things interesting, though, Congress can appoint "officers of Congress."

    b. Congress can depart from the Constitution's default rule of presidential appointment with Senate confirmation only for "inferior officers." So you may have to figure out whether somebody is "inferior."

4. Removal of executive officers.

   a. Congress has constitutional authority to impeach but cannot otherwise increase its power to remove executive officers.

   b. There is no constitutional provision expressly declaring presidential authority to remove executive officials. The scope of this authority—and Congress's power to restrict it—has long been contentious. The Supreme Court's current view, in essence, is that Congress cannot impose restrictions on presidential removal authority that would unduly interfere with the President's power to discharge the executive power. Applying this "test," the Court has upheld statutory provisions requiring good cause for the removal of some executive officials. (It is a safe bet, however, that the Court would not tolerate efforts by an overreaching Congress to require cause for removal of officials such as the Secretary of State.)

5. There are numerous other legislative and executive controls over agencies that can check illegal, mistaken, or impolitic agency action. For instance,

   a. Congress exercises control over agencies through oversight hearings and appropriations. It cannot, however, exercise control over agencies via the "legislative veto," as explained below.

   b. Congress typically expressly delegates rulemaking power to the head of an agency rather than to the President. Nonetheless, for decades, presidents of both parties have used executive orders to require many agencies to submit their rules to centralized White House review.

A. Separation of Powers

1. In General

The United States Constitution and state constitutions separate government into the legislative, executive, and judicial branches. Administrative agencies are units of government created by statute to carry out specific tasks in implementing the statute. Usually, the agencies fall within the executive branch of government; however, some important agencies are independent of the executive branch. (*See infra* p. 18 *et seq.*, discussing constitutionality of independent agencies.)

2. Judicial Enforcement of Separation of Powers

The courts are often called upon to decide whether particular statutes involving administrative agencies violate constitutional doctrines mandating separation of powers. For purposes of an administrative law course, the most important separation-of-powers doctrines include the Nondelegation Doctrines, which limit congressional power to authorize agencies to function as junior varsity legislatures and courts, as well as doctrines allocating power to appoint and remove executive officials. Administrative law is thus deeply concerned with how much power agencies can wield and who controls that power.

3. Formalism vs. Functionalism

The numerous cases decided by the Supreme Court in the area of separation of powers tend to fall into two groups: formalist and functionalist. Formalist cases base their analyses on relatively simple, bright-line tests rooted in constitutional language and structure. Formalist cases ostensibly pay little attention to the practical advantages and disadvantages of the scheme under consideration. [*See, e.g.,* **INS v. Chadha,** 462 U.S. 919 (1983) (rejecting legislative vetoes) (*see infra,* p. 21); **Clinton v. City of New York,** 524 U.S. 417 (1998) (rejecting line-item vetoes) (*see infra,* p. 22)]

Functionalist cases tend to focus on the practical impact of the disputed statute, such as whether it serves a useful purpose in government or appears to be an attempt by one branch to interfere with the functions of another branch. [*See, e.g.,* **Commodity Futures Trading Comm'n v. Schor,** 478 U.S. 833 (1986) (adopting multi-factor test for determining whether agency adjudication infringes Article III judicial power) (*see infra,* p. 11); **Morrison v. Olson,** 487 U.S. 654 (1988) (adopting functional test for determining whether restrictions on presidential removal of executive officials infringes Article II presidential power) (*see infra,* p. 18)]

4. Checks and Balances

The Constitution contains numerous checks and balances so that each branch has the means to defend itself from overreaching by the other branches (*e.g.,* the executive branch can block legislation by vetoing it). The courts also protect the checks and balances system. For example, a statute that invalidly attempts to permit legislation without giving the President the power to veto it (a "legislative veto") is invalid. (*See infra,* p. 21.)

B. Nondelegation Doctrine (Legislative Power)

1. Introduction to the Nondelegation Doctrine

According to the Supreme Court, Congress ***cannot delegate*** its ***legislative*** power. In practice, Congress does so constantly by enacting statutes that confer broad rulemaking powers on administrative agencies. The Supreme Court has addressed this tension by holding that a delegation of rulemaking power does not violate the Nondelegation Doctrine so long as Congress includes some "intelligible principle" limiting the scope of the delegation. Courts sometimes deploy the canon of constitutional avoidance to construe a statutory delegation narrowly to avoid a nondelegation problem.

2. Nondelegation Doctrine—Evolution of the Case Law

To understand the modern cases, it is helpful to chart the historical development of the Nondelegation Doctrine. The basic story is that the courts have been very tolerant of broad delegations except during the aberrational year of 1935, when the Supreme Court struck two provisions of the National Industrial Recovery Act, which granted vast powers to the President (with the aid of private parties) to respond to the Great Depression.

a. Early Cases—Formulas to Legitimate Delegation

From the earliest times, Congress delegated to agencies effective power to make law as they implement statutes. The Supreme Court upheld such delegations by employing various formulas of judicial review that allowed the agencies to exercise more and more power.

(1) Ascertainment of Facts

An agency could effectively exercise legislative power if such power was ostensibly limited to ascertaining whether a "fact" had occurred.

Example: Congress gave the President power to raise tariff schedules if a foreign country imposed a duty on American products that the President considered "reciprocally unequal and unreasonable." The Court upheld this delegation of power on the theory that the President was not exercising any lawmaking function, but was simply authorized to ***ascertain a "fact"*** (*i.e.,* the existence of unreasonable foreign duties) that would suspend a congressional statute allowing free imports. [**Field v. Clark,** 143 U.S. 649

(1892)] *Note:* Obviously, the President's decisions would turn on international economic and political issues and would be based on judgment rather than mere ascertainment of "fact."

(2) Filling in Details

Under another formula, a delegation of legislative power to make rules to implement a vague statute was upheld on grounds that the agency was merely "filling in the details."

 Example: Congress gave the Secretary of Agriculture the power to make rules and regulations protecting the national forests. The Court held that no legislative power had been delegated—only the power to *fill in details*. [**United States v. Grimaud**, 220 U.S. 506 (1911)]

(3) Finding an "Intelligible Principle"

Modern cases typically uphold legislative delegations by finding that Congress has set an *"intelligible principle"* or a "primary standard" for the agency to follow. When Congress establishes such a principle or standard, at least it has made the fundamental policy decisions that the agency only needs to implement. [**J.W. Hampton & Co. v. United States**, 276 U.S. 394 (1928) (President has power to impose tariffs to "equalize" differences in production costs.)] The principle or standard usually furnishes very little actual guidance to the agency.

b. The National Industrial Recovery Act Cases—The 1935 Anomaly

(1) Background

In early cases, the Supreme Court legitimized every congressional delegation of legislative power to an agency. However, in the 1930s, the Court twice invalidated such delegations.

(a) Comment

This retreat arose as a result of the far-reaching New Deal statutes passed by Congress to counter the effects of the Depression. In particular, the National Industrial Recovery Act ("NIRA"), passed in 1933, gave unusually broad powers to the President. The Supreme Court was extremely hostile to this sort of aggressive interference with the free market.

(2) *Panama Refining:* The "Hot Oil" Case

The first of these cases involved a NIRA provision that allowed the President to ban the shipment in interstate commerce of oil produced in violation of state regulations ("hot oil"). The Supreme Court held that this power was an ***unconstitutional delegation*** on the ground that there were ***no standards*** in the Act to guide the President's exercise of discretion. Although there were various declarations of policy in section 1 of the Act, the Court found them unduly vague and conflicting. [**Panama Refining Co. v. Ryan**, 293 U.S. 388 (1935)]

(a) Dissenting Argument

Justice Cardozo dissented, pointing out that the President's delegated power (to ban the shipment of hot oil) was clearly defined—his only discretion being whether to do so. Cardozo argued that section 1 of the Act provided ample guidance since it stated that the purposes of the Act were to conserve natural resources, prevent unfair competitive practices, and utilize the productive capacity of industry. Since Congress could not, at a given moment, predict whether these purposes would be served by banning the shipment of hot oil, it had left this decision to the President.

(3) The *Schechter Poultry* Case

The second case concerned a NIRA delegation that gave the President power to adopt codes of fair competition in cooperation with members of an industry. These codes were to set forth schedules of wages and prices and other rules that would be binding upon entire industries. This delegation was vastly broader than the narrow provision in the *Panama Refining* case and was also held invalid. [**Schechter Poultry Corp. v. United States**, 295 U.S. 495 (1935)]

(a) Rationale

Again, the Supreme Court found an absence of standards to guide the President in deciding what regulations to impose upon the various industries. The Court was also heavily influenced by the lack of hearings or other procedures (even publication) in adopting the codes, and was concerned by the role of private industry in regulating itself—*i.e.,* that large companies might succeed in having rules adopted that would harm their competitors.

c. Post-NIRA Cases from the Twentieth Century

All subsequent Supreme Court cases involving the delegation issue have uniformly ***upheld*** broad delegations of rulemaking power to agencies—even those with vague (or sometimes no) standards. (However, no delegations of power since the 1930s have been as broad as those under the NIRA.)

(1) Public Interest

The Court has upheld delegations based on meaningless standards such as the power to act "as public convenience, interest or necessity requires." [**Federal Radio Comm'n v. Nelson Brothers**, 289 U.S. 266 (1933)]

(2) Fair Prices

During World War II, Congress authorized the Price Administrator to fix maximum prices, which "in his judgment shall be generally fair and equitable and will effectuate the purposes of this Act," namely to prevent wartime inflation and profiteering. The Court upheld the delegation because Congress obviously could not set prices itself. "Congress is not confined to that method of executing its policy which involves the least possible delegation of discretion. . . . Only if we could say that there is an absence of standards for the guidance of the Administrator's action, so that it would be impossible in a proper proceeding to ascertain whether the will of Congress has been obeyed, would we be justified in overriding its choice of means." [**Yakus v. United States**, 321 U.S. 414 (1944)]

(3) No Standards

Indeed, delegations have been upheld even though Congress provided *no* standards at all.

> **Example:** The Court sustained a delegation to the Secretary of the Interior to apportion Colorado River water in times of shortage, even though there were no standards as to how this was to be done. (Three dissenters questioned the constitutionality of such a delegation.) [**Arizona v. California**, 373 U.S. 546 (1963)]

EXAM TIP	

Remember that even though the Court has **upheld broad delegations** of legislative power to agencies, the courts often give **lip service** to the Nondelegation Doctrine and usually look for some standards. Thus you should do so as well when you analyze an exam question that raises the issue of delegation.

(4) Economic Stabilization

In the 1970s, Congress enacted several vague statutes giving the President broad economic powers. Although the *Schechter* and *Panama Refining* cases posed potential problems for these statutes, post-1930s cases upholding broad delegations, especially *Yakus*, suggested that Congress essentially had a free hand.

(a) The *Meat Cutters* Case

Although the Supreme Court did not consider the anti-inflation statutes, an important lower court decision upheld the Economic Stabilization Act of 1970. This Act authorized the President to stabilize wages and prices at levels not lower than those on May 15, 1970, with such adjustments as might be necessary to prevent "gross inequities." [**Amalgamated Meat Cutters v. Connally**, 337 F. Supp. 737 (D.D.C. 1971) (three-judge court)]

1) The court held that the statute—under which the President had imposed a wage-price freeze—*sufficiently "marked out" the field* in which the President was to act by setting a base date and providing for adjustment of inequities. Legislative history and previous wage-price control statutes were held to indicate the congressional intent.

2) The court also found it relevant that Congress had provided a relatively **short life span** for executive authority (so that frequently Congress would have to reexamine the President's actions) and that judicial review was available.

3) Significantly, the court in *Meat Cutters* warned the agency to set some **administrative standards** by promulgating regulations. It implied that if the agency failed to narrow the statute by enacting regulations, the whole scheme might later be held unconstitutional. However, in **Whitman v. American Trucking Associations**, 531 U.S. 457 (2001), the Supreme Court stated that if a statute is invalid because of a lack of standards, the defect cannot be repaired by the agency.

d. The Nondelegation Doctrine Today—*Whitman v. American Trucking Associations*

Following the well-worn path it has followed ever since the aberrations of *Schecter* and *Panama Refining,* the Supreme Court's most recent pronouncement on the Nondelegation Doctrine, **Whitman v. American Trucking Associations,** 531 U.S. 457 (2001), found that the statute in question contained the "intelligible principle" necessary to uphold the delegation.

(1) The D.C. Circuit Tries the *Meat Cutters* Suggestion

The Clean Air Act instructs the Environmental Protection Agency ("EPA") to adopt ambient air quality standards "which in the judgment of the Administrator . . . and allowing an adequate margin of safety, are requisite to protect the public health." This statute obviously gave the EPA little guidance on where to set the standard; it did not indicate how much pollution is too much. The lower court held that the statute violated the nondelegation doctrine, but it would have allowed the EPA to cure this problem by providing the missing intelligible principle itself via regulation. [**American Trucking Ass'ns v. EPA**, 175 F.3d 1027 (D.C. Cir. 1999)]

(2) The Supreme Court Rejects That Suggestion

Contra the D.C. Circuit, the Supreme Court held that if a statute violates the Nondelegation Doctrine, an agency cannot cure it by adopting a narrowing construction. The very act of doing so, the Court explained, would require the agency to legislate in violation of the doctrine. The Court also held that the statute in question did provide a sufficiently intelligible principle. That principle arose from the word "requisite," meaning not higher or lower than necessary to protect the public health with an adequate margin of safety, without considering any other factors (such as the cost of the regulations). As a result, the statute did not unlawfully delegate legislative power to the EPA. [**Whitman v. American Trucking Ass'ns**, *supra*]

EXAM TIP — *gilbert* LAW SUMMARIES

If you are given a statute on your exam and need to figure out if it violates the Nondelegation Doctrine, bend over backwards to find some ***intelligible principle within the statute***. And remember that the agency cannot fix the problem by adopting some limiting principle. The limiting principle must be ***in the statute!***

(a) Rationale for Refusing to Find a Violation

The Court stated: "[Congress] must provide substantial guidance on setting air standards that affect the entire national economy. But even in sweeping regulatory schemes we have never demanded, as the court of appeals did here, that statutes provide a 'determinate criterion' for saying 'how much of the regulated harm is too much.' . . . 'A certain degree of discretion, and thus of lawmaking, inheres in most executive or judicial action.' "

e. Dissents Advocating Revival of the Nondelegation Doctrine

Although the Nondelegation Doctrine appears to be a dormant issue, there is often some support on the Supreme Court for reviving it. Some concurring and dissenting opinions call for Congress to make the difficult and fundamental policy choices, rather than passing them on to the agencies. If these views become the majority on the Supreme Court, it is quite possible that the Nondelegation Doctrine will be revived. [*See, e.g.,* **Whitman v. American Trucking Ass'ns**, *supra* (Thomas dissent would reject the "intelligible principle" rule.); **Industrial Union Dep't v. American Petroleum Inst.**, 448 U.S. 607 (1980) (Rehnquist concurrence); **American Textile Manufacturers Inst. v. Donovan**, 452 U.S. 490 (1981) (Rehnquist and Burger dissent)]

f. Delegations to Federal Judges

Congress may delegate rulemaking powers to federal judges when the issue has an appropriate relationship to the judicial function and the delegation entails no danger of undermining the integrity of the judicial branch or expanding its powers beyond constitutional bounds. [**Mistretta v. United States**, 488 U.S. 361 (1989) (upholding constitutionality of sentencing guidelines promulgated by commission that includes federal judges as members)]

g. Delegations to Private Parties

Delegation of rulemaking powers to private parties carries with it the risk that the private parties will use their powers to gain an advantage over their competitors.

(1) State Cases

Numerous cases at the state level have found such delegations invalid. For example, the Texas Supreme Court invalidated a delegation of power to a private foundation that had the power to impose assessments on cotton farmers to eradicate the boll weevil. The decision was based on a multifactor analysis that particularly stressed the absence of meaningful review of the foundation's activity by a state agency, the fact that it was run by cotton farmers who had a pecuniary interest in the program and who lacked any training or experience, and the absence of standards to guide the foundation. [**Texas Boll Weevil Eradication Found., Inc. v. Lewellen**, 952 S.W.2d 454 (Tex. 1997)]

(2) Federal Cases

At the federal level, one case in the 1930s invalidated a delegation of power to coal companies and unions to make contracts that would bind other coal companies. [**Carter v. Carter Coal Co.**, 298 U.S. 238 (1936)] Since that time, however, the federal courts have *upheld* such delegations, but in each case there were some *safeguards* against private abuse of power. [*See* **United States v. Rock Royal Coop.**, 307 U.S. 533 (1939) (private companies could veto rules but not initiate them); **Todd & Co. v. SEC**, 557 F.2d 1008 (3d Cir. 1977) (trade association could make rules but SEC could review and veto them). *But see* **Ass'n of American Railroads v. U.S. Dep't of Trans.**, 721 F.3d 666 (D.C. Cir. 2013) (invalidating an "unprecedented" delegation that: (a) gave Amtrak, a private entity, as much authority as the Federal Railroad Administration ("FRA") to draft regulations; and (b) gave Amtrak a veto over FRA regulatory preferences)] In essence, private entities may "help a government agency make its regulatory decisions," but the government must not cede regulatory control to them. [**Id.**]

3. Nondelegation and the Canon of Constitutional Avoidance

Even if a broad delegation of rulemaking authority is valid under the Nondelegation Doctrine, courts may *set aside particular rules* under the "ultra vires" doctrine—*i.e.,* if the court finds that the agency has adopted a rule outside the scope of its delegated power. Determining the scope of delegated power requires courts to construe agency enabling acts—the statutes that create and empower agencies. As part of this process, courts sometimes invoke the "canon of constitutional avoidance." This tool of statutory construction teaches that courts should, where reasonably possible, avoid construing a statute in a way that raises a serious constitutional question. If a court can reject a rule as ultra vires based on a narrow construction of an agency's statutory authority, then the court can avoid resolving whether that statutory authority, more generously construed, would be unconstitutional.

a. Constitutional Avoidance and OSHA

The Occupational Health and Safety Administration ("OSHA") has statutory authority to adopt workplace safety standards "reasonably necessary or appropriate to provide safe or healthful employment and places of employment." The agency adopted an extremely burdensome regulation that set benzene concentrations at one part per million. This was the lowest level that was economically feasible for the chemical industry and below any level scientifically proved to be dangerous. The Court expressed severe doubts about the breadth of the delegation to OSHA, which left unclear whether the agency was to balance costs and benefits. As a result, the Court narrowly construed the statute, finding that OSHA's authority to ensure a "safe" work environment only allowed it to eliminate "significant risk of harm." Since OSHA had made no such finding, its rule was invalid. [**Indus. Union Dep't v. American Petroleum Inst.**, 448 U.S. 607 (1980)] In a concurring opinion, Justice Rehnquist argued that the statute violated the nondelegation doctrine because Congress, not the Court, must supply an ascertainable standard.

In a subsequent case, when OSHA made the required finding that a significant health risk existed, a majority of the Court upheld a rule setting permissible concentrations of cotton dust at the lowest feasible level. It held that the statute should be construed *not* to permit OSHA to conduct a cost-benefit analysis of the rule. Two justices dissented, arguing that the statute was an invalid delegation of legislative power. [**American Textile Mfrs. Inst. v. Donovan,** 452 U.S. 490 (1981)]

b. **An Example from the States**

A state statute allowed the agency to "deal with any matters affecting the public health." The agency adopted elaborate anti-smoking rules, such as banning smoking in various public places and requiring smoke-free work areas. The court held that the rules were ultra vires, in part because the relatively standardless delegation of power left it to the agency to balance health concerns against cost and privacy interests. Moreover, the legislature itself had tried and failed to adopt anti-smoking legislation, which suggests that the agency should not have tried to fill the gap on its own. [**Boreali v. Axelrod**, 71 N.Y.2d 1 (1987)]

EXAM TIP

On your exam, do not dispose of a Nondelegation Doctrine question without considering whether you might use its constitutional avoidance "shadow" to argue for a narrow construction of the agency's authority.

c. **Deploying the Canon to Avoid Other Constitutional Issues**

A court might believe the statute or the rule violates a constitutional right or important civil liberty; however, to avoid a difficult constitutional question, the court can construe the statute narrowly and invalidate the particular rule on ultra vires rather than substantive constitutional grounds.

Example—denial of passports: The Secretary of State adopted a rule denying passports to Communists, acting under a statute providing that the Secretary "may grant and issue passports . . . under such rules as the President shall designate." The Court construed the statute narrowly, holding that it did not confer authority to deny passports for political activity, thus invalidating the regulation. The Court thereby avoided having to deal with difficult constitutional issues concerning the right to travel. [**Kent v. Dulles**, 357 U.S. 116 (1958)] *Note:* In a later case, the Court upheld a regulation prohibiting the issuance of passports for travel to Cuba. Here the court found that Congress had intended the Secretary to impose area restrictions; thus, this regulation was within the delegated power. [**Zemel v. Rusk**, 381 U.S. 1 (1965)]

Compare: The Supreme Court is not always consistent on this point. It has refused to construe a statute narrowly so as to invalidate regulations that raised serious constitutional questions about free speech and the right to abortion. It construed the statute broadly so as to uphold the regulation and also squarely upheld the constitutional validity of the challenged regulation. The opinion suggests that the Court was anxious to reach and decide the substantive constitutional issues. [**Rust v. Sullivan**, 500 U.S. 173 (1991) (upholding a regulation prohibiting personnel in federally funded family planning centers from discussing abortion with patients)]

C. Nondelegation Doctrine (Judicial Power)

1. Introduction

Article III, § 1, of the Constitution provides that "[t]he judicial Power of the United States, shall be vested in one supreme Court, and in such inferior Courts as the Congress may from time to time ordain and establish." To protect the decisional independence of federal judges, this section also provides that they "shall hold their Offices during good Behaviour" and "receive for their Services[ ] a Compensation[ ] [that] shall not be diminished."

The Supreme Court insists that this **judicial power** cannot be shared across branches. [**Stern v. Marshall,** 131 S.Ct. 2594 (2011)] Nonetheless, administrative agencies "adjudicate" disputes in countless contexts. The trick, therefore, is to determine the point at which administrative adjudication crosses the line into an impermissible usurpation of "judicial power." Regrettably, the precedents and analysis involved are more difficult and convoluted than in the analogous context of determining whether an agency's rulemaking usurps legislative power.

2. The *Schor* Framework for Determining Article III Violations

In **Commodity Futures Trading Commission v. Schor,** 478 U.S. 833 (1986), the Court declared that whether agency adjudication infringes the judicial power depends on pragmatic consideration of factors including:

> [a] the extent to which the "essential attributes of judicial power" are reserved to Article III courts, and, conversely, the extent to which the non-Article III forum exercises the range of jurisdiction and powers normally vested only in Article III courts, [b] the origins and importance of the right to be adjudicated, [c] and the concerns that drove Congress to depart from the requirements of Article III.

Whether a party has consented to adjudication by a non-Article III tribunal is also relevant. [**Id.**; **Stern v. Marshall,** 131 S.Ct. 2594 (2011)] Applying these factors, the Court concluded that the CFTC could adjudicate a common-law claim for debt brought by a commodities broker as a compulsory counterclaim against his unhappy client, Schor, who had filed a statutory claim for reparations against the broker before the CFTC.

a. Essential Attributes of Judicial Power

This *Schor* factor inquires how closely the agency's adjudicative powers approximate those of a federal court. In upholding the constitutionality of agency adjudication in *Schor*, the Court observed that: (1) the agency exercised authority over a narrow and "particularized area of law" rather than the broad jurisdiction of a federal court; (2) the agency's orders were not self-executing but instead required judicial enforcement; (3) the agency's actions were subject to substantial judicial review; and (4) the agency did not exercise powers associated with district courts such as presiding over jury trials.

b. Origins and Importance of the Right—The Public/Private Rights Distinction

In part, this *Schor* factor refers to the difficult distinction between "public" and "private rights." The archetypical "public right" involves a dispute between a private party and the government over matters that could have been determined exclusively by the political branches in any event. To illustrate, consider that sovereign immunity, absent waiver by Congress, blocks actions against the federal government. As Congress enjoys total control over *whether* a private party can sue the government, it arguably follows that Congress also can control *how* such actions proceed and can assign them to non-Article III adjudication.

An archetypical "private right" involves a dispute between two private parties rooted in state-based, common law. A contract dispute between two private parties is a good example. Congress had nothing to do with creating these sorts of rights, which, in many cases, are much older than the United States.

Note well—the public-private distinction has never been clear, and it has grown fuzzier in recent years.

(1) Private Disputes over Public Rights

Even though a dispute is between two private parties, it may nonetheless implicate a public right where "the claim at issue derives from a federal regulatory scheme" or where "resolution of the claim by an expert government agency is deemed essential to a limited regulatory objective within the agency's authority." [*Stern, supra,* p. 11] For instance, a statutory scheme required companies to share data but also required suitable compensation. The right to compensation, although it ran between private parties, was integrally related to the statutory scheme. It was therefore, in effect, a matter of public right that could be determined by an arbitrator. [**Thomas v. Union Carbide Agric. Prods. Co.,** 473 U.S. 568 (1985)]

(2) Significance of the Public/Private Distinction

The significance of pigeonholing a right as "public" or "private" is not as clear as one might like. In recent decades, the view that federal agencies cannot adjudicate "private rights" has enjoyed considerable support on the Court. [**Northern Pipeline Constr. Co. v. Marathon Pipe Line Co.,** 458 U.S. 50 (1982) (plurality) (holding that Congress could grant adjudicatory authority to non-Article III judges only for territorial courts, courts-martial, or for determining public rights)]

In *Schor, supra,* p. 11, the Court rejected this categorical approach. The origins of a claim in state-based common law are significant because these sorts of claims have historically been determined within the federal system by Article III judges. Encroachment in this area therefore raises greater separation-of-powers concerns, calling for more searching review. Thus, the conclusion that a matter involves a "private right" weighs against allowing non-Article III adjudication but does not categorically block it.

Later cases involving bankruptcy judges (who are not Article III judges) contain language or reasoning that seems to contradict *Schor*'s flexible approach. [**Granfinanciera S.A. v. Nordberg,** 492 U.S. 33 (1989) (stating that if a statutory cause of action does not implicate a "public right," then "Congress may not assign its adjudication to a specialized non-Article III court"); ***Stern,*** *supra,* p. 11 (holding that a bankruptcy court could not determine a defamation claim that did not turn on a public right)] [*See also infra,* p. 13 for further discussion of the implications of *Stern* for *Schor*-style analysis]

(3) Two Paths Through the Thicket

The "private rights" problem is acute where an agency adjudicates a claim between two private parties—especially if that claim is rooted in state-based common law. The case law suggests two ways of approaching this problem to uphold an agency's adjudicatory authority. First, using the *Schor* approach, one might argue that an agency may, under some circumstances, adjudicate private rights, such as the common-law claim for debt involved in *Schor* itself. Second, an agency can try to take advantage of the fuzziness of the public/private rights distinction. Along these lines, the agency might argue that a claim involving two private parties should be regarded as "public" because it is "integrally related to a particular federal government action." [*Stern, supra,* p. 11; ***Thomas,*** *supra,* p. 12]

(4) State Courts and the Public/Private Right Distinction

Some state court cases also invalidate transfers to agencies of the power to decide private disputes. [**Wright v. Central DuPage Hosp. Ass'n.**, 347 N.E.2d 736 (Ill. 1976) (transfer of right to decide medical malpractice disputes)]

c. Concerns That Drove Congress

This *Schor* factor communicates the common-sense idea that administrative adjudicatory power is more likely to be upheld where it can be characterized as playing an important role in furthering a legitimate congressional statutory scheme.

d. Consent of the Parties

Maintenance of an independent judiciary protects individuals from arbitrary government action by ensuring neutral decisionmaking. In *Schor, supra,* p. 11, the Court observed that, insofar as Article III protects an individual right, it is waivable. Consent does not fully dispose of separation-of-powers concerns, however, because Article III protects the structural role of independent courts as part of the overall system of checks and balances. Parties cannot waive this structural protection. [**Id.**] Nonetheless, a party's consent to non-Article III adjudication remains a factor bearing on whether it infringes on the judicial power. [*Stern, supra,* p. 11]

e. Questions About *Schor* Raised by Stern

Many of the Court's most important explorations of the constitutional limits on adjudication by non-Article III tribunals have involved challenges to the authority of bankruptcy judges, who lack the constitutional tenure and salary protections of Article III judges. [***Northern Pipeline,*** *supra,* p. 12; ***Granfinanciera,*** *supra,* p. 12] In 2011, the Court decided another such case, ***Stern,*** *supra,* p. 11, which addressed whether a bankruptcy court could constitutionally determine a compulsory counterclaim for tortious interference. The majority concluded that this exercise of jurisdiction violated Article III because: (1) the claim did not implicate public rights; and (2) the bankruptcy court was not acting as an "adjunct" to an Article III court. The dissent, authored by Justice Breyer, observed that this approach seemed to ignore the *Schor* framework. Presumably in response, the majority expressly limited the implications of *Stern* for agency authority, observing that the bankruptcy and agency contexts are "markedly distinct" and that "we do not in this opinion express any view on how the [public rights] doctrine might apply in that different context." The tension between the two approaches, however, remains.

3. An Older, Overlapping Framework—Non-Article III "Adjuncts"

Crowell v. Benson, 285 U.S. 22 (1932), is associated with the idea that agency adjudication does not infringe on the judicial power so long as Article III courts retain sufficient power of review. In other words, it is okay for agencies to act as assistants or *adjuncts* to the federal courts. The federal statute at issue in *Crowell* created a workers' compensation scheme that required payments from employers to employees for injuries on navigable waters. As liability ran between private individuals, the Court categorized the claims as a matter of "private right." Nonetheless, Congress could entrust initial adjudication to an agency because its determinations were subject to sufficient control by Article III courts. These controls included: (a) the availability of judicial proceedings to set aside compensation orders and a requirement of judicial proceedings to enforce them; (b) de novo review of issues of law; and (c) rationality review of non-jurisdictional fact determinations. The *Crowell* majority insisted, however, that Article III courts must maintain plenary control over findings of "jurisdictional fact" that speak to the power of the agency to act. In *Crowell*, these included whether the claimant was an employee, and whether he was injured on navigable waters. This "jurisdictional fact" caveat has been severely criticized and has for the most part faded out of administrative law.

4. Administrative Authority to Adjudicate Penalties

An agency's authority to impose penalties for the violation of a regulation or statute generally depends on whether the penalty is a criminal sanction or a civil penalty.

a. Criminal Sanctions

The legislature may authorize an agency to *enact* a regulation, the violation of which is a crime—as long as *prosecution* for the violation is left to the courts. [**United States v. Grimaud,** 220 U.S. 506 (1911)]

(1) Agency May Not Imprison

Imprisonment for violating a regulation can be imposed only by the courts, and not by an agency. [**Wong Wing v. United States**, 163 U.S. 228 (1896)]

(a) Exceptions

Temporary confinement of aliens by administrative order, when incidental to exclusion or expulsion, is accepted. Similarly, preventive *quarantine* of persons with infectious diseases is permitted.

b. Civil Penalties

Many state and federal statutes allow agencies to *impose civil penalties* for violation of statutes or regulations.

(1) Importance of "Civil" vs. "Criminal" Penalty Distinction

Generally, if the penalty is labeled "civil" rather than "criminal," it can be assessed by an agency (instead of a court) without the protections afforded under criminal law. [**Waukegan v. Pollution Control Bd.**, 311 N.E.2d 146 (Ill. 1974); *and see* **Helvering v. Mitchell**, 303 U.S. 391 (1938) (agency can adjudicate the amount of tax owed by a taxpayer and can assess a penalty for fraud)]

(a) Double Jeopardy

Double jeopardy protects a defendant only against multiple criminal punishments. Normally, the imposition of civil penalties plus criminal penalties is not a violation of double jeopardy. Only in rare circumstances will a penalty that the legislature has described as civil be deemed by the court as criminal so as to trigger double jeopardy protection. [**Hudson v. United States**, 522 U.S. 93 (1997)]

(b) Jury Trial

Moreover, a penalty can be imposed *without* a jury trial—despite the Seventh Amendment—if a "public right" created by statute is being enforced. [**Atlas Roofing Co. v. Occupational Safety & Health Review Comm'n.**, 430 U.S. 442 (1977) (penalties up to $1,000 for serious violations, up to $10,000 for willful or repeated violations)]

(2) Punitive Damages

The California Supreme Court has held that, although agencies can be empowered to award both damages and civil penalties, they cannot be empowered to award punitive damages against one private litigant in favor of another. This invades the judicial province. [**McHugh v. Santa Monica Rent Control Bd.**, 777 P.2d 91 (Cal. 1989)]

D. Executive Controls Over Administrative Action

1. Appointment Power

One of the primary means of controlling agencies is appointing the people who run them. This is primarily a presidential (or gubernatorial) responsibility. **Article II, § 2, cl. 2** of the Constitution provides:

> ... he shall nominate, and by and with the advice and consent of the Senate, shall appoint ambassadors, other public ministers and consuls, judges of the Supreme Court, and all other officers of the United States, whose appointments are not herein otherwise provided for, and which shall be established by law: but the Congress may by law vest the appointment of such inferior officers, as they think proper, in the President alone, in the courts of law, or in the heads of departments.

a. "Officers of the United States"

The constitutional text controls appointments of "Officers of the United States." In the abstract, these are persons who "exercis[e] significant authority pursuant to the laws of the United States." [**Buckley v. Valeo**, 424 U.S. 1 (1976)] In *Buckley*, the Court determined that FEC Commissioners wielding extensive rulemaking and adjudicative powers were "Officers of the United States."

(1) There are also Officers of Congress

The Constitution does not authorize congressional appointment of Officers of the United States. Congress may, however, appoint *Officers of Congress* to "perform duties ... in aid of those functions that Congress may carry out itself." [***Buckley**, supra*] For instance,

Congress needs to gather information to legislate. Therefore, Congress can grant Officers of Congress powers of an "investigative or informative nature." [**Id.**]

(2) Employees

Not everyone who works for the federal government is an "officer." Most are "employees," who are "lesser functionaries subordinate to officers of the United States." [***Buckley**, supra*] In ***Landry v. FDIC***, the D.C. Circuit held that administrative law judges who do not render final agency decisions are employees rather than inferior officers. [204 F.3d 1125 (D.C. Cir. 2000)] [*Cf.* **Free Enter. Fund v. Pub. Co. Accounting Oversight Bd.**, 130 S.Ct. 3138 (2010) (noting that the issue of whether ALJs are officers is disputed)]

b. Appointment of "Inferior" Officers

The default mechanism for appointment of Officers of the United States is presidential nomination and Senate approval. Congress may, however, "by law vest the appointment of such inferior officers, as they think proper, in the President alone, in the courts of law, or in the heads of departments." **U.S. Const. Art. II, § 2, cl. 2.**

(1) Who Are You Calling "Inferior"?

"'[I]nferior officers' are officers whose work is directed and supervised at some level by other officers appointed by the President with the Senate's consent." [**Free Enter. Fund v. Pub. Co. Accounting Oversight Bd.**, 130 S.Ct. 3138 (2010)] In other words, an "inferior officer" is one who has a "superior" other than the President.

(2) Court Martial Judges

The Court upheld the appointment by the Secretary of Transportation of judges of the Coast Guard Court of Criminal Appeals because the judges are inferior officers. They are subordinate both: (a) to the Judge Advocate General, who exercises administrative control over them and can remove them without cause, and (b) to the Court of Appeals for the Armed Forces, which reviews their decisions. [**Edmonds v. United States**, 520 U.S. 651 (1997)]

(3) Independent Counsel

Under a sunsetted provision of the Ethics in Government Act of 1978, a panel of federal court judges had power to appoint independent counsel to investigate and prosecute executive branch officials. In a decision with strong political overtones, the Supreme Court concluded that these terrifically powerful officials were "inferior officers" and therefore could be appointed by judges rather than by the President. Grounds for this conclusion included: independent counsels were subject to removal for cause by the Attorney General, their duties were limited to the investigation of certain crimes, and their positions were temporary. [**Morrison v. Olson**, 487 U.S. 654 (1988)]

(4) Public Company Accounting Oversight Board Members

Congress created this agency in the aftermath of major accounting scandals to oversee auditing of public companies subject to securities laws. PCAOB has extensive rulemaking, adjudicatory, and enforcement powers. The Board is also, however, subject to extensive oversight by the SEC, which has authority to alter the Board's rules or sanctions. By statute, the SEC can remove Board members for good cause. As discussed below in p. 19, the Supreme Court threw out the good-cause limitation on SEC removal authority. Having thus increased the SEC's power over the Board, the Court easily concluded that Board members were "inferior officials" who thus could be appointed by the SEC rather than the President. [**Free Enter. Fund v. Pub. Co. Accounting Oversight Bd.**, 130 S.Ct. 3138 (2010) (observing that the power to remove at will is a "powerful tool for control")]

c. Recess Appointments

What if the President needs to appoint an officer subject to Senate confirmation when the Senate is unavailable? The framers thought of that problem and included the following constitutional provision:

> The President shall have power to fill up all vacancies that may happen during the recess of the Senate, by granting commissions which shall expire at the end of their next session.

Art. II, § 2, cl. 3.

(1) The D.C. Circuit on Recess Appointments in 2013

Recess appointments have provided a means for presidents to avoid the senatorial confirmation process, which has grown increasingly contentious and difficult in recent decades. In *Noel Canning v. NRLB*, 705 F.3d 490 (2013), the D.C. Circuit issued an opinion that pretty much eliminates this power. The court held that "recess" in this context refers solely to the period between sessions of the Senate. As the court seemed to accept the premise that the Senate is in charge of determining whether it is in "session," it follows that the Senate can block the President from making recess appointments. Further constricting the President, the court also held that the recess appointment power applies only to a vacancy that arises during the recess in which the power is deployed. (You will want to check on whether the Supreme Court has upheld or tossed *Noel Canning*.)

SUMMARY OF APPOINTMENTS OF OFFICERS AND GOVERNMENTAL EMPLOYEES

	PERMISSIBLE METHOD OF APPOINTMENT	EXAMPLES
SUPERIOR OFFICERS	Must be appointed by President with consent of the Senate	Cabinet officials; agency heads
INFERIOR OFFICERS	Statute may vest appointment in President, heads of departments, or courts of law. Senate consent not needed. Subject to control by superior officers.	Courts-martial judges who can be removed without cause; special prosecutors; PCAOB members
OTHER EMPLOYEES	May be appointed in any manner Congress prescribes	ALJs who cannot make final decisions; most other people working for the federal government, *e.g.*, computer technicians, administrative assistants, etc.

2. Removal Power

The flip-side of the appointment power is the removal power. Unlike the appointment power, no specific constitutional provision limits presidential authority to remove agency officials. The scope of this power has long been contested ground between the President and Congress.

a. Clash of Titans: Unitary Executive vs. Independent Agencies

Although no specific constitutional provision controls presidential removal power, the Constitution does vest the "executive power" in the President (**Art. II, § 1, cl. 1**), and it also charges the President with the duty to "take care that the laws be faithfully executed" (**Art. II, § 3**). Adherents of the "unitary executive" theory contend that the President, to wield his executive power properly, must have plenary authority to remove agency officials. Congress has nonetheless frequently protected various agency officials by requiring "good cause" for their removal. We refer to agencies that are headed by officials enjoying such protection as "independent agencies." Notwithstanding the objections of the unitary-executive camp, independent agencies form a deeply embedded part of the federal bureaucracy.

b. Evolution of the Constitutional Law of Independent Agencies

(1) 1926: The President Must Have Plenary Removal Power over Executive Officials

In *Myers v. United States*, 272 U.S. 52 (1926), the Court rejected as unconstitutional a statutory provision that required Senate consent for removal of postmasters. The Court reasoned that the President must have broad power of removal over all executive officers to ensure that his policies will be carried out by persons enjoying his full confidence.

(2) 1935: Quasi-Legislative/Quasi-Judicial Independent Agencies

In *Humphrey's Executor v. United States*, 295 U.S. 602 (1935), the Court held that Congress could constitutionally impose a for-cause limitation on presidential removal of commissioners of the FTC. The Court's rationale relied heavily on the FTC's rulemaking and adjudicatory authority. In light of these powers, the agency was not so much "executive" in nature as "quasi-legislative" and "quasi-judicial." As such, Congress could properly limit executive control over the agency by restricting presidential removal authority.

(3) 1988: Don't Interfere with the President Too Much

In the aftermath of Watergate, the Ethics in Government Act of 1978 authorized appointment of "independent counsel" to investigate and prosecute executive branch officials. Independent counsel could be removed by the Attorney General only for good cause. The *Humphrey's Executor* framework allowing such restrictions on removal for quasi-legislative/quasi-judicial agencies could not apply to independent counsel because prosecution has long been considered a core executive power.

The Court nonetheless upheld the constitutionality of the removal restriction in *Morrison v. Olson*, 487 U.S. 654 (1988). The Court explained that the "real question" when assessing the constitutionality of removal restrictions is whether they "are of such a nature that they impede[ ] the President's ability to perform his constitutional duty" to discharge the executive power and "take care that the laws be faithfully executed." The Court concluded the good-cause limitation on removal of independent counsel did not violate this standard. These officers have "limited jurisdiction and tenure and lack[ ] policymaking or significant administrative authority." Also, the good-cause restriction still left the President with authority to make sure that independent counsel performed their tasks competently and legally. As such, the Court could "not see how the President's need to control the exercise of . . . discretion [by independent counsel was] so central to the functioning of the Executive Branch as to require . . . that the counsel be terminable at will by the President." The Court conceded, however, that there "are some 'purely executive' officials who must be removable by the President at will if he is to be able to accomplish his constitutional role."

(4) 2010: Double For-Cause Limits Interfere Too Much

In the aftermath of major accounting scandals, Congress created the Public Company Accounting Oversight Board, granting it extensive regulatory powers over auditing of public companies. By statute, members were subject to removal for cause by the SEC. In *Free Enter. Fund v. Public Co. Accounting Oversight Bd.*, 130 S.Ct. 3138 (2010), the Court *assumed* that the President could remove SEC Commissioners only for cause. This meant that Congress had given two layers of good-cause protection to Board members from the President—that is: Board members were protected from removal by the SEC Commissioners, who were in turn protected from removal by the President. This double layer of protection interfered too much with presidential executive authority and was therefore unconstitutional. The Court dealt with this problem by invalidating the Board's good-cause protection from the SEC.

(5) Sidebar on Legislative Courts

Even without a statute limiting the President's removal power, the Court held that the President could not remove a member of the War Claims Commission without cause. The Commission had a judicial function (adjudicating claims of persons suffering damage from the enemy during World War II), which made removal without cause inappropriate. [**Weiner v. United States**, 357 U.S. 349 (1958)]

c. No Congressional Removal (Other than by Impeachment)

Congress may not retain the power to remove (or share in the process of removing) officials engaged in executive functions other than by impeachment. For example, a statute required the Comptroller General to determine whether the annual federal budget deficit would exceed targets in the statute, a matter involving considerable expertise and judgment. If the deficit exceeded the targets, mandatory budget cuts followed. The Comptroller General could be removed only by Congress—not by the President. The statute was held unconstitutional because the Comptroller General would be engaged in executive action, but Congress retained the power to control him through its removal power. [**Bowsher v. Synar,** 478 U.S. 714 (1986)]

3. Fiscal Power

The President (through the Office of Management and Budget ("OMB"), a White House staff agency) can control administrative requests to Congress for appropriations or changes in legislation.

4. Organizational Power

The President has extensive statutory powers to create, abolish, and reorganize agencies within the executive branch.

5. Centralized Review of Rulemaking

By a series of executive orders issued over several decades, presidents of both parties have imposed substantial controls over major rulemaking by executive agencies. [*See especially* **Executive Order 12,866**, *infra*, p. 98] E.O. 12,866 requires executive agencies to assess the costs and benefits of many significant regulatory actions. These actions are subject to review by the Office of Information and Regulatory Affairs ("OIRA"), which is a division of the OMB. The executive order procedure enables the President to exert control over the rulemaking function of all executive branch agencies to make sure the rules implement the President's program.

6. Direction of Agency Heads

Statutes usually delegate authority to agency heads, not to the President, to adopt rules or take other action. It is unclear whether the President has legal authority to direct agency heads in the executive branch to take action that the heads do not wish to take, but modern Presidents assert that they have such power. Proponents of the unitary executive believe that it would not be constitutional to vest such power in any office below that of the President. Other scholars say that statutes granting discretionary authority to agency heads mean that the President lacks such power. This important issue has not been settled by the Supreme Court. As a practical matter, however, agency heads tend to listen closely to the President who appointed them.

7. Inspectors General

Inspectors general are posted throughout the federal government to audit federal agencies and departments for fraud, waste, or abuse. [**Inspector General Act of 1978**, 5 U.S.C. app. 3]

8. Ombudsman

Ombudsmen investigate and correct public complaints about specific administrative action. An ombudsman has no formal powers, but agencies normally follow the advice of an ombudsman who has decided that an agency has acted illegally or improperly. Many state and federal agencies employ ombudsmen.

9. Gubernatorial Veto of Rules

Governors in some states have the power to veto rules. [*See* **1981 Model State APA § 3–202**]

SUMMARY OF EXECUTIVE CONTROLS OVER ADMINISTRATIVE ACTION

- ☑ *Appointment power*—power of executive to appoint agency heads, superior officers (with consent of Senate) and inferior officers;
- ☑ *Removal power*—but Congress can impose good-cause limitations on removal so long as they do not unduly interfere with the President's ability to perform her constitutional duty;
- ☑ *Fiscal power*—can request Congress to fund/defund agency;
- ☑ *Organizational power*—to create, abolish, reorganize agencies within the executive branch;
- ☑ *Rulemaking power*—centralizing control over agency rulemaking via executive orders requiring, inter alia, cost/benefit analysis;
- ☑ *Inspector General*—audit for fraud, waste, and abuse; and
- ☑ *Ombudsmen*—investigate and correct complaints from public.

E. Legislative Controls Over Administrative Action

1. Introduction

Aside from passing legislation that alters, amends, or repeals existing regulatory statutes, Congress or state legislators have numerous tools to engage in oversight of the actions of administrative agencies.

2. Standing Committees

Standing committees of the federal or state legislatures keep abreast of agency activities in particular areas, often by holding oversight hearings. Testifying at such hearings often consumes large quantities of the executive officials' time. Standing committees sponsor legislation to amend existing laws to deal with problems discovered during the oversight process.

3. Review Committees

Numerous states have administrative rules review committees ("ARRCs") that routinely review the legality and desirability of agency rules. In some of those states, if an ARRC disapproves a rule, the agency has the burden of proof of validity of the rule on judicial review. [**1981 Model State APA § 3–204(d)**]

4. Investigations

Other legislative committees concerned with general government operations may investigate the conduct of particular agencies. Occasionally, Congress appoints "watchdog" committees to examine the operations of particular agencies and to publicize controversial administrative actions. The General Accountability Office ("GAO"), headed by the Comptroller General, is a congressional watchdog agency that investigates executive branch agencies to see whether they are acting legally and efficiently.

5. Appropriations

In making appropriations, the legislature may increase or decrease the resources that an agency has available to enforce existing laws. By cutting appropriations to an agency, the legislature can express its disapproval of the actions the agency has taken. Occasionally, in appropriations bills, Congress will enact an "earmark" that prohibits an agency from spending money on a rulemaking project or on enforcement of an existing rule.

6. Appointments

The Senate must consent to presidential appointments of high-level administrative and executive positions. However, Congress cannot itself make appointments of persons who will engage in rulemaking, adjudication, or core executive functions. [*See, supra,* pp. 15, 19]

7. Legislative Veto—A Power Congress Used to Have

a. Congressional Vetoes

Congress cannot retain a "legislative veto" of administrative adjudication or rulemaking. [**INS v. Chadha,** 462 U.S. 919 (1983)] Prior to the *Chadha* decision, Congress employed the legislative veto to overturn administrative rules (and sometimes adjudications) after they were adopted.

Some statutes allowed Congress to veto agency action by resolution of both houses, sometimes by resolution of only one house, but always *without* the President's signature. The *Chadha* decision invalidated all legislative vetoes (including two-house veto provisions) on the bases of: (i) bicameralism, which requires that legislative action be taken only by agreement of both houses; and (ii) the lack of a presidential signature (or repassage of the bill by each house by a two-thirds vote).

b. State Legislative Vetoes

Most state decisions agree with *Chadha*. [*See, e.g.,* **Missouri Coal. for the Env't v. Joint Comm. on Admin. Rules,** 948 S.W.2d 125 (Mo. 1997)] However, one state has upheld a legislative veto statute. [**Mead v. Arnell,** 791 P.2d 410 (Idaho 1990)]

c. Congressional Review Act

Congress passed the Congressional Review Act ("CRA") [5 U.S.C. §§ 801–808] to reclaim some of the ground it lost because of the *Chadha* case. The CRA requires that all rules of general applicability be submitted to Congress and to the General Accountability Office ("GAO") before they take effect. In the case of a "major rule," the rule cannot take effect for at least sixty calendar days after it is submitted to Congress. In the case of either major or non-major rules, Congress can veto the rule by enacting a joint resolution of disapproval. A joint resolution of disapproval is like a statute; it must be approved by both houses and signed by the President (or passed by a two-thirds majority over the President's veto). The statute provides for a fast track for congressional consideration of proposed rules. If a rule goes into effect and then is disapproved by Congress, the rule is treated as if it had never taken effect. Additionally, if a rule is disapproved, the agency may not reissue the rule in substantially the same form unless Congress enacts legislation allowing it to do so.

8. Presidential Line Item Vetoes

The Line Item Veto Act was an attempt by Congress to limit government spending. It gave the President power to veto a single appropriation out of a large appropriation bill without having to veto the entire bill. Similarly, the President could veto a single tax benefit without vetoing the entire tax bill. The Supreme Court struck down the Line Item Veto Act because it allowed the President to amend a law without going through the legislative process. It refused to find an analogy to the case law upholding delegation of rulemaking power, given that the rulemaking delegation cases do not allow the President to actually change the text of laws enacted by Congress. Rulemaking delegations are intended to carry out a congressional purpose, but the Line Item Veto Act allows the President to act contrary to congressional purpose. [**Clinton v. City of New York,** 524 U.S. 417 (1998)]

9. Miscellaneous Controls

Legislators may participate in notice and comment rulemaking or make ex parte contacts with agencies engaged in rulemaking. They may also engage in "status inquiries" to agencies about pending adjudicatory matters involving their constituents. Such status inquiries are not prohibited ex parte contacts. However, legislators should not attempt to influence pending adjudications, *e.g.,* by holding a hearing and criticizing agency adjudicators about preliminary rulings in the case. [*See* **Pillsbury Co. v. FTC,** 354 F.2d 952 (5th Cir. 1966) (such legislative interference denied due process to party litigating against the agency)]

SUMMARY OF VALID LEGISLATIVE CONTROLS OVER ADMINISTRATIVE ACTION

CONGRESS HAS THE FOLLOWING CONTROLS OVER ADMINISTRATIVE ACTION

- ☑ *Legislative control*—passing legislation that amends or repeals existing regulatory statutes;
- ☑ *Standing committees* (often by oversight hearings)—sponsor legislation that amends or repeals existing legislation;
- ☑ *Investigations*—monitoring by specially appointed "watchdogs" or the GAO;
- ☑ *Appropriations*—increasing or decreasing funding to agencies;
- ☑ *Appointments*—the United States Senate consents to high-level appointments;
- ☑ *Congressional Review Act*—allows Congress (with Presidential approval) to override agency rules;
- ☑ *Participation in rulemaking procedures*—*e.g.,* submitting comments in notice and comment rulemaking; and
- ☑ *"Status inquiries"*—submitted to agencies about pending adjudicatory matters.

Chapter Two
The Due Process Right to a Hearing

CONTENTS	PAGE
Key Exam Issues	26
A. **Interests Protected by Due Process—"Liberty" and "Property"**	26
B. **Timing of the Hearing**	33
C. **Elements of the Hearing**	36
D. **Issues That Do Not Require a Hearing for Resolution**	39
E. **The State Action Requirement for Triggering Due Process**	42

Key Exam Issues

This chapter addresses the constitutional requirements of procedural due process, except for the requirement of an unbiased decisionmaker, which is discussed in Chapter 4 (Adjudicative Integrity). Chapter 3 focuses on adjudicatory requirements imposed by statute or agency rule rather than by the Constitution. In analyzing a client's rights to a hearing, always consider *all alternative sources* of procedural protection: constitutional, statutory, and agency regulation.

When assessing a due process problem, you will typically have to consider two different types of issues. The first is whether due process guarantees apply to the action in question—*i.e.*, has due process been triggered? Assuming that the answer to this first question is a yes, the second assesses what procedures due process requires in the context at issue—*i.e.*, how much process is due?

1. *Has due process been triggered?*

    a. *The Adjudication/Rulemaking Distinction.* Due process draws a distinction between adjudications that turn on individualized facts (*i.e.*, who did what to whom) and rulemakings that turn on matters of "legislative fact" and policy judgments. Procedural due process guarantees apply to the former, not the latter. Thus, you may have a due process right to a hearing to determine whether you broke the speed limit; you do not have a due process right to participate in legislative proceedings to determine the speed limit.

    b. *The State Action Requirement.* Due process constrains governmental action, not private action. Sometimes, however, actions by private actors may be chargeable to the state.

    c. *Are "liberty" or "property" at stake?* The Constitution's due process guarantees apply to deprivations of "life, liberty, or property." For the most part, your administrative law course won't worry about the "life" interest, leaving it to other courses. You will, however, likely focus on some of the extensive case law examining the limits of "liberty" and "property."

2. *How much process is due (and when)?* This question arises because a claimant contends that due process demands that the government add some particular element to its procedures or change their timing. For example, a claimant might demand an evidentiary hearing prior to the deprivation at issue. In assessing such claims, courts apply a balancing test that examines three factors:

    a. The strength and nature of the private interest affected;

    b. The incremental benefits of adding the requested procedure; and

    c. The governmental interest in not providing the requested procedure.

A. Interests Protected by Due Process—"Liberty" and "Property"

1. Procedural Due Process

Constitutional due process under the Fifth and Fourteenth Amendments generally requires that federal and state governments provide notice and some kind of hearing before taking an action that deprives an individual of "liberty" or "property." An impartial decision-maker must also be provided.

a. Purposes of Procedural Due Process

As a basic ingredient of administrative law, the right to notice and a hearing provides vital protection against arbitrary government action. It helps to insure that decisions will be based only upon facts developed in the hearing. It helps to instill a feeling of fair treatment in the affected person. It also promotes participation and dialogue by affected individuals in the decisionmaking process. [**Marshall v. Jerrico Inc.,** 446 U.S. 238 (1980)]

b. Distinguish—Substantive Due Process

Substantive due process means that government must *justify* deprivations of liberty or property. In the case of economic interests, such action triggers only rational basis scrutiny by courts. Courts often state that governmental action that "shocks the conscience" may violate substantive due process. [**County of Sacramento v. Lewis,** 523 U.S. 833 (1998)] But deprivations of certain fundamental interests (e.g., control over one's own body or deprivations of rights protected by the Bill of Rights) trigger strict judicial scrutiny. *Note:* Administrative law courses concentrate on procedural due process; substantive due process is considered in constitutional law courses.

2. "Liberty"

The "liberty" interest protected by due process has been broadly defined. It includes the right to contract, engage in common occupations, marry, establish a home, bring up children, worship freely, and acquire useful knowledge—in short, the right to enjoy the qualities of life recognized as essential to the pursuit of happiness. [**Bd. of Regents v. Roth,** 408 U.S. 564 (1972)] Some examples of deprivation of liberty follow.

a. Imposition of "Stigma-Plus"

Government action that imposes a stigma may amount to a deprivation of liberty if the action also carries legal consequences.

(1) Public and Allegedly False Information

To trigger a deprivation of liberty, stigmatic information must be ***both public and allegedly false.*** Thus, liberty interests were not implicated where the reasons for discharge were not made public [**Bishop v. Wood,** 426 U.S. 341 (1976)], or where the derogatory information was true. [**Codd v. Velger,** 429 U.S. 624 (1977)]

(2) The "Plus" Part of "Stigma-Plus"

To trigger a name-clearing hearing, government imposition of a stigma must generally be accompanied by some other action that has legal, rather than practical, consequences ("stigma-plus").

> **Example—stigma-plus:** A state official labeled Plaintiff a public drunkard, meaning that Plaintiff could not legally buy alcohol. The combination of the stigma, along with the legal prohibition against buying alcohol, met the stigma-plus requirement. [**Wisconsin v. Constantineau,** 400 U.S. 433 (1971)]

> **Example—stigma-plus:** The "plus" for stigma-plus can take the form of loss of government employment where the government gives stigmatizing, public reasons for termination and the plaintiff contests those reasons. [**Hammer v. City of Osage Beach, Missouri,** 318 F.3d 832 (2003) (citing **Board of Regents v. Roth,** 408 U.S. 564 (1972) (stating that "a government employee has a liberty interest in his or her good name and reputation, which is entitled to protection when he or she is fired based on allegations of

dishonesty, immorality, or illegality")] Thus, City Manager's liberty interest was implicated where Mayor released press release accusing City Manager of illegal on-the-job conduct in connection with termination of City Manager's at-will employment. [**Hammer,** *supra.*]

Example—no stigma-plus: The sheriff circulated handbills to merchants describing Plaintiff as a shoplifter. This was highly damaging, but did not deprive Plaintiff of liberty absent some action by the government changing Plaintiff's legal rights. The sheriff's action might be tortious (thus giving rise to a tort action under state law), but it did not trigger an obligation to provide a name-clearing hearing. [**Paul v. Davis,** 424 U.S. 693 (1976)]

Example—no stigma-plus: After Plaintiff resigned from his government job as a psychologist, his supervisor sent an unfavorable letter to another government hospital, which then refused to hire Plaintiff. Because Plaintiff resigned rather than being discharged, the derogatory letter did not meet the stigma-plus requirement. [**Siegert v. Gilley,** 500 U.S. 226 (1991)]

EXAM TIP

For your exam, remember that "stigma" alone is insufficient to trigger the right to a hearing—some *adverse legal consequence* resulting from the agency action is required.

b. Deprivation of Constitutional Rights

Government action against a person that *violates substantive constitutional rights* is a deprivation of liberty. For example, discharging an employee for engaging in protected speech would violate the First Amendment; the action would also trigger procedural protection. However, the Court has held that agencies need *not* provide a prior hearing in such cases. The person's interests can be vindicated in an action for damages in federal court under the Civil Rights Act. [42 U.S.C. § 1983; **Perry v. Sindermann,** 408 U.S. 593 (1972)] More direct infringements on First Amendment interests (such as refusal of parade permits or seizure of allegedly obscene books) require the state to provide prior notice and a hearing.

c. Deportation of Aliens

Deportation is a deprivation of liberty and triggers a right to a hearing. [**Wong Yang Sung v. McGrath,** 339 U.S. 33 (1950)] However, there is *no right* to a hearing in connection with *exclusion* of an alien attempting to enter the country—even where the alien asserts a right to enter. [**United States *ex rel.* Knauff v. Shaughnessy,** 338 U.S. 537 (1950)]

d. The Liberty Interest in Prison After Criminal Conviction

Imprisonment for a crime is the ultimate deprivation of liberty. Criminal procedure provides the process due in such cases, and, for most purposes, it extinguishes the liberty interest during incarceration. Nonetheless, the Due Process Clause of its own force protects prisoners from deprivations outside the scope of their sentences. Also, a liberty interest "may arise from an expectation or interest created by state laws or policies." [**Wilkinson v. Austin,** 545 U.S. 209 (2005)]

(1) Liberty Interests Protected in Prison Independent of State Regulation

(a) *Transfer from prison to mental hospital.* [**Vitek v. Jones**, 445 U.S. 480 (1980) (transfer of inmate from prison to mental hospital not "within the range of confinement justified by imposition of a prison sentence"; consequences of involuntary commitment for mental illness are "qualitatively different" from those of criminal conviction)]

(b) *Involuntary administration of psychotropic drugs to prisoners.* [**Washington v. Harper**, 494 U.S. 210 (1990) (prisoner possessed "significant liberty interest in avoiding the unwanted administration of antipsychotic drugs under the Due Process Clause of the Fourteenth Amendment")]

(c) *Decisions inevitably lengthening prisoner's term of confinement,* for example by canceling "good time credits."

(d) *Transfer to a "super-max" prison* with unusually harsh conditions of confinement. [**Wilkinson v. Austin**, 545 U.S. 209 (2005)]

(2) Liberty Interests in Prison Created by State Laws or Policies

State laws or policies governing the length or terms of confinement may, under some circumstances, create a liberty interest protected by due process. [**Sandin v. Conner**, 515 U.S. 472 (1995)]

(a) Early Release Cases and the "Entitlement" Approach to Finding a Liberty Interest

There is no constitutional right to a reduction in sentence for good behavior. A state may, however, create an entitlement to a reduction that it cannot take away without respecting due process. In a series of cases in the 1970s and 1980s, the Court held that a state creates a liberty interested protected by due process where the state uses mandatory language to trigger early release based on specified findings. [**Wolff v. McDonnell**, 418 U.S. 539 (1974) (prisoner had liberty interest in "good time" credits established by state policy); **Bd. of Pardons v. Allen**, 482 U.S. 369 (1987) (parole system providing that inmate shall be released if certain findings were made created liberty interest in parole); **Greenholtz v. Nebraska Penal Inmates**, 442 U.S. 1 (1979) (similar)]. As noted in the next paragraph, later cases have undermined this approach to finding a liberty interest based on mandatory language in a state law or policy.

(b) *Sandin*'s Stricter Approach to the Liberty Interest

In more recent cases, the Court has expressed concern that finding liberty interests based on mandatory language in state regulations is counterproductive because it discourages states from adopting regulations and encourages excessive litigation by prisoners. The task of finding liberty interests should focus not on whether a state uses mandatory language but instead on the nature of the deprivation. A state regulation governing use of a restraint may create a liberty interest where the restraint "imposes atypical and significant hardship on the inmate in relation to the ordinary incidents of prison life." [**Sandin v. Conner**, 515 U.S. 472 (1995)]

In *Sandin,* the Court held that a 30-day period of administrative segregation for a prisoner serving a 30 years-to-life sentence did not satisfy this standard. In a later case, the Court held that transfer to "Supermax" conditions, including solitary confinement for an indefinite period, did trigger due process. [**Wilkinson v. Austin**, 545 U.S. 209 (2005)]

e. Expulsion or Suspension from School

Expulsion or suspension from public school or college may amount to a deprivation of liberty and trigger due process protection. [**Goss v. Lopez,** 419 U.S. 565 (1975)]

(1) Expulsion from College

Due process requires that expulsion from a public college *for disciplinary reasons* be accompanied by adequate procedural safeguards, including an oral hearing and a right to present evidence. [**Papish v. Univ. of Missouri,** 410 U.S. 667 (1973)]

(2) Academic Dismissals

There is *no right* to a hearing in connection with a dismissal for academic deficiencies. The only requirement is that the school must inform the student of academic problems in time for her to try to correct them and that the decision be carefully and deliberately made. [**Univ. of Missouri v. Horowitz,** 435 U.S. 78 (1978)] *Rationale:* Subjective academic judgments are not susceptible to review by trial-type proceedings and it would be disruptive to project the courts into this arena.

(3) High School Suspensions

A suspension from high school is an invasion of liberty. In the case of a suspension lasting 10 days or less, the required procedure is merely a conference with the disciplinarian and an opportunity for the student to state her side. No greater formality is required. [**Goss v. Lopez,** *supra,* p. 30] In a case of a suspension lasting more than 10 days, a more formal hearing may be required.

EXAM TIP

Don't be fooled by an exam question that deals with a student's expulsion from a private school. Remember that due process is triggered **only by government action.** However, expulsion from private schools does trigger a right to a hearing under the laws of some states. In addition, such a hearing might be available under a theory of express or implied contract.

3. "Property"—Old and New

The word "property" includes far more than money, land, or chattels. It includes "entitlements," such as welfare or legally protected employment relationships or licenses. Under prior law, such entitlements were considered "privileges" rather than rights, and thus revocable by the government without providing any procedure, but the right-privilege distinction has been abolished. If the benefit in question can be denied or withdrawn at the discretion of a government official, it is not treated as "property." But if the benefit can be denied or withdrawn only pursuant to non-discretionary standards, it is treated as "property." This type of property-by-entitlement is often called "New Property."

a. Welfare

A person receiving welfare or other government benefits under statutory and administrative standards defining eligibility has an interest in continued receipt of the benefits. If the state wants to terminate the benefits, it must provide notice and a hearing before doing so. [**Goldberg v. Kelly,** 397 U.S. 254 (1970) (termination of welfare payments under Aid to Families with Dependent Children ("AFDC") program deprived recipient of due process)] *Goldberg* is the leading modern case holding that due process protects "entitlements." Welfare cannot be terminated on the theory that its receipt was a mere privilege; instead, it is a form of "New Property."

(1) Post-*Goldberg* Approach

Goldberg appears to find that welfare is a protected interest under due process by balancing the individual's need for the payments against the government's need to terminate payments prior to a hearing. Subsequent cases, starting with *Roth, supra,* p. 27, take a different approach. Whether a person has a protected interest depends on whether that interest falls under "liberty" or "property," not on a balancing process. Welfare is "property" because the recipient has an "entitlement" to receive it if she meets the statutory criteria. Balancing is then used only to determine what process is due and when it is due. [**Mathews v. Eldridge,** 424 U.S. 319 (1976); *see infra,* pp. 34, 36]

b. Government Employment

A government job is "property" where the jobholder is protected by law from discharge without cause. For example, a tenured teaching job or a civil service job is a form of property. [**Cleveland Bd. of Educ. v. Loudermill,** 470 U.S. 532 (1985)] On the other hand, if the government employee can be fired without cause (*e.g.,* an untenured teacher), the job is not "property" and thus is not protected as "property" by due process. [**Bd. of Regents v. Roth,** *supra,* p. 27]

(1) Constrained Discretion Creates "New Property"

Thus, the key to defining "property" for due process purposes is whether a statute or other source of law constrains the decisionmaker's *discretion.* If the employee may be fired only for good cause, his job is property. But if the employee can be fired for *any reason,* his job is not property. *Note:* If the holder of an unprotected job is fired for reasons that impose a "stigma-plus," the discharge is an invasion of liberty and entitles the victim to a name-clearing hearing (*see supra,* p. 27).

(2) De Facto Tenure

Even if state law provides that government employees have no tenure and can be discharged without cause, an employee may show that she has "de facto" tenure. This is a right arising out of *implied contract* that protects employees against discharge without good cause. If de facto tenure exists, the employee is entitled to a hearing to establish grounds for nonretention. [**Perry v. Sindermann,** *supra,* p. 28]

(3) State Law

The issue of whether an ambiguous state statute actually constrains official discretion is a matter of state law. [**Bishop v. Wood,** 426 U.S. 341 (1976) (affirming questionable construction of state law by federal district judge that "permanent" police officer who could be dismissed if his work was "not satisfactory" had no property interest and thus could be dismissed without a hearing)]

(4) Limited Power of State to Prescribe Procedure

Once a state creates a tenured job, it cannot define procedural protections for that job that fall below the minimal protections of due process as established by federal constitutional law. [**Cleveland Bd. of Educ. v. Loudermill**, *supra*, p. 31 (disapproving contrary holding in plurality opinion in **Arnett v. Kennedy**, 416 U.S. 134 (1974))]

The *Arnett* plurality thought that an employee had to take the "bitter with the sweet," meaning that the state could both create the entitlement to job protection (the "sweet") and the procedure for protecting it (which might be "bitter"). But *Loudermill* holds that due process, not state law, provides the procedure for protecting the job, once the state has surrounded the job with protection against discharge for good cause. Before the discharge, the employer must provide notice, an explanation of charges, and an oral or written opportunity to respond. A full-fledged oral hearing, including confrontation, can be delayed until *after* the discharge. [**Cleveland Bd. of Educ. v. Loudermill**, *supra*]

c. Utility Service

Receipt of municipal utility service can be a "property" right that cannot be cut off without a hearing if there is a factual dispute such as whether the recipient made payments. [**Memphis Light, Gas & Water Div. v. Craft**, 436 U.S. 1 (1978)]

d. Licenses

Professional licenses are a form of "property" protected by due process insofar as they can be withdrawn only for defined reasons (*e.g.*, misconduct), not at the discretion of a government official. Thus, the government must provide notice and a hearing before invoking sanctions against a licensee such as suspension or revocation. The idea that a license to do business is a mere privilege, which can be granted or rescinded at pleasure, has now been rejected.

SUMMARY OF INTERESTS PROTECTED BY DUE PROCESS — *gilbert LAW SUMMARIES*

THE DEPRIVATION OF LIBERTY OR PROPERTY BY A GOVERNMENT AGENCY GENERALLY TRIGGERS THE RIGHT TO NOTICE AND A HEARING. EXAMPLES INCLUDE:

LIBERTY	PROPERTY
☑ Imposition of **stigma-plus**	☑ Deprivation of **welfare** based on statutory entitlement
☑ Deprivation of **constitutional right**	☑ Deprivation of **government employment** protected against discharge without cause
☑ **Deportation** of aliens	
☑ Deprivation of **physical liberty**	☑ Deprivation of municipal **utility services**
☑ **Expulsion or suspension** from school	☑ Deprivation of **licenses**
	☑ Deprivation of **real or personal property**

e. Domestic Violence Restraining Orders

A state statute provided that the police "shall" arrest a person who violates a domestic violence restraining order. Wife got an order requiring Husband to stay away from her and the children but Husband violated the order and kidnapped and murdered the children. The police failed to enforce the order. Wife sought damages on the ground that failure to enforce the order violated her due process rights. Although the statute appears to create an entitlement by the use of the word "shall," the Court rejected the claim. Such police decisions are *historically discretionary,* not mandatory. In addition, the right to enforcement had *no "monetary value."* [**Town of Castle Rock v. Gonzales,** 545 U.S. 748 (2005)]

f. Applications for Benefits

The Supreme Court has not definitively determined whether the entitlement approach to recognizing "New Property" applies to *applications* for benefits as well as to *revocations* of benefits. [**Am. Mfrs. Mutual Ins. Co. v. Sullivan,** 526 U.S. 40, 61 n.13 (1999) (reserving question of whether an applicant may have a property interest in "claims for payment")] Most lower courts take the view that the entitlement approach does apply to applications as the alternative would seem to be that the government can arbitrarily deny them. [**Kapps v. Wing,** 404 F.3d 105, 115 (2nd Cir. 2005) (collecting authority)]

4. Deprivation

Procedural due process applies only if the government "deprives" a person of liberty or property. The meaning of "deprivation" is not clear under present law.

a. Indirect Deprivations

Due process applies only in the case of a *"direct"* deprivation of liberty or property. Thus, if the state has taken action against one person that injures a second person, the injured person may not have any due process rights because her "deprivation" was "indirect." [**O'Bannon v. Town Court Nursing Center,** 447 U.S. 773 (1980)]

Example: Patients in a licensed nursing home have no right to a hearing before the government terminates the home's license. The home would have a right to a hearing (*cf. supra,* p. 32), and the patients would have a right to a hearing if their government benefits were cut off on individualized grounds (*cf. supra,* pp. 30–31), but they have no right to a hearing relating to disqualification of the home because the harm to them is indirect. [**O'Bannon v. Town Court Nursing Center,** *supra*]

Example: A decision by the police not to enforce a domestic violence restraining order against Husband only indirectly harms Wife and therefore does not deprive Wife of property. [**Town of Castle Rock v. Gonzales,** *supra,* p. 33]

B. Timing of the Hearing

1. General Rule

The general rule is that a hearing must occur *before* the deprivation of liberty or property occurs. The timing of the hearing is frequently of great importance, because if the state acts first and holds a hearing later, the damage to the person from even a temporary loss of liberty or property may be irreparable. [**Goldberg v. Kelly,** *supra,* p. 30]

2. Emergency Exception

There has always been an exception for emergency action: To protect the public health or safety, the government sometimes must act without providing any procedure at all—even though post-deprivation procedures may not be effective protection. [**North Amer. Cold Storage Co. V. Chicago,** 211 U.S. 306 (1908) (destruction of rotting food held in cold storage); **Fahey v. Mallonee,** 332 U.S. 245 (1947) (bank is failing and jeopardizing depositors' interests)]

3. Balancing Test

Under current law, the timing issue is analyzed by a balancing test. This test has led the Court to decide in numerous cases that a state is entitled to act first and hold a hearing later (or provide only abbreviated procedures first and a full hearing later). [**Mathews v. Eldridge,** 424 U.S. 319 (1976)]

a. Factors

Applying the *Mathews* balancing test, the court considers:

(i) *The nature of the private interest* affected;

(ii) *The risk to that interest* posed by a challenged procedure and the likelihood that a different procedure would better protect that interest; and

(iii) *The burden on government* from imposing the different procedure.

4. Application of the Balancing Test of *Mathews*

a. The Pre-*Mathews* Regime: Welfare Benefits in *Goldberg*

Prior to its decision in *Mathews,* the Supreme Court held in *Goldberg* that a trial-type hearing must be provided to a welfare beneficiary before termination of benefits. The Court reasoned that welfare benefits are provided only to very poor people; if they are erroneously cut off, the damage done to the recipient may be irreparable.

b. Social Security Disability Benefits in *Mathews*

In *Mathews,* the benefit in question was *social security disability payments* rather than *welfare*. The Court set forth its new balancing test for determining due process requirements and used it to distinguish disability payments from welfare payments to justify the conclusion that the government need not provide a full-blown evidentiary hearing prior to cutting off disability benefits.

(1) Private Interest

Recipients of disability benefits need not be poor. Therefore, in many cases, the recipients will not be placed in "brutal need" if their benefits are erroneously cut off. Also, recipients can fall back on welfare during that period.

(2) Risk of Error

Unlike welfare cases that often turn on credibility disputes, disability cases are usually decided based on written medical reports. Therefore, the risk of error in delaying a hearing is less.

(3) Government Interest

In both welfare and disability cases, the government has a strong interest in cutting off benefits before a hearing. Otherwise, people who are not entitled to benefits can stall the termination decision while waiting for a hearing, and it is practically impossible for the government to recoup the benefits later.

c. Employment Discharge

Under the *Mathews* balancing test, the government can suspend an employee from a tenured or civil service job ***without providing a full hearing*** in advance. However, there must be an adequate ***predischarge procedure*** to establish that there is probable cause for discharge. [**Cleveland Bd. of Educ. v. Loudermill,** *supra,* p. 31]

(1) Probable Cause Procedure

Thus, a civil service employee is entitled to notice, an explanation of the employer's evidence against him, and an opportunity to present his side of the story orally or in writing. In addition, he is entitled to a ***full hearing after the discharge*** within a reasonable time. [**Cleveland Bd. of Educ. v. Loudermill,** *supra,* p. 31]

(2) Suspension Without Pay in Emergency

In emergency situations, the employer can suspend an employee without any pretermination procedure and without pay, provided that a reasonably prompt post-suspension hearing is provided. [**Gilbert v. Homar,** 519 U.S. 1052 (1997) (suspension of campus police officer for drug offense); **FDIC v. Mallen,** 486 U.S. 230 (1988) (suspension of bank officer indicted for crime)]

d. Licenses

The general rule is that a hearing is required ***before suspension or revocation*** of a license. [**Bell v. Burton,** 402 U.S. 535 (1971) (suspension of license of uninsured motorist involved in auto accident)] However, in various circumstances the state has been allowed to ***suspend first*** and provide a hearing later.

(1) Unsafe Driver

Where a driver has a series of traffic tickets and there is little room for the decisionmaker to exercise discretion, the state is allowed to suspend the license before granting a hearing. [**Dixon v. Love,** 431 U.S. 105 (1977)] Similarly, it may summarily suspend the driver's license of a person who refuses to take a breath test after being arrested for drunken driving. [**Mackey v. Montrym,** 443 U.S. 1 (1979)]

(2) Professional License

The state was entitled to suspend a horse trainer for 15 days after testing disclosed the presence of drugs in horses. The test provided the requisite probable cause. However, a prompt post-suspension hearing must be provided. [**Barry v. Barchi,** *supra,* p. 32]

e. Creditors' Remedies

Whether a creditor can seize a debtor's property before judicial determination that a debt is actually owed is unclear. The issue requires careful *Mathews* balancing.

(1) Absolute Rule

Early cases followed *Goldberg* and held that a creditor could ***not*** seize a debtor's property prior to a judicial determination of probable cause. [**Sniadach v. Family Fin. Corp.,** 395 U.S. 337 (1969); **Fuentes v. Shevin,** 407 U.S. 67 (1972) (replevin statute)]

(2) Judicial Determination

Later cases discarded this absolute rule. They **upheld** such seizures if there was an adequate determination by a judge (rather than a court clerk) of probable cause to believe that the debtor really owed the debt and the creditor's legitimate interests required summary action. [**Mitchell v. W.T. Grant Co.,** 416 U.S. 600 (1974) (judicial authorization of the seizure)]

(3) Exigent Circumstances

Summary seizure of a debtor's property is not permissible, even upon approval by a judge, where the creditor shows no legitimate need for this drastic procedure (such as a preexisting interest in the property or concern that the debtor would conceal the property). [**Connecticut v. Doehr,** 501 U.S. 1 (1991)]

EXAM TIP

It is helpful to remember that government deprivation of a constitutionally protected interest (*e.g.,* liberty or property) generally requires **at least** a procedure **to determine whether probable cause exists before the deprivation** occurs. The major exceptions include situations where public safety is threatened or the affected individual has been accused of a crime, especially if that crime affects the public interest. A full hearing is usually required before permanent deprivation of a right is allowed.

C. Elements of the Hearing

1. Same *Mathews* Balancing Test

In early due process cases, the Supreme Court prescribed fixed lists of the elements that a due process hearing must contain. [**Goldberg v. Kelly,** 397 U.S. 254 (1970)] In more recent cases, however, the Court has employed the *Mathews* balancing test *to decide what elements* the hearing must contain. [*See supra,* p. 34] Thus, the same balancing analysis is used both for timing and for establishment of the precise ingredients of the notice and hearing process.

2. Elements of Due Process

Due process hearings generally require:

(i) Fair *notice;*

(ii) *Confrontation* of adverse witnesses;

(iii) An *impartial decisionmaker;* and

(iv) A *statement of reasons.*

However, the exact circumstances are critical, and *Mathews* balancing may require more or less formality in a given context.

a. Notice

The right to a hearing entails timely and adequate notice of what the government intends to do and of the procedure by which the individual can present objections. [**Memphis Light, Gas & Water Div. v. Craft,** 436 U.S. 1 (1978)]

(1) *Mathews* Not Applied to Notice for Civil Actions

Under traditional civil procedure principles, the test for determining the adequacy of notice is whether the form of notice used was "reasonably calculated under all the circumstances to apprise interested parties of the pendency of the action and afford them an opportunity to present their objections." [**Mullane v. Central Hanover Bank,** 339 U.S. 306 (1950)] As a result, the Court upheld notification by certified mail of a pending asset forfeiture, even though the recipient was in prison and the prison failed to deliver the letter. [**Dusenbery v. United States,** 534 U.S. 161 (2002)] However, when a certified letter warning of a foreclosure sale is returned to the government unclaimed, and the government does nothing else to follow up, the notice does not meet due process standards. [**Jones v. Flowers,** 547 U.S. 220 (2006)] Surprisingly, neither case relied on *Mathews* balancing. (*See supra,* p. 34 *et seq.*) Instead, they relied on *Mullane.*

(2) Fair Warning of What the Law Requires

If a person is subject to sanctions for violating an agency regulation, the regulation must give fair warning that particular conduct is prohibited. In some cases, conduct might violate one reasonable interpretation of a regulation but be in compliance with a different reasonable interpretation of the same regulation. In such situations, due process prohibits the government from sanctioning the person for violating the regulation. The agency might avoid this problem by publishing an interpretive rule that furnishes fair warning of the agency's interpretation. [**Trinity Broad. Co. v. FCC,** 211 F.3d 618 (D.C. Cir. 2000) (FCC's interpretation of regulation was valid but failed to give fair notice so that applicant for renewal of license could not be penalized for violating regulation); **Gen. Electr. Co. v. EPA,** 53 F.3d 1324 (D.C. Cir. 1995) (civil penalty for violating regulation concerning disposal of toxic chemical held invalid due to lack of notice)]

b. Oral Testimony and Confrontation of Witnesses

In many cases, due process requires that persons threatened with deprivation of liberty or property be afforded an opportunity to present their arguments and evidence orally and confront adverse witnesses—especially where credibility is at issue. [*Goldberg, supra,* p. 30] Nevertheless, the requirements of due process are flexible, and the Court increasingly has dispensed with oral testimony or cross-examination when it seemed unnecessary or counterproductive. For example, adversarial trial-type procedure is not required in connection with:

(1) *The commitment of children to mental institutions* [**Parham v. J.R.,** 442 U.S. 584 (1979)];

(2) *Short-term suspensions from school* [**Goss v. Lopez,** *supra,* p. 30];

(3) *The transfer of prisoners to mental institutions* [**Vitek v. Jones,** *supra,* p. 29]; or

(4) *The transfer of prisoners to a super-max prison.* [**Wilkinson v. Austin,** *supra,* p. 29—prisoner may attend hearing and offer pertinent information in writing but may not call witnesses]

c. Impartial Decisionmaker

An impartial decisionmaker is essential to due process. This means a decisionmaker who is not biased, has no conflict of interest, and has not prejudged the facts of the case. (Impartiality of decisionmakers is discussed in detail *infra,* p. *78 et seq.*)

d. Findings and Reasons

Due process may require a decisionmaker to *state reasons* for its conclusions. In **Goldberg v. Kelly,** *supra,* p. 30, which involved termination of welfare benefits, the Court held that due process required the decisionmaker to give reasons and identify supporting evidence based on legal rules and evidence presented at the hearing.

e. Right to Counsel

For criminal cases, the Sixth Amendment requires appointment of counsel for indigent defendants. [**Gideon v. Wainwright**, 372 U.S. 335 (1963)] By contrast, for civil matters, the scope of any constitutional right to counsel is determined by application of the *Mathews* balancing test. [**Turner v. Rogers**, 131 S.Ct. 2507 (2011)]

(1) Counsel at the Party's Expense

In the pre-*Mathews* case of *Goldberg,* the Court held that a welfare beneficiary threatened with loss of benefits had a right to bring counsel to the evidentiary hearing. [**Goldberg v. Kelly,** *supra,* p. 30]

By contrast, in the post-*Mathews* case of **Walters v. Nat'l Assoc. of Radiation Survivors**, 473 U.S. 305 (1985), the Court determined that a statute that effectively blocked use of counsel at proceedings to determine veterans' benefits did not violate due process. A statute providing for veteran's benefits claims limited the amount a claimant can pay an attorney to $10. (The statute has since been repealed.) This meant that attorneys were barred from Veteran's Administration claims procedures (except for pro bono attorneys). However, free assistance was available to claimants from nonlawyer representatives employed by veterans' groups. The Court upheld the statute under the *Mathews* factors (*see supra,* p. 34). The most important reasons were the congressional policy against diversion of any portion of a recovery to attorneys, the availability of nonlawyer representatives, and the fact that Veteran's Administration proceedings are informal and nonadversarial. Although the services of an attorney would be helpful in complex cases, these cases were too rare to invalidate a statute that applies to millions of claims every year.

(2) Appointed Counsel

Even where a party has a right to employ counsel, the Supreme Court has indicated that the state is *usually not required* to provide counsel. [**Goldberg v. Kelly,** *supra,* p. 29]

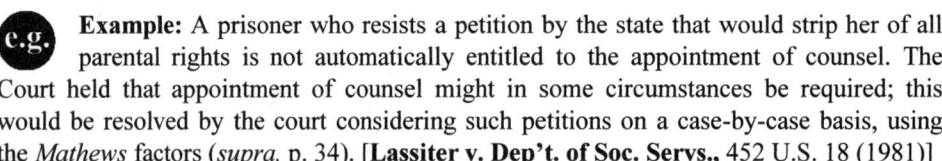

Example: A prisoner who resists a petition by the state that would strip her of all parental rights is not automatically entitled to the appointment of counsel. The Court held that appointment of counsel might in some circumstances be required; this would be resolved by the court considering such petitions on a case-by-case basis, using the *Mathews* factors (*supra,* p. 34). [**Lassiter v. Dep't. of Soc. Servs.**, 452 U.S. 18 (1981)]

Example: A non-custodial parent was not entitled to appointed counsel to defend him at civil contempt proceedings for nonpayment of support that could lead to incarceration. [**Turner v. Rogers**, 131 S.Ct. 2507 (2011)]

But see: A four-justice plurality would have held that due process requires representation by counsel for transfer from a prison to a mental hospital. [**Vitek v. Jones**, 445 U.S. 480 (1980)]

But see also: Fundamental fairness requires appointment of counsel for some but not all probation revocation hearings. Counsel should generally be provided where the probationer makes a colorable claim that (1) he did not violate the terms of release; or (2) he has a substantial justification that renders revocation inappropriate and that justification is difficult to present. [**Gagnon v. Scarpelli**, 411 U.S. 778 (1973)]

f. State Law Judicial Remedies as Sufficient Due Process

In some situations, the *ex post* judicial remedies provided by state tort or contract actions provide the process that is constitutionally due to remedy a deprivation of liberty or property.

Example—corporal punishment at school: Paddling a high school student is a deprivation of liberty, but a state law tort action for damages against the teacher for excessive punishment provides all the process that the student is due. The Court decided that the burden on the school of holding a prior administrative hearing on whether to paddle a student outweighed any possible benefit to the student. [**Ingraham v. Wright**, 430 U.S. 651 (1977)]

Example—contract payment: Where the property claimed is a right to be paid under a contract, a state law contract action provides all the process that is due. [**Lujan v. G & G Fire Sprinklers**, 532 U.S. 189 (2001)] In *Lujan*, the state withheld payment from a subcontractor deemed to be in breach of contract. Thus, the subcontractor was deprived of money owed to it without any hearing on whether the withholding was justified. The Court held that no administrative hearing was required because the subcontractor could sue the state for breach of contract in state court and all factual issues would be determined in the state court action.

Example—negligent or intentional misconduct: Due process does not require a prior hearing before negligent or intentional destruction by prison guards of a prisoner's property. Here, the core problem is that no prior hearing is practically possible as the officials are acting in an unauthorized way that violates state policy. An ex post state law tort action provides all the process that is due. [**Parratt v. Taylor**, 451 U.S. 527 (1981) (negligent destruction); **Hudson v. Palmer**, 468 U.S. 517 (1984) (intentional destruction)]

D. Issues That Do Not Require a Hearing for Resolution

1. Procedural Due Process Does Not Apply to "Rulemaking"

a. The *Due Process* Distinction Between Rulemaking and Adjudication

Due process draws a functional distinction between rulemaking and adjudication. Understood in this sense, an agency engages in rulemaking where it makes policy decisions based on its understanding of *"generalized"* or *"legislative" facts*. These are facts that are **common to large groups** of people or businesses. For instance, whether carbon dioxide is a greenhouse gas or whether tax rates should go up are matters of legislative fact.

An agency adjudicates where it applies law to *"individualized"* or *"adjudicative"* facts. These are who-did-what-to-whom facts that relate to particularized situations. For instance, whether you attended your last administrative law class is a matter of adjudicative fact. Adjudicative facts often require a determination of credibility or state of mind and are thus suitable for trial-type hearings.

b. Due Process Does Not Require a Hearing to Resolve Legislative Facts

Due process does not require a hearing to resolve matters of legislative fact. The intuition here is that, where the same facts hold for many people, it is impracticable and unhelpful to require that they all be permitted to testify.

c. Due Process May Require a Hearing to Resolve Adjudicative Facts

The need to resolve adjudicative facts about particularized circumstances is a necessary prerequisite for triggering procedural due process rights. An intuition here is that allowing a person to share information about her particularized circumstances contributes to accurate decisionmaking and fundamental fairness. Note, however, that a need to resolve adjudicative facts will not trigger procedural due process where other requirements are not satisfied (*e.g.*, where no deprivation of life, liberty, or property is at stake).

d. Application of Rulemaking—Adjudication Distinction

(1) Traditional Leading Cases—*Londoner/Bi-Metallic*

The rulemaking-adjudication distinction was first drawn in two early cases involving taxation, **Londoner v. Denver**, 210 U.S. 373 (1908), and **Bi-Metallic Investment Co. v. State Board of Equalization**, 239 U.S. 441 (1915). We therefore often refer to the *Londoner/Bi-Metallic* distinction.

(a) An Adjudication—*Londoner*

A city ordinance levied assessments on property owners for street improvements. The decision to pave the streets and the determination of the total paving cost did not require a trial-type hearing. However, the division of costs among particular owners did require a hearing because there was a question of how much each piece of property had benefited. [**Londoner v. Denver,** 210 U.S. 373 (1908)]

(b) A Rulemaking—*Bi-Metallic*

A state board increased the valuation of all property in Denver by 40%. The Court rejected the claim of a Denver taxpayer to a right to a hearing on the reevaluation. [**Bi-Metallic Inv. Co. v. State Board of Equalization,** 239 U.S. 441 (1915)] The Court explained: "Where a rule of conduct applies to more than a few people, it is impracticable that everyone should have a direct voice in its adoption. . . . Their rights are protected in the only way [possible] in a complex society, by their power, immediate or remote, over those who make the rule." As *all* Denver property taxpayers had a stake in the across-the-board increase in valuation, *none* had a procedural due process right for an adjudicative hearing to contest the legislative fact of whether Denver properties had been systemically undervalued.

The Court distinguished *Londoner* in a famous passage, explaining that in the earlier case, **"a relatively small number of persons ... were exceptionally affected in each case on individual grounds."** Thus, *Londoner* involved individualized, adjudicative facts about specific properties.

(2) Modern Applications

The Court has often drawn on *Londoner* and *Bi-Metallic* in evaluating due process.

> **Example—railroad rates:** Due process does not require a hearing when an agency adopts a general rule raising the rates charged by all railroads for using freight cars owned by other railroads. The disputed facts are not individualized but apply to all railroads. [**United States v. Fla. E. Coast Ry.,** 410 U.S. 224 (1973)]

> **Example—food stamp reductions:** Nor does due process apply to a legislative amendment to the formula for computing food stamp benefits that has the effect of lowering benefits for many persons. Similarly, there is no right to advance notice or to a hearing with respect to the automatic recalculation required by this amendment. However, if an individual claims that because of facts specific to her the calculation was erroneous, she has a right to a hearing with respect to determination of such facts. [**Atkins v. Parker,** 472 U.S. 115 (1985)]

2. Immaterial Issues

Due process does not require the state to provide a hearing if the issue in dispute is not relevant to the statutory scheme. [**Conn. Dep't. of Pub. Safety v. Doe,** 538 U.S. 1 (2003) (convicted sex offender has no right to hearing to prove that he is not dangerous before being placed on a public website because dangerousness is irrelevant to whether person's name and photo will be placed on the website)]

3. Issues Conclusively Determined by Agency Rule

An agency often can preempt a right to a hearing to determine facts by *legislatively determining the questions* at issue. If the rule is valid, then no additional factfinding, and thus no trial-type hearing, is required. However, the agency should ordinarily permit a person to petition for a waiver of the rule on the theory that the person's individualized circumstances are unusual and not contemplated by the rule. [**United States v. Storer Broad. Co.,** 351 U.S. 192 (1956)]

a. A Few Examples

> **Example:** The FCC has statutory authority to grant broadcast licenses in the "public interest." It promulgated a rule that capped the number of licenses a given entity could obtain. Storer contended it was entitled to a "full and fair hearing" as to whether it would serve the public interest for it to obtain a license beyond the cap. The Court rejected this argument, accepting that the FCC had already determined via rule that granting licenses beyond the cap would not serve the "public interest." [*Storer, supra*]

> **Example:** The National Labor Relations Board ("NLRB") must decide on the appropriate bargaining unit for the organization of employees. An NLRB rule established that there should be eight such units in hospitals. The Court upheld this rule, holding that the statute gave the NLRB power to resolve bargaining unit issues either by adjudication or rulemaking. If the eight-unit test proves unsuitable for certain hospitals, the NLRB retains the power to make exceptions in extraordinary circumstances. [**Am. Hosp. Assoc. v. NLRB,** 499 U.S. 606 (1991)]

> **Example:** A statute granted disability benefits only if an individual could not engage in any gainful activity by reason of the disability. Rather than make this determination on a case-by-case basis, the agency by rule adopted a "grid" system that indicated whether a disabled person with particular qualifications could obtain a job. The Court held that the applicant was not entitled to a hearing (under the Constitution or the statute) on the issues settled by the rule. [**Heckler v. Campbell,** 461 U.S. 458 (1983)]

b. Waivers

Agency rules are often either over- or under-inclusive. They may be fair and reasonable when applied to most of the persons to whom they apply, but unfair and unreasonable when applied to persons whose circumstances are different from the norm. As a result, an agency typically entertains a petition for a waiver of the rule in an unusual case (and the rule itself may allow such a petition). However, an agency is entitled to be restrictive in its waiver decisions out of concern that granting one such request could trigger a flood of similar requests and create so many exceptions that the exceptions would become the rule. As a result, courts are likely to be deferential in reviewing an agency decision to reject a request for a waiver. [**Yetman v. Garvey,** 261 F.3d 664 (7th Cir. 2001) (rejecting waiver requests from a Federal Aviation Administration rule prohibiting commercial airlines from hiring pilots over the age of sixty)]

4. Administrative "Summary Judgment"

Sometimes, even though a hearing would ordinarily be required, the agency can require private parties to make a preliminary showing that individualized facts are at issue. If the party is unable to do so, it would be a waste of time and money to hold a hearing. Thus, the agency is permitted to use a sort of administrative summary judgment procedure. [**Weinberger v. Hynson, Westcott & Dunning, Inc.,** 412 U.S. 609 (1973)]

E. The State Action Requirement for Triggering Due Process

1. Due Process and the State Action Requirement

Due process requirements of the Constitution apply only to state actors—with the Fifth Amendment applying to the federal government and the Fourteenth Amendment applicable to the states (including their instrumentalities, such as cities).

For instance, if you attend a state law school, then due process principles apply to its actions. If you attend a private law school, they do not.

2. Distinguishing State and Non-State Action—Fair Attribution Test

The state action requirement for due process requires courts to draw a line between state and non-state actors. The Supreme Court has declared that, for an action to be fairly attributable to a state, two conditions must be satisfied. First, "the deprivation must be caused by the exercise of some right or privilege created by the State or by a rule of conduct imposed by the state or by a person for whom the State is responsible." Second, "the party charged with the deprivation must be a person who may fairly be said to be a state actor." Expanding on this second, circular condition, the Court explained that it can be satisfied where an actor is a state official, or he "has obtained significant aid from state officials," or "his conduct is otherwise chargeable to the State." [**Lugar v. Edmonson Oil Co., Inc.,** 457 U.S. 922 (1982)]

DETERMINING IF DUE PROCESS HAS BEEN TRIGGERED

PREREQUISITE	SUMMARY
ADJUDICATION	For this purpose, adjudications turn on individualized, "adjudicative" facts; rulemakings turn on "legislative facts."
STATE ACTION	To trigger due process, an action must be by the state or chargeable to it.
DEPRIVATION	The deprivation must not be indirect.
LIBERTY OR PROPERTY	The state must have deprived the claimant of "liberty" or "property." Legal entitlement may be "new property."

HOW MUCH PROCESS IS DUE? AND WHEN? CONSIDER THE *MATHEWS* FACTORS:

DETERMINING HOW MUCH PROCESS IS DUE

- Consider the strength and nature of the private interest affected;
- Consider the incremental benefits of adding the requested procedure;
- Consider the government's interest in refusing the requested procedure.

Example of a private "state actor": Creditor sued on a debt in Virginia state court and, pursuant to state statute, sought prejudgment attachment of debtor's property based on ex parte proceeding. Acting on creditor's petition, court clerk issued a writ of attachment, which was later executed by Sheriff. Debtor later brought § 1983 action against creditor. The Supreme Court held that the creditor could be characterized as a "state actor" given its "joint participation with state officials in seizing debtor's property. [**Lugar v. Edmonson Oil Co., Inc.,** *supra*]

Example of a private actor that stayed that way: Private insurers, pursuant to state statute, withheld workers' compensation payments for disputed medical treatments pending "utilization review" to determine if treatments were reasonable and necessary. Claimants sued private insurers under § 1983. The Supreme Court ruled that private insurers' actions could not be fairly attributable to the state. The mere fact that a private entity is subject to extensive state regulation does not make that entity a "state actor" for the purpose of applying due process. A private entity's actions are fairly attributable to the state where the state exercises "coercive power" or provides "significant encouragement" guiding the private entity. State's decision to allow insurers to withhold payment during proceedings to determine the validity of claims did not constitute the type of "encouragement" necessary to attribute private entity's decisions to the state. [**Am. Mfrs. Mut. Ins. Co. v. Sullivan,** 526 U.S. 40 (1999)]

Chapter Three
Adjudicative Procedures

CONTENTS	PAGE
Key Exam Issues	46
A. Overview of the APA's Procedural Template	46
B. A Summary of APA Requirements for Formal Adjudication	50
C. Triggering Formal Adjudication Under the APA	50
D. Agency Adjudicators	53
E. Prehearing Process for Formal Adjudication	53
F. The Process of Proof at the Hearing for a Formal Adjudication	56
G. Agency Decisions and Explanations	62
H. Procedures for Informal Adjudication	66
I. Declaratory Orders	67
J. Agency Adjudication and Retroactivity	68
K. Choosing Between Adjudication and Rulemaking to Develop Policy	70

Key Exam Issues

The previous chapter considered procedural requirements for agency adjudication based on the due process guarantees of the United States Constitution. In addition to the Constitution, statutes and agency rules often specify procedures for adjudications. Therefore, when determining the adequacy of agency adjudicatory procedures, you should always look to all three of these sources of law. Some key points to remember are:

1. The federal Administrative Procedure Act ("APA") provides a detailed procedural template for what is commonly termed "formal adjudication" (a/k/a "on the record" or "trial-type" adjudication). Your exam is pretty likely to require you to figure out whether an agency must use formal adjudication to determine some matter. The APA provides that formal adjudication is required where *some other statute* (*i.e.*, the agency's enabling act) requires an agency to adjudicate a matter "on the record after opportunity for agency hearing." 5 U.S.C. § 554(a). You will need to pay careful attention to how various courts interpret this "trigger" language.

2. If formal adjudication is required, you may need to determine whether the agency's procedures comply. To do so, you will need to study the APA's requirements for formal adjudication, which are largely to be found in 5 U.S.C. §§ 554, 556–57.

3. A good deal of your basic administrative law course will be devoted to learning the APA's requirements. You should always bear in mind, however, that due process, agency enabling acts, and agency rules might trump or supplement the APA's procedural requirements. This point is especially important as applied to "informal adjudications," which the APA itself leaves largely uncontrolled.

4. Agencies commonly adopt procedural regulations to guide their adjudications. For instance, although the APA's statutory "rule of evidence" pretty much allows admission of any relevant evidence, an agency might adopt rules that hew much more closely to the Federal Rules of Evidence. These procedural rules, once adopted, bind the agency until they are properly changed.

5. Many agencies possess both adjudicatory and rulemaking power. They can thus develop policies like courts via case-law or like legislatures via statute-like rules. Given the advantages of rulemaking, you might think that agencies would be required to favor this policy-making mechanism over adjudication. The law has not developed this way. Under the famous (in administrative law circles) *Chenery* doctrine, agencies have broad discretion to choose between adjudication and rulemaking to develop law and policy.

A. Overview of the APA's Procedural Template

1. The APA's Four Basic Procedural Types

The APA provides a short menu of basic procedural schemes that apply broadly across many agencies. This menu is based on two dichotomies. First, the APA distinguishes between "rulemaking" and "adjudication." Second, the APA distinguishes between proceedings that require a trial-type hearing and those that do not. It is common in administrative law parlance to describe trial-type proceedings as "formal" and other proceedings as "informal." Combining these two dichotomies creates the APA's basic menu of procedural options:

a. Formal Adjudication

The APA creates a template for what are commonly called "formal," or "on-the-record," or "trial-type" proceedings at 5 U.S.C. §§ 554, 556–57. We commonly call agency adjudications that follow this template, "formal adjudications." Two of the main tasks of this chapter are: (1) figuring out when an agency must use formal adjudication; and (2) figuring out what procedures formal adjudication requires.

b. Informal Adjudication

The majority of agency adjudications fall into the residuary "informal adjudication" category. The APA imposes very few procedural requirements on informal adjudications. *See* 5 U.S.C. § 555. Note, however, that procedural requirements for informal adjudication may be imposed by due process, the agency's enabling act, or agency regulations.

c. Formal Rulemaking

Like formal adjudication, formal rulemaking follows the procedural template established in 5 U.S.C. §§ 556–57. It is commonly understood that this trial-type template provides a particularly bad way to go about the policymaking task of creating a rule. [**United States v. Fla. E. Coast Ry.**, 410 U.S. 224 (1973)] Formal rulemaking is therefore seldom used, and courts resist reading agency enabling acts as requiring it.

d. Informal Rulemaking

Informal rulemaking, like informal adjudication, is a residuary category—rulemaking that isn't formal is informal. The default mechanism for creating an informal "legislative" rule (*i.e.*, a rule with the force of law) is the notice-and-comment procedures established by 5 U.S.C. § 553. You will likely spend a good bit of time discussing these procedures in your Administrative Law class. Agencies need not, however, use these procedures to create interpretive rules, policy statements, or procedural rules. Agencies can also avoid notice-and-comment where they have good cause to do so. Determining the scope of these exceptions is another important task for your Administrative Law course.

THE APA'S QUARTET	ADJUDICATION	RULEMAKING
FORMAL	Trial-type, on-the-record proceeding. §§ 554, 556–57	Trial-type, on-the-record proceeding. §§ 553 (except for (c)), 556–57
INFORMAL	APA imposes very few procedural requirements. General provisions of § 555 apply.	Default procedure of notice and comment, subject to various exceptions. § 553.

2. The APA's Clumsy Rulemaking/Adjudication Distinction

The APA provides a set of definitions at 5 U.S.C. § 551 that distinguish adjudication from rulemaking. For reasons that should be plain in a moment, these definitions are not very helpful. It is nonetheless important that you work through these definitions if only so you understand why they are problematic.

a. "Adjudication"

The APA defines "adjudication" as the "agency process to formulate an order." [APA § 551(7)] To understand this definition, we have to learn what the APA means by "order," and to understand that term, we have to learn what the APA means by "rule" and "rulemaking":

(i) A *"rule"* is "the whole or a part of any agency statement of general or particular applicability and future effect designed to implement, interpret, or prescribe law or policy or describing the organization, procedure, or practice requirements of an agency." [APA § 551(4)]

(ii) *"Rulemaking"* is the "agency process for formulating, amending, or repealing a rule." [APA § 551(5)]

(iii) An *"order"* is the "whole or a part of a final disposition . . . of an agency *in a matter other than rulemaking* but including licensing." [APA § 551(6)]

If you track through the preceding definitions, you will see that "adjudication" is the agency process for producing an "order," which is a "final disposition" in any proceeding that is not "rulemaking."

b. The Oddest Part of the APA's Definition of "Rulemaking"

Did you see it? Note that the definition of "rule" includes agency statements of "general or particular applicability" and "future effect." Everything has either general or particular applicability, and every agency action contemplates future effect. So the definition of "rule" just can't be right. Courts and litigants therefore usually ignore it—which is typically safe to do because whether a proceeding involves rulemaking or adjudication is generally pretty obvious.

Example: Agency orders A to desist from false advertising. Under the APA, this disposition might be considered a rule since it is of "particular applicability" and "future effect." Yet invariably such action is treated as "adjudication," not "rulemaking."

c. Distinguish the *Constitutional* Dichotomy Between Rulemaking and Adjudication from the APA's

Administrative law distinguishes between rulemaking and adjudication on two different levels. As just discussed, we have the APA's definitional dichotomy, which is formalistic, poorly drafted, and widely ignored. Recall that there is also, however, a functional, constitutional distinction between rulemaking and adjudication that bears on whether a proceeding implicates procedural due process. Understood in this sense, rulemaking is policymaking based on generalized (legislative) facts, and it does not implicate procedural due process. Adjudication determines the rights of parties based on application of individualized (adjudicative) facts to law, and it triggers procedural due process protections for deprivations of liberty or property. [*Supra*, p. 40 *et seq.* (discussing the *Londoner/Bi-Metallic* dichotomy)]

(1) Due Process Can Apply to a Statutory Rulemaking

Here is a slightly tricky point: An agency might use the *statutory* forms of rulemaking to resolve a matter that falls on the adjudication side of the *constitutional* rulemaking/adjudication dichotomy. In this kind of rare situation, a party could invoke due process to claim greater procedural protections in a matter that an agency has treated as a rulemaking. [**Sangamon Valley Television Corp. v. United States,** 269 F.2d 221 (1959) (applying due process principles to an agency's informal rulemaking that resolved "conflicting private claims to a valuable privilege" (*i.e.*, allocation of a television license))]

3. Other Sources of Law That Might Alter or Supplement APA Procedures

When determining the procedures an agency must use for a particular proceeding, it is important to remember that other sources of law may trump or supplement APA requirements.

a. Due Process

Constitutional procedural requirements rooted in due process trump the APA, of course. This point is largely academic as applied to formal adjudications because the APA's template provides so many procedural protections for that context that it is unlikely due process would require more. The APA imposes almost no procedural requirements on informal adjudication, however. Where an informal adjudication threatens a deprivation of liberty or property, due process may fill this procedural void.

b. Agency Enabling Acts

The APA's structure enables Congress to choose from a standardized set of options when setting agency procedures. E.g., Congress can create an agency and instruct it to use the APA's template for "formal adjudication." Many agency statutes, however, contain specific procedural provisions that trump the APA's default settings. Therefore, when determining agency procedures required by statute, you must always consider both the agency's enabling act as well as the APA.

c. Agency Rules

An agency often has discretion to develop its own procedural rules to govern its proceedings. These rules must, of course, be consistent with statutory or constitutional requirements. If an agency adopts such rules, it must follow them until they are properly changed.

SOURCES OF LAW TO CHECK FOR ADJUDICATIVE PROCEDURE	
DUE PROCESS	Applicable to deprivations of liberty or property even in absence of statutory or regulatory requirements.
AGENCY ENABLING ACT	Can trump the default statutory template of the APA.
APA	Relatively detailed procedures for formal adjudication (§§ 554, 556–57); very little for informal adjudication (§ 555)
AGENCY PROCEDURAL RULES	Generally bind the agency until properly changed—particularly if the rule creates important procedural benefit for individuals

B. A Summary of APA Requirements for Formal Adjudication

The APA sets forth procedural requirements that govern both formal adjudication and formal rulemaking at §§ 556–57. It adds requirements particular to formal adjudication at § 554. In addition, the APA includes some basic requirements at § 555 that apply to all agency proceedings generally.

In a concurring opinion in **Citizens Awareness Network, Inc. v. U.S.**, Judge Lipez summarized the requirements that these statutory provisions together impose on formal adjudication:

1. The agency must give notice of legal authority and matters of fact and law asserted. § 554(b).

2. The oral evidentiary hearing must be presided over by an officer who can be disqualified for bias. § 556(b).

3. Presiding officers cannot have ex parte communications. §§ 554(d), 557(d)(1).

4. Parties are entitled to be represented by attorneys. § 555(b).

5. The proponent of an order has the burden of proof. § 556(d).

6. A party is entitled to present oral or documentary evidence. § 556(d).

7. A party is entitled "to conduct such cross-examination as may be required for a full and true disclosure of the facts." § 556(d).

8. Orders can be issued only on consideration of the record of the hearing. § 556(d).

9. The transcript of testimony and exhibits is the exclusive record for decision and shall be made available to parties. § 556(e).

10. The decision must include "findings and conclusions, and the reasons or basis therefor, on all the material issues of fact, law, or discretion presented on the record." § 557(c)(3)(A).

[391 F.3d 338 (1st Cir. 2004) (Lipez, J., concurring) (citing Richard J. Pierce, Jr., **Administrative Law Treatise** § 8.1 (4th ed. 2002)]

C. Triggering Formal Adjudication Under the APA

1. Agency Enabling Acts Pull the Trigger

The APA itself does not determine which categories of agency adjudication require formal procedures. Instead, the APA provides that formal adjudication procedures apply where Congress states in an agency's enabling act that adjudications are "to be determined on the record after opportunity for agency hearing." § 554(a). So, to figure out whether formal adjudication is required for some category of agency action, you must comb through the agency's enabling act for language sufficient to pull this trigger in the APA. If there is no such statutory language, the APA formal adjudication provisions *do not apply*.

2. Courts Do Not Take a "Magic Words" Approach to the Trigger

Administrative law would have one less issue to worry about if courts took the view that an agency's enabling act requires formal adjudication only if the act uses the precise phrasing that adjudications must be determined "on the record after opportunity for agency hearing." As courts have not taken this approach, we are left with the problem of determining what other language is sufficient to pull the trigger. For instance, should a statutory requirement of a "public hearing" that does not refer to a "record" requirement be enough to pull the trigger? As explained in the next subsection, lower courts have adopted differing approaches to this problem.

a. But Courts Do Take Something Close to a "Magic Words" Approach to Triggering Formal *Rulemaking*

Looking ahead to rulemaking, the APA provides that formal rulemaking must be used where an agency's enabling act requires rules "to be made on the record after opportunity for an agency hearing." § 553(c). The APA's triggers for formal proceedings are thus linguistically the same for both adjudication and rulemaking. Courts nonetheless construe these triggers very differently, largely because formal rulemaking is regarded as very inefficient. As a result, language in an agency enabling act that may be sufficient to trigger formal adjudication won't be sufficient to trigger formal rulemaking. [**United States v. Fla. E. Coast Ry.**, 410 U.S. 224 (1973) (requirement that agency determine rates "after hearing" did not trigger formal rulemaking for industry-wide ratemaking proceeding)]

3. Three Circuit Court Approaches to the Formal Adjudication Trigger

a. *Chevron* Deference to the Agency's Interpretation

Under the increasingly dominant view, reviewing courts should defer to an agency's reasonable and reasoned conclusion that ambiguous statutory language does not pull the trigger for formal adjudication. [**Dominion Energy Brayton Point, LLC v. Johnson**, 443 F.3d 12 (1st Cir. 2006); **Chem. Waste Mgmt., Inc. v. EPA**, 873 F.2d 1477 (D.C. Cir. 1989)]

(1) Did "After Public Hearing" Pull the Trigger?

Dominion involved permitting for the discharge of heated water from a nuclear power plant. *Chemical Waste* involved procedures for issuing corrective action orders. In both cases, the pertinent statute instructed EPA to take action after an opportunity for a "public hearing." EPA determined that this language did not require it to use formal adjudication. The First and D.C. Circuits upheld the agency's decisions.

(2) Application of *Chevron* Deference

In *Dominion* and *Chemical Waste*, the courts determined that the deference doctrine of **Chevron, USA, Inc. v. Natural Resources Defense Council**, 467 U.S. 837 (1984), applied to the question of whether EPA's enabling acts required formal adjudication. (For discussion of this important doctrine, see *infra*, p. 150 *et seq.*) In essence, *Chevron* instructs courts to defer to an agency's reasonable interpretation of a statute that the agency administers. The *Dominion* and *Chemical Waste* courts held that EPA had reasonably explained that the phrase "after public hearing," as used in the pertinent enabling acts, did not trigger formal adjudication. Hence, the courts deferred to the agency.

b. Presumption of Formality for Statutory Hearings Subject to Judicial Review

(1) The *Seacoast* Presumption That the First Circuit Abandoned

Dominion overruled an earlier First Circuit case that established a presumption that formal adjudication is required for statutorily-required hearings subject to judicial review. A core rationale for this presumption is that the adversarial-style proceedings of formal adjudication are helpful for establishing the specific factual findings on which adjudications generally turn. [**Seacoast Anti-Pollution League v. Costle,** 572 F.2d 872 (1st Cir.), *cert. denied,* 439 U.S. 824 (1978)]

(2) But That Some Courts Still Follow

Although the First Circuit has overruled its *Seacoast* presumption in favor of formality, the Ninth Circuit continues to follow a similar approach. [**Marathon Oil Co. v. EPA,** 564 F.2d 1253 (9th Cir. 1977)]

c. Presumption of Informality Absent the "Magic Words"

(1) The *City of West Chicago* Approach

The Seventh Circuit has conceded that the magic words "on the record" are not required to trigger formality. In the absence of this statutory phrase, however, "Congress must clearly indicate its intent to trigger the formal, on-the-record hearing provisions of the APA." [**City of W. Chicago v. NRC,** 701 F.2d 632 (7th Cir. 1983)]

(2) Facts from *City of West Chicago*

Kerr-McGee Corporation requested that the Nuclear Regulatory Commission ("NRC") grant an amendment to Kerr-McGee's "source material" license that would allow it to demolish buildings used to produce thorium and store contaminated soil on site. Section 189(a) of the Atomic Energy Act of 1954 required the NRC to grant a "hearing" if requested by an interested person before approval of such a license. The parties disputed whether this "hearing" requirement triggered formal adjudication. The Seventh Circuit, motivated in part by a concern to avoid burdening the NRC with unnecessary hearings, applied the presumption against formality just described. Finding no evidence of a clear congressional intent to require formality in the legislative history, the court affirmed the NRC's conclusion that formal adjudication was not required.

EXAM TIP

Many exam questions will require you to determine whether an agency must use formal adjudication. As explained above, different circuits have adopted different approaches. If the exam question makes clear which circuit you are in, then use that circuit's approach. Otherwise, analyze all the possibilities.

---

4. Two State Approaches to the Trigger Problem

The 1961 Model State APA followed the federal APA; no formal adjudication is required unless some other statute requires a formal hearing. The 1961 statute has been adopted in about half of the states. [*See, e.g.,* **Greenwood Manor v. Iowa Dep't of Pub. Health,** 641 N.W.2d 823 (Iowa 2002) (application of Iowa version of 1961 Act)] However, several states, such as Wisconsin and Florida, take a different approach. They require an appropriate adjudication procedure in *every* case of adjudication, whether or not some other statute requires it. An "appropriate" procedure means that the hearing procedure is as formal as the situation calls for. This approach was followed in the 1981 Model State APA, but the 1981 Act has been adopted in very few states. [*See* 1981 Model State APA §§ 4–101, 4–201]

e.g. Example: Under a Wisconsin statute, a person is entitled to a hearing if a substantial interest of the person is injured by the agency action and there is a dispute of material fact. Thus, a local agency required by a state agency to line sewer tunnels with concrete was entitled to a formal hearing. The cost of lining the tunnels was very substantial, so the local agency that wanted to avoid these costs was suffering injury to a "substantial interest." [**Milwaukee Metro. Sewerage Dist. v. Wis. Dep't of Nat. Res.,** 375 N.W.2d 648 (Wis. 1985)]

D. Agency Adjudicators

1. Formal Adjudication: ALJ or Agency Head

The APA contemplates that either agency heads or administrative law judges ("ALJs") will preside at the taking of the evidence for formal adjudications. [APA § 556(b)] Congress may, of course, alter this default rule. [**Id.**] As a practical matter, most hearings for formal adjudication are conducted by ALJs. These professional fact finders were formerly called "hearing officers." The typical pattern is that the ALJ renders an initial decision, and the final agency decision is made by the agency heads who review the ALJ's decision. In some agencies, the function of reviewing ALJ decisions is delegated to a judicial officer rather than to the agency heads.

2. Non-APA Cases

Many important adjudications do not require formal adjudication under the APA, and thus need not be determined by ALJs. Agencies often provide for such matters to be determined in the first instance by "administrative judges" or "AJs." The big difference between an ALJ and an AJ (other than the missing "L") is that the former are protected by the APA's provisions specifically designed to promote decisional independence. [*See infra,* p. 76 *et seq.*] The latter are not. Due process will, however, apply to AJ determinations that implicate deprivations of liberty or property.

E. Prehearing Process for Formal Adjudication

1. Notice

All APAs contain provisions relating to notice. The federal act provides that persons entitled to notice of an agency hearing shall be timely informed of: (i) the time, place, and nature of the hearing; (ii) the legal authority and jurisdiction under which the hearing is to be held; and (iii) the matters of fact and law asserted. [APA § 554(b)] Statutes and regulations relating to specific agencies frequently provide for additional notice requirements.

2. Parties and Intervention

a. Purpose of Intervention

In addition to the named parties, additional parties often seek to intervene in agency proceedings. They do so because their legal rights or other legal interests may be affected by the proceeding, and they believe that their positions will not be adequately represented by the named parties and the agency staff.

b. Discretion

Generally, agencies permit such intervention as long as the new party or parties will *not unduly complicate the proceeding.* [APA § 555(b)] Often, the intervention is conditional: The intervenors can participate on some issues but not all, or are limited in their use of discovery or cross-examination. [**Office of Communications of the United Church of Christ v. FCC**, 359 F.2d 994 (D.C. Cir. 1966) (TV viewers have right to intervene to protest renewal of station's license, but FCC can adopt rules to limit the number of parties)]

c. Relation Between Intervention and Standing

The criteria for intervention and standing to seek judicial review are not the same, even though some earlier cases seem to equate the two situations. For example, a party that lacks standing might be entitled to intervene if it could make a significant contribution to the administrative proceeding. [**Koniag, Inc. v. Andrus**, 580 F.2d 601 (D.C. Cir. 1978)] By the same token, a party that can meet the requirements for standing might still be denied the right to intervene if intervention would unduly complicate the proceeding or otherwise violate the agency's own rules. [**Envirocare of Utah, Inc. v. Nuclear Regulatory Comm'n**, 194 F.3d 72 (D.C. Cir. 1999)]

Example: The Nuclear Regulatory Commission's statute allows intervention "on the request of any person whose interest may be affected by the proceeding." Petitioner Envirocare ("E") has an NRC license to dispose of nuclear waste. E wishes to intervene in NRC proceedings that consider whether to give a similar license to Q. E fears that the NRC will not compel Q to meet all of the high standards that E was required to meet. The NRC refused to allow E to intervene in Q's case, even though E probably could meet the requirements for standing to challenge the NRC decision in court. One reason for the NRC's decision was that E's participation would unduly complicate Q's case. Under *Chevron* (discussed in p. 150 *et seq., infra*), the court must defer to the NRC's reasonable construction of the ambiguous word "interest" in the statute. [*Envirocare, supra*]

3. Discovery

There is no APA requirement for discovery in agency proceedings. [**Citizens Awareness Network v. United States**, 391 F.3d 338 (1st Cir. 2004) (NRC does not violate APA by doing away with discovery and substituting a system of mandatory disclosure of expert witness reports)] Similarly, most states *do not provide* any rights to prehearing discovery to parties to administrative proceedings. However, in some states, parties to administrative proceedings have the same rights to prehearing discovery (*e.g.*, to take depositions) as do litigants in civil cases. [1981 Model State APA § 4–210(a)] In one state, the court held that, as a matter of common law, an administrative respondent in a license revocation case should have the same access to the documents and interviews in agency files as a criminal defendant would have. [**Shively v. Stewart**, 65 Cal. 2d 475 (1966)]

EXAM TIP

Keep in mind that an agency hearing, even a formal adjudication, is *not a court case*. Therefore some of the rules of procedure that apply in court cases do not necessarily apply in agency hearings. Prehearing discovery is one area where the agency rules usually differ from court rules.

a. Subpoena Power

Normally, all parties to administrative proceedings have subpoena power so that they can compel the presence of witnesses at the hearing. Similarly, by using a subpoena duces tecum, parties can compel witnesses to bring documents with them. Agency procedural rules can require a showing that the subpoenaed evidence will be relevant and that the scope of the subpoena is reasonable. [APA § 555(d)]

b. Freedom of Information Act

An individual can often obtain important information in government files by making a request under the Freedom of Information Act or corresponding state statutes. (*See infra* Chapter 6.) This information may be quite useful for purposes of pretrial discovery.

4. Settlement and Alternative Dispute Resolution

As in civil litigation, parties to administrative litigation try to settle their cases without trial. In 1990, Congress amended the APA to require agencies to explore and use alternative dispute resolution ("ADR") techniques in all agency functions, including adjudication and rulemaking. [Administrative Dispute Resolution Act, P.L. 101–552]

a. APA Amendments

The ADR Act amended the APA by changing section 556(c)(6), and by adding section 556(c)(7) and (8) to encourage the use of ADR techniques to settle disputes and to permit an ALJ to require participation in settlement conferences.

b. ADR Techniques

The ADR Act amended Title 5 of the United States Code to add new sections authorizing and encouraging agencies to use the whole range of ADR techniques: settlement negotiations, conciliation, facilitation, mediation, fact finding, minitrials, and arbitration.

c. When ADR Is Used

Despite the statute's requirement to explore the use of ADR, ADR *procedures are voluntary*; regulated parties cannot be compelled to use them. The statute also suggests that there are situations in which ADR is not appropriate, such as when an authoritative resolution of the matter is required for precedential value.

F. The Process of Proof at the Hearing for a Formal Adjudication

1. Burden of Proof

The rules relating to the burden of producing evidence and the burden of persuasion in administrative hearings are roughly the same as in civil litigation.

a. Placement of Burden

Under the federal APA, "... the proponent of a rule or order has the burden of proof.... A sanction may not be imposed or rule or order issued except on consideration of the whole record or those parts thereof cited by a party and supported by and in accordance with the reliable, probative and substantial evidence." [APA § 556(d)]

(1) Burden of Persuasion

APA section 556(d), which places the burden of proof on the proponent of a rule or order, refers to the *burden of persuasion,* not the burden of going forward with the evidence. Thus, an applicant for a benefit must prove his case by a preponderance of the evidence.

Example: The Supreme Court overturned an agency decision that held that the applicant would win if the applicant's and the employer's evidence were evenly balanced. The agency's view (known as the "true doubt" rule) violates section 556(d) by failing to place the burden of proof on the applicant. [**Dir., Office of Workers' Comp. v. Greenwich Collieries,** 512 U.S. 267 (1994)]

(2) Proving an Exception

The burden of proving an exception to the applicability of a statute lies with the party asserting that exception. [**NLRB v. Ky. River Cmty. Care, Inc.,** 532 U.S. 706 (2001)]

Example: By statute, employers must bargain with a union representing their employees, if the employees vote for representation. The statute does not apply to employees who are "supervisors." Although the NLRB has the burden of proof to establish that the duty to bargain has arisen, the employer has the burden to show that particular employees are supervisors. [**NLRB v. Ky. River Cmty. Care, Inc.,** *supra*]

b. Standard of Proof

The general rule is that a case must be proved by a *preponderance of the evidence*—not the higher standards such as clear and convincing evidence or beyond a reasonable doubt. [**Steadman v. SEC**, 450 U.S. 91 (1981)] *Note:* The *Steadman* case involved sanctions against a licensee for fraud. In a contract case, fraud must be proved by clear and convincing evidence, but this is not required in administrative proceedings.

2. Evidentiary Rules for Administrative Proceedings

a. Admissibility of Evidence

The federal APA provides: "Any oral or documentary evidence may be received, but the agency as a matter of policy shall provide for the exclusion of irrelevant, immaterial, or unduly repetitious evidence." [APA § 556(d)] Thus, as far as the APA is concerned, the general rule is that *any relevant evidence* is admissible in administrative proceedings, *regardless of the rules of evidence* applicable in civil litigation. Thus, hearsay evidence is admissible regardless of whether it falls under one of the hearsay exceptions.

But note: An agency may adopt stricter rules of evidence by procedural rule.

EXAM TIP

An important area where agency procedure differs from court procedure concerns admissible evidence. The APA's "rule of evidence" in § 556(d) is, to say the least, very lax compared to the Federal Rules of Evidence. Remember to check available agency rules, however, as they may adopt a stricter approach.

---

b. Reliance on Hearsay Alone

While hearsay evidence is often freely admissible in administrative cases, there is a split in authority on whether the agency can rely on *hearsay alone* in making a finding.

(1) State Courts—Conflict over the "Residuum Rule"

Many state courts follow the rule that the agency's decision must be based on at least *some* (a "residuum" of) evidence that is *not* hearsay. [**Gehin v. Wis. Group Ins. Bd.**, 692 N.W.2d 572 (Wis. 2005) (retaining residuum rule and collecting authority from other states following it)]

(a) Illustration

In *Gehin, supra*, the Wisconsin Group Insurance Board based its finding that Gehin was not disabled on three written medical reports—*i.e.,* hearsay. The claimant herself and a doctor testified in her favor. The Wisconsin Supreme Court held that the Board's reliance on pure hearsay violated the residuum rule and that this hearsay did not constitute, by itself, substantial evidence.

(2) Federal Rejection of Residuum Rule

The residuum rule does not apply in the review of the decisions of federal agencies. [**Richardson v. Perales,** 402 U.S. 389 (1971)]

(a) Potential Weakness of *Perales*

The *Perales* case is somewhat weak authority because it was decided on alternative grounds. The ultimate fact issue in *Perales* was whether a claimant was permanently disabled. The reports of several doctors were introduced in opposition to the claim. The doctors were not called to testify, and the claimant did not seek to subpoena them. The Court upheld the decision denying benefits even though the doctors' hearsay reports were the only evidence against the claimant. Thus, the Court appeared to reject the residuum rule. The Court noted, however, that the claimant had waived his right of cross-examination by failing to subpoena the doctors. Thus, it can be argued that the *Perales* decision might have gone the other way if the claimant had attempted unsuccessfully to subpoena the doctors. [*But see, e.g.*, **Passmore v. Astrue,** 533 F.3d 658 (8th Cir. 2008) (holding that claimant did not have an absolute right to subpoena and cross-examine a physician who authored a medical report used against him; upholding ALJ's denial of subpoena)]

(3) Unreliable Hearsay Doesn't Constitute Substantial Evidence with or Without a Residuum Rule

Of course, even where the residuum rule does not apply, a decision based solely on *unreliable* hearsay evidence should be set aside.

Example: The Army deprived Plaintiff of security clearance on the basis of various incidents that it claimed jeopardized security. Plaintiff denied or adequately explained each of the incidents. All of the Army's evidence was based on hearsay (the statements of one Hiley), and it did not produce Hiley to testify (he was unavailable). There was great personal hostility between Plaintiff and Hiley. The court held that substantial evidence did not support the Army's decision because the hearsay evidence was not sufficiently credible. [**Hoska v. Dep't of the Army,** 677 F.2d 131 (D.C. Cir. 1982)]

(4) Reliance on Hearsay Alone Can Violate Due Process

Hearsay evidence is evidence of a statement made by an *out-of-court* declarant that is offered to prove the truth of the statement. Thus, the opponent of the hearsay is denied the right to confront the declarant. In an extreme case, reliance on hearsay alone could violate the due process right to confront witnesses. This might occur if the hearsay does not fall within any judicial exception to the hearsay rule, if credibility issues were critical, and especially if the declarant were available but the agency failed to produce the declarant despite a timely request to do so. [*See* **Ezeagwuna v. Ashcroft,** 325 F.3d 396 (3d Cir. 2003) (highly unreliable double hearsay that was sole basis for rejecting an asylum petition violated due process)]

3. Exclusive Record Principle

As you might expect, for formal or "on the record" proceedings, an agency may not rely on evidence that is *outside the record*. Under the federal APA, "the transcript of testimony and exhibits, together with all papers and requests filed in the proceeding, constitutes the exclusive record for decision. . . ." [APA § 556(e)] However, this basic principle has a number of limitations:

a. Physical Inspections

Agency decisions can be based upon physical inspections or tests, provided that these are conducted in a way that is fair to the parties involved.

b. Assistance to Adjudicators

Administrative law judges and agency heads are entitled to the assistance of law clerks and other staff members to help them understand the evidence, find testimony in the record, and write the decision. Just as a judge can have a law clerk, administrative judges are entitled to similar assistance. Of course, the assistant cannot supplement the facts in the record; she can merely help the decisionmaker to understand the record or give advice about law or policy. (*See infra,*

p. 83, discussing bar on ex parte contacts in formal adjudication) Moreover, the staff advisor cannot have been an adversary in the case—that is prohibited by separation of functions provisions. (*See infra*, p. 76 *et seq.*)

c. Official Notice

A trier of fact is permitted to take official notice of factual material. Official notice is similar to judicial notice in that it relieves the party who has the burden of proof of producing facts to prove the matter asserted. Noticed material is treated as evidence. Official notice is a great time saver; it allows matters that are unlikely to be disputed to be treated as proved. Nevertheless, the opponent generally must have an opportunity to rebut it. Unlike courts, agencies can take official notice of "technical or scientific materials within the agency's specialized knowledge," even though such items are not necessarily indisputable.

Example: A medical panel can take official notice of community standards of medical practice. [**Franz v. Bd. of Med. Quality Assurance**, 31 Cal. 3d 124 (1982)]

(1) Opportunity to Contradict

APA section 556(e) provides: "When an agency decision rests on official notice of a material fact not appearing in the evidence in the record, a party is entitled, on timely request, to an *opportunity to show the contrary.*"

(a) Criteria for Rebuttal

Agencies have discretion to determine whether to allow rebuttal of noticed facts. They need not, for instance, allow an opportunity to rebut a proposition like, "the earth revolves around the sun." Reviewing courts are more likely to require an opportunity to rebut noticed facts where they involve *adjudicative facts,* are subject to *dispute,* or are *critical* to the result.

Example—immigration: An immigration judge took official notice of the following facts without furnishing an opportunity for rebuttal: (i) Violeta Chamorro had been elected president of Nicaragua; (ii) her coalition gained a majority in parliament; (iii) the Sandinistas had been ousted from power; and (iv) Plaintiff's family had nothing more to fear from the Sandinistas. The court held that the first two facts were both legislative and indisputable, and no rebuttal opportunity was required. The third fact was legislative but disputable. The fourth fact was adjudicative and disputable. The judge should have provided an opportunity for rebuttal of the third and fourth facts. [**Castillo-Villagra v. INS**, 972 F.2d 1017 (9th Cir. 1992)]

(b) Timing of the Opportunity to Rebut

In a typical formal adjudication, the parties present their cases to an administrative law judge ("ALJ"), who prepares a decision subject to plenary review by the agency heads. As they review the ALJ's decision, the agency heads may take official notice of facts that the ALJ did not. This creates a problem: When should the agency heads furnish the affected party an opportunity to rebut the noticed facts? Some cases allow agencies to furnish this opportunity through a motion to reopen the case after the agency heads issue a decision. [**Rhoa-Zamora v. INS**, 971 F.2d 26 (7th Cir. 1992)] Contrary authority exists that the agency heads must furnish this opportunity before they issue a decision. [**Castillo-Villagra v. INS,** *supra*, p. 59]

d. Use of Expertise in Evaluating Evidence

Agency fact finders become experts in deciding particular types of cases. This expertise enables them to make predictions about the future and allows them to disbelieve the testimony of expert witnesses and rely on their own expertise instead. Generally, use of this expertise is allowed: "The presiding officer's experience, technical competence, and specialized knowledge may be utilized in evaluating evidence." [1981 Model State APA § 4–215(d)]

Example: An expert fact finder is not bound by expert testimony as to the cause of an injury. [**McCarthy v. Sawyer-Goodman Co.,** 215 N.W. 824 (Wis. 1927) (agency finding that hernia was not caused by industrial injury upheld)]

(1) Matters of Prediction

Likewise, precise support in the record is not required to uphold an agency's conclusion as to matters of prediction or allocation of resources.

Example—prediction of effect of decreased railroad rates: An agency order decreasing railroad rates—based upon its predictions as to the effect of the decrease on traffic—was upheld without supporting evidence in the record. The Court took into consideration the agency's experience with the railway and the experimental nature of the decrease. [**Mkt. St. Ry. v. R.R. Comm'n,** 324 U.S. 548 (1945)]

(2) Limitation—Conjecture

However, an agency will *not* be permitted to rely upon its own expertise where the matter is *not technical* and the agency is clearly indulging in *conjecture.* [**F.A. McDonald Co. v. Indus. Comm'n,** 26 N.W.2d 165 (Wis. 1947)]

(3) Limitation—Lack of Reasons

Reliance on expertise will be sharply scrutinized when the agency, without giving warning at the hearing, disregards the testimony of an expert witness and substitutes its own conclusions:

> A rejection of unopposed testimony by a qualified and disinterested expert on a matter susceptible of reasonably precise measurement, without the agency's developing its objections at a hearing, ought to be upheld *only when the agency's uncommunicated criticisms* appear to the reviewing court to be *both so compelling and so deeply held* that the court can be fairly sure the agency would not have been affected by anything the witness could have said had he known of them; *and* [when] the Court would have been bound to affirm, despite the expert's hypothetical rebuttal, out of deference for the agency's judgment on so technical a matter.

[**Davis & Randall, Inc. v. United States,** 219 F. Supp. 673 (W.D.N.Y. 1963)]

(4) Case-by-Case Review of Agency Invocation of "Expertise"

Results in this area vary on a case-by-case basis. Much depends on the credibility of the administrator's opinion, its presentation on appeal, the susceptibility of the issue to precise proof, the agency's demonstrated expertise, whether an opportunity to contradict the evaluation was ever provided, and judicial confidence in the fairness of the agency and its procedures.

SUMMARY OF EXCLUSIVE RECORD PRINCIPLE

RULE	The transcript of testimony and any exhibits constitute the *exclusive record* for decision; the agency cannot rely on evidence outside of that record.
LIMITATIONS	• Physical inspection or test allowed • Assistance of agency staff allowed as long as they stick to record • Official notice of facts allowed but an opportunity to rebut may be required (especially for facts that are adjudicative, contested, and important) • Agency expertise may be used to evaluate evidence and make predictions

4. Right of Cross-Examination

a. The APA's General Provision

In APA formal hearings, parties normally have the opportunity to cross-examine adverse witnesses. The APA provides that a party is entitled "to conduct such cross-examination as may be required for a full and true disclosure of the facts." [APA § 556(d) (fifth sentence)] Under this provision, an agency typically need not provide for cross-examination when the issues turn on technical or economic matters rather than on credibility because cross-examination is not required "for a full and true disclosure of the facts" in such situations.

Example: The Nuclear Regulatory Commission revised its rules for nuclear reactor licensing cases to dispense with full rights of cross-examination. Under the new rules, a party seeking to cross-examine a witness must first seek permission from the hearing officer and must establish that cross is "necessary to ensure the development of an adequate record for decision." The court upheld the new rule, but noted that parties must have the right to cross-examination when they can make a sufficient showing that it is needed. [**Citizens Awareness Network v. United States**, 391 F.3d 338 (1st Cir. 2004)]

b. An APA Carve-Out

However, "[i]n [formal] rulemaking or determining claims for money or benefits or applications for initial licenses an agency may, when a party will not be prejudiced thereby, adopt procedures for the submission of all or part of the evidence in written form." [APA § 556(d) (sixth sentence)]

G. Agency Decisions and Explanations

1. Types of Decisions for Formal Adjudication

APA § 557(b) describes the types of decisions that an ALJ may issue as part of a formal adjudication.

a. Initial Decision

An ALJ may issue an **"initial decision."** These decisions become final unless they are appealed to the agency.

(1) Note—Agency Control over ALJ Initial Decisions

On review of the initial decision, the agency has all the powers it would have had in making the initial decision. [APA § 557(b)]

b. Recommended Decision

The agency—in specific cases or by general rule—may require the entire record developed by the ALJ to be certified to the agency itself for decision. In such cases, the ALJ merely makes a "recommended decision." [APA § 557(b)]

c. Tentative Decision

In initial *license* proceedings, or in formal *rulemaking* where a hearing on the record is required, the agency itself can issue a tentative decision. [APA § 557(b)(1)]

TYPES OF ADJUDICATORY DECISIONS UNDER § 557(b)	
TYPE OF DECISION	
INITIAL	— ALJ hears evidence "on the record"; decision final unless appealed to the agency
RECOMMENDED	— ALJ develops record for agency so agency can decide; ALJ recommends decision
TENTATIVE	— In initial license proceedings or formal rulemaking where a hearing on the record is required, the ***agency itself*** may issue a tentative decision

2. Statutory Duty to Explain Decisions in Formal Adjudication

The APA provides: "All decisions, including initial, recommended, and tentative decisions, are a part of the record and shall include a statement of—(A) *findings and conclusions,* and the *reasons or basis* therefor, on all the material issues of fact, law, or discretion presented on the record; and (B) the appropriate rule, order, sanction, relief, or denial thereof." [APA § 557(c)]

a. Party Must Have Opportunity to Submit Own Findings

Section 557(c) also provides that, for formal adjudications, before a decision is made on the findings of fact and conclusions of law—or before the agency decides to review the administrative law judge's decision—the parties must have a reasonable opportunity to submit their *own proposed findings and conclusions,* or their *exceptions to the decisions* already made. The record must show the administrative law judge's ruling as to each finding, conclusion, or exception thus presented. [APA § 557(c)]

b. Adoption of ALJ Decisions by Agency Heads

Frequently, an administrative law judge decides a case, rendering a decision that includes findings and reasons. The agency heads summarily affirm the ALJ decision. The heads are not required to state findings and reasons; by adopting the ALJ's decision, the heads state the same findings and reasons as the ALJ. [**Guentchev v. INS**, 77 F.3d 1036 (7th Cir. 1996)] However, if the agency heads state that the ALJ reached a "substantially correct result," the heads have not summarily affirmed the ALJ, and the reviewing court cannot be sure precisely which of the ALJ's findings or reasons the heads have adopted. [**Armstrong v. Commodity Futures Trading Comm'n**, 12 F.3d 401 (3d Cir. 1993)] As a result, the agency's affirmation may be vacated.

3. Other Sources of a Duty to Explain Adjudicatory Decisions

a. Section 555 of the APA

Section 555 of the APA applies to agency proceedings generally, *without regard to their formality*. It provides that, except where its grounds are self-explanatory, an agency must give a "brief statement" explaining its grounds for denying a "written application, petition, or other request of an interested person made in connection with any agency proceeding." [APA § 555(e)]

b. Agency Enabling Acts or Procedural Rules

An agency's enabling act or its procedural rules might require an explanation. A duty to explain need not appear on the face of an agency enabling act for a court to find one. Courts have inferred a statutory duty of an agency to give reasons for its actions from the availability of judicial review—*i.e.*, where judicial review is based on an agency's rationale for its action, the agency must explain that rationale. [**Dunlop v. Bachowski**, 421 U.S. 560 (1975) (determining that, to enable judicial review, Secretary of Labor had to declare reasons for refusing to bring suit to set aside an election)]

c. Due Process

An agency might have a duty to explain under the fact-sensitive balancing test of **Mathews v. Eldridge.** [424 U.S. 319 (1976) (see *supra*, p. 34)]. In the pre-*Mathews* case of **Goldberg v. Kelly**, the Supreme Court held that due process imposed a duty of explanation on the decisionmaker in a welfare termination case. [397 U.S. 254 (1970) (see *supra,* p. 30)]

4. Purposes for Explaining

The requirement that findings and conclusions be stated assures that the fact finder will carefully evaluate the evidence and consider its discretionary choices. Furthermore, without adequate findings and conclusions by the agency, the courts would have no way of determining the basis on which the agency had acted, and the parties could not decide whether to seek review. [**Dunlop v. Bachowski**, *supra*]

5. Courts Will Not Supply Explanations

Administrative decisions will be reviewed and enforced only on the basis of findings and conclusions that are a *part of the record.* Courts will not infer or imply other findings in order to uphold agency action—or accept "post hoc" rationalizations supplied in the briefs.

Example: In the first *Chenery* case [**SEC v. Chenery Corp.**, 318 U.S. 80 (1943) (*Chenery I*)], the SEC rejected a reorganization plan that insiders had proposed to preserve their control of a company. The agency relied on judicially-created equity doctrine for this result. The Supreme Court vacated the SEC's decision as the agency had misapplied these doctrines. The Court refused to consider whether different reasons that the agency had not relied upon contemporaneously could support the agency's decision. To do so would require the Court to make decisions that Congress had assigned to the agency.

SUMMARY OF ISSUES AT EACH STAGE OF FORMAL ADJUDICATION

PREHEARING PROCESS

Proper Notice — check statutory requirements

Intervention — allowed if does not complicate proceeding

Discovery — generally not allowed, but check statute; subpoenas allowed

Opportunity for Settlement or Mediation

HEARING PROCESS

Burden of Proof — on proponent of rule or order, normally by a preponderance of the evidence

Admissibility of Evidence — generally any relevant evidence may be received in formal proceedings under the APA; but check agency procedural rules.

Cross-Examination — parties are entitled "to conduct such cross-examination as may be required for a full and true disclosure of the facts."

Exclusive Record Principle — decision must be based on record; some limitations on this rule (e.g., official notice)

POST-HEARING PROCESS

Findings and Reasons — must be stated

H. Procedures for Informal Adjudication

1. Gap in APA Coverage

The federal APA sets forth detailed procedural rules for formal adjudication. By contrast, the APA sets out only very meager requirements for "informal adjudication," which covers a vast range of agency decisionmaking.

a. APA Provisions

The APA sets forth a few provisions applicable to informal adjudication.

(1) Right to Counsel; Right to Appear

Rights to appear and to counsel under the APA depend on whether one is a "person compelled to appear in person," a "party," or an "interested person."

"*A person compelled to appear in person* before an agency or representative thereof is entitled to be accompanied, represented, and advised by counsel or, if permitted by the agency, by other qualified representative."

"*A party* is entitled to appear in person or by or with counsel or other duly qualified representative in an agency proceeding."

"So far as the orderly conduct of public business permits, *an interested person* may appear before an agency or its responsible employees for the presentation, adjustment, or determination of an issue, request, or controversy in a proceeding, whether interlocutory, summary, or otherwise, or in connection with an agency function."

[APA § 555(b)]

(2) Timely Conclusion

The APA requires the agency to conclude matters within a reasonable time. [APA § 555(b)]

(3) Explanation of Denial

The APA also requires an agency to give prompt notice and explanation of the denial of any application, petition, or other request. [APA § 555(e)]

(4) Enforcement of Subpoenas

The APA provides that subpoenas and reports can be enforced only as authorized by law. [APA § 555(c), (d)]

(5) Licensing Provisions

The APA requires a prior warning and opportunity to correct the problem in cases of license revocation or suspension. However, this provision does not apply in cases of willfulness or in which public health, interest, or safety requires otherwise. Also, when a licensee applies to renew a license, the former license does not expire until the application has been finally determined by the agency. [APA § 558(c)]

2. Filling the Gap with Due Process

Of course, where an agency threatens to deprive a person of liberty or property, it must honor due process requirements in informal adjudications.

3. Filling the Gap with Another Statute

An agency's enabling act may, even if it does not trigger formal adjudication under the APA, contain various statutory requirements for agency adjudications. In many such cases, agencies hold trial-type hearings that are similar to those required by the APA, except that the agencies do not employ ALJs as their hearing officers.

4. Filling the Gap with Procedural Regulations

Note also that if an agency provides procedural protections in its regulations, the agency will be required to follow *its own regulations* even if it was not legally required to adopt them.

5. Courts Don't Get to Fill the Gap

Courts lack authority to create additional procedures for informal adjudications untethered to any requirement imposed by positive law (*e.g.*, the Constitution or the agency's enabling act). [**Pension Benefit Guar. Corp. v. LTV Corp.**, 496 U.S. 633 (1990) (applying the *Vermont Yankee* principle to informal adjudication)]

I. Declaratory Orders

1. Introduction

One important type of formal agency adjudication is the declaratory order. Persons subject to agency regulation often need guidance on how the agency will interpret the law. In most cases, they can obtain this guidance through seeking formal or informal advice from the agency staff, but the agency is *not bound* by this advice. (*See infra*, p. 88 *et seq.* for discussion of estoppel.) If the person seeks *authoritative guidance*, he may seek a declaratory order from the agency. This is the administrative equivalent of a declaratory judgment in court; *i.e.*, it is an authoritative statement on how the law will be applied but without seeking any other remedy.

2. APA Provisions

The federal act provides: "The agency . . . as in the case of other orders, and in its sound discretion, may issue a declaratory order to terminate a controversy or remove uncertainty." [APA § 554(e)]

3. Broad Power

In construing APA § 554(e), the Supreme Court has ruled that wherever the agency could have conducted its usual trial-type hearing (*e.g.*, to revoke a license), it may enter a declaratory order instead. [**Red Lion Broad. Co. v. FCC**, 395 U.S. 367 (1969)]

a. Implied Power

Some commentators feel that an agency also has the *implied power* to issue a declaratory order in cases *not* requiring a hearing.

4. Judicial Review

Declaratory orders are reviewable by the courts in the same manner as any other administrative order. [*See* **Red Lion Broad. Co. v. FCC**, *supra*]

J. Agency Adjudication and Retroactivity

1. Overview of the Problem

At least as a default, we think of adjudication as retroactive in the sense that a "new rule" developed in a case of first impression (whether by a court or an agency) should apply to the parties of that case. This practice creates obvious possibilities for unfairness and surprise to the parties, which in turn suggests that agencies should have discretion to apply new doctrines developed in adjudication prospectively—that is, agencies should be able to announce a "new rule" in an adjudication but hold back on applying it until later cases. As discussed below, one school of thought would forbid purely "prospective adjudication" on the ground that "rules" with solely future effect should be created through the APA's rulemaking procedures. [**NRLB v. Wyman-Gordon Co.**, 394 U.S. 759 (1969); **Bowen v. Georgetown Univ. Hosp.**, 488 U.S. 204, 220–21 (1988) (Scalia, J., concurring) ("adjudication could not be purely prospective, since otherwise it would constitute rulemaking")] As a practical matter, however, agencies can avoid the force of *Wyman-Gordon* and engage in prospective adjudication. Also, where an agency does attempt to apply its adjudication retroactively, a reviewing court may overrule it.

2. *Wyman-Gordon* Sort of Bars Prospective Adjudication

Cobbling together the opinions of a plurality and a dissent, the Supreme Court seemed to prohibit agencies acting under the APA from adopting purely *prospective rules* by means of adjudication rather than rulemaking. [**NLRB v. Wyman-Gordon Co.**, 394 U.S. 759 (1969)]

a. One Majority Rejected Prospective Adjudication

Wyman-Gordon followed an earlier case, *Excelsior Underwear,* 156 N.L.R.B. 1236 (1966), in which the NLRB held that a company must furnish the union with a list of all employees for electioneering purposes. In *Excelsior,* the new policy was announced by the NLRB as *prospective* only; *i.e.*, it was not applied to the parties in the *Excelsior* case. A majority of the Supreme Court in *Wyman-Gordon* determined that the *Excelsior* rule was invalid because a purely prospective order should be *adopted as a rule* under § 553—in compliance with the statutory provisions for rulemaking.

b. A Different Majority Upheld the Agency's Order Anyway

The Court nonetheless enforced the NLRB's order in *Wyman-Gordon*. The plurality took the view that the order should be sustained because it involved a *separate* adjudication than *Excelsior*. Put another way, the conclusion that *Excelsior* had produced a defective rule did not prevent the NRLB from applying its adjudicative authority to develop the same doctrine in a later, proper adjudication. The concurrence took the view that agencies can engage in purely prospective adjudication in any event. As a result, *Wyman-Gordon* has had little practical effect because there is no effective sanction against the agency's adoption of a prospective-only adjudication on which it can rely in future decisions that have retroactive effect.

c. Dissenting Opinion

Dissenting judges in *Wyman-Gordon* disagreed with this outcome. Since the Board in *Wyman-Gordon* had relied on *Excelsior*, and since *Excelsior* was incorrectly decided, the Court should have overturned the decision in *Wyman-Gordon*. An agency decision that rests on an invalid precedent is itself invalid, even though the decision might have been legally supportable on other grounds. [**SEC v. Chenery Corp.**, 318 U.S. 80 (1943) (*"Chenery I"*)]

3. Retroactive Application of Agency Adjudications

The default is that agency adjudications, like judicial decisions, are retroactive. Courts sometimes deprive agency adjudications of retroactive effect, however, in fairness to the affected parties.

a. The (Very) General Rule from *Chenery II*

The *Chenery* litigation arose out of an SEC decision rejecting a reorganization plan for a public utility company. The statute requiring the reorganization plan required that it be "fair" and "equitable." In administrative proceedings leading up to *Chenery I*, the SEC explained its rejection by invoking judicially-created equitable principles. In *Chenery I,* the Supreme Court determined that the agency had misapplied these principles and vacated and remanded. [**SEC v. Chenery Corp.,** 318 U.S. 80 (1943)] On its next try, the agency rejected the reorganization plan because it was not "fair" or "equitable" within the meaning of the controlling statute. (See the difference? In the first try, the agency relied on judicial precedent; in the second, it relied on its own construction and application of a statute it administered.) Among other objections, Chenery complained that this order was unfairly retroactive. The Supreme Court rejected this argument, observing:

> That such action might have a retroactive effect was not necessarily fatal to its validity. Every case of first impression has a retroactive effect, whether the new principle is announced by a court or by an administrative agency. But such retroactivity must be balanced against the mischief of producing a result which is contrary to a statutory design or to legal and equitable principles. If that mischief is greater than the ill effect of the retroactive application of a new standard, it is not the type of retroactivity which is condemned by law.

[**SEC v. Chenery Corp.,** 332 U.S. 194 (1947) (*"Chenery II"*)]

b. More Factors to Apply

A court deciding whether a new case-law rule is unfairly retroactive should balance at least five factors: (i) whether the case is *one of first impression,* (ii) whether the new rule *represents an abrupt departure* from well-established practice as opposed to filling a void in an unsettled area of the law, (iii) the extent to which *the party relied on prior law,* (iv) the *degree of burden* that a retroactive order imposes, and (v) the *statutory interest* in applying a new rule to the case at hand. [**Clark-Cowlitz Joint Operating Agency v. FERC,** 826 F.2d 1074 (D.C. Cir. 1987), *cert. denied*, 485 U.S. 913 (1988); **Retail, Wholesale, & Dep't Store Clerks Union v. NLRB,** 466 F.2d 380 (D.C. Cir. 1972)]

Example: The NLRB held that the employer committed an unfair labor practice in refusing to rehire strikers when jobs opened up after the strike. This was a change in the law. The NLRB not only required the strikers to be rehired, it also required the employer to pay back wages. The court upheld the order to rehire the strikers but reversed the requirement of back pay. The employer relied on well-established precedent in refusing to rehire the strikers. Consequently, the requirement that the employer pay back wages had an unnecessarily harsh retroactive effect and was an abuse of discretion. [**Retail, Wholesale, & Dep't Store Clerks Union v. NLRB,** *supra*]

e.g. **Example:** The NLRB reversed itself several times on the question of whether a nonunion employer had to allow an employee to bring a co-worker with him to an investigatory interview with the employer. Changing its view once again, the NLRB imposed sanctions on an employer that had refused to allow an employee to bring a co-worker with him. The court held that this retroactive adjudication was an abuse of the NLRB's discretion because the employer could not have anticipated that the NLRB would change its position. [**Epilepsy Found. of Ne. Ohio v. NLRB,** 268 F.3d 1095 (D.C. Cir. 2001)]

K. Choosing Between Adjudication and Rulemaking to Develop Policy

1. The Basic Rule—Broad Agency Discretion

Legislatures make law via statutes; they cannot adjudicate. Courts "make law" by deciding cases; they cannot legislate. A typical agency, by contrast, enjoys both adjudicative and rulemaking powers. Rulemaking is commonly understood to possess several major advantages as a policymaking tool over adjudication—*e.g.*, it provides better notice to interested parties, results in clearer law, is generally applicable, and is almost always prospective. One might therefore conclude that the legal system should require agencies to develop law and policy via rulemaking. Courts have declined to do so, however, in part because they do not wish to interfere with the complicated agency task of setting priorities and allocating resources. An agency that enjoys both adjudicative and rulemaking power generally has broad discretion to choose which one to use to develop law and policy as it implements a statutory scheme. [**SEC v. Chenery Corp.,** 332 U.S. 194 (1947) ("*Chenery II*") ("the choice made between proceeding by general rule or by individual, ad hoc litigation is one that lies primarily in the informed discretion of the administrative agency")]

2. Factors That Favor Use of Adjudication

In *Chenery II, supra,* the Supreme Court identified several factors that may favor the use of adjudication, notwithstanding the various advantages of rulemaking:

> [1] [P]roblems may arise in a case which the administrative agency could not reasonably foresee, problems which must be solved despite the absence of a relevant general rule. [2] Or the agency may not have had sufficient experience with a particular problem to warrant rigidifying its tentative judgment into a hard and fast rule. [3] Or the problem may be so specialized and varying in nature as to be impossible of capture within the boundaries of a general rule. In those situations, the agency must retain power to deal with the problems on a case-to-case basis if the administrative process is to be effective.

[**SEC v. Chenery Corp.,** 332 U.S. 194 (1947)]

3. Judicial Review for Abuse of Discretion

In administrative law, agency discretion is seldom absolute. Courts review an agency's choice between adjudication and rulemaking for "abuse of discretion." Generally speaking, litigants are very unlikely to prevail against a federal agency on this ground. A few examples follow.

a. Application—*Chenery II*

As discussed above, *Chenery II* addressed the propriety of the SEC's adjudicative decision to reject a public utility company's reorganization plan because it was not "fair" and "equitable" within the meaning of the relevant statute. In particular, the agency objected to management trading during the pendency of the reorganization that would have enabled it to retain control of the company. Chenery contended that no preexisting law proscribed its conduct and that the agency should have used its rulemaking powers to develop its new position rather than adjudication. The Supreme Court rejected this argument, declining to hold "that the Commission, which had not previously been confronted with the problem of management trading during reorganization, was forbidden from utilizing this particular proceeding for announcing and applying a new standard of conduct."

b. Application—*Bell Aerospace*

In *Bell Aerospace,* the Supreme Court held that the NLRB could determine via adjudication that "buyers" at a firm were not "managerial employees"—a characterization that bore on whether the buyers were covered by the National Labor Relations Act. The Court noted that use of adjudication was especially apt because the term "buyer" does not have a well-defined meaning across the industry. Therefore, it was "doubtful whether any generalized standard could be framed which would have more than marginal utility." [**NLRB v. Bell Aerospace Co.,** 416 U.S. 267 (1974)]

c. Application—*Ford Motor Co.*—A Rare Agency Loss

In *Ford Motor Co.,* an automobile dealership objected to an FTC order concluding that the dealer had engaged in an unfair trading practice in violation of § 5 of the FTC Act. The conduct at issue related to allocation of "surpluses" generated by retail sale of repossessed vehicles. The Ninth Circuit concluded that the FTC's decision to proceed by adjudication rather than rulemaking constituted an abuse of discretion. It declared that, as a general matter, agencies should proceed by rulemaking where they seek "to change the law and establish rules of widespread application." [Query: Is this too aggressive to square with cases like *Chenery II* and *Bell Aerospace*?] The court determined that the agency's condemnation of a widespread industry practice amounted to a generally applicable change in law. The court drew further support for its position from the pendency of an FTC rulemaking addressing car dealerships' accounting for deficiencies arising in connection with repossession. If it made sense to address deficiencies by rulemaking, then surpluses could be addressed that way, too. [**Ford Motor Co. v. FTC,** 673 F.2d 1008 (9th Cir.1981), *cert. denied*, 459 U.S. 999 (1982)]

4. Another Approach—Required Rulemaking

a. Duty to Adopt Rules—*Oregon*

Some states have been far more aggressive than the federal courts in requiring agencies to adopt regulations to limit their discretion. In *Megdal v. Oregon State Board of Dental Examiners,* a state board revoked a dentist's license for "unprofessional conduct" because he made a false statement on his malpractice insurance application. The court held that the agency was required to adopt rules defining the meaning of this broad term before a licensee could be disciplined. This would serve the purpose of giving fair notice to licensees and confining the board's exercise of discretion. The decision was based on a finding that the legislature so intended, not on due process. [**Megdal v. Oregon State Board of Dental Examiners,** 605 P.2d 273 (Or. 1980)]

b. 1981 Model Act Approach

The 1981 Model State APA moved strongly in the direction of required rulemaking.

(1) Preference for Rulemaking over Adjudication

The Model Act requires an agency to adopt rules in preference to making policy through adjudication. The agency shall "as soon as feasible and to the extent practicable, adopt rules . . . embodying appropriate standards, principles, and procedural safeguards that the agency will apply to the law it administers. . . ." [1981 Model State APA § 2–104(3)]

(2) Replacement of Adjudicatory Law with Rules

Second, if the agency has previously been making law and policy through case-by-case adjudication, the Act requires that the agency replace the case law with rules. Each agency shall "as soon as feasible and to the extent practicable, adopt rules to supersede principles of law or policy lawfully declared by the agency as the basis for its decisions in particular cases." [1981 Model State APA § 2–104(4)]

Chapter Four
Adjudicative Integrity

CONTENTS	PAGE
Key Exam Issues	74
A. **Constitutional Combination and Statutory Separation of Functions**	74
B. **Controlling Other Forms of Bias**	78
C. **Legislative Pressure on Agency Adjudicators**	81
D. **Ex Parte Communications**	82
E. **Decisionmaker Familiarity with the Case**	84
F. **Consistency Across Cases**	86

Key Exam Issues

This chapter examines statutory and constitutional requirements designed to protect the integrity and independence of administrative adjudicators and adjudication. These include due process principles and APA provisions that curb bias and ex parte contacts. This chapter also discusses doctrines that help ensure that an agency's decisions are consistent and coherent with each other—*i.e.*, res judicata, stare decisis, and estoppel.

Issues that may be especially likely to crop up in your administrative law course include:

1. **ALJ independence:** Various statutory provisions create extensive protections designed to enhance ALJ decisional independence. Be alert to whether the *ALJ's independence was protected* as provided in the APA.

2. **Combination and separation of functions:** Due process does not categorically bar agencies from combining functions that separation-of-powers doctrine seems to assign to different branches. For example, agencies make rules, bring enforcement actions, and adjudicate them. Note well, however, that the APA provides significant protections against the *same person engaging in both adversary and adjudicatory responsibility.* Make sure that these statutory **separation-of-functions** provisions were observed.

3. **Due process and bias:** Due process guarantees an impartial adjudicator. Make sure that both the ALJ and agency heads were *free from bias* in the form of prejudgment of the factual issues, animus against the party, or economic conflict of interest.

4. **Ex parte contacts:** Make sure that *no illegal ex parte communications* were made to adjudicatory decisionmakers.

5. **Effects of earlier decisions:** Finally, see whether the decision was constrained by the requirements of *res judicata, equitable estoppel, or stare decisis*.

A. Constitutional Combination and Statutory Separation of Functions

1. Overview of the Problem

Administrative agencies often make the rules, investigate violations, prosecute the offenders, and adjudicate the cases. Such concentrations of power might seem a flagrant violation of separation of powers, but they are a fact of life in the modern administrative state. Combination of functions also implicates an obvious due process concern insofar as one might reasonably conclude that an entity that prosecutes a matter cannot fairly adjudicate it. Nonetheless, the Supreme Court has held that combining enforcement and adjudicatory powers in one agency does not violate due process per se. [**Withrow v. Larkin,** 421 U.S. 35 (1975)] Administrative law does not ignore the problem of potential bias from combination of functions, however. Instead, rather than rely primarily on due process, the law's basic strategy for combatting this problem is to rely on statutory provisions that require separation of functions within an agency. [*See esp.* APA § 554(d)]

2. Agencies Can Combine Functions Consistent with Due Process

Under due process, the agency heads can engage in the functions of investigation and prosecution, then adjudicate the case. [**Withrow v. Larkin,** *supra*]

Example: In *Withrow,* the heads of a state medical licensing board held an investigatory hearing against a doctor, recommended to the district attorney that the doctor be prosecuted, and then adjudicated the revocation of the doctor's license. The Supreme Court upheld the procedure under due process. It was concerned that a contrary decision could disrupt the functioning of many federal, state, or local agencies in which agency heads combine adversarial and adjudicatory functions. The Court also considered it significant that APA § 554(d) (below), which requires separation of functions, contains an exception for agency heads.

a. But Combination at Lower Levels Might Violate Due Process

However, a mixing of functions in the same person *below the level of agency heads* may be a violation of due process, given that other staff members may be assigned to carry out different functions. [**Goldberg v. Kelly,** *supra,* p. 30 (in welfare decisions, a staff member who adjudicates a dispute should not have participated in making the determination under review); **Nightlife Partners v. City of Beverly Hills,** 108 Cal. App. 4th 81 (2003) (due process violated when adversarial staff member in zoning dispute furnishes ex parte advice to decisionmaker)]

EXAM TIP

For your exam, you should avoid oversimplified statements involving combination of functions and due process. Absent unusual circumstances, the combination of functions in the same agency doesn't violate due process. For that reason, it does not violate due process if an *agency head* investigates a case and then adjudicates the same case. However, it might violate due process if a *lower-level staff member* both investigates and adjudicates (or gives ex parte advice to an adjudicator) because a different staff member could have been assigned to carry out the adjudicatory or advisory function.

b. The Split-Enforcement Model

Just because Congress can, consistent with due process, combine enforcement and adjudicatory functions in an agency doesn't mean that it always does so. Congress has split the adjudicatory function from the law enforcement function for some agencies. For example, the Occupational Safety and Health Administration ("OSHA") *enforces* the worker safety laws and adopts regulations to implement them. However, when OSHA seeks *sanctions* against employers who violated the rules, the case is tried by the Occupational Safety and Health Review Commission ("OSHRC"), a separate agency that employs its own ALJs and is headed by officials who exclusively adjudicate cases.

(1) Judicial Deference Where the Split Agencies Disagree

When OSHA and OSHRC differ on a question of law they jointly administer, the courts must decide which agency is owed deference. The Supreme Court held that the courts should defer to OSHA's interpretations, not OSHRC's, because OSHA was likely to have greater expertise and familiarity with its own regulations. [**Martin v. Occupational Safety and Health Review Comm'n,** 499 U.S. 144 (1991)]

3. Statutory Separation of Functions for Formal Adjudication

Consistent with *Withrow, supra*, the APA contemplates that agency heads may play a role both in enforcement decisions and adjudication. *E.g.,* the agency may both authorize initiation of an enforcement action and then later adjudicate the same matter. At the ALJ level, however, the APA insists on strict separation of functions—adjudicators may not work for enforcers, and enforcers may not adjudicate. [APA § 554(d)]

a. Adjudicators May Not Work for Prosecutors

Section 554(d) provides that an ALJ may not "be responsible to or subject to the supervision or direction of an employee or agent engaged in the performance of an *investigative or prosecuting* function for an agency."

b. Adversaries May Not Adjudicate

Section 554(d) further provides: "An employee or agent engaged in the performance of investigative or prosecuting functions for an agency in a case may not, in that or a factually related case, *participate or advise in the decision*, recommended decision, or agency review . . . except as witness or counsel in public proceedings."

Note that the separation of functions rule applies on a case-specific basis: It applies only if a staff member has been an adversary in the case under decision or a factually related case. A person who has been an adversary in a factually similar but unrelated case can serve as an adjudicator in a later case. [**Marshall v. Cuomo**, 192 F.3d 473 (4th Cir. 1999) (staff member not disqualified as adviser even though he was an adversary in a similar case brought earlier against the very same respondent)]

Example: Agency brings an enforcement action against Acme Co. for violation of its regulations. Claire is a staff member of Agency who investigated Acme and advised that the agency issue a complaint against Acme. Floyd is another Agency staff member who is an expert in the area, but has not been involved in the case against Acme. Under section 554(d), Claire cannot furnish ex parte advice to the heads of Agency in the Acme case. However, Floyd can furnish ex parte advice to the agency heads in the Acme case.

c. APA Exceptions Allowing Combination of Functions

APA restrictions on the combination of functions above do *not* apply in several situations. Pay special attention to the third one!

  (i)   Applications for initial licenses [APA § 554(d)(A)];

  (ii) Proceedings involving the rates, facilities, or practices of public utilities or carriers [APA § 554(d)(B)]; or

  (iii) *The agency itself* or any member or members of the body comprising the agency [APA § 554(d)(C)].

EXAM TIP

Remember that to help ensure fair and unbiased adjudication, below the level of the agency heads, the APA generally **prohibits** an employee of the investigative or prosecuting arm of an agency *from supervising or directing* an ALJ, or from participating or advising in the decision of a case that she investigated or prosecuted, except in initial license applications and in most cases involving public utilities or carriers.

d. More on the "Agency Heads" Exception

The last exception permits agency heads to prosecute, investigate, and subsequently adjudicate the same case. The exception also covers the personal staff members of agency heads, who can participate in discussions about whether to issue a complaint and can later advise the agency heads in the final decision of the case. [**Grolier, Inc. v. FTC**, 615 F.2d 1215 (9th Cir. 1980)]

(1) Scope of Exception for Agency Heads

The agency heads exception applies *only if the individual was a member of the agency throughout the entire case*. It does not allow an individual to serve as a prosecutor and then adjudicate the same case after being appointed a member of the agency. [**Amos Treat & Co. v. SEC**, 306 F.2d 260 (D.C. Cir. 1962)] Similarly, a staff member, such as the personal adviser to the agency head, cannot participate in a decision to initiate prosecution and then serve as an administrative law judge in the same case. [**Grolier, Inc. v. FTC**, *supra*]

(2) Advisers and Agency Heads

Despite the agency heads exception, staff members who engaged in investigation and prosecution of a case probably cannot furnish ex parte advice to the agency heads when they make the final decision in the same case. Agency heads may be advised only by persons who have not engaged in prosecution or investigation. [*See, e.g.*, **Greene v. Babbitt**, 943 F. Supp. 1278 (W.D. Wash. 1996) (policy and legal advice by prosecutor to agency head violated § 554(d))] However, *before* the decision is made to engage in adjudication, the agency heads are permitted to discuss a case with prosecutors and investigators to decide whether to issue a complaint or designate a matter for hearing; they can then make the final decision in the same case. [*See* **Env't Def. Fund v. EPA**, 510 F.2d 1292 (D.C. Cir. 1975)]

4. Additional Statutory Protections for ALJ Independence

a. In-House ALJs in the Federal System

In the federal government and in most states, ALJs nominally work for the agency for which they decide cases—*e.g.*, an ALJ who adjudicates matters for the FTC is an FTC employee (or maybe an officer). To preserve ALJ decisional independence, in addition to requiring separation-of-functions under § 554(d), the APA provides that these judges must:

(i) *Be hired by a process controlled by the Office of Personnel Management* (rather than by the employing agency);

(ii) *Be assigned to cases by rotation,* as far as practicable;

(iii) *Not perform duties inconsistent with their duties as administrative law judges*;

(iv) *Be removed only for good cause*, as determined by the Merit Systems Protection Board (and not removed by the agency that had appointed them); and

(v) ***Be entitled to compensation*** set by the Office of Personnel Management ***independent of agency recommendations*** or ratings (so their pay could not be cut by the agency if it disapproved of their decisions).

(1) Agency Power to Guide ALJs via General Policies

Agencies cannot interfere with the decisional independence of their ALJs by influencing specific decisions, but they can adopt policies to guide the ALJ's decision of classes of cases. Agencies also can take reasonable measures to improve the consistency of ALJ decisions or to increase ALJ productivity. [**Nash v. Bowen**, 869 F.2d 675 (2d Cir. 1989)]

b. Central Panel Alternative for Protecting ALJ Independence

In over 20 states, ALJs operate in a "central panel." This means they do not work for the agencies but are assigned out to the various agencies when needed to conduct a hearing. The advantage of this arrangement is that the ALJs are perceived as being independent of the agency that is prosecuting the case. The disadvantage is that the ALJs are less specialized and possess less expertise than those who decide cases only for a single agency.

B. Controlling Other Forms of Bias

1. Proscribed Forms of Bias

An adjudicative decisionmaker is disqualified from deciding a case in which the decisionmaker is biased. The prohibited forms of bias include: (i) prejudgment of the facts, (ii) pecuniary bias, and (iii) personal animus against a party. A biased decisionmaker is prohibited both by procedural due process and by the APA.

2. Prejudgment of the Facts

When the decisionmaker has a fixed opinion regarding the facts about the parties that are at issue in the case, the decisionmaker must be disqualified. [**Cinderella Career & Finishing Schools, Inc. v. FTC**, 425 F.2d 583 (D.C. Cir. 1970) (adjudicator should be disqualified where "a disinterested observer may conclude that the [agency] has in some measure adjudged the facts as well as the law of a particular case in advance of hearing it")]

a. Public Statements Concerning Adjudicative Facts

In some cases, prejudgment of the facts is revealed by extra-judicial statements made by the decisionmaker.

Example—congressional report: An FTC Commissioner had previously served as counsel to a Senate subcommittee investigating the drug industry, during which time he had made statements indicating his belief that American Cyanamid had violated antitrust laws, and had helped draft a committee report critical of the company. This was held sufficient to disqualify him from FTC hearings involving the same company and issues. [**Am. Cyanamid Co. v. FTC**, 363 F.2d 757 (6th Cir. 1966)]

Example—public speech: Statements in a speech that indicated an agency head had already made up his mind about the guilt of a party showed the Commissioner had prejudged the facts even though he did not mention the party by name. [**Cinderella Career &

Finishing Schools, Inc. v. FTC, 425 F.2d 583 (D.C. Cir. 1970); *and see* **Bakalis v. Golembeski**, 35 F.3d 318 (7th Cir. 1994) (adjudicator made public statements that the college president should be dismissed before deciding the case)]

b. Legislative Facts, Law, or Policy

Prejudgment of issues of law, policy, or legislative fact do not require disqualification. (Recall that legislative facts are generalized facts bearing on policy; adjudicative facts are particularized facts about individual parties.) Otherwise, the expertise acquired by an agency would be a handicap rather than an advantage. [**FTC v. Cement Inst.**, 333 U.S. 638 (1948) (prior FTC report that a type of pricing system violated Sherman Act did not disqualify it from proceeding against cement companies using that pricing system); **Cent. Platte Natural Res. Dist. v. Wyoming**, 513 N.W.2d 847 (Neb. 1994) (hearing officer not disqualified because of prejudgment about water rights by reason of prior exposure to facts of water rights case)]

c. Contacts with Facts Arising While Decisionmaker Is in Role

A decisionmaker is not disqualified by reason of exposure to facts of a dispute while carrying out an assigned task for the agency (*i.e.*, while "in role"), absent a strong showing that the decisionmaker has a closed mind on the issue.

> **Example**—ALJ: An ALJ is not disqualified simply because he has already heard and decided the same case at an earlier time. [**NLRB v. Donnelly Garment Co.**, 330 U.S. 219 (1947)]

> **Example**—pre-decisional conference: Agency heads are not disqualified from deciding a case in which they previously heard evidence from agency prosecutors and decided to issue a complaint. [**Withrow v. Larkin**, *supra*]

> **Example**—press release: The customary issuance of press releases prior to adjudication—warning consumers there is "reason to believe" a law has been violated—does *not* unfairly bias the adjudicative proceedings. Although fact finders may be subject to pressure to vindicate the charges in the press release, such an element of "prejudgment" is inevitable where the agency has the power to both prosecute and adjudicate. [**FTC v. Cinderella Career & Finishing Schools, Inc.**, 404 F.2d 1308 (D.C. Cir. 1968)]

3. Financial Bias

A decisionmaker who has a financial or other personal interest in the case to be decided should be disqualified. [**Tumey v. Ohio**, 273 U.S. 510 (1927) (a judge whose compensation depended on fines paid by persons he convicted is disqualified); **Aetna Ins. Co. v. Lavoie**, 475 U.S. 813 (1986) (a judge who is conducting personal litigation involving the same legal issue as in present case must be disqualified)]

a. Institutional Interest

Bias may also be established if the adjudicating agency would benefit significantly from a decision against a party. [**Ward v. City of Monroeville**, 409 U.S. 57 (1972) (traffic court judge disqualified because he was also mayor and fines went into the city budget); **AEP Chapter Housing Ass'n v. City of Berkeley**, 114 F.3d 840 (9th Cir. 1997) (rent control agency not disqualified even though about 5% of its budget depends on registration fees it collects from landlords found to be subject to rent)]

(1) Prosecutors Distinguished

A prosecuting agency that does no adjudication is not disqualified even though it retains the penalties it collects. [**Marshall v. Jerrico, Inc.**, 446 U.S. 238 (1980)] In dictum, however, the Court indicated that a prosecutorial agency might be disqualified upon a much clearer showing of financial bias.

b. Professional Interest—Licenses

A recurring problem is whether a professional interest in a case should disqualify a decisionmaker. This problem arises frequently in connection with licensing boards. A board that licenses doctors is not disqualified from deciding a case that will add or subtract one more doctor from the group of doctors in a large city or state. But if the decisionmaker was the only doctor in a town, he might well be disqualified from deciding whether a second doctor should receive a license to practice in the town. [**Stivers v. Pierce**, 71 F.3d 732 (9th Cir. 1995) (dictum)]

(1) Optometry Cases

By statute, a majority of the agency heads of the optometry board must be independent optometrists (*i.e.*, not employees of corporations such as Wal-Mart). The agency is considering whether to revoke the licenses of all employed optometrists. The agency is not disqualified from deciding this case, absent a more focused showing that they cannot decide it fairly. [**Friedman v. Rogers**, 440 U.S. 1 (1979)] However, this case seems inconsistent with an earlier one, which held that if *all* of the agency heads had to be independent optometrists, a court could find that the agency is biased against employed optometrists. [**Gibson v. Berryhill**, 411 U.S. 564 (1973)]

4. Animus Toward a Party

A decisionmaker should be disqualified if it can be shown that she is personally hostile toward a party or a group to which the party belongs. This sort of personal hostility is often referred to as "animus." [**Berger v. United States,** 255 U.S. 22 (1921) (judge's statements evidenced hostility toward Germans)] Some cases indicate that an adjudicator should be disqualified if she has been the subject of personal abuse or criticism from a party. [*See, e.g.*, **Mayberry v. Pennsylvania,** 400 U.S. 455 (1971) ("no one so cruelly slandered is likely to maintain that calm detachment necessary for fair adjudication")]

a. Conduct at Hearing

Normally, an adjudicator's conduct toward a party at the hearing does not establish animus or prejudgment of the facts, even though the adjudicator speaks harshly and critically about the party, rules against the party on every issue, and disbelieves all its witnesses. [*See, e.g.*, **NLRB v. Pittsburgh Steamship Co.**, 337 U.S. 656 (1949); **McLaughlin v. Union Oil Co.**, 869 F.2d 1039 (7th Cir. 1989)] Such conduct simply reflects the opinions the decisionmaker has formed about the party based on what transpired at the hearing. Nevertheless, animus or prejudgment of the facts may be suggested by comments at the hearing together with highly irregular hearing procedures. [**Stivers v. Pierce**, 71 F.3d 732 (9th Cir. 1995) (harshness, harassment, and delays at the hearing combined with other evidence of pecuniary interest and personal animus)]

5. The Rule of Necessity

If the only adjudicators with power to hear and decide a case are biased, they are still permitted to hear and decide the case under the rule of necessity. Otherwise, nobody could decide the case and wrongdoers might go unpunished. [**Brinkley v. Hassig**, 83 F.2d 351 (10th Cir. 1936)] However, judicial review is likely to be more stringent than usual. In some states, the problem can be avoided because the authority that appointed the biased administrator is empowered to appoint a substitute for the purpose of hearing the case.

6. APA Provision on Bias

APA section 556(b) provides: "On the filing in good faith of a timely and sufficient affidavit of personal bias or other disqualification of a presiding or participating employee, the agency shall determine the matter as a part of the record and decision in the case." This provision contemplates that, upon complaint of bias, an ALJ will step aside ("recuse" herself). If she fails to do so, the agency heads (and the reviewing court) will consider the ALJ's failure to recuse herself as one of the issues in the case. The same principles apply to agency heads. If an agency head is biased, she should recuse herself. Note that if an agency head refuses to recuse herself, the APA does not indicate whether the other agency heads have power to disqualify her from voting.

a. Timing

A party must challenge a biased decisionmaker by filing the affidavit referred to in section 556(b) as soon as the party learns the pertinent facts. A failure to make an immediate disqualification motion is a waiver of the right to do so. [**Marcus v. Dir., Office of Workers' Comp. Programs**, 548 F.2d 1044 (D.C. Cir. 1976)]

C. Legislative Pressure on Agency Adjudicators

Congressional pressure on agency adjudicators while a case is in the hearing stage may deprive the parties to the adjudication of due process. [*See, e.g.,* **Koniag, Inc. v. Andrus,** 580 F.2d 601 (D.C. Cir. 1978); **Pillsbury Co. v. FTC,** 354 F.2d 952 (5th Cir. 1966)]

1. Illustration—*Pillsbury* Case

In *Pillsbury Co.,* an initial FTC decision was severely criticized in a congressional subcommittee hearing. The FTC chairman was closely questioned, and other FTC members were also present. The chairman then withdrew from further proceedings in the matter, but others who were present and questioned did take part in the final decision against Pillsbury. The court found this congressional intervention unwarranted and a *violation of due process. But note:* Nevertheless, the FTC was not permanently disqualified from hearing the case because during the thirteen years since the case began, there had been a sufficient change in personnel so that the matter could be remanded to the FTC for decision.

2. Narrow Application of *Pillsbury*

Courts in subsequent cases have been very cautious in their application of the *Pillsbury* rule. Thus, interference in a pending case *prior* to the time the case enters the hearing phase is less likely to require reversal than interference *after* it reaches the hearing phase. [*See, e.g.,* **DCP Farms v. Yeutter,** 957 F.2d 1183 (5th Cir. 1992)]

3. Causing Consideration of Irrelevant Factors

Congressional pressure that caused the agency to consider an irrelevant factor in making a discretionary decision would render the agency decision arbitrary and capricious. [*See* **D.C. Fed'n of Civic Ass'ns v. Volpe,** 459 F.2d 1231 (D.C. Cir. 1971), *cert. denied,* 405 U.S. 1030 (1972) (agency approved construction of bridge only after Congressmen threatened to withhold funding of the D.C. subway unless bridge was built)]

Courts appear quite cautious in applying this standard to invalidate agency decisions. They are concerned that a rigid application of the standard would interfere with legitimate congressional oversight as well as impair agency flexibility in dealing with Congress. [**ATX, Inc. v. Dep't of Transp.**, 41 F.3d 1522 (D.C. Cir. 1994) (introduction of bills in Congress did not pressure agency); **DCP Farms v. Yeutter**, *supra* (pressure concerned relevant rather than irrelevant factor)]

D. Ex Parte Communications

Both due process and APA provisions governing formal proceedings control ex parte contacts during adjudication. Such contacts may also run afoul of agency procedural regulations.

1. Limits on Ex Parte Contacts in Formal Proceedings, APA § 557(d)

The APA prohibits any interested person *outside* the agency from making (or causing to be made) any ex parte communication relevant to the merits to a member of the agency, an ALJ, or any other employee who is or may reasonably be expected to be involved in the decisional process. [APA § 557(d)(1)] This APA provision applies to *formal rulemaking* as well as to *formal adjudication, but not to informal adjudication or informal rulemaking.*

a. "Interested Person"

The term "interested person" is broadly applied. It means anyone outside the agency whose interest in the proceedings is greater than that of the general public.

Example: Albert Shanker, prominent head of a teachers' union, is an "interested person" with respect to a case involving an illegal strike by a federal employees' union. [**Prof'l Air Traffic Controllers Org. v. Fed. Labor Relations Auth.**, 672 F.2d 109 (D.C. Cir. 1982)]

b. Outside the Agency but Inside the Government

The President and members of the White House staff are considered persons outside the agency and may not engage in ex parte contact with adjudicators. [**Portland Audubon Soc'y v. Endangered Species Comm.**, 984 F.2d 1534 (9th Cir. 1993) (contacts between White House staff and "God Squad" members adjudicating whether to grant exceptions to the Endangered Species Act violated APA § 557(d))] Similarly, "market monitors" are outside the Federal Energy Regulatory Agency ("FERC") and cannot engage in ex parte contacts with FERC decisionmakers—no matter how useful such contacts might be for the regulatory scheme. [**Elec. Power Supply Ass'n v. FERC**, 391 F.3d 1255 (D.C. Cir. 2004)]

(1) Distinguish—Informal Rulemaking

The President and members of his staff may participate ex parte in *informal rulemaking* proceedings (unless this is prohibited by a specific statute). [**Sierra Club v. Costle**, 657 F.2d 298 (D.C. Cir. 1981)] Section 557(d)'s limits on ex parte contacts do not apply to informal proceedings.

c. "Ex Parte Communication"

An ex parte communication is defined as an oral or written communication that is not on the public record with respect to which reasonable prior notice to all parties was not given.

However, a request for a "status report" is not considered an ex parte communication. [APA § 551(14)]

d. Relevant to the Merits

A communication is relevant to the merits if it concerns any substantive issue in the case (*i.e.*, whether it is an issue of fact, law, policy or discretion). However, communications concerning procedural issues or settlement are not considered relevant to the merits. [**La. Ass'n of Indep. Producers v. Fed. Energy Regulatory Comm'n**, 958 F.2d 1101 (D.C. Cir. 1992)] Similarly, so-called status inquiries (whether from members of Congress or from the parties) are not considered ex parte communications. [APA § 551(14); **Massman Construction Co. v. TVA**, 769 F.2d 1114 (6th Cir. 1985) (request by party to find out when decision would be issued was permissible status inquiry)]

e. Effect of Ex Parte Contact

If an ex parte contact is made in violation of the APA during formal proceedings, the writing must be placed on the record and a memorandum of any oral contact must be prepared and placed on the record. The agency may, to the extent consistent with the interests of justice and the policy of the underlying statute, require the party who made the communication to show cause why the claim should not be dismissed, denied, disregarded, or adversely affected. [APA § 557(d)(1)(C), (D)]

f. Judicial Review

A reviewing court has discretion whether to vacate a decision tainted by ex parte contacts. It should consider whether the contacts irrevocably tainted the proceeding so as to make the ultimate agency judgment unfair. The court will consider such factors as (i) whether the communication probably influenced the decision, (ii) whether the party who made the contact benefited by it, (iii) whether the opponents had adequate opportunity to respond, and (iv) whether vacating the decision would serve any useful purpose. [**Prof'l Air Traffic Controllers' Org. v. Fed. Labor Relations Auth.**, *supra* (many improper contacts, but remand would be futile; strong dissent)]

g. Reciprocal Prohibition for Agency Employees

The APA also prohibits ex parte communications relevant to the merits *by* agency employees involved in the decisional process *to* interested persons outside the agency. [APA § 557(d)(1)(B)]

2. Additional Limits on Ex Parte Contacts in Formal Adjudication, APA § 554(d)

In addition to imposing separation of functions below the level of agency heads (*see supra*, p. 76 *et seq.*), § 554(d) contains an additional bar on ex parte contacts. It provides that, except as authorized by law, an ALJ may not "consult a person or party on a fact in issue, unless on notice and opportunity for all parties to participate." In dictum, the Supreme Court stated that this provision applies to conferences between an ALJ and "any person or party, including other agency officials." [**Butz v. Economou**, 438 U.S. 478 (1978)] *But see supra,* p. 58 (discussing permissible staff assistance to ALJs).

3. Due Process and Ex Parte Contacts

The APA provisions discussed above do not apply to informal proceedings. Due process does apply to informal adjudications, however, where deprivations of liberty or property are at issue. Undisclosed ex parte contacts from outsiders may violate due process. [**Idaho Historic Pres. Council, Inc. v. City Council of Boise,** 8 P.3d 646 (Idaho 2000) (Council denied due process in receiving but not disclosing ex parte contacts in a land use dispute); *see* **Sierra Club v. Costle**, 657 F.2d 298 (D.C. Cir. 1981) ("Where agency action resembles judicial action, where it involves ... 'conflicting private claims to a valuable privilege,' the insulation of the decisionmaker from ex parte contacts is justified by basic notions of due process to the parties involved.")]

E. Decisionmaker Familiarity with the Case

1. Overview of the Problem

A typical agency is a large, complex bureaucracy. The agency heads who run them have many different responsibilities that they cannot possibly discharge by themselves. The expertise and knowledge residing at the agency may be spread across thousands of people. These facts of bureaucratic life create a basic problem: When an agency head issues an order, how much of the underlying facts and record must that agency head actually understand?

Over time, the Supreme Court has developed a very practical answer to this question. Old case law indicates that the person who decides a case must be familiar with the record. Subsequent cases, however, make it extremely difficult to investigate the mental processes of an administrator to determine if this obligation has been fulfilled—a "strong showing" of bad faith is required. The Supreme Court has, however, used the threat of allowing burdensome investigations into the mental processes of administrators as a means to require agencies to provide contemporaneous explanations for their actions.

2. Theoretical Obligation—"The One Who Decides Must Hear"

In a pre-APA case, the Supreme Court stated, "[t]he one who decides must hear." [**Morgan v. United States,** 298 U.S. 468 (1936) (*Morgan I*)] Taken literally, this language would seem to preclude the practice of having ALJ's preside at the taking of evidence. More practically, it may be understood to require that the agency head be at least somewhat familiar with the evidence and argument presented at the hearing in order to render a valid decision. It is unclear whether the *Morgan I* rule is based on procedural due process or on an interpretation of the applicable statutory requirement that the agency provide a "full hearing."

Example: In *Morgan I* (there were four *Morgan* cases), the Department of Agriculture conducted a lengthy inquiry into the reasonableness of stockyard rates. A trial examiner heard the evidence, and the Secretary of Agriculture allegedly set the rate schedule without hearing or reading any of the evidence or argument presented at the hearing. The parties were never advised of the proposed rate schedule or of the trial examiner's findings. The Court held that the parties had been denied a "full hearing": "If the one who determines the facts which underlie the order has not considered evidence or argument, it is manifest that the hearing has not been given." *Note:* The Court conceded that the evidence could be taken by an examiner and sifted and analyzed by subordinates. But the person responsible for making the final decision had to be ***familiar*** with the record.

a. Delegation of Decisionmaking

Agencies may meet the requirements of *Morgan I* by delegating decisionmaking authority to lower level personnel if such delegation is permissible under the agency's statute.

Example: Petitions for review in labor cases were required by statute and agency regulation to be decided by the NLRB or by a three-member panel of the Board. When a decision was made by one member and the legal aides for two others, it was held invalid as a violation of the *Morgan I* rule. [**KFC Nat'l Mgmt. Corp. v. NLRB,** 497 F.2d 298 (2d Cir. 1974)]

b. Failure to Hear Oral Argument

Failure to actually hear the oral argument does not require reversal *if* the decisionmaker is nonetheless familiar with the record, given that oral argument is not constitutionally required even in a "trial-type" hearing. [*See* **FCC v. Station WJR,** 337 U.S. 265 (1949)]

c. A *Morgan I*-style Problem for ALJs

APA section 554(d) requires that "the employee who presides at the reception of evidence . . . shall make the recommended decision or initial decision . . . ***unless he becomes unavailable*** to the agency." However, if issues of credibility are involved, it is improper to have a substitute ALJ prepare the findings and conclusions and issue a decision. Thus, APA section 554(d) does not confer *complete* discretion to substitute trial examiners. [**Gamble-Skogmo, Inc. v. FTC,** 211 F.2d 106 (8th Cir. 1954) (examiner had reached retirement age, but could have continued at discretion of the agency)]

3. Practical Reality

Generally speaking, allowing parties to investigate the knowledge and memories of agency heads regarding the various orders and rules that they issue makes very little sense. For one thing, such investigations, if allowed to accumulate, could be highly time consuming and disruptive. For another, administration of a complex agency is necessarily a collaborative task that requires agency heads to rely on their subordinates. Recognizing these realities, in *Morgan IV*, the Supreme Court held that it is ***improper to question*** the decisionmaker as to his mental processes. [**United States v. Morgan,** 313 U.S. 409 (1941) (*Morgan IV*)]

a. Effect of *Morgan IV*

As a practical matter, *Morgan IV* substantially undercut the impact of *Morgan I* by making it very difficult to determine whether the one who decided has honored the obligation to "hear."

b. A Threatened Exception for Lack of Findings

In one of the most important cases of the modern administrative law canon, the Supreme Court suggested that where a decisionmaker fails to offer a contemporaneous explanation for a decision, she might be cross-examined in court to determine the reasons for the decision—an important departure from *Morgan IV*. [**Citizens to Preserve Overton Park v. Volpe,** 401 U.S. 402 (1971)] *Overton Park* involved an informal adjudication for which the APA imposed no express requirement of explanation. [*Cf.* § 557(b) (requiring explanations for formal proceedings)] The Court's opinion amounted to a not-so-veiled threat to agencies that, if they don't explain such decisions when they make them, then they might have to explain them later during litigation.

Subsequent decisions dialed back this threat. So long as an agency offers an explanation for its action, even a "curt" one, courts should remand to the agency to fix explanatory defects rather than use judicial proceedings to determine the agency's reasons. [**Camp v. Pitts,** 411 U.S. 138 (1973)]

c. Exception for "Bad Faith or Improper Behavior"

Inquiry into the decisionmaker's reasoning is not allowed "absent a strong showing of bad faith or improper behavior." [**Citizens to Preserve Overton Park v. Volpe,** *supra*] Such improper behavior must first be shown by external facts. It would be improper to take the depositions of the decisionmakers to determine whether they had the necessary familiarity with the case or were biased. [**San Luis Obispo Mothers for Peace v. Nuclear Regulatory Comm'n,** 789 F.2d 26 (D.C. Cir. 1986)]

F. Consistency Across Cases

1. Introduction

Courts have developed various doctrines to ensure consistency across cases, including res judicata, stare decisis, and equitable estoppel. Consistency in administrative adjudication is good, but it competes with the need for agency flexibility to adapt to new circumstances and implement complex statutory duties. Reflecting this balance, res judicata applies to administrative adjudication, but not as strictly as in the courts; a very weak form of stare decisis applies to agencies. Federal courts have sent mixed signals regarding equitable estoppel. Most Supreme Court decisions are markedly hostile to estopping the government; lower court decisions nonetheless sometimes apply it.

2. Res Judicata

The rules of res judicata and collateral estoppel (*i.e.,* claim preclusion and issue preclusion) apply to administrative adjudicatory decisions, although not as strictly as they apply to judicial decisions.

a. General Rule

When an administrative agency acts in a judicial capacity and resolves issues of fact properly before it, and the parties had a full and fair opportunity to litigate, the decision generally has *preclusive effect* on future agency and court decisions. [**United States v. Utah Constr. & Mining Co.,** 384 U.S. 394 (1966); Restatement (Second) of Judgments § 83]

b. Preclusion Against the Government

The government can be precluded from relitigating issues of fact or law after losing a case. [**United States v. Stauffer Chem. Co.,** 464 U.S. 165 (1984) (government loses on legal issue in Circuit 1; it cannot relitigate *same issue* against *same party* in Circuit 2); **FTC v. Texaco,** 517 F.2d 137 (D.C. Cir. 1975) (decision by one agency precludes relitigation by a second)]

c. Nonmutual Collateral Estoppel

The Supreme Court has broadly endorsed nonmutual collateral estoppel. This means that a party who loses in one case is precluded from relitigating the same issues in another case even though in the second case he faces a different opponent. [**Parklane Hosiery Co. v. Shore,** 439 U.S. 322 (1979)]

Example: In *Parklane Hosiery Co.,* a stockholder's class action was brought against the defendant corporation and its officers and directors, claiming the corporation's proxy statement was false and misleading. Before this action came to trial, the SEC brought suit against the same defendants making a similar claim. The district court entered a declaratory judgment for the SEC. The plaintiffs in the class action then moved for summary judgment on issues relating to the proxy statement, arguing that defendants were estopped from relitigating the issues already resolved in the SEC action. The Supreme Court agreed, holding that the defendants were collaterally estopped on the issues resolved in the SEC action because they were already afforded a "full and fair" opportunity to litigate these issues.

(1) Exception for the Government

Nonmutual collateral estoppel does not apply against the United States. Thus, if the government loses an earlier district court decision and does not appeal, it can relitigate the *same issue* against *other parties*. [**United States v. Mendoza**, 464 U.S. 154 (1984)]

EXAM TIP

It is important to remember that while the government may not relitigate the *same issue* against the *same party* after it loses a case, it may relitigate the *same issue* against a *different party* after it loses. The rationale may help you remember the distinction. The government can relitigate an issue it lost against different parties because it should not be compelled to appeal every case it loses. Moreover, the government should be able to relitigate and create a conflict between circuits so the issue can "percolate" to the Supreme Court for resolution.

d. Exceptions to Administrative Res Judicata

Res judicata applies less strictly in the administrative context than in the judicial. Numerous exceptions to res judicata have been recognized.

(1) Statutory Policy

When the legislature indicates that a prior agency decision should not be preclusive, the issue can be relitigated later. [**Univ. of Tenn. v. Elliott**, 478 U.S. 788 (1986)]

Example: In *University of Tennessee,* Elliott alleged that he had been fired from a state job because of racial discrimination. He lost a state administrative decision. He then sued in federal court under 42 U.S.C. § 1983 and under Title VII of the Civil Rights Act of 1964. The Court held that the prior adjudication precluded Elliott from relitigating under section 1983 but *not under Title VII.* Congress wanted to preserve a federal court remedy for antidiscrimination plaintiffs.

(2) Other Factors

The second tribunal has the discretion to decide whether to preclude a litigant, and many factors might cause an adjudicator to permit relitigation. [*See, e.g.,* Restatement (Second) of Judgments § 83(3) (first decision not preclusive if the scheme of remedies permits assertion of second claim despite adjudication of the first)] Fairness in applying res judicata might also come into play. For example, if different rules of evidence, burden of proof, cross-examination or discovery might have changed the result in the first case, the first decision should not preclude the second. [**North Carolina v. Chas. Pfizer & Co.**, 537 F.2d 67 (4th Cir.), *cert. denied,* 429 U.S. 870 (1976) (FTC findings of antitrust violation do not preclude court because of different procedural and evidentiary practices); Restatement (Second) of Judgments § 83(2)]

3. Stare Decicis

a. The Very Weak "Stare Decisis" Force of Agency Decisions

Agencies are free to change legal or policy positions taken in prior adjudicatory decisions provided they recognize that they are changing course and give a rational explanation for doing so. [**FCC v. Fox Television Stations, Inc.,** 556 U.S. 502 (2009); **Atchison, Topeka & Santa Fe Ry. v. Wichita Bd. of Trade,** 412 U.S. 800 (1973)] Moreover, if a party attacks an existing agency precedent as irrational, the agency must explain why it rejected this claim and adhered to existing precedent. [**Flagstaff Broad. Fed'n v. FCC,** 979 F.2d 1566 (D.C. Cir. 1992)]

b. Judicial Stare Decisis and the Problem of Agency Nonacquiesence

In some contexts, courts regard the stare decisis force of judicial decisions as strictly binding. For instance, one panel of a circuit court may not overrule an earlier panel decision. Parties seeking such a result need en banc or Supreme Court review. In other contexts, courts regard precedents as presumptively binding or persuasive. For instance, the Supreme Court is not strictly bound by its earlier precedents but regards them as presumptively controlling.

Agencies complicate the problem of judicial stare decisis—both because they are part of a different branch of government and because federal agencies typically have nationwide jurisdiction. To pose the problem in more concrete terms, agencies have to determine how much weight to give to a precedent issued by a particular lower court as they discharge their functions across the country. The agency will obey a court's mandate in the case that gave rise to it. In later cases, however, the agency must determine whether to honor the court's precedent.

It is generally accepted that an agency may choose the path of "nonacquiescence" in a case involving litigation in a different jurisdiction—*i.e.*, when litigating in the 7th Circuit, the agency need not follow a legal precedent established in the 1st Circuit. [**Nielsen Lithographing Co. v. NLRB,** 854 F.2d 1063 (7th Cir. 1988) (observing that an agency need not "knuckle under to the first court of appeals (or the second, or even the twelfth) to rule adversely" to the agency.]

The practice of "intracircuit nonacquiesence"—defying a circuit precedent in the same circuit—is more controversial. The issue is less likely to arise, however, insofar as an agency should expect the circuit court itself to regard its own precedent as strictly binding. Therefore, an agency that ignores circuit precedent in that same circuit should plan on losing, absent en banc or Supreme Court review.

4. Equitable Estoppel

Agencies often furnish oral or written advice to members of the public in need of guidance. Guidance can also be furnished more formally through agency guidelines or interpretive bulletins. Sometimes, an agency decides that its earlier guidance was wrong, and it wishes to issue a subsequent decision that retracts it retroactively. This pattern raises the problem of whether equitable estoppel may block the agency from doing so.

a. Estoppel and Apparent Authority in the Private Sector

In the private sector, a person who detrimentally and reasonably relies on statements made by another can often claim that the latter is estopped from changing its position. Similarly, in the private sector, a principal is bound by the actions of its agent under either actual or apparent authority. Apparent authority arises if the principal has caused third parties reasonably to believe that the agent has authority to act—even if the agent has no such authority.

b. Estopping the Government Under State Law

The law of many states permits the government to be estopped very much as a private sector entity might be. [*See, e.g.,* **Foote's Dixie Dandy, Inc. v. McHenry,** 607 S.W.2d 323 (Ark. 1980) (mistaken advice to taxpayer about whether form must be filed)]

c. Estopping the Government Under Federal Law

Traditionally, the federal government has been ***immune*** from estoppel and apparent authority. Unless a statute prevents the government from changing its mind (and there are numerous such statutes), it is free to do so despite the harm caused by detrimental reliance. The Supreme Court has not entirely closed the door on estoppel, but its most recent cases suggest that it is rarely appropriate.

Notwithstanding this tendency in the Supreme Court cases, lower court cases have sometimes estopped the government in particularly compelling fact situations, especially where the government performs a proprietary function (such as making contracts). [*See, e.g.,* **Portmann v. United States,** 674 F.2d 1155 (7th Cir. 1982) (mistaken advice by post office clerk that package was insured; estoppel applies)]

(1) Supreme Court Cases

The Supreme Court decisions vacillate; some suggest that estoppel is possible against the government, but others suggest that it is never possible.

(a) Money Judgment Cases

It is clear that estoppel *cannot* be used to obtain a money judgment against the government. [**Office of Personnel Mgmt. v. Richmond**, 496 U.S. 414 (1990)]

1) *Richmond* Case

P was receiving a government pension. He sought advice about whether he could take a job without decreasing the pension. Officials advised him that he could. The advice was wrong because the applicable statute had changed and the officials did not know about the change. P took the job and his pension was reduced. Because P sought a money judgment, the Court held that the government could not be estopped. Such payment would violate the applicable statute and thus violate the Appropriations Clause of the Constitution, which prohibits disbursements except pursuant to congressional appropriations. Dictum in the decision suggests that most justices would never allow an estoppel claim, even for nonmonetary benefits, but the Court did not eliminate this possibility. [**Office of Personnel Mgmt. v. Richmond,** *supra*]

2) *Community Health* Case

Prior to *Richmond*, dictum in one Supreme Court decision was more favorable towards estoppel. [**Heckler v. Cmty. Health Servs.,** 467 U.S. 51 (1984)] Although the Court in that case found that a hospital's reliance on erroneous oral advice was neither detrimental nor reasonable, the decision suggested that estoppel could lie under more compelling facts. Dictum in the *Richmond* case appears far more hostile to such claims.

3) *Merrill* Case

Earlier cases revealed strong hostility to estoppel and apparent authority. Unlike *Richmond*, they do not rest on the Appropriations Clause. For example, a wheat farmer wrongly advised that federal crop insurance would cover his crop could not recover when the crop was destroyed. [**Fed. Crop Ins. Corp. v. Merrill**, 332 U.S. 380 (1947)]

(b) Immigration Cases

In immigration and naturalization cases, the Supreme Court has indicated that the government *can be estopped* if it is guilty of *"affirmative misconduct."* Note that the relief being sought (*i.e.,* United States residency or citizenship) is nonmonetary, so that the Appropriations Clause problem identified in *Richmond* is not present. However, it is not clear what is required to show "affirmative misconduct."

1) *Hibi* Case

At a minimum, the government's failure to act does *not* qualify as "affirmative misconduct." Where the government failed to advise certain noncitizens that they qualified for naturalization, and failed to provide any means for exercising that right, the government was not estopped. [**INS v. Hibi**, 414 U.S. 5 (1973)]

2) *Moser* Case

One early Supreme Court case might be an example of "affirmative misconduct." The government mistakenly advised an alien that applying for a draft exemption would not forfeit the right to apply for citizenship. The alien was later permitted to apply for naturalization because he had reasonably relied on this advice. [**Moser v. United States**, 341 U.S. 41 (1951)]

(c) Civil or Criminal Sanctions

Mistaken government advice might negate the mental state required for a criminal conviction. [**United States v. Pa. Indus. Chem. Co.**, 411 U.S. 655 (1973) (government estopped to prosecute chemical company that reasonably relied on regulations that appeared to permit conduct in question)] Similarly, a party who engages in conduct that appears to be legal under a reasonable interpretation of regulations cannot be subject to civil penalties when the agency interprets the regulations in an unexpected manner that causes the party's conduct to be a violation of the regulations. [**Gen. Elec. Co. v. EPA**, 53 F.3d 1324 (D.C. Cir. 1995) (order imposing civil money penalty for violating regulation concerning disposal of toxic chemical remanded because EPA did not provide company with fair warning of its interpretation of regulations, which were unclear)]

Chapter Five
Rulemaking Procedures

CONTENTS	PAGE
Key Exam Issues	92
A. **Introduction**	93
B. **Legal Effect of Rules—The Legislative/Nonlegislative Distinction**	99
C. **The Notice-and-Comment Rulemaking Process**	102
D. **Exceptions to Notice-and-Comment Rulemaking Requirements**	109
E. **Impartiality of Rulemakers**	116
F. **The Rulemaking Record**	118

Key Exam Issues

In analyzing rulemaking procedures, consider the following:

1. **Legislative or Executive Controls**

   Other than the APA, do any legislative or executive controls apply, such as the requirement to provide a regulatory impact statement or an environmental impact statement?

2. **APA Procedures—Formal or Informal Rulemaking?**

   Does the agency's enabling act require that rulemaking be determined "on the record after an opportunity for agency hearing"? If so, then the agency will need to use the formal, on-the-record procedures of 5 U.S.C. §§ 556–57.

3. **APA Procedures—Informal (a/k/a Notice-and-Comment) Rulemaking**

   If notice-and-comment is required, are the APA's requirements spelled out in 5 U.S.C. § 553 satisfied? These include:

   a. *Notice* of proposed rulemaking. Two issues to watch here include: (i) Did the agency disclose the scientific and technical data on which it relied? and (ii) Was the agency's final rule sufficiently close to the proposed rule to avoid another round of notice-and-comment?

   b. *Public participation* through the comment process.

   c. A *statement of basis and purpose*. Watch for whether this statement responded to all material comments.

4. **Exceptions to APA Procedures**

   The notice-and-comment procedures of 5 U.S.C. § 553 provide the APA's default mechanism for creating a rule. There are numerous exceptions to this default rule, however. So before rushing off to notice-and-comment, check whether any of the following exceptions apply—especially the ones in bold:

   a. Military or foreign affairs function;

   b. Agency management or personnel;

   c. Public property, loans, grants, benefits, or contracts;

   d. **Procedural rules;**

   e. **Good cause exception;**

   f. **Interpretive rules or policy statements [a/k/a "guidance documents"].**

5. **Limits on Judicial Control—the *Vermont Yankee* Principle**

   The Supreme Court has made clear that courts have no authority to impose additional procedural requirements for rulemaking beyond those specified by Congress or adopted by an agency or (in rare circumstances) required by due process. Congress and the agencies, not the courts, are supposed to be in charge of determining agency rulemaking procedures.

A. Introduction

1. What We Mean by a "Rule"

a. Definitions

(1) "Rule"

A "rule" is "the whole or a part of an agency statement of *general or particular applicability* and *future effect* designed to implement, interpret, or prescribe *law or policy* or describing the organization, procedure, or practice requirements of an agency...." [APA § 551(4)] [For discussion of the problematic nature of this definition, *see supra*, p. 48]

(2) "Rulemaking"

"Rulemaking" is the "agency process for formulating, amending, or repealing a rule." [APA § 551(5)] (That wasn't so bad, was it?)

(3) "Regulation"

The term "regulation" is synonymous with "rule," and the terms are used interchangeably.

b. Characteristics of a "Rule"

Thus, an administrative "rule" (as opposed to an "order"—used in the APA to describe the results of adjudication) is:

(1) *Addressed to future* situations;

(2) *Usually addressed to a class* of persons (although APA § 551(4) provides for "particular applicability" as well); and

(3) *Often needs to be made specific* by subsequent adjudication involving particular parties.

c. Sometimes, a "Rule" Can Affect a Class of One

As long as a rule is *stated in general terms,* APA rulemaking procedures can apply even though only a single company is affected by the rule.

Of course, the courts must be alert for situations in which the proceeding in question is really an adjudication (*i.e.,* involving the determination of *individualized, adjudicative facts about a single company*) rather than rulemaking. If in substance the agency was engaged in adjudication rather than rulemaking, adjudicatory procedure would apply and, if a deprivation of liberty or property was involved, due process would apply as well. [*See* **Anaconda Co. v. Ruckelshaus**, 482 F.2d 1301 (10th Cir. 1973)]

Example: In *Anaconda,* the agency proposed a rule about pollution from a particular smelting process in a single county. Only one company actually engaged in that process in that county. However, the rule appeared to apply to a general class (which could, in theory, expand to cover others in the future), and thus was considered a rule, as defined in the APA, not an adjudication. Moreover, even if due process did apply, the court thought that the notice and comment rulemaking procedures would satisfy due process since the facts at issue could be fairly and efficiently determined through the rulemaking process.

d. **Classifying Agency Action Under the APA**

It can be difficult to classify various forms of agency action. The action might be rulemaking, adjudication, or neither. Some actions have important practical consequences but do not fall into either the rulemaking or adjudication categories of the APA—*e.g.*, a press release stating that probable cause justifies an enforcement action against a regulated entity.

(1) Legal Consequences of Classification as Rulemaking or Adjudication

If the action is rulemaking and does not fall into an exception, then the agency must engage in notice and comment before adopting it (or, in rare situations, use formal, "on the record" procedures).

If the action is adjudication, however, and if there is no external requirement of a hearing triggering formal adjudication, the agency is subject to very few statutory procedural obligations. [*See supra,* p. 66 *et seq.* (discussing informal adjudication)]

(2) Distinguishing Rulemaking and Adjudication in APA Terms

The issue of whether an agency action is a "rulemaking" or an "adjudication" in terms of the APA rarely arises in litigation. Occasionally, however, a party will successfully argue that an action that an agency treated as an informal adjudication should have been regarded as a rulemaking that required notice-and-comment. Notwithstanding the APA's defective definition of "rule," this type of argument is more likely to succeed if the action has broad applicability and prospective effect. [**Sugar Cane Growers Cooperative of Florida v. Veneman,** 289 F.3d 89 (D.C. Cir. 2002)—agency's announcement of the terms of subsidy program that would apply to all future applicants was rulemaking that should have used notice-and-comment]

Example: Agency determines that the eviction procedures in State W provide tenants in public housing with adequate procedural protections. This determination has the legal consequence of allowing local public housing authorities to dispense with grievance procedures before evicting tenants. Held: Agency's determination should be treated as rulemaking rather than adjudication since it affects broad classes of individuals and has purely future effect. Consequently, Agency was required to engage in rulemaking procedures before adopting it. [**Yesler Terrace Community Council v. Cisneros,** 37 F.3d 442 (9th Cir. 1994)]

RULEMAKING VS. ADJUDICATION— A SUMMARY

RULEMAKING	ADJUDICATION
• Usually prospective rather than retroactive	• Usually retroactive and therefore can disappoint reliance interests
• Applies across the board (but maybe to a very small class)	• Often singles out an individual or individual company
• Conducive to broad public input	• Input only comes from parties to the case
• Not subject to restrictions regarding separation of functions. Informal rulemaking not subject to limits on ex parte contacts.	• Subject to restrictions regarding separation of functions and ex parte contact
• Publication in C.F.R. and Federal Register promotes accessibility	• Less readily accessible to nonparties

2. Sources of Rulemaking Procedure

Your basic administrative law class will focus to a considerable extent on the APA's procedural requirements for rulemaking. Other important sources of procedural requirements for rulemaking include: agency enabling acts, statutory requirements for "impact statements," agency rules, and presidential executive orders.

a. Due Process (Is Mostly Inapplicable)

Recall that constitutional law draws a distinction between rulemaking based on generally applicable, "legislative" facts and adjudications, which apply law to adjudicative facts to determine legal rights. [*See supra* pp. 39–40] Procedural due process does not apply to rulemaking understood in this sense.

(1) A Narrow, Quasi-Exception

As this chapter details, the APA creates a statutory template for rulemaking. On rare occasions, agencies have used the statutory forms of rulemaking to determine what are, from a constitutional perspective, adjudications. In such cases, the agency's "rulemaking" would be subject to procedural due process. [**Sangamon Valley Television Corp. v. United States,** 269 F.2d 221 (1959) (applying due process principles to an agency informal rulemaking that resolved "conflicting private claims to a valuable privilege" (*i.e.*, allocation of a television license))]

b. The APA (!)

(1) Informal Rulemaking

Section 553 of the APA creates a template for informal or "notice-and-comment" rulemaking. Notice-and-comment is the default method for creating legislative rules.

(2) Formal Rulemaking

An agency must use formal or "on the record" procedures of §§ 556–57 to promulgate rules that are "required by statute to be made on the record after opportunity for agency hearing." [APA § 553(c) (last sentence)]

Recall that §§ 556–57 apply to both formal adjudication and formal rulemaking. In essence, they create a template for decisionmaking that can resemble a bench trial. Section 556: (1) provides for decisionmaking by ALJs; (2) grants powers to persons presiding at hearings (*e.g.*, to administer oaths); (3) determines matters such as cross-examination rights, admissibility of evidence, and burden of proof; and (4) defines the "record." Section 557: (1) identifies types of decisions (*e.g.*, "initial" or "recommended"); (2) requires these decisions to include appropriate findings, conclusions, and reasons; and (3) bars ex parte contacts. For further discussion of these various requirements, *see supra* Chapters 3 & 4 on formal adjudication.

A broad consensus exists that using the trial-type procedures of §§ 556–57 to create a broadly applicable rule is extremely inefficient and encourages gamesmanship. The Supreme Court has therefore signaled that courts should avoid construing agency statutes as requiring formal rulemaking. [**United States v. Florida East Coast Railway,** 410 U.S. 224 (1973) (holding that requirement that agency create a rule "after hearing" did not trigger formal rulemaking under the APA)]

c. Agency Enabling Acts/Hybrid Rulemaking

In numerous agency enabling acts, Congress has imposed specific rulemaking procedures (such as cross-examination) that are not required by the APA's informal rulemaking provisions. Yet Congress has not fully converted these rulemaking processes into formal rulemaking. As a result, these agency-specific procedures are referred to as "hybrid rulemaking," since they fall in between formal and informal rulemaking. [*See, e.g.,* **Association of National Advertisers, Inc. v. FTC,** 627 F.2d 1151 (D.C. Cir. 1979)—requirement that FTC allow cross-examination before adopting rules does not convert rulemaking into adjudication]

d. Generally Applicable Statutes (Other Than the APA)

Congress has adopted a number of statutes over the years designed to force agencies to give heightened consideration to various sensitive values as part of rulemaking. Examples include

(1) National Environmental Policy Act

The National Environmental Policy Act ("NEPA"), 42 U.S.C. §§ 4321–4347d, requires agencies that recommend legislation or take any "major" federal action (including rulemaking) to make an environmental assessment of the action, including consideration of less environmentally damaging alternatives.

(2) Regulatory Flexibility Act

The Regulatory Flexibility Act ("RFA"), 5 U.S.C. §§ 601–12, requires consideration of the effects of proposed rules on small businesses. The notice of rulemaking must include an initial regulatory flexibility analysis that focuses on the impact of the rule on small business and highlights alternatives that might minimize the burden. The final rule must respond to comments raised by the initial analysis and explain why less burdensome alternatives were rejected.

(3) Paperwork Reduction Act

The Paperwork Reduction Act, 44 U.S.C. §§ 3501–20, grants the Office of Management and Budget (OMB) authority to control gathering of information—in part to minimize the paperwork requirements that the government creates. Notice-and-comment rules that require collection of information are subject to clearance procedures at OMB.

(4) Unfunded Mandates Reform Act

The Unfunded Mandates Reform Act, 2 U.S.C. chs. 17A, 25, is supposed to make Congress and agencies stop and think, as it were, before imposing a mandate on state, local, and tribal entities. It requires agencies to include a regulatory impact statement with the notice of proposed rulemaking for rules that are likely to cause state, local, and tribal governments, or the private sector, to expend more than $100 million (in 1995 dollars, adjusted annually for inflation).

(5) Information Quality Act

The Information Quality Act, 44 U.S.C. § 3516 Note, was enacted in 2000 as an amendment to the Paperwork Reduction Act. It requires agencies to adopt guidelines to maximize the quality of the information they disseminate and to establish mechanisms for correction of agency information. The implications of the IQA for rulemaking are still evolving. [*See* Jeffrey S. Lubbers, *A Guide to Federal Agency Rulemaking* (5th ed., 2012)]

(6) E-Government Act of 2002

The E-Government Act of 2002, 44 U.S.C. § 3501 Note, requires agencies, to the extent practicable, to accept electronic submissions in rulemaking and to maintain a rulemaking docket accessible by Internet.

(7) Congressional Review Act

The Congressional Review Act ("CRA") [5 U.S.C. §§ 801–808] creates a fast-track system for legislative rejection of agency rules. Rejection of a rule under the CRA has happened just once, which is not surprising given that it requires both houses of Congress and the President to concur or a congressional override of a presidential veto. [For more detail on the CRA, *see supra,* p. 22.]

e. Agency Procedural Rules

Agencies commonly promulgate procedural rules to govern their rulemaking.

f. Executive Orders

(1) Question of Authority

The scope of presidential power to control rulemaking has been a strongly contested issue in administrative law. On the one hand, Congress typically delegates rulemaking authority by statute not to the President but to agency heads. On the other hand, the President is the "head" of the executive branch, which suggests he has considerable authority (both de jure and de facto) to instruct agency heads how to perform their work.

(2) E.O. 12,866 and Cost-Benefit Analysis

Over the last several decades, each president has relied on executive orders requiring executive agencies to engage in cost-benefit analysis as part of rulemaking for "significant regulatory actions." At present, the primary template for this cost-benefit analysis remains an executive order issued by President Clinton, E.O. 12,866, 58 Fed. Reg. 51735 (1993)). [*See also* E.O. 13,563, 76 Fed. Reg. 3821 (Jan. 21, 2011) (Obama administration order "supplemental to and reaffirm[ing] the principles, structures, and definitions" of E.O. 12,866)] Agencies submit their regulatory assessments to centralized review by the Office of Information and Regulatory Affairs (OIRA), which is a part of the Office of Management and Budget (OMB).

E.O. 12,866 does not apply to "independent" agencies. Also, it does not require cost-benefit analysis where such balancing is forbidden by law.

g. Judicially-Imposed Procedures—*Vermont Yankee* Principle

One of the canonical cases you are sure to study in your administrative law casebook is **Vermont Yankee Nuclear Power Corp. v. NRDC**, 435 U.S. 519 (1978). It holds that courts have **no authority** to fashion new procedural requirements for rulemaking beyond those adopted by Congress and agencies or required (in rare instances) by due process. *Vermont Yankee* has not, however, stopped courts from adopting extremely expansive constructions of the APA's statutory requirements for notice-and-comment rulemaking. [*See infra,* p. 102 *et seq.* (discussing judicial glosses on APA requirements of notice and explanation for rules)]

3. Advantages of Rulemaking as Technique for Policy Making

As noted earlier (p. 70), agencies are often free to make policy through adjudication of individual cases or by rule. Advantages of proceeding by rule include:

- Rules are ordinarily *prospective* rather than retroactive; therefore, they are less likely to disappoint well-founded reliance interests.

- Rules *apply across the board,* so no individual or company is singled out for special and potentially unfair treatment in an enforcement action.

- The informal rulemaking process of notice-and-comment is designed to gather ***broad public input,*** thus improving the quality of the rules. The adjudication process, by contrast, generally furnishes input from the parties to the case.

- Rules are published in the Federal Register and the Code of Federal Regulations, thus making them ***more accessible and transparent*** than adjudicatory opinions.

4. Retroactive Rules

Legislative rules are ordinarily prospective in application, although interpretive rules are frequently retroactive. Absent an ***express grant of authority*** from Congress, agencies are not authorized to adopt retroactive legislative rules. [**Bowen v. Georgetown University Hospital,** 488 U.S. 204 (1988)]

a. Application

In *Georgetown University Hospital,* an agency adopted a rule in 1981. A later court decision invalidated the rule because it was not adopted with the appropriate notice and comment procedure. In 1984, the agency adopted the same rule after notice and comment—but made it retroactive to 1981. The Court found no express grant of authority that permitted the agency to adopt retroactive regulations. Consequently, under the rule of construction adopted by the majority, the retroactive effective date was invalid.

(1) Justice Scalia's Alternative Approach

In a concurring opinion, Justice Scalia argued that the APA by its own terms prohibits retroactive rules. Section 551(4) defines "rule" as an agency statement of "future effect." This means, he argued, that the rule must be prospective, not retroactive, unless Congress has specifically authorized retroactive rules.

(2) The Primary/Secondary Distinction

Justice Scalia's *Bowen* concurrence also contained an influential discussion of the difference between primary and secondary retroactivity. The clear-statement rule in *Bowen* applies to the former, which alters "the past legal consequences of past actions." For instance, suppose yesterday you drove 50 mph in a 60 mph zone. Today, the speed limit is reduced to 40 mph, and you are handed a ticket for breaking the speed limit yesterday—that's primary retroactivity. Secondary retroactivity has exclusively future legal effects, but these future effects affect the value of past transactions. For instance, imposing much lower speed limits may reduce the value of the very fast car you purchased last year. These lower speed limits do not, however, carry any *legal* consequences for you based on your *past* action of purchasing the very fast car. *Bowen* does not bar agency rules with secondarily retroactive effects, but of course such rules can run afoul of other restrictions on agency authority.

EXAM TIP

If you see a legislative rule applied retroactively on an exam, remember that *such rules cannot have primary retroactive effect absent clear authorization from Congress—which you probably won't find.* Look at your facts—first determine whether the adopted rule will change the legal consequences of past actions, *e.g.*, by making acts illegal that were previously legal. If so, then check to see if Congress has specifically authorized the adoption of retroactive rules for that matter. If there is no congressional authorization, then you should find the rule invalid.

B. Legal Effect of Rules—The Legislative/Nonlegislative Distinction

1. Some Rules Have the "Force of Law," and Some Don't

You will encounter several different ways that administrative law categorizes rules. One of the more important distinctions is between "legislative" and "nonlegislative" rules. As the name suggests, "legislative" rules, in essence, make law—no matter what you may have learned in high school about legislatures being in charge of such things. Nonlegislative rules are not technically binding as law but may nonetheless enjoy huge practical force on regulated parties.

2. Legislative Rules

Legislative rules carry the force of law. In other words, so long as a legislative rule falls within the scope of an agency's delegated rulemaking power, it is *as binding as a statute* on regulated parties, agencies, and courts. Courts often refer to nonprocedural legislative rules as "substantive rules."

a. Legislative Rules Bind the Agency

An important implication of this point is that an agency is bound by its legislative rules until it properly changes them, which can be quite time consuming and expensive. [*See, e.g.*, **Arizona Grocery Co. v. Santa Fe Railway,** 284 U.S. 370 (1932)—agency was bound by railroad rates it had previously adopted; rates could not be retroactively repealed]

b. Broad Construction of Legislative Rulemaking Authority

An agency has legislative rulemaking authority only if Congress has delegated such power to it. Given the importance of this power, one might reasonably expect courts to insist that Congress grant such authority clearly. Instead, courts broadly construe general grants of rulemaking authority as including the power to make legislative rules. For instance, in **National Petroleum Refiners Association v. FTC,** the court held that a grant of authority to the agency "to make rules and regulations for the purpose of carrying out [the Act]" included the power to create legislative rules. [482 F.2d 672 (D.C. Cir. 1973), *cert. denied,* 415 U.S. 951 (1974)] The court's analysis stressed the advantages of adopting generally applicable binding rules to regulate unfair trade practices rather than merely attacking them on a case-by-case basis.

c. Special Considerations for "Procedural" Rules

The general rule that legislative rules bind agencies until properly changed applies to procedural rules that create important procedural benefits for individuals. [**Vitarelli v. Seaton,** 359 U.S. 535 (1959); **Morton v. Ruiz,** 415 U.S. 199 (1974) (agency must follow procedural rules that affect the rights of individuals until they are properly changed)]

The Supreme Court has taken a more relaxed to approach, however, to procedural rules adopted merely to aid "the orderly transaction of business." A party wishing to contest an agency's failure to follow such a rule must show "substantial prejudice." [**American Farm Lines v. Black Ball Freight Service,** 397 U.S. 532 (1970)]

3. Nonlegislative Rules

Agencies frequently adopt rules that do *not* have binding legislative effect—*i.e.*, they do not change the law. These *nonlegislative rules* are nonetheless extremely significant as sources of guidance to agency staff, regulated parties, and courts.

a. Types of Nonlegislative Rules Include:

Interpretive rules, which set forth the agency's interpretation of statutes or prior legislative rules; and

Policy statements, which set forth the manner in which the agency intends to exercise its discretionary power.

Together, these types of nonlegislative rules are sometimes called "guidance documents."

b. Nonlegislative Rules Do Not "Bind" the "Agency" (*i.e.*, the Agency Heads)

The D.C. Circuit has held that an agency is not bound by its interpretive rules or policy statements and can depart from them whenever it wishes. The court's basic rationale for this position is that if a rule *binds* the agency then it is, by definition, legislative. So nonlegislative rules cannot bind the agency. [**Vietnam Veterans of America v. Secretary of the Navy**, 843 F.2d 528 (D.C. Cir. 1988)] It does not follow, however, that an agency's departure from a nonlegislative rule is immune from attack. A party might, for instance, persuade a court that the agency's departure was arbitrary or otherwise illegal.

(1) But Interpretive Rules Can Bind Agency Staff

Within an agency hierarchy, agency staffers are generally expected to follow the instructions of their superiors. Therefore, even though an interpretive rule lacks binding force as "law," it will bind agency staff as instructions from their superiors. An interpretive rule does not become legislative even though it binds agency personnel, including ALJs. [**Warder v. Shalala**, 149 F.3d 73 (1st Cir. 1998)]

c. An Example

Suppose that Congress passed a statute that states, "It is illegal to pollute." The statute also creates a Pollution Commission ("PC") that has legislative rulemaking authority as well as authority to adjudicate violations of the statute and order civil penalties.

Suppose the PC issues a legislative rule "barring the wearing of ugly shirts because they constitute visual pollution." If the rule was properly promulgated and fell within the agency's legal authority, then it has created binding law. The agency could bring an enforcement action against you and win if it proved you wore an ugly shirt. It would be pointless to argue your ugly shirt does not constitute "pollution" because this point was already been determined by binding law in the form of a legislative rule.

Suppose instead the PC issues an interpretive rule stating its view that "the term 'pollution' as used by the statute includes visual pollution such as that caused by wearing loud and ugly shirts." You wear an ugly shirt and the agency brings an enforcement action against you. The dispositive legal issue will not be whether you wore an ugly shirt. Rather, the dispositive legal issue will remain whether you "pollute[d]" in violation of statute. You might be able to argue successfully that the statute doesn't properly apply to you—*e.g.*, because the statutory term "pollution" does not include "visual pollution" notwithstanding the agency's contrary view.

Of course, even though the agency's interpretive rule lacks "binding" force in a technical sense, it still may be of immense practical importance for several reasons. First, an agency is quite likely to follow the positions it stakes in interpretive rules (and policy statements) even though they don't technically bind agency heads. Second, courts typically extend some measure of respect or deference to agencies on judicial review of nonlegislative rules. Third, life is easier when you don't fight with the agency. As a practical matter, it often makes more sense to follow rather than contest an agency's rules regardless of whether they have "legislative" force.

C. The Notice-and-Comment Rulemaking Process

1. Notice-and-Comment as the Default Procedure for Rulemaking

Section 553 of the APA provides that agencies are to use notice-and-comment procedures to create rules unless some sort of exception applies. These exceptions are discussed *infra* in subsection D of this chapter.

2. Notice of Proposed Rulemaking

Prior to adopting a rule, an agency must **publish in the Federal Register** (a daily publication of the federal government) a notice of proposed rulemaking, unless persons subject to the rule are named and either are **personally served or otherwise have actual notice.** Notice is sometimes also given on the agency's website. Additionally, there is a government-wide website (www.regulations.gov) that allows the public to search for all pending proposed rules on a given subject. The notice must include:

(i) A statement of the **time, place, and nature** of public rulemaking proceedings;

(ii) Reference to the **legal authority** under which the rule is proposed; and

(iii) Either the **terms or substance of the proposed rule** or a **description of the subjects and issues** involved. Ordinarily, the agency publishes the entire text of a proposed rule in the Federal Register.

[APA § 553(b)]

3. Disclosure of Data in the Notice (and Later)

As part of a notice for a rule, an agency is required to publish or make available critical data, such as scientific methodology, so that persons commenting on the rule can make meaningful submissions and criticisms. [**Chamber of Commerce v. SEC,** 443 F.3d 890 (D.C. Cir. 2006); **Portland Cement Association v. Ruckelshaus,** 486 F.2d 375 (D.C. Cir. 1973), *cert. denied,* 417 U.S. 921 (1974); **United States v. Nova Scotia Food Products,** 568 F.2d 240 (2d Cir. 1977)]

a. Limitation

Only basic data must be supplied, not every bit of background information in the agency file. [**B.F. Goodrich Co. v. DOT,** 541 F.2d 1178 (6th Cir. 1976)]

b. After Comment Period Closes

If an agency adds critical material to the record after the comment period closes, the rule may be overturned because the public had no opportunity to comment on the material. [**Idaho Farm Bureau Federation v. Babbitt,** 58 F.3d 1392 (9th Cir. 1995)] However, less critical material added to the record to respond to public comments might not trigger a reversal. [**Rybachek v. EPA,** 904 F.2d 1276 (9th Cir. 1990)]

c. Impact of *Vermont Yankee* Case

As discussed *infra,* p. 98, **Vermont Yankee Nuclear Power Corp. v. National Resources Defense Council,** 435 U.S. 519 (1978), prohibits courts from adding procedural requirements to the APA rulemaking provisions. It has yet to be decided whether case law aggressively requiring disclosure of scientific and technical data is consistent with *Vermont Yankee*. The text of the APA's notice provision does not expressly require such disclosures. Arguably, however, the disclosure principle can be derived from the APA notice provisions. Alternatively, the disclosure principle may be consistent with the APA because nondisclosure of critical matters prevents outsiders from commenting on pertinent issues so that the agency fails to consider relevant factors, thus rendering the rule arbitrary and capricious. [**United States v. Nova Scotia Food Products,** 568 F.2d 240 (2d Cir. 1977)]

4. Public Participation

The APA provides that "after notice required by this section, the agency shall give interested persons an opportunity to participate in the rulemaking through submission of written data, views, or arguments with or without opportunity for oral presentation." [APA § 553(c)]

a. Time for Comments

The APA does not make clear how long a period must be allowed for the public to submit comments on a proposed rule. Probably a reasonable time under the circumstances must be provided. [**Florida Power & Light Co. v. United States,** 846 F.2d 765 (D.C. Cir. 1988)—15 day period not unreasonable where agency already received a substantial number of comments which affected the contents of the final rule]

(1) Caution

Do not confuse the question of how much time must be allowed for the public to comment on a proposed rule with the different issue of the ***effective date of the final rule.*** Unless an exception applies, the agency must allow 30 days *after* publishing a final rule before the rule becomes effective. [APA § 553(d)]

b. Oral Presentation

Notice-and-comment under the APA does not require oral argument, much less trial-type procedure. As a matter of custom, however, many agencies schedule a public meeting where members of the public can make oral arguments. Some statutes impose additional procedural requirements on top of the APA, such as a requirement of oral argument or even cross-examination on disputed issues of material fact. Rulemaking that is modified by the addition of ad hoc procedural requirements is called "hybrid rulemaking."

c. Electronic Rulemaking

Most rulemaking is now handled electronically. In part, this is a result of the E-Government Act of 2002, 44 U.S.C. § 3501 Note, which requires agencies, to the extent practicable, to accept electronic submissions in rulemaking and to maintain a rulemaking docket accessible by Internet. You should be sure to spend some time checking out the federal government's central portal for participating in rulemaking at **www.regulations.gov**. At this site, you can search for pending rules, examine rulemaking dockets, submit comments, etc.

5. Revisions to Proposed Rules—Logical Outgrowth Limit

As finally adopted, the rule may be quite different from the version initially published in the Federal Register. This may occur because public comments caused the agency to make changes in the rule. However, the agency is not required to provide a new notice and start the procedure all over again, just because the final rule is different from the proposed rule. That would discourage the agency from making changes to its proposed rule even when it is persuaded by arguments made in the comments.

However, such changes must be a *"logical outgrowth" of the proposed rule.* If the changes are not a "logical outgrowth" of the original proposal, the public would not have received adequate warning from the proposed rule. The public would not have realized that an entirely different rule was on the table and therefore they would have lost the opportunity to comment on it. [**Long Island Care at Home, Ltd. v. Coke,** 127 S.Ct. 2339 (2007)—change from proposed to final rule was reasonably foreseeable; *but see* **Natural Resources Defense Council v. EPA,** 279 F.3d 1180 (9th Cir. 2002)—final rule was radically different from proposal and failed to provide fair warning to commenters; **Chocolate Manufacturers Association v. Block,** 755 F.2d 1098 (4th Cir. 1985)—same]

EXAM TIP

For your exam, remember that the final version of the adopted rule may be different from the original proposed rule published in the Federal Register. The "differing" rule may still be adopted as long as the final rule is a *logical outgrowth* of the proposed rule.

---

6. Statement of Basis and Purpose

The APA provides: "After consideration of the relevant matter presented [by the comment process], the agency shall incorporate in the rules adopted a concise general statement of their basis and purpose." [APA § 553(c)] This provision requires that the agency: (i) actually *consider the comments* it has received and *respond to material comments;* and (ii) *prepare a statement of reasons* for the rule.

a. "Concise and General"

Don't take the "concise" part literally. The courts have interpreted this provision to require a statement of findings and reasons as part of the final rule. This statement enables a reviewing court "to see what major issues of policy were ventilated by the informal proceedings and why the agency reacted to them as it did." As a result, the statements cannot really be either "concise" or "general." [**United States v. Nova Scotia Food Products Corp.,** 568 F.2d 240 (2d Cir. 1977); **Automotive Parts & Accessories Association v. Boyd,** 407 F.2d 330 (D.C. Cir. 1968)]

b. Response Requirement

The statement of basis and purpose must contain a response to significant and material comments made by the public, explaining why those suggestions were not followed or how problems raised by the public were resolved. [**United States v. Nova Scotia Food Products Corp.,** *supra;* **Rodway v. USDA,** 514 F.2d 809 (D.C. Cir. 1975)]

c. Post Hoc Rationalizations

In supporting the rule on judicial review, the agency is *limited to the reasons articulated* in the statement of basis and purpose. The agency may not concoct additional explanations at the time of judicial review. [**Motor Vehicle Manufacturers Association v. State Farm Mutual Auto Insurance Co.,** 463 U.S. 29 (1983)]

7. Publication

After adopting a rule, an agency must publish it in the Federal Register. This publication requirement covers legislative rules, generally applicable interpretive rules and policy statements, and procedural rules. [APA § 552(a)(1)] Legislative rules are then codified in the Code of Federal Regulations ("CFR"), which is broken down by agencies and indexed. "Except to the extent that a person has actual and timely notice of the terms thereof, a person may not in any manner be required to resort to, or be adversely affected by, a matter required to be published in the Federal Register and not so published." [APA § 552(a)(1)]

8. Delayed Effective Date

Unless an exception applies, the required publication of a final rule in the Federal Register is to be made not less than 30 days before the effective date of a rule. [APA § 553(d)] This provision applies only to substantive, not to procedural rules, and is intended to provide time for regulated persons to accommodate themselves to a new rule. [*Cf.* discussion of Congressional Review Act, *supra,* p. 22 ("major rules" cannot take effect until 60 days after submission to Congress)]

a. Exceptions

The grace period requirement does not apply:

(1) To a substantive rule that grants or recognizes an exemption or relieves a restriction;

(2) To interpretive rules and statements of policy; or

(3) For good cause found and published with the rule.

9. Right to Petition

An agency must give an interested person the right to petition for the "issuance, amendment, or repeal of a rule." [APA § 553(e)] Although § 553 does not impose a time limit for action on such petitions nor require the agency to state reasons when it rejects a petition, another provision requires "prompt notice" of the denial of a petition and a "brief statement of the grounds for denial." [APA § 555(e)]

10. Judicial Remedies

a. In General—To Vacate or Not to Vacate

If a court finds that a rule was invalidly adopted (either because the APA requirements were not followed or because the rule is found to be substantively invalid), the court has two choices: (i) it can **vacate the rule,** which invalidates the rule and requires the agency to start over, or (ii) it can **remand without vacation to the agency** for further consideration, which allows the agency to keep the rule in effect, remedy the problem, and re-adopt the rule. Which approach to take is a matter for the ***discretion*** of the reviewing court, which should consider, among other factors, the seriousness of the violation and the damage to the public interest that would occur if the rule is set aside. [**Sugar Cane Growers Cooperative of Florida v. Veneman,** 289 F.3d 89 (D.C. Cir. 2002); **Checkosky v. SEC,** 23 F.3d 452 (D.C. Cir. 1994)] Notably, the dissenting judge in *Checkosky* argued that remanding without vacating is contrary to the APA. Section 706(2)(A) of the APA provides that a reviewing court faced with an agency action that it has found substantively or procedurally invalid "***shall***" (not "may") "hold unlawful and set aside" such agency action.

b. Particular Issues Relating to Petitions for Rulemaking

(1) Denial of Rulemaking Petition Is Reviewable

The Supreme Court has confirmed that an agency's refusal to institute a rulemaking proceeding after a member of the public petitions for one is judicially reviewable. [**Massachusetts v. EPA,** 127 S.Ct. 1438 (2007)] In the *Massachusetts* case, the EPA rejected a petition for rulemaking to limit greenhouse gas emissions from new motor vehicles. The Court held that an agency's denial of a rulemaking petition is reviewable (in contrast to agency refusals to take enforcement action, which are presumptively unreviewable because they are committed to agency discretion. *See* §§ 742–43, *infra.*)

(2) Petition as a Prerequisite for Seeking an "Update"

A party who believes that an existing agency rule should be updated must first petition the agency to institute a rulemaking proceeding. The party is not permitted to seek judicial review of an existing rule—on the theory that the existing rule that was once reasonable has become unreasonable—without first petitioning the agency to amend it. [**Auer v. Robbins,** 519 U.S. 452 (1997)]

(3) Scope of Review

Although the *Massachusetts* case reviewed issues of legal error and abuse of discretion in connection with EPA's decision to reject a rulemaking petition, the scope of review of such actions is normally quite narrow. The court is likely to defer to the agency's decision not to allocate resources to the particular project requested by the public or to its determination that the petition failed to present persuasive grounds for a change in policy. [**Professional Pilots Federation v. FAA,** 118 F.3d 758 (D.C. Cir. 1997); **WWHT, Inc. v. FCC,** 656 F.2d 807 (D.C. Cir. 1981)]

11. Courts Don't Get to Add Procedures—*Vermont Yankee* Again

The Supreme Court has emphatically held that Congress and the agencies, not the courts, are in charge of determining rulemaking procedures. Courts are not free to require the agencies to follow additional rulemaking procedures not prescribed in the APA, such as oral argument or cross-examination. [**Vermont Yankee Nuclear Power Corp. v. National Resources Defense Council,** 435 U.S. 519 (1978)]

a. Core Rationales

Rationales for *Vermont Yankee* include: (a) Congress put agencies, not courts, in charge of agency procedures; (b) allowing courts to impose more procedures on agencies would create uncertainty as to the legality of agency procedures; and (c) agencies would tend to respond to this uncertainty by adding procedures just to avoid potential reversal, impairing administrative processes.

b. Two Narrow Exceptions

In *Vermont Yankee, supra,* the Court acknowledged that additional procedures ***could be required*** in proceedings styled as rulemakings where a very small number of persons would be "exceptionally affected" by a proposed rule, each upon individual grounds. Such proceedings are "quasi-judicial" in nature and may trigger due process, which gives courts a legal basis for determining procedures. [*See supra* pp. 39–40 (discussing the constitutional distinction between rulemaking and adjudication)] *Vermont Yankee* also noted "a totally unjustified departure from well-settled agency procedures of long standing might require judicial correction."

12. Negotiated Rulemaking

Numerous agencies have experimented with negotiated rulemaking, in which all affected interests are called together by the agency to try to reach a consensus. The agreed-upon rule is then the subject of ordinary notice and comment procedure.

a. Negotiated Rulemaking Act

In 1990, Congress enacted several pieces of legislation to encourage alternate dispute resolution ("ADR") techniques in administrative law, including the Negotiated Rulemaking Act ("NRA"). [5 U.S.C. §§ 581 *et seq.*] Congress found that "negotiated rulemaking can increase the acceptability and improve the substance of rules, making it less likely that the affected parties will resist enforcement or challenge such rules in court. It may also shorten the amount of time needed to issue final rules."

(1) When Negotiated Rulemaking Used

The NRA provides that an agency head can propose negotiated rulemaking if it would be in the public interest to do so. In making this determination, the agency head should consider whether there are a *limited number of identifiable interests* that will be significantly affected by the rule and a reasonable likelihood that a committee can be convened with a balanced representation of *persons who can represent those interests* and are willing to negotiate in good faith to reach a consensus on the proposed rule.

(2) Procedure

The agency must publish a *notice in the Federal Register* announcing its use of negotiated rulemaking, together with a list of proposed committee members, a proposed agenda, a timetable, and other information. Additional persons can apply for membership on the committee. The public has 30 days to *file comments* on this announcement. After considering comments, if the agency wishes to proceed, it establishes a negotiated rulemaking committee (generally of fewer than 25 persons) and provides appropriate administrative support to the committee.

(3) Agency Participation

An agency representative participates in the committee deliberations. The committee can appoint a facilitator to chair the meetings and assist the members in negotiating.

(4) Agency Discretion to Reject the Negotiated Outcome

Suppose an agency participates in a negotiated rulemaking, agrees to a particular rule, then changes its mind and proposes a different rule. *Held:* The agency is permitted to do this. It cannot bind itself to adopt whatever rule the negotiated rulemaking committee came up with. [**USA Group Services, Inc. v. Riley**, 82 F.2d 708 (7th Cir. 1996)]

(5) Judicial Review

The NRA provides that agency action relating to establishing, assisting, or terminating a negotiated rulemaking committee shall *not* be subject to judicial review. If the negotiated rulemaking procedure produces a rule, the rule may be judicially reviewed, and if so it may not be accorded any greater deference by a court than a normal rule.

THE APA'S REQUIREMENTS FOR NOTICE-AND-COMMENT RULEMAKING

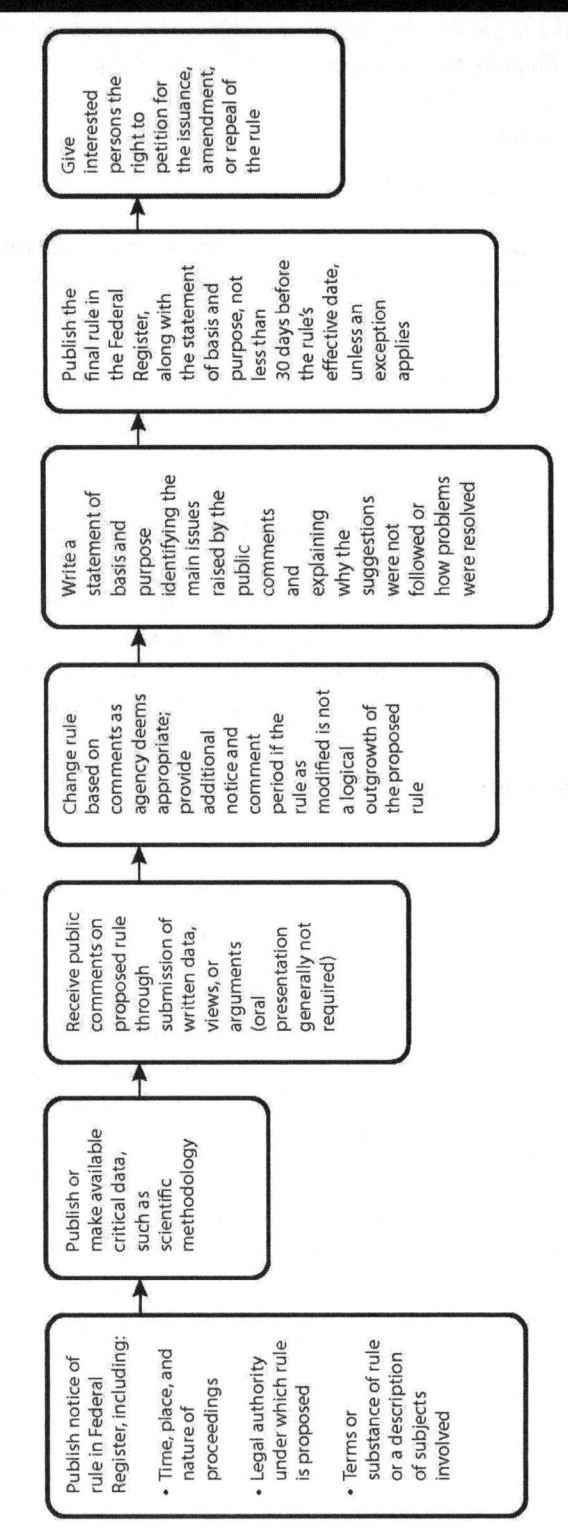

D. Exceptions to Notice-and-Comment Rulemaking Requirements

1. Introduction

Section 553 of the federal APA establishes notice-and-comment as the default means for rulemaking but also creates numerous exceptions to this requirement. One exception, for formal rulemaking, requires agencies to use burdensome, "trial-type" procedures for rulemaking. The other exceptions, by contrast, identify situations in which an agency need not use notice-and-comment at all.

2. Formal Rulemaking

An agency must use formal or "on the record" procedures of §§ 556–57 to promulgate rules that are "required by statute to be made on the record after opportunity for agency hearing." [APA § 553(c) (last sentence)] [*See supra*, p. 96 (discussing formal rulemaking)]

3. Categorical Exceptions to Notice-and-Comment

Section 553's rulemaking requirements do not apply to a ***military or foreign affairs*** function of the United States or a matter relating to ***agency management or personnel*** or to ***public property, loans, grants, benefits, or contracts.*** [APA § 553(a); **Humana of South Carolina v. Califano**, 590 F.2d 1070 (D.C. Cir. 1978)—a regulation limiting amount hospital can charge Medicare patients relates to "benefits" and thus is exempt from APA rulemaking requirements] These very broad exceptions are construed narrowly by the courts on the theory that Congress wanted notice-and-comment rulemaking procedure to apply whenever practical.

4. Procedure Exception

"Rules of agency organization, procedure, or practice" are exempted from both ***notice and comment*** requirements and from the ***delayed effective date*** provision, but ***not*** from the right to petition requirement. [APA § 553(b)(A)]

A procedural rule "does not itself alter the rights or interests of parties, although it may alter the manner in which the parties present themselves or their viewpoints to the agency." [**Electronic Privacy Information Ctr. v. U.S. Dept. of Homeland Sec.**, 653 F.3d 1 (D.C. Cir. 2011)]. To distinguish "procedural" rules from "substantive" rules, the courts consider whether a rule "encodes a substantive value judgment." [**Public Citizen v. Dept. of State**, 276 F.3d 634 (D.C. Cir. 2002) (State Department adopted rule that it would not search for documents in response to a FOIA request created after the date of the requester's letter; as this rule applied to all FOIA requests regardless of subject matter, it did not encode a substantive value judgment)] The D.C. Circuit has added the important qualification that judgments "about what mechanics and processes are most efficient" do not fall into the category of "substantive value judgments" for the purpose of applying the exemption from notice-and-comment for procedural rules. Most procedural rules rest to some degree on efficiency judgments, so accepting them as "substantive value judgments" would effectively destroy the APA's exemption for procedural rules. [**JEM Broadcasting Co., Inc. v. FCC**, 22 F.3d 320 (D.C. Cir. 1994) (FCC rules that required dismissal of flawed license applications without leave to amend were procedural even though they might be said to express a value judgment regarding applications with errors)]

The D.C. Circuit has also explained that the difference between substantive and procedural rules is "one of degree" that links to whether "the substantive effect is sufficiently grave so that notice and comment are needed to safeguard the policies underlying the APA." [**Electronic Privacy,** *supra*] Where impacts are grave, there is a greater need for public participation and for the agency to gather information, which calls for narrow construction of the procedural exemption. [**Id.**]

5. Good Cause Exception

The APA's good cause exception applies both to the notice and comment requirements and also to the delayed effective date provision.

a. APA Provisions

Notice and comment is excused "when the agency for good cause finds (and incorporates the finding and a brief statement of reasons therefor in the rules issued) that notice and public procedure thereon are ***impracticable, unnecessary, or contrary to the public interest.***" [APA § 553(b)(B)] To dispense with the 30-day delayed effective date provision, a federal agency must find good cause to do so. [APA § 553(d)(3)]

b. Unnecessary Exception

(1) Definition of "Unnecessary"

A rule falls under the "unnecessary" prong of the good cause rule if it is totally noncontroversial. Minor, technical amendments of rules are often adopted without prior notice and comment under the "unnecessary" prong, but if the rule would be of consequence to members of the public, the agency must provide notice and comment procedure. [**Utility Solid Waste Activities Group v. EPA,** 236 F.3d 749 (D.C. Cir. 2001)—technical amendment to repair an error in the rule, resulting from an erroneous use of WordPerfect find/replace command in drafting the original rule, was of great consequence to the public, so rulemaking procedure was not "unnecessary"]

(2) Direct Final Rules

A common federal practice that relies on the "unnecessary" exception is referred to as "direct final rules." Under this approach, an agency will publish notice that it proposes to adopt a rule without public participation because the agency believes it would not be necessary. If within a short period (often 30 days), a single member of the public submits an adverse comment, the rule is withdrawn and resubmitted as a proposed rule as to which public comments are invited. If no adverse comments are received, the agency adopts the rule at the end of the 30-day period without further procedures.

c. Impracticable or Contrary to the Public Interest

"Impracticable" means a situation in which the execution of agency functions would be prevented by prior notice and comment. "Contrary to the public interest" means that the interests of the public would be defeated by advance notice. [Attorney General's Memorandum on the APA 30–31 (1947)] The courts are quite strict in requiring that a real emergency situation be present before an agency is allowed to dispense with prior notice and comment.

(1) Emergencies

Typically, agencies are able to sustain good cause claims in the case of a public health or safety emergency or an environmental crisis. [**Jifry v. FAA,** 370 F.3d 1174 (D.C. Cir. 2004)—rules provide for automatic suspension of pilot license upon notification that pilot constituted a security risk; national security requires immediate implementation; **Northern Arapahoe Tribe v. Hodel,** 808 F.2d 741 (10th Cir. 1987)—urgent need for hunting regulations where the season had already begun and herds could dwindle to extinction]

(2) Public Interest

In other situations, prior announcement of a proposed rule would have negative economic effects. For example, prior announcement of a price freeze might cause prices to shoot up before the rule could become effective. [**DeRieux v. Five Smiths, Inc.,** 499 F.2d 1321 (Temp. Emer. Ct. App. 1974)]

(3) Statutory Deadlines

Still another situation where good cause can be claimed occurs if the rules must be adopted by a statutory deadline and it is not possible to conduct notice and comment proceedings before the deadline. [**Sepulveda v. Block,** 782 F.2d 363 (2d Cir. 1986)] However, a time crunch occurring because of the agency's own inaction or procrastination does not constitute good cause. [**NRDC v. Abraham,** 355 F.3d 179 (2d Cir. 2004)—emergency rule adopted to delay the effective date of a rule adopted by outgoing administration; emergency was of the agency's own making and does not qualify as good cause]

(4) Interim-Final Rules

Federal agencies that adopt rules under the "impracticable" or "contrary to the public interest" prongs of the good cause exception often do so in the form of so-called "interim-final" rules. Pursuant to this practice, a rule is adopted without prior notice and comment under the good cause exception, but the public is invited to submit comments on the rule after it becomes effective. The agency commits itself to consider those comments, then to modify the rule before making it final. Thus, the interim-final rule serves not only as an immediately effective rule, but also as a proposed rule: it gives notice to the public that the agency is considering a final rule and invites public comment on that rule. Some decisions hold that the agency's open-minded consideration of these post-effective comments is a relevant factor in determining whether the agency had good cause for adopting the interim-final rule in the first place. [**Mid-Tex Electric Cooperative v. Federal Energy Regulatory Commission,** 822 F.2d 1123 (D.C. Cir. 1987)]

6. Interpretive Rules

a. Definition

Interpretive rules provide guidance to the public by explaining the meaning of particular terms in a statute or a previous rule. However, because interpretive rules, by definition, do not exercise delegated legislative power, they are not legally binding on outsiders. An outsider could be prosecuted for violating the statute or a legislative rule, but not an interpretive rule. (For further discussion of this point, *see supra* pp. 99–101 (distinguishing the force of legislative from nonlegislative rules.)

(1) Procedures

The APA does not require notice-and-comment for interpretive rules. [APA § 553(b)(A)] Agencies often voluntarily engage in notice-and-comment before adopting them, however. Interpretive rules of general applicability must be published in the Federal Register. [APA § 552(a)(1)(D)]

b. Distinguishing Interpretive from Legislative Rules

Suppose an agency invokes the interpretive-rule exception to adopt a rule without notice-and-comment. A party might later attack the validity of the rule on the ground that it is actually a legislative rule that required notice-and-comment. It is therefore important to be able to distinguish these two types of rule. Doing so is difficult because, as you have learned in several contexts in law school by now, the line between interpretation and creation is not clear.

(1) Agency Intent

Some courts focus on the agency's intention. A rule is legislative if the agency had power to make legislative rules *and* intended to use it. By contrast, a rule is interpretive if the agency did not intend to use any legislative power it might have. [**General Motors Corp. v. Ruckelshaus**, 742 F.2d 1561 (D.C. Cir. 1984) (a rule is legislative where "agency intends to create new law, rights, or duties"; a rule is interpretive if it "simply states what the administrative agency thinks that statue means"; in choosing between these categories, "the agency's own label, while relevant, is not dispositive"]

(2) Does It Look Like Something Is Being "Interpreted"?

Sometimes courts focus on whether a rule has a tight enough linguistic connection to a statute (or another rule) to qualify as "interpretive." A gloss that provides "crisper more detailed lines" may be properly "interpretive." [**American Mining Congress v. MSHA**, 995 F.2d 1106 (D.C. Cir. 1993) (agency letter declaring that certain x-ray results qualified as a "diagnosis" of a lung disease fell within the interpretive rule exemption).

Specific agency rules based on very vague language, however, are more likely to be regarded as legislative in nature. [**Catholic Health Initiatives v. Sebelius**, 617 F.3d 490 (D.C. Cir. 2010) (detailed provisions regarding reimbursement for insurance premiums paid by medical providers could not be regarded as an interpretation of the statutory phrase "reasonable costs"); **Hoctor v. United States Department of Agriculture**, 82 F.3d 165 (7th Cir. 1996) (requirement of an eight foot fence to contain wild animals was not an interpretation of earlier legislative regulation that required "appropriate" housing of wild animals).

Also, an agency rule will more likely be regarded as legislative if the agency relies on factual and policy rationales for the rule rather than linguistic analysis. [**Syncor Internat'l Corp. v. Shalala**, 127 F.3d 90 (D.C. Cir. 1997) (FDA rule asserting regulatory authority over Positron Emission Tomography radiopharmaceuticals rested on changes in technology and wider use of procedures; these policy related rationales indicated that the rule was legislative)]

(3) Did the Rule Make "New Law"?

Some cases place emphasis on whether a rule has created a new binding norm—*i.e.*, new law. [**Air Transport Association of America, Inc. v. FAA**, 291 F.3d 49 (D.C. Cir. 2002)—legislative rule required minimum rest period for flight personnel prior to "scheduled completion of any flight segment"; FAA letter explained that this phrase included rescheduled flight times based on actual flying conditions; D.C. Circuit held that this letter qualified as interpretive rule as it did not carry "force and effect of law" but instead was "fairly encompassed within the required rest regulation"; **American Mining Congress v. Mine Safety & Health Admin.**, 995 F.2d 1106 (D.C.Cir.1993) (a rule is legislative if it "amends" a prior legislative rule in the sense that the later rule repudiates or is irreconcilable with the earlier one).

Along these lines, courts sometimes check whether a rule must be legislative by inquiring whether "in the absence of a legislative rule by the agency, the legislative basis for agency enforcement would be inadequate." [**American Mining Congress v. Mine Safety & Health Admin.**, 995 F.2d 1106 (D.C.Cir.1993)] This language sounds a bit more intimidating than it is. Various statutes bar actions that violate "such rules and regulations as the [agency] may proscribe." Such a provision, by itself, forbids or requires nothing. Any subsequent rule that creates binding obligations cannot be an "interpretation" of the statute but must instead create new law. [**Id.**]

(4) Ouch! Some Amendments to Interpretive Rules Are Legislative—*Alaska Prof. Hunters* Problem

A recurring problem occurs where an agency changes a well-established interpretation of a legislative rule. Suppose we have three rules. First, there is a legislative rule. Next, there is an interpretive rule that puts some gloss on the legislative rule. Last, there is a new rule that abandons the old interpretive rule by adopting a new gloss on the legislative rule. You might think that this new rule, insofar as it simply adopts a new interpretation of the legislative rule, should count as an interpretive rule that does not require notice-and-comment. Many courts agree. [*See, e.g.,* **Abraham Lincoln Memorial Hosp. v. Sebelius,** 698 F.3d 536 (7th Cir. 2012); **Chief Probation Officers v. Shalala,** 118 F.3d 1327 (9th Cir. 1997)—later rule is invalid only if inconsistent with an earlier legislative rule, not an earlier interpretive rule]

Some courts, most notably the D.C. Circuit, do not. Motivated by a concern to protect the reliance interests of regulated parties, the D.C. Circuit has stated that "[w]hen an agency has given its regulation a definitive interpretation, and later significantly revises that interpretation, the agency has in effect amended its rule, something it may not accomplish without notice-and-comment." Put another way, after the legislative rule "absorbs" a definitive interpretation, any attempt to change that interpretation also changes the underlying legislative rule. [**Alaska Professional Hunters Association v. FAA,** 177 F.3d 1030 (D.C. Cir. 1999) (rejecting FAA "Notice to Operators" that applied commercial pilot regulations to Alaska guide pilots in contravention of contrary, decades-old interpretation); *see also* **MetWest Inc. v. Secretary of Labor,** 560 F.3d 506 (D.C. Cir. 2009) (emphasizing that the *Alaska Prof. Hunters* doctrine requires substantial and justifiable reliance); **Shell Offshore Inc. v. Babbitt,** 238 F.3d 622 (5th Cir. 2001) (approving the D.C. Circuit's *Alaska Prof. Hunters* reasoning)]

HOW COURTS DISTINGUISH BETWEEN INTERPRETIVE AND LEGISLATIVE RULES

APPROACH	SUMMARY
AGENCY INTENT	A rule is legislative if the agency **had power** to make it legislative **and intended** to use it.
IDENTIFY INTERPRETATION	A rule is not interpretive unless it **explains the meaning** of language in an existing statute or regulation.
IDENTIFY NEW LAW	If a rule spells out a **duty "fairly encompassed" in an existing regulation,** the rule is interpretive. If, on the other hand, the rule makes up a new legal obligation, then it must be legislative.
CHANGE OF DEFINITIVE INTERPRETATION	In the D.C. Circuit, where an agency abandons an old, definitive interpretation of a legislative rule in favor of a new interpretation, the new "interpretation" may be regarded as legislative.

7. Policy Statements

a. Definition

A policy statement indicates the manner in which an agency intends to exercise a discretionary function, such as future prosecutions, investigations, or enforcement actions.

b. Procedures

The APA does not require notice-and-comment for policy statements. [APA § 553(b)(A)] Statements of general policy must be published in the Federal Register. [APA § 552(a)(1)(D)]

c. Distinguishing Policy Statements from Legislative Rules

Policy statements announce how an agency *intends* to exercise discretion, but they cannot *bind* the agency because, if they do, they create a legislative rule. [**American Bus Ass'n v. United States,** 627 F.2d 525 (D.C. Cir. 1980) (a policy statement must "genuinely leave[ ] the agency and its decisionmakers free to exercise discretion")] A policy statement is "tentative" in the sense that parties must have an opportunity to persuade the agency to exercise discretion differently than the policy statement.

(1) Both Language and Practice Are Relevant

An agency rule will be treated as "binding as a practical matter . . . if it either appears on its face to be binding . . . or is applied by the agency in a way that indicates it is binding." [**General Electric Co. v. EPA,** 290 F.3d 377 (D.C. Cir. 2002)—purported guidelines for treating PCBs were definitive rather than tentative and also were applied by agency in a binding manner; **CropLife America v. EPA,** 329 F.3d 876 (D.C. Cir. 2003)—agency decision that it will not consider certain type of studies in pesticide registration cases is binding on the staff and cannot be a policy statement]

Of particular note, even if an agency rule *states* that it is not binding, a court may determine that it is a binding legislative rule if the agency treats that rule as binding. [**U.S. Tel. Ass'n v. FCC,** 28 F.3d 1232 (D.C. Cir. 1994) (FCC issued purportedly nonbinding statement containing detailed fee schedule for monetary forfeitures; in holding that the schedule should have been subjected to notice-and-comment, the D.C. Circuit observed that the FCC had deviated from this scheme only 8 times in 300 cases)]

(2) Enforcement Guidelines

When a purported policy statement precludes the staff from taking enforcement action if a certain standard is not met, the document is not treated as a policy statement because it is binding on the staff. Persons who believe the enforcement policy is too lenient would have no way of challenging it unless notice and comment is provided. [**Community Nutrition Institute v. Young,** 818 F.2d 943 (D.C. Cir. 1987)—FDA "action level" that it would take no enforcement action against corn having less than certain toxin level required notice and comment]

EXCEPTIONS TO APA RULEMAKING REQUIREMENTS — gilbert LAW SUMMARIES

CATEGORICAL EXCEPTIONS	• APA provisions do not apply to *agency management or personnel matters* • APA provisions do not apply to *public property, loans, grants, benefits, or contracts*
PROCEDURE EXCEPTION	• Rules of agency organization, procedure, or practice are exempted from *notice and comment requirements* and from *delayed effective date* provision, but *not* from the right to petition requirement
GOOD CAUSE EXCEPTION	• Notice and comment requirements excused where agency for good cause finds them *impracticable, unnecessary, or contrary to the public interest* • *30-day delayed effective date* provision may be excused for good cause
INTERPRETIVE RULES	• Notice and comment requirements and delayed effective date provisions do not apply to *interpretative rules*
POLICY STATEMENTS	• Notice and comment requirements and delayed effective date provisions do not apply to *general statements of policy*

E. Impartiality of Rulemakers

1. Overview: "Unbiased" Rulemaking Is Problematic

Adjudicators are supposed to be rigorously fair and unbiased. Along these lines, as discussed in Chapters 3 and 4, the APA includes various requirements designed to assure that formal adjudications are fair. These include separation of functions and bans on ex parte contacts.

The concept of "bias" doesn't neatly translate into rulemaking—we expect policymakers to bring their expertise and values to the task of policymaking. Consistent with this point, the APA's rules designed to promote fair adjudication do not apply to the legislative process of *informal* rulemaking.

2. Ex Parte Contacts and Formal Rulemaking

Formal rulemaking is an uncomfortable hybrid. On the one hand, rulemaking is a legislative process, which suggests a flexible approach to controlling communications with decisionmakers. On the other, formal rulemaking requires an agency to use the "on the record" or trial-type procedures specified by 5 U.S.C. §§ 556–57. The limits on ex parte communications specified by § 557(d) therefore apply to formal rulemaking. [*See supra,* pp. 82–83 (discussing § 557(d)'s limits on ex parte contacts)]

3. Ex Parte Contacts and Informal Rulemaking

Generally, the public submits comments on proposed rules, and the comments are part of a public file. However, persons who are concerned about a proposed rule may sometimes wish to make ex parte contacts with the decisionmakers in addition to (or instead of) putting comments on the public record. Under current case law, this practice does not violate the APA, but some regulatory statutes (and agency rules) do require ex parte contacts to be disclosed and included in the rulemaking record.

a. *Sangamon* Rule

In some situations, a proceeding that an agency has styled as a rulemaking is really more like adjudication in the sense that it decides a dispute between several outside parties based on adjudicative facts. In this situation, *due process* may bar ex parte contacts from the disputants to the decisionmaker. [**Sangamon Valley Television Corp. v. United States,** 269 F.2d 211 (D.C. Cir. 1959); *see also supra,* p. 48 (discussing how an agency determination may amount to an "adjudication" under due process principles even though the agency has styled it as a rulemaking)]

b. *Home Box Office* Rule

In one important case, the court invalidated a generally applicable rule that appeared to be the result of an ex parte deal between the cable television and over-the-air television industries. The court felt that this was fundamentally unfair to members of the public who were cut out of the backroom dealing. Moreover, the court could not properly review a rule that resulted from ex parte contact rather than from the record that was made by public comments. The court therefore announced a rule barring ex parte contacts with agency officials and employees involved in the decisional process of an informal rulemaking after issuance of the notice of proposed rulemaking. [**Home Box Office, Inc. v. FCC,** 567 F.2d 9 (D.C. Cir.), *cert. denied,* 434 U.S. 829 (1977)]

c. *Home Box Office* Narrowed Almost Out of Existence

The biggest doctrinal problem with *Home Box Office* is its lack of textual support in the APA, which contains no limits on ex parte contacts for notice-and-comment rulemaking but expressly bars them for formal rulemaking. *Home Box Office* therefore seems to run afoul of the *Vermont Yankee* principle that courts don't get to add procedures to the informal rulemaking process. It is also dubious from a policy point of view insofar as we may want rulemakers to enjoy a free flow of information from informal contacts with regulated parties and regulatory beneficiaries.

Later cases have seriously undercut *Home Box Office.* The general consensus now is that ex parte contacts in notice-and-comment rulemaking **are permissible,** unless: (a) the *Sangamon* rule applies, *supra,* p. 116; (b) a statute other than the APA prohibits such contacts or requires them to be disclosed on the record; or (c) the agency has adopted procedural rules limiting ex parte contacts (which some have done in the wake of *HBO*). [**Action for Children's Television v. FCC,** 564 F.2d 458 (D.C. Cir. 1977); **Sierra Club v. Costle,** 657 F.2d 298 (D.C. Cir 1981)]

4. Legislative or Executive Interference

Generally there is **no prohibition** against either legislative or executive attempts to influence rulemakers through ex parte communications in informal rulemaking. [**Sierra Club v. Costle,** *supra*]

a. Presidential Communications

Sierra Club involved meetings between the agency head and the White House staff regarding a rule limiting emissions from coal-fired plants. The court thought these were wholly appropriate since the President is constitutionally responsible for all executive branch decisions. Also, the executive has a legitimate interest in coordinating rulemaking across agencies that might otherwise be subject to tunnel vision. [**Sierra Club v. Costle,** *supra*] For discussion of centralized "White House" review of rulemaking pursuant to executive order, see *supra,* pp. 97–98.

b. Congressional Pressure and "Relevant Factors"

Sierra Club also discussed meetings between EPA and Senator Byrd of West Virginia—an important coal-producing state. The court rejected contentions that these contacts were improper, noting "Americans rightly expect their elected representatives to voice their grievances and preferences concerning the administration of our laws." [**Id.**]

Congressional pressure becomes improper where a congressperson forces an agency to base a rulemaking decision "upon factors not made relevant by Congress in the applicable statute." [**Id.**] The idea behind "relevant factors" is that Congress grants discretion to an agency to further some set of goals, and it expects the agency to take certain factors in consideration when exercising that discretion. An agency should not let "irrelevant factors" affect its judgment. To give an easy example, an EPA Administrator should not consider her ownership of stock in coal companies when determining whether to adopt a rule allowing greater emissions from coal-fired plants. In **D.C. Federation of Civic Associations v. Volpe**, a congressperson threatened to hold up appropriations for a subway system until the agency approved plans for a bridge. Congress did not contemplate that the agency would determine where to put a bridge based on how this would affect money for a subway. The court therefore set aside the decision to build the bridge because of this pressure. [459 F.2d 1231 (D.C. Cir. 1971), *cert. denied,* 405 U.S. 1030 (1972)]

The court in *Sierra Club* distinguished *D.C. Federation* on the ground that there was no evidence that Senator Byrd had done anything but express his views on the substance of the rule—conduct that was entirely appropriate in a democracy.

5. Bias

The rules guaranteeing an impartial adjudicator do **not apply** in rulemaking since rulemaking is intended to be a political process. A rulemaker is disqualified only upon a "clear and convincing showing that he has an unalterably closed mind on matters critical to the disposition of the rulemaking." [**Association of National Advertisers v. FTC,** 627 F.2d 1151 (D.C. Cir. 1979), *cert. denied,* 447 U.S. 921 (1980); **C & W Fish Co. v. Fox,** 931 F.2d 1556 (D.C. Cir. 1991)] (If you are having trouble imagining how this standard could be satisfied, then you are paying attention.)

Example: In the *National Advertisers* case, the FTC was considering rules restricting advertising on children's television. The chairman had given several speeches indicating his intense antagonism to advertising directed toward children. The court found that these speeches did not establish the "closed mind" that would disqualify the chairman.

6. Separation of Functions

The rules requiring separation of adversary staff members from the decisionmaking function do not apply in rulemaking. [**United Steelworkers of America v. Marshall,** 647 F.2d 1189 (D.C. Cir. 1980), *cert. denied,* 453 U.S. 913 (1981)—outside consultants and advocates for worker protection rule permitted to advise Assistant Secretary of Labor] [*Cf. supra,* pp. 76–77 (discussing the "separation of functions" requirements for formal adjudication)]

F. The Rulemaking Record

1. Introduction

Frequently, agency rules are challenged before the courts. An important issue that arises on review is the nature of the record before the court—*i.e.*, what evidentiary materials the parties may use when attacking or defending the rule. Where formal or "on the record" proceedings are challenged, this issue is easy to resolve because the APA defines what belongs in the record. [5 U.S.C. § 556(e)] Also, some statutes establish hybrid rulemaking procedures that use notice-and-comment but also specify well-defined records. [*See, e.g.*, Clean Air Act provisions at 42 U.S.C. § 7607(d)]

Determining the record for informal proceedings is more problematic. In a case involving informal adjudication, the Supreme Court indicated that the administrative record was, in essence, the information that was before the agency at the time of the decision. [**Citizens to Preserve Overton Park v. Volpe,** 401 U.S. 402 (1971)] Transposing this idea to informal rulemaking, the "record" should include materials before the agency at the time the rule was adopted, including, at the very least, the notice of proposed rulemaking, public comments, transcript of a public hearing (if any), and the agency's statement of basis and purpose.

In many circumstances, the agency may wish to submit additional materials to establish the reasonableness of its rule. Similarly, the challengers may wish to submit materials to show the unreasonableness of the rule. The degree to which they can do so is unsettled.

2. Rules on Scientific Evidence and Contemporaneous Rationales

Note that judicially-crafted rules governing the rulemaking process block certain kinds of efforts to supplement the administrative record. For instance, the courts have interpreted § 553 to require disclosure of the scientific and technical data on which an agency relies in crafting a notice of proposed rulemaking. [*See supra,* p. 102] Also, the contemporaneous rationale rule holds that an agency's discretionary action must be judged based on the rationale the agency gave at the time it took the action. [*See supra,* p. 64 (discussing *Chenery* rule); *infra,* p. 163 (discussing review for reasoned decisionmaking)] Thus, the required scientific data and contemporaneous rationale have to be part of the preexisting administrative record, and an agency cannot fix deficiencies by later efforts to supplement.

3. Closed Record Approach

Generally speaking, courts favor a "closed" record, limiting the record to material before the agency at the time it made the decision. [**American Radio Relay League, Inc. v. FCC,** 524 F.3d 227 (D.C. Cir. 2008) (Tatel, J., concurring) (observing that, "to review an agency's action fairly, [a court] should have before it neither more nor less information than did the agency when it made its decision"); **Southwest Center for Biological Diversity v. U.S. Forest Service**, 100 F.3d 1443 (9th Cir. 1996) ("Judicial review of an agency decision typically focuses on the administrative record in existence at the time of the decision and does not encompass any part of the record that is made initially in the reviewing court.")]

4. Exceptions

There are narrow exceptions to the closed record requirement. For instance, supplementation may be justified by a "strong showing of bad faith or improper behavior." [**IMS, P.C. v. Alvarez,** 129 F.3d 618 (D.C. Cir. 1997)] Some courts have recognized that supplementation may be allowed to assist the court in understanding technical material in the record. [**Southwest Center,** *supra*.]

5. State Law

Numerous state decisions reject the concept of exclusive record and allow introduction of factual materials on judicial review. [*See* **Liberty Homes v. Department of Industry,** 401 N.W.2d 805 (Wis. 1987)]

Chapter Six
Obtaining Information and Attorney's Fees

CONTENTS	PAGE
Key Exam Issues	122
A. **Agency Acquisition of Information**	123
B. **Constitutional Protection from Agency Information Gathering**	126
C. **Freedom of Information Act**	129
D. **Government in the Sunshine Act**	140
E. **Attorney's Fees**	141

Key Exam Issues

An agency must be able to acquire information as a basis for both adjudicative and rulemaking proceedings. This chapter considers the agency's power to obtain information, and the corresponding rights of the public to obtain and refrain from giving information. It also considers the agency's obligation to hold public meetings and the circumstances in which the agency can or must pay the attorney's fees of private parties.

Exam questions in these areas are likely to focus on the following topics:

1. **Agency Seeks Information from the Private Sector**

    When the agency tries to get information from a private party, it may:

    a. **Subpoena information**

    In such cases, consider whether the subpoena is *"reasonable"*—*i.e.*, for a proper purpose and not excessively burdensome. Also think about any applicable *constitutional privileges* (*e.g.*, self-incrimination, unlawful search or seizure) or any *common law privileges* (*e.g.*, attorney-client privilege) that are violated by the subpoena.

    b. **Conduct a physical search**

    Ask yourself if the search requires a *warrant* (*i.e.*, the industry is not pervasively regulated), and if a warrant is required, has it been obtained?

2. **Private Party Seeks Information from an Agency**

    When someone in your fact pattern is trying to get information from the agency, consider the following:

    a. **Freedom of Information Act**

    First, check whether the information is *required to be published or made generally available* under the Freedom of Information Act ("FOIA"). If the agency is not required to make such information available, specific documents can still be *requested* unless they fall under an exception to the Act. (Watch especially for the inter- or intra-agency memorandum exception for predecisional, nonfactual documents.)

    b. **Sunshine Act**

    Remember that many agency meetings must be open to the public.

3. **Attorney's Fees**

    The general rule is that private parties *cannot recover* attorney's fees from the government. However, there are many *statutory exceptions* to this rule to consider. For instance, some statutes authorize courts to award reasonable attorney's fees to "prevailing parties" or where "appropriate." More generally, the Equal Access to Justice Act provides for an award of fees to a party that prevails against the government in civil litigation unless the government's position was substantially justified.

A. Agency Acquisition of Information

1. Methods of Obtaining Information

Most information acquired by agencies is obtained voluntarily. However, an agency may also be entitled to compel information through (i) *subpoena* power; (ii) required *reports*; (iii) physical *inspections*; or (iv) *investigatory hearings.*

a. APA Provisions on Gathering of Information

(1) *Section 555(c) provides:* "Process, requirement of a report, inspection, or other investigative act or demand may not be issued, made, or enforced, except as authorized by law. A person compelled to submit data or evidence is entitled to retain or, on payment of lawfully prescribed costs, procure a copy or transcript thereof, except that in a nonpublic investigatory proceeding the witness may for good cause be limited to inspection of the official transcript of his testimony."

(2) *Section 555(d) provides:* "Agency subpoenas authorized by law shall be issued to a party on request and, when required by rules of procedure, on a statement or showing of general relevance and reasonable scope of the evidence sought. On contest, the court shall sustain the subpoena or similar process or demand to the extent that it is found to be in accordance with law. In a proceeding for enforcement, the court shall issue an order requiring the appearance of the witness or the production of the evidence or data within a reasonable time under penalty of punishment for contempt in case of contumacious failure to comply."

2. Agency Power to Subpoena

A subpoena (sometimes called a "civil investigative demand" or "CID") requires an individual to appear and give information. A subpoena duces tecum requires the production of documents. An agency has no inherent subpoena power; it must be conferred by statute. [APA § 555(c)] If the subject of an agency subpoena refuses to comply voluntarily, the agency must seek judicial enforcement of its request. If the judicial order is ignored, the court may hold the resisting party in contempt.

a. Fourth Amendment Limitations

The agency need *not show probable cause* for the investigation. (However, it must comply with the "reasonableness" requirements of the Fourth Amendment; *see below.*)

Example—probable cause unnecessary: The Walsh-Healy Act required government contractors to comply with prevailing wage rates. The Secretary of Labor issued a subpoena for wage information concerning a factory that processed raw materials for ultimate purchase by the government. Even though there was no probable cause to suspect that wages were too low, or even that the factory was subject to the Act, the Court held that the district court must enforce the subpoena. [**Endicott Johnson Corp. v. Perkins,** 317 U.S. 501 (1943)]

(1) Subpoena Must Be "Reasonable"

An agency subpoena must be "reasonable" within the meaning of the Fourth Amendment. That is, the subpoena must be *specific* as to what is sought, and the object of the subpoena must be *relevant* to subject matter that the agency is *authorized* to investigate. Relevance means that the information might be useful to the agency's investigation. [**Oklahoma Press Publishing Co. v. Walling**, 327 U.S. 186 (1946)—subpoena for corporate records upheld as reasonable]

(2) Legal Issues

Normally a court will not consider legal issues at the subpoena enforcement stage (*e.g.*, whether the suspected conduct is a violation of statute). Nevertheless, if the subpoena shows on its face that the agency has no jurisdiction, the court will refuse to enforce the subpoena. [**Major League Baseball v. Crist**, 331 F.3d 1177 (11th Cir. 2003)—subpoena obviously invalid given that baseball is exempt from antitrust laws]

(3) Burdensomeness of Subpoena

Generally the fact that compliance with a subpoena will be expensive and burdensome is not a defense. [**CAB v. Hermann**, 353 U.S. 322 (1957)—upholding a subpoena for all the books, records and documents of an airline and its stockholders for a period of 38 months] Occasionally, however, a court will scale down a request that is deemed unduly burdensome or require the agency to be more specific in its requests. [*See* **Hunt Foods & Industries, Inc. v. FTC**, 286 F.2d 803 (9th Cir. 1960)] A trial court has substantial discretion to limit the burden of a subpoena (*e.g.*, by requiring the agency to inspect documents at the subpoenaed party's place of business). [**CAB v. Hermann**, *supra*]

(4) Review for Improper Purpose

A court that is requested to enforce a subpoena may consider whether the agency's request is actually designed to *harass or intimidate*, rather than to obtain information. However, a difficult burden of proof must be met to show harassment. [**Shasta Minerals & Chemical Co. v. SEC**, 328 F.2d 285 (10th Cir. 1964)]

b. Third Party Subpoenas

Frequently, an agency will conduct an investigation of someone (the "target") and will subpoena information from someone else about the target. Absent some statutory limitation, the target is not entitled to notice of the third-party subpoena, even though the third party may voluntarily comply with the subpoena before the target can intervene and raise objections that the subpoena seeks irrelevant or privileged information. [**SEC v. Jerry T. O'Brien, Inc.**, 467 U.S. 735 (1984)]

3. Agency Power to Make Physical Inspections

Enforcement of health, safety, and welfare laws often requires government officials physically to inspect homes and businesses or conduct physical tests of employees. Although such searches fall within the Fourth Amendment prohibition on unreasonable searches and seizure, the requirements for obtaining a warrant are lenient, and in many situations no warrant is required at all.

a. Home Inspections

For administrative inspections of homes, warrants are generally required.

Example: A building inspector must obtain a warrant before inspecting a dwelling for housing code violations unless a householder's consent is first obtained. [**Camara v. Municipal Court**, 387 U.S. 523 (1967)—tenant jailed for refusing entry to city inspectors attempting to inspect his residence without a warrant]

(1) Probable Cause

It is not necessary to cite specific reasons to obtain a warrant. Probable cause is satisfied if information as to the neighborhood indicated the likelihood of violations. In the case of a health or public safety emergency (*e.g.*, extreme structural decay, rodent feces), no warrant would be required. [**Camara v. Municipal Court**, *supra*]

b. Warrants Required for Some Business Inspections

Whether a warrant will be required for an administrative business inspection is much less certain.

(1) General Rule

Earlier cases simply applied *Camara* to the business inspection situation. [**See v. Seattle**, 387 U.S. 541 (1967)—inspection of locked warehouse by fire inspector requires warrant]

(2) OSHA Inspection

Similarly, a warrant must be obtained to inspect business premises for compliance with employee safety rules, despite the danger that the employer might conceal defects while the inspector gets a warrant. [**Marshall v. Barlow's Inc.**, 436 U.S. 307 (1978)] However, the inspecting agency need not demonstrate probable cause to believe that a violation of the law has occurred. Under *Barlow's*, the inspector needs to show only that the choice of this particular employer was based on reasonable standards, such as statistical sampling techniques.

c. Exceptions

A statute can validly authorize ***warrantless*** inspections of "pervasively" regulated businesses.

(1) Requirements for Warrantless Inspection

The business must be subject to close and detailed regulation, and the statute must meet Fourth Amendment reasonableness standards. This requires that:

(a) There be a *substantial government interest* in the regulatory scheme;

(b) Warrantless inspections are *necessary* to further that scheme; and

(c) The statute must *perform the functions of a warrant* by advising the owner of the business that *periodic searches will be made* and the statute must *limit the time, place, and scope* of the inspections.

(2) Application

(a) Auto Junkyards

A New York statute validly permits warrantless inspection of auto junkyards. The state has a substantial interest in preventing auto theft; unannounced searches of junkyards are necessary to further that scheme (because stolen property disappears quickly); the statute provides for frequent and regular inspections of licensed premises; they are limited in time, place, and scope. The fact that such searches are used primarily to turn up evidence of crime is irrelevant in light of their regulatory nature. [**New York v. Burger**, 482 U.S. 693 (1987)]

(b) Gun and Liquor Dealers

On similar reasoning, warrantless inspection of liquor and gun dealers has been upheld. [**United States v. Biswell**, 406 U.S. 311 (1972)—guns; **Colonnade Catering Corp. v. United States**, 397 U.S. 72 (1970)—liquor]

(c) Mines

Underground mines must be inspected four times each year. The regularity and consistency of such inspections make them distinguishable from the OSHA inspections involved in **Marshall v. Barlow's Inc.** (*supra*, p. 116). [**Donovan v. Dewey**, 452 U.S. 594 (1981)]

B. Constitutional Protection from Agency Information Gathering

1. Introduction

The constitutional protections available to suspects in criminal cases are not applicable to administrative investigations, even though such investigations may lead to adjudicatory proceedings that could impose heavy penalties.

2. Privilege to Refuse to Furnish Information

Witnesses called to testify at an agency investigatory hearing or at an agency adjudicatory hearing may assert the *Fifth Amendment privilege* against self-incrimination in refusing to answer specific questions, but they cannot refuse to take the stand as they can in a criminal case.

a. When Privilege Arises

If the information requested could supply a link in a chain leading to criminal conviction, the witness may claim the privilege.

(1) Immunity

The agency can often rely on an immunity statute to compel incriminating testimony. [*See* **Kastigar v. United States**, 406 U.S. 441 (1972)]

(2) Privilege Limited to Natural Persons

The custodian of the records of an entity (such as a corporation or partnership) *cannot* claim any Fifth Amendment privilege for such papers, even if the act of producing them might be incriminatory, since the custodian holds such papers in a representative capacity. [**Braswell v. United States**, 487 U.S. 99 (1988)] The privilege against self-incrimination is *not available* to a corporation, a union, or a partnership. [**Bellis v. United States**, 417 U.S. 85 (1974)]

b. Scope of Fifth Amendment Privilege

(1) Private Papers

The Fifth Amendment does not protect a witness's private papers or business records from disclosure even if the content of those documents is incriminating. [**United States v. Doe**, 465 U.S. 605 (1984)] However, the Fifth Amendment does apply to compelled production of the documents if the act of producing them would be incriminating. Thus production of papers might be, in effect, incriminating testimony that the papers actually existed or that they were in the witness's possession or were authentic. [**Fisher v. United States**, 425 U.S. 391 (1976)]

(2) Search Warrant

Private papers can be seized pursuant to the authority of a valid search warrant. The Fifth Amendment does not apply, since the person from whom the documents are seized has not been compelled to admit anything about the documents. [**Andresen v. Maryland**, 427 U.S. 463 (1976)]

(3) Required Records

The Fifth Amendment privilege does *not* extend to records that are *required to be kept*. [**Shapiro v. United States**, 335 U.S. 1 (1948)]

Example: In *Shapiro*, persons subject to maximum price regulations were required to preserve all records of sales and produce them for examination. The Court held that there was no Fifth Amendment protection as to records required to be kept by statute, as long as the records were relevant to an activity that Congress could regulate.

(a) Distinguish—Records of Criminal Activity

The potential scope of *Shapiro* has been *limited* in cases involving statutory requirements that persons engaged in criminal activity retain records that would prove their criminality. [**Marchetti v. United States**, 390 U.S. 39 (1968)]

Example: *Marchetti* involved a prosecution for failure to register and provide detailed information concerning payment of a gambling tax. The Court held that the statute required a gambler to incriminate himself.

c. Availability of Other Privileges

The ***attorney-client*** privilege is available. [**Fisher v. United States**, *supra*] The ***accountant-client*** privilege is not available. [**Couch v. United States**, *supra*] There is no privilege for accountant's work papers analogous to the attorney work product privilege. [**United States v. Arthur Young & Co.**, 465 U.S. 805 (1984)]

3. Rights to Procedural Due Process in Investigations

a. Notice and Hearing

The due process rights of notice and hearing—usually accorded in administrative adjudications (*see supra*, p. 36 *et seq.*)—are ***not*** available in investigatory hearings.

(1) Illustration

The United States Civil Rights Commission conducted hearings on voting irregularities in the South and was alleged to have violated due process by failing to give notice of the charges, failing to disclose the names of informants, and failing to allow cross-examination. The Supreme Court held that these procedural protections were *not* required because the hearings were merely "investigatory." [**Hannah v. Larche**, 363 U.S. 420 (1960)] *Note:* The fact that criminal prosecutions might follow the Commission's report was held not to make the hearings part of the criminal process.

EXAM TIP

Don't fall prey to an exam question that involves an investigatory hearing on a fundamental right. Remember that due process will *not* be triggered in an investigatory hearing *just because* a fundamental right is involved. For example, the Supreme Court held that due process procedural protections were not needed in hearings on voting irregularities conducted by the U.S. Civil Rights Commission because the hearings were merely "investigatory."

(2) Distinguish—Proceedings Accusatory in Nature

However, where the investigatory hearings appear to be part of a *prosecutorial process*, due process will be implicated. [**Jenkins v. McKeithen**, 395 U.S. 411 (1969)—agency that made specific findings of guilt had to comply with due process]

4. Right to Counsel

A witness required to appear before an investigatory hearing is entitled to the representation of counsel. APA section 555(b) provides: "A person compelled to appear in person before an agency or representative thereof is entitled to be accompanied, represented and advised by counsel or, if permitted by the agency, by other qualified representative."

5. Use of Information from Unlawful Searches

Even though evidence seized in an unlawful search is inadmissible in a criminal proceeding, it may be admitted in a federal administrative proceeding. [**United States v. Janis,** 428 U.S. 433 (1976)—evidence obtained pursuant to defective state search warrant admissible in federal civil tax proceeding; **INS v. Lopez-Mendoza,** 468 U.S. 1032 (1984)—civil deportation proceeding]

A four-justice plurality in *Lopez-Medoza* indicated that the exclusionary rule should apply in civil deportation proceedings to "egregious violations of Fourth Amendment or other liberties that might transgress notions of fundamental fairness and undermine the probative value of the evidence obtained." Four dissenting justices would have applied the exclusionary rule without insisting on an especially egregious violation. As that makes eight justices, a number of circuit courts have held that *Lopez-Mendoza* is subject to an "egregious violation" exception. [*See, e.g.*, **Gonzalez-Rivera v. INS,** 22 F.3d 1441 (9th Cir. 1994) (border patrol officer's stop of deportee based solely on his Hispanic appearance held to be an "egregious constitutional violation"; **Almeida-Ameral v. Gonzales**, 461 F.3d 231 (2nd Cir. 2006) (stating exclusion under *Lopez-Mendoza* appropriate in case of "egregious violation that was fundamentally unfair" or a violation that "undermined the reliability of the evidence in dispute")]

EXAM TIP

On an exam question covering use of information from unlawful searches, remember the general rule that evidence seized in an unlawful search **may be admitted in a federal administrative proceeding.** Consider the exception only if you encounter an especially "egregious" violation—such as the stop in *Gonzalez-Riviera* based on race.

C. Freedom of Information Act

1. In General

The Freedom of Information Act ("FOIA") is set forth at 5 U.S.C. § 552. The Act provides a comprehensive statement of the rights of *private parties* to obtain information in the possession of the government. Although its primary purpose is to provide information to the general public, the Act can also be useful as a method of discovery for those litigating against the government.

a. "Agencies" Covered

Under FOIA, the term "agency" covers "any executive department, military department, Government corporation, Government controlled corporation, or other establishment in the executive branch of the Government (including the Executive Office of the President), or any independent regulatory agency...." § 552(f)(1).

b. Entities Not Subject to the Act

(1) Entities Not in Executive Branch of the Federal Gov't

FOIA does not cover, inter alia, Congress, the courts, state governments, or municipal governments.

(2) The President

Notwithstanding FOIA's otherwise broad coverage of the executive branch, it does not require disclosure from the President nor from offices within the Executive Office of the President that function only to advise or assist the President rather than exercise independent authority. [**Kissinger v. Reporters Committee for Freedom of the Press**, 445 U.S. 136 (1980); **Citizens for Responsibility & Ethics in Washington v. Office of Administration**, 566 F.3d 219 (D.C. Cir. 2009)]

2. Three Levels of Disclosure—Publication, Inspection, Production on Request

a. Publication of Procedures and Rules

Section 552(a)(1) requires that each agency publish (in the Federal Register) a description of its organization, the party from whom the public can obtain information, a statement of its *procedures*, and its general *rules, policies,* and *interpretations.* A person cannot be bound or adversely affected by any matter that should have been published but was not, unless she has actual notice thereof.

> **Example:** This provision was applied to invalidate eligibility rules for Indian welfare payments, where the Bureau of Indian Affairs failed to publish the rules in the Federal Register. [**Morton v. Ruiz,** 415 U.S. 199 (1974)]

b. Records Available for Public Inspection

Section 552(a)(2) requires that each agency make available for public inspection and copying: its *opinions* in decided cases, its statements of *policy and interpretations* not published in the Federal Register, and any administrative staff manuals that affect the public. Generally, these documents are available in hard copy in agency "reading rooms," but those generated after 1996 must be available in electronic form and thus are posted on agency websites.

(1) Definition of Terms

(a) "Opinion" vs. "Memorandum"

A distinction must be drawn between "opinions," which are to be made available under section 552(a)(2), and predecisional "memoranda."

> **Example:** A communication from the FTC to its staff, explaining the effect of an agency order, is an "opinion." But memoranda from staff members to the Commissioners—and from individual Commissioners to staff—are predecisional "intra-agency memoranda." [**Sterling Drug, Inc. v. FTC**, 450 F.2d 698 (D.C. Cir. 1971)]

(b) "Interpretations"

Policy statements and interpretations of *general* applicability must be published in the Federal Register pursuant to § 552(a)(1). Section 552(a)(2)'s requirement that policy statements and interpretations be available for inspection thus refers to guidance documents of specific rather than general applicability, such as letters sent to individuals who requested guidance. Among other things, an "interpretation" includes a private ruling by the IRS (*e.g.*, in a letter advising as to tax consequences of a particular transaction). [**Tax Analysts & Advocates v. IRS**, 505 F.2d 350 (D.C. Cir. 1974)]

(2) Invasion of Privacy

Identifying details in all required publications can be deleted to prevent unwarranted invasions of privacy.

c. Agency Records to Be Produced on Request

Section 552(a)(3)(A) establishes a default rule that agencies must provide certain "records" on request—that is:

> ... [E]ach agency, upon any request for records which (i) reasonably describes such records and (ii) is made in accordance with published rules stating the time, place, fees (if any), and procedures to be followed, shall make the records promptly available to any person.

As detailed below, this duty to disclose is subject to numerous exemptions.

(1) FOIA on "Records"

FOIA itself does not offer a full definition of "record." It does, however, provide that the term "record" is not limited by format. [§ 552(f)(2)(A)]

(2) Definition of "Agency Records"

The Supreme Court has explained that "agency records" are records that: (a) an agency creates or obtains; and (b) are controlled by the agency at the time of the FOIA request." [**DOJ v. Tax Analysts**, 492 U.S. 136 (1989)]

(a) Factors Relating to "Agency Control"

Agency "control" over records depends on a four-factor inquiry:

(1) the intent of the document's creator to retain or relinquish control over the records;

(2) the ability of the agency to use and dispose of the record as it sees fit;

(3) the extent to which agency personnel have read or relied upon the document; and

(4) the degree to which the document was integrated into the agency's record system or files.

[**Consumer Fed'n of Am. v. Dep't of Agric.**, 455 F.3d 283 (D.C.Cir.2006)] The third and fourth of these factors are most important.

(b) No Obligation to Obtain Records Not in Agency Control

An agency only need disclose records that actually were *in its control* at the time they were requested. In general, an agency has no obligation to obtain records requested under FOIA if those records have escaped agency control by the time of the request. [**Kissinger v. Reporters Committee for Freedom of the Press**, 445 U.S. 136 (1980)]

(c) A Partial Exception for Records in Possession of Grantees

In **Forsham v. Harris**, the Supreme Court held that a private research organization does not become an "agency" creating "agency records" by virtue of using federal funding to generate information. [445 U.S. 169 (1980)]

In 1999, Congress partially overruled *Forsham* to make some data generated by private entities using federal funding available under FOIA. In response to a FOIA request, agencies must request and grant recipients must provide "research data relating to published research findings produced under an award that were used by the Federal Government in developing an agency action that has the force and effect of law." [Office of Management & Budget Circular A-110.36(d)(1)]

(d) "Agency Records" Need Not Be Stored by the Agency

Records can be under agency control even though they are not physically in agency custody. Under relatively recent amendments, FOIA specifically provides that "record" includes any information that would otherwise qualify for such status even though it is maintained not by an agency but by "an entity under Government contract, for the purposes of records management." [§ 552(f)(2)(B)]

(e) Storage Format Doesn't Matter

FOIA specifies that "record" includes "any information that would be an agency record ... when maintained by an agency in any format, including an electronic format." [§ 552(f)(2)(A)]

(f) Congressional Records Aren't Covered

Unlike agency records, "congressional records" are not covered by FOIA. A record may be in the possession of an agency but still be a "congressional record." This determination depends on whether Congress demonstrated a contemporaneous intention to retain control over the record in question. [*See, e.g.*, **Goland v. CIA**, 607 F.2d 339 (D.C. Cir. 1978) (Congress manifested intent to maintain control over hearing transcript in agency's custody by labeling it "secret")]

(g) Personal Records Aren't Covered

An agency official's "personal" records are not agency records. Factors bearing on this determination include: (1) the purpose for creating the document; (2) its integration into agency filing; and (3) its use to conduct agency business. [**Consumer Fed'n of Am. v. Dep't of Agric.**, 455 F.3d 283 (D.C.Cir.2006) (official's calendar that he relied on for personal use not an "agency record")]

(3) Procedures

The FOIA contains detailed procedures governing, among other things, timelines for responding to requests, expedited processing, search and duplication fees, waivers of fees, and intra-agency appeals. Here are just a few highlights:

(a) "[A]ny Person" Can Make a Request

In general, the right to obtain documents under FOIA does not relate to the identity of the requester. Subject to very limited exceptions, properly requested records are to be made available to "any person."

FOIA uses the APA's definition of "person," which includes "an individual, partnership, corporation, association, or public or private organization other than an agency." [5 U.S.C. § 551(2)] The definition of excluded "agencies" is somewhat complex, but basically includes federal executive and independent agencies. [5 U.S.C. § 551(1)] Thus, neither EPA nor the SEC, for example, can make a proper FOIA request.

(b) Reasonable Requests That Follow Regulations

An agency's duty to disclose is triggered by a FOIA request that "reasonably describes" the records sought and "is made in accordance with published rules stating the time, place, fees (if any) and procedures to be followed." [5 U.S.C. § 553(3)(A)(i), (ii)] A "reasonable description" should enable an agency employee to locate a record with "reasonable amount of effort." Courts reject overly broad "fishing expeditions." [*See* **USDOJ Guide to the FOIA** 47 (2009)]

(c) Agency Denials—Reasons and Right to Appeal

If an agency denies a FOIA request, it must inform the requester of the agency's reasons and the right to appeal within the agency. If this appeal fails, the agency must inform the requester of the right to seek judicial review. [§ 552(a)(6)(A)(i)–(ii)]

(d) The *Glomar* Response

Agencies sometimes refuse either to confirm or deny the existence of records where doing so would itself endanger national security. This is called the ***Glomar*** response. [**Phillippi v. CIA,** 546 F.2d 1009 (D.C. Cir. 1976)]

(e) De Novo Judicial Review

If an agency refuses to disclose, district courts have jurisdiction "to order the production of any agency records improperly withheld." [§ 552(a)(4)(B)]

(f) *Vaughn* Index

On judicial review of a denial of a FOIA request, the agency bears the burden of justifying withholding. Agencies typically discharge this burden by producing a *Vaughn* index that identifies withheld records and explains why one or more exemptions to disclosure are applicable. [**Vaughn v. Rosen**, 484 F.2d 820 (D.C. Cir. 1973), *cert. denied*, 415 U.S. 977 (1974)]

(g) In Camera Review

Courts have discretion to conduct *in camera* review to determine whether withholding is justified. [APA, § 552(a)(4)(B)] Such review is especially appropriate in sensitive national security cases.

(h) Attorney's Fees

A court "may assess against the United States reasonable attorney fees and other litigation costs reasonably incurred in any case under this section in which the complainant has substantially prevailed." [§ 552(a)(4)(E)(i)]

3. Exemptions to the Act

APA section 552(b) sets out nine exemptions to FOIA.

a. Exemption 1: National Security

FOIA exempts matters that are "(A) specifically authorized under criteria established by an Executive order to be kept secret in the interest of national defense or foreign policy and (B) are in fact properly classified pursuant to such Executive order." [§ 552(b)(1)]

b. Exemption 2: Internal Matters

FOIA exempts matters "related solely to the internal personnel rules and practices of an agency." [§ 552(b)(2)]

(1) Recent Narrowing

Until recently, Exemption 2 had a broad and complex reach with some material covered by a "High 2" exemption and some covered by a "Low 2" exemption. High 2 covered disclosure of agency internal procedures that might lead to circumvention of the law. Low 2 covered trivial internal matters of little broader interest. In **Milner v. Dept. of the Navy**, 131 S.Ct. 1259 (2011), the Supreme Court threw out this bifurcated scheme in favor of a "plain meaning" approach to Exemption 2, which covers "only records relating to issues of employee relations and human resources." Exemption 2 therefore did not apply to the Navy records at issue, which related to safe storage of munitions.

c. Exemption 3: Matters Exempted by Other Statutes

FOIA incorporates by reference other statutes that exempt records from disclosure. To qualify under Exemption 3, a statute must: (a) leave the agency with no discretion to disclose; or (b) specify "particular criteria for withholding or refer[ ] to particular matters to be withheld." Also, statutes enacted after 2009 must specifically cite to Exemption 3 itself to qualify for its coverage. [§ 552(b)(3)]

d. Exemption 4: Trade Secrets and Confidential/Financial Information

FOIA exempts "[1] trade secrets and [2] commercial or financial information obtained from a person and privileged or confidential." [§ 552(b)(4)]

(1) Trade Secrets

The D.C. Circuit has defined "trade secret" as "a secret, commercially valuable plan, formula, process, or device that is used for the making, preparing, compounding, or processing of trade commodities and that can be said to be the end product of either innovation or substantial effort." [**Public Citizen's Health Research Group v. FDA**, 704 F.2d 1280 (D.C. Cir. 1983)]

(2) Commercial or Financial Information

Courts have broadly construed "commercial" to include any matter in which an entity has a commercial interest. [**Public Citizens**, *supra*] "Financial" information is not limited to business related settings but can also include personal financial information.

(3) Confidential

Information is "confidential" where disclosure is likely: "(1) to impair the Government's ability to obtain necessary information in the future; or (2) to cause substantial harm to the competitive position of the person from whom the information was obtained." [**Nat'l Parks and Conservation Ass'n v. Morton**, 498 F.2d 765 (D.C. Cir. 1974)] These two prongs are sometimes called the "impairment prong" and the "competitive harm" prong.

Courts have also recognized that information may be treated as "confidential" in order to protect the government's interest in "administrative efficiency and effectiveness." [**Critical Mass Energy Project v. Nuclear Regulatory Commission**, 975 F.2d 871 (D.C. Cir. 1992) (en banc)]

(a) Information Voluntarily Shared with the Government

Courts follow the categorical rule that information that a party submits to the government voluntarily is "confidential" if it is "of a kind that would customarily not be released to the public by the person from whom it was obtained." [**Critical Mass,** *supra*] The idea behind this rule is that outsiders will be less likely to volunteer sensitive information to the government if it will be disclosed pursuant to a FOIA request.

(b) Compelled Information

The concern that release of information in response to a FOIA request will impair the flow of such information to the government has much less force as applied to information that outsiders have been compelled to disclose to the government. The idea here is that the force of legal compulsion will generally provide sufficient impetus for proper reporting.

The applicability of Exemption 4 to compelled information therefore generally turns on application of the "competitive harm" prong. This harm must flow from "affirmative use of proprietary information by competitors." [**Public Citizen Health Research Group v. FDA,** 704 F.2d 1280 (D.C. Cir. 1983)]

(4) Exemption 4 Doesn't Require Agencies to Keep Secrets, but the Trade Secrets Act Does

The Freedom of Information Act does not restrict the government from disclosing confidential information if it wishes to do so. In other words, it does not protect the company that submitted the material from disclosure by the agency. [**Chrysler Corp. v. Brown**, 441 U.S. 281 (1979)]

A different federal statute, the Trade Secrets Act ("TSA"), furnishes protection to submitters against disclosure of confidential information submitted to the government. [18 U.S.C. § 1905] Under the TSA, it is a crime for a government employee to disclose trade secrets and similar confidential statistical, financial, or technical material unless disclosure is "authorized by law." If an agency proposes to disclose material in violation of the TSA, the submitter of the material can obtain judicial review under the APA.

(a) Relation of TSA to Exemption 4

The scope of § 1905 is at least as broad as the FOIA exemption for trade and commercial secrets. Thus, if material falls within Exemption 4, and if no valid agency rule permits disclosure, the agency cannot disclose it voluntarily. [**CNA Financial Corp. v. Donovan,** 830 F.2d 1132 (D.C. Cir. 1987)]

e. Exemption 5: Inter- or Intra-Agency Memoranda

This exemption applies to "inter-agency or intra-agency memorandums or letters which would not be available by law to a party other than an agency in litigation with the agency." [§ 552(b)(5)]

(1) Criteria—Discovery Standards

In essence, if a document would be privileged from disclosure in civil litigation, then Exemption 5 protects it from disclosure in the FOIA context. [**NLRB v. Sears, Roebuck & Co.**, 421 U.S. 132 (1975)] Agencies commonly invoke the work product doctrine and attorney-client privilege familiar to you from Civil Procedure. They also commonly invoke the "deliberative process" privilege.

(2) Deliberative Process Privilege

The deliberative process privilege protects predecisional, deliberative memoranda (*i.e.,* those involving recommendations to decisionmakers to help them decide) from disclosure. The theory is that disclosure of such documents may inhibit frank discussion within the agency. However, post-decisional memoranda, meaning those that explain policy or decisions *already made*, do not ordinarily come within the exemption.

(a) Pre- and Post-Decisional Memoranda at NLRB

A person complaining of an unfair labor practice may appeal to the General Counsel of the NLRB if the regional director refuses to prosecute the charge. The General Counsel will recommend either that a complaint be issued or that the charge be terminated. This decision will be communicated to the regional director in an "appeal memorandum." Under the unusual procedures of the NLRB, the General Counsel's decision not to issue a complaint is final and not reviewable by the agency heads. The Supreme Court held that appeal memoranda that give the reasons for *refusing to issue a complaint*, and which thus end the case, are post-decisional memoranda that must be disclosed on request. In addition, they are "final opinions" and thus subject to routine disclosure under section 552(a)(2). But memoranda that recommend *issuance of a complaint* are "predecisional," and therefore protected by the exemption. [**NLRB v. Sears, Roebuck & Co.,** *supra*]

(b) Factual Material Not Exempt

The deliberative process privilege under section 552(b)(5) applies only to *policymaking* material, and does not protect *factual* statements per se. [**EPA v. Mink,** 410 U.S. 73 (1973)] Factual matters may be withheld, however, where disclosure would harm the deliberative process. [**Petroleum Information Corp. v. Department of Interior,** 976 F.2d 1429 (D.C. Cir. 1992)]

(3) Attorney Work-Product Privilege

There is an important distinction between how this privilege, applicable to work product prepared in anticipation of litigation, applies in civil litigation and how it applies in the FOIA context. The Supreme Court has held that Exemption 5 applies unless the work product at issue would be "routinely or normally disclosed on a showing of relevance." [**FTC v. Grolier,** 462 U.S. 19 (1983)] In civil litigation, factual work product enjoys only limited protection and can be obtained on a showing of sufficient need. In the FOIA context, however, such materials are subject to absolute protection under Exemption 5 because they are not routinely disclosed on a showing of relevance.

(4) Presidential Privilege

Exemption (5) of the FOIA also includes the presidential communications privilege. The presidential privilege covers communications to and from the President, as well as those to or from members of the White House staff who have significant responsibility for formulating advice to be given to the President. This privilege covers both predecisional and postdecisional communications, as well as factual materials. [See *In re* **Sealed Case,** 121 F.3d 729 (D.C. Cir. 1997) (presidential privilege applies to grand jury subpoena to White House staff members); **Judicial Watch, Inc. v. United States Department of Justice,** 365 F.3d 1108 (D.C. Cir. 2004) (presidential privilege does not extend to documents concerning pardon applications that are not solicited by or received by the President or his senior advisers).

f. Exemption 6: Invasion of Personal Privacy

Exemption 6 covers "personnel and medical files and similar files the disclosure of which would constitute a clearly unwarranted invasion of personal privacy." [§ 552(b)(6)]

(1) Personnel and Medical Files and Similar Files

Any information that "applies to a particular individual" satisfies this threshold requirement for Exemption 6 protection. [**United States Dept. of State v. Washington Post Co.,** 456 U.S. 595 (1982)]

(2) Privacy Interest

The concept of "privacy" under FOIA is broad. For instance, "[i]nformation such as place of birth, date of marriage, employment history, and comparable data" although not "normally regarded as highly personal," should be exempt from disclosure that would cause a "clearly unwarranted invasion of personal privacy." [**Id.**] Even information that has been publicly available may be subject to a privacy exemption if it has become "practicably obscure." [**United States Dept. of Justice v. Reporters Committee for Freedom of the**

Press, 489 U.S. 749 (1989) ("rap sheets" implicated privacy interest under Exemption 7(C))] To trigger a privacy protection, however, the privacy interest at stake must be "substantial" rather than "de minimis." [**Multi Ag Media LLC v. USDA,** 515 F.3d 1224 (D.C. Cir. 2008)]

(3) Balancing Private and Public Interest

If disclosure implicates a substantial privacy interest, then harm to that privacy interest must be balanced against the public interest in disclosure. This public interest must relate to FOIA's purpose, which is to further transparency and accountability through disclosure of information regarding agencies' performance of their statutory duties. [**Reporters Committee,** *supra*] The interest in disclosure of high level official misconduct is therefore especially strong. The requester's personal reasons for seeking disclosure have no bearing on assessment of the public interest. [**Id.**]

(4) Illustration

A union requested the home addresses of federal government employees so it could contact them. The public's interest in this information was "virtually non-existent" as disclosure would not inform citizens "about what their government is up to." By contrast, the privacy interest of the employees was "not insubstantial," even though their home addresses might be publicly available in phone books and the like. Therefore, the information was exempted from disclosure under FOIA. [**United States Department of Defense v. Federal Labor Relations Authority,** 510 U.S. 487 (1994)]

g. Exemption 7: Law Enforcement Records

This exemption is a bit of a mouthful. It covers "records or information compiled for law enforcement purposes, but only to the extent that the production of such law enforcement records or information"

(A) could reasonably be expected to interfere with enforcement proceedings,

(B) would deprive a person of a right to a fair trial or an impartial adjudication,

(C) could reasonably be expected to constitute an unwarranted invasion of personal privacy,

(D) could reasonably be expected to disclose the identity of a confidential source, . . . and, in the case of a record or information compiled by criminal law enforcement authority in the course of a criminal investigation or by an agency conducting a lawful national security intelligence investigation, information furnished by a confidential source,

(E) would disclose techniques and procedures for law enforcement investigations or prosecutions, or would disclose guidelines for law enforcement investigations or prosecutions if such disclosure could reasonably be expected to risk circumvention of the law, or

(F) could reasonably be expected to endanger the life or physical safety of any individual . . . [§ 552(b)(7)]

(1) Exemption 7(C)'s Protection of Privacy

This exemption for personal privacy in law enforcement documents offers somewhat stronger protection than the protection that Exemption 6 extends to "personnel and medical files." Exemption 6 requires a showing that the disclosure would constitute a "*clearly unwarranted* invasion of personal privacy." Exemption 7(C) requires only a showing that disclosure "*could reasonably be expected* to constitute an unwarranted invasion of personal privacy."

(a) Illustration of Exemption 7(C)

Death scene photographs of Vincent Foster, a Clinton aide, were "compiled for law enforcement purposes." Family members of Foster had a cognizable privacy right in controlling their distribution in light of common law and cultural traditions. To overcome this privacy interest, it is not enough for a requester to assert a public interest in revealing negligent or improper conduct. Rather, the requester "must produce evidence that would warrant a belief by a reasonable person that the alleged Government impropriety might have occurred." The requester did not satisfy this standard, and Exemption 7(C) therefore applied. [**National Archives and Records Administration v. Favish**, 541 U.S. 157 (2004)]

EXAM TIP

For your exam, be sure to remember that there are essentially two personal privacy exemptions for FOIA requests with different exemption standards. One exemption is for *personnel records and the like*, which is triggered by a *"clearly unwarranted"* invasion of privacy. However, law enforcement records containing private information are less likely to be released—the exemption standard for such records is a *reasonable expectation* that the records constitute an unwarranted invasion of personal privacy.

h. Exemption 8: Bank Regulations

Exemption 8 covers matters that are "contained in or related to examination, operating, or condition reports prepared by, on behalf of, or for the use of an agency responsible for the regulation or supervision of financial institutions." [§ 552(b)(8)]

i. Exemption 9: Natural Resources

And finally, Exemption 9 covers "geological and geophysical information and data, including maps, concerning wells." [§ 552(b)(9)]

SUMMARY OF EXEMPTIONS UNDER THE FREEDOM OF INFORMATION ACT

EXEMPTION	EXTENT OF EXEMPTION
NATIONAL SECURITY MATTERS	*Blanket exemption*, but a court may *inspect material in camera* to ensure it was categorized properly
INTERNAL POLICY RULES AND PRACTICES	Meant to make *relatively trivial* agency rules exempt from disclosure.

EXEMPTIONS IN OTHER STATUTES	Statute must either *require that all material be withheld* or must *particularly spell out* criteria for withholding
COMMERCIAL TRADE SECRETS	Exemption for secret, commercially valuable *production processes*
COMMERCIAL OR FINANCIAL INFORMATION THAT IS PRIVILEGED OR CONFIDENTIAL	If material is *voluntarily* provided to the government, it is "confidential" if such material is *not ordinarily released* to the public. If the government *compelled* the disclosure, it is "confidential" if disclosure would *cause substantial harm* to the competitive position of the submitter
CERTAIN INTER- AND INTRA-AGENCY MEMORANDA	1) Material that *would not be available "by law"* (*i.e.*, that ordinarily would not be discoverable in civil litigation) *need not be disclosed* 2) *Predecisional* memoranda need not be disclosed; *factual* statements are not protected
PRESIDENTIAL PRIVILEGE	Covers *both* pre- and postdecision material, *and* factual statements. Privilege may give way in a *criminal proceeding*
PERSONAL PRIVACY	Personnel, medical, and similar files are exempted if disclosure would constitute a *clearly unwarranted invasion of personal privacy.* The general public's need for disclosure is balanced against the privacy interest
LAW ENFORCEMENT	1) Exempt if disclosure would generally *interfere with current or future investigations* 2) *Privacy exemption:* Law enforcement records are exempt if disclosure *could reasonably be expected to constitute an unwarranted invasion of personal privacy*
BANK REGULATIONS	*Examination, operating or condition reports* used or prepared by regulating agencies are exempt
NATURAL RESOURCES	*Geological and geophysical information* is exempt

4. Exclusions—Which Are Very Different from Exemptions

Section 552(b) provides that certain categories of records, though subject to FOIA, are *exempt* from disclosure. When claiming immunity from disclosure under an exemption, agencies generally acknowledge withholding documents and explain why. [*supra,* p. 132] Sometimes an agency will deploy the *Glomar* response, refusing to admit or deny the existence of responsive records. [*supra,* p. 132]

By contrast, § 552(c) provides that an agency may treat certain especially sensitive law enforcement records as "not subject to the requirements" of FOIA. These *exclusions* relate, inter alia, to records that might harm ongoing investigations, reveal information about informants, or relate to foreign intelligence or international terrorism. [§ 552(c)(1)–(3)] Where requested records falls into an exclusion, an agency may respond to a request that no records subject to FOIA exist.

D. Government in the Sunshine Act

1. General Rule

The Government in the Sunshine Act requires that, generally, agencies hold their meetings *open to the public.* [5 U.S.C. § 552b]

a. Definition of Agency

An agency for this purpose means one headed by a collegial body of two or more members and any subdivision thereof authorized to act on behalf of the agency. [§ 552b(a)(1)]

b. Definition of Meeting

A meeting for this purpose is defined as the deliberations of agency members that determine or result in the conduct or disposition of official agency business. [§ 552b(a)(2)]

c. Consultations

The Sunshine Act does not apply to an informal international conference between a committee of FCC members and counterpart European agencies. The conference concerned only an exchange of views about licensing issues, not a decision on discrete proposals on which an agency subdivision might act. [**FCC v. ITT World Communications,** 466 U.S. 463 (1984)]

2. Exceptions

The Sunshine Act sets forth many exceptions to the open meeting rule. Many of them parallel exemptions to the Freedom of Information Act. [*See supra*, p. 133 *et seq.*] In general, where the agency can refuse to disclose documents under the Freedom of Information Act, it can close meetings to prevent disclosure of similar information. [*See* § 552b(c)(1)–(10)] Examples of exceptions to open meeting requirements include meetings likely

   (i) To involve accusing any person of a crime or formally censuring any person;

   (ii) To disclose information prematurely that would significantly frustrate implementation of a proposed agency action; or

   (iii) To concern the agency's issuance of a subpoena or its participation in civil litigation or the initiation, conduct, or disposition of any formal agency adjudication.

[APA § 552b(c)(5), (9)(B), (10)]

E. Attorney's Fees

1. General Rule

The general rule in American law is that all parties bear their own attorney's fees. [*See* **Alyeska Pipeline Service Co. v. Wilderness Society**, 421 U.S. 240 (1975)]

2. Specific Statutory Provisions

Nevertheless, many specific provisions of federal law provide for the award of attorney's fees to private parties. For example, the Freedom of Information Act provides for such awards [*supra*, p. 133], and so do various environmental and civil rights provisions [*e.g.*, 42 U.S.C. § 1988].

a. Prevailing Parties

These fee-shifting statutes often provide for an award of attorney's fees to "prevailing parties." Generally, a prevailing party is one who has secured judicial relief by prevailing on the merits of at least some of its claims through a judgment or a consent decree. [**Buckhannon Board & Care Home, Inc. v. West Virginia Department of Health and Human Resources,** 532 U.S. 598 (2001)]

(1) Voluntary Change Will Not Warrant Fee Award

However, a party is *not* entitled to a fee award simply because its lawsuit brought about the desired effect through a *voluntary change* in the defendant's conduct. For example, in **Buckhannon Board & Care Home**, *supra*, the plaintiff filed suit hoping to invalidate a state statute as preempted by federal law. As a result of the lawsuit, the state legislature changed the statute and the defendant moved to dismiss the lawsuit as moot. Although the plaintiff's lawsuit was the "catalyst" for the legislative action, the plaintiff was not a "prevailing party" because the change did not come about as the result of a judicial judgment or consent decree.

(2) The FOIA Exception to *Buckhannon*

The *Buckhannon* test creates the danger that the government will avoid payment of attorney's fees by "voluntarily" changing its position just before an anticipated loss on the merits. The Open Government Act of 2007, Pub.L. No. 110–175, 121 Stat. 2524, eliminated this problem in the context of FOIA claims. A FOIA complainant who has "substantially prevailed" is eligible for reasonable attorney's fees. A complainant may substantially prevail by obtaining relief by "a voluntary or unilateral change in position by the agency, if the complainant's claim is not insubstantial." [5 U.S.C. § 552(a)(4)(E)(ii)(II)] In other words, Congress has reinstated the "catalyst" theory of attorney's fees for FOIA.

b. Awarding Fees "If Appropriate"

Some statutes call for awarding attorney's fees "if appropriate." The Supreme Court has stated that this standard requires a claimant to show "some degree of success on the merits," which must be more than a "trivial success" or a "purely procedural victor[y]." [**Ruckelshaus v. Sierra Club**, 463 U.S. 680 (1983); *cf.* **Hardt v. Reliance Standard Life Ins. Co.,** 560 U.S. 242 (2010) (applying *Ruckelshaus* approach to ERISA claim involving denial of disability insurance benefits; concluding that petitioner had achieved sufficient success on the merits to be eligible for fee award where district court stated it was inclined to rule in petitioner's favor but nonetheless remanded to insurance carrier for reconsideration of benefit claim, which insurer then granted)]

3. General Authorization—Equal Access to Justice Act

Under the Equal Access to Justice Act ("EAJA"), an agency shall award attorney's and expert's fees to a "prevailing party" in a formal adjudication where the United States was represented by counsel unless the agency's position was "substantially justified" or special circumstances make an award unjust. [5 U.S.C. § 504] In addition, a court shall award fees against the government under the same standard in any civil action (excluding actions sounding in tort, but including judicial review of agency action) brought by or against the United States. [28 U.S.C. § 2412(d)] Under both sections 504 and 2412(d), the agency has the burden to show that its conduct was "substantially justified." To sustain its burden of substantial justification, the agency must establish that its position was justified to a degree that could satisfy a reasonable person and had a reasonable basis in both law and fact. [**Pierce v. Underwood,** 487 U.S. 552 (1988)]

4. Amount

Where a statute calls for the award of fees, the court should set the attorney's fees by multiplying the hours spent on the matter (if reasonable) by a reasonable hourly rate. This product is called the "lodestar" and is presumed to be a reasonable fee.

a. Setting the Rate

The hourly rate is based on rates charged in the market by comparably qualified attorneys for comparable services—not the amount charged to the client (if anything). [**Blum v. Stenson,** 465 U.S. 886 (1984)] The fee can vastly exceed the amount of damages recovered by the client. [**City of Riverside v. Rivera,** 477 U.S. 561 (1986) (rejecting "the proposition that fee awards . . . should necessarily be proportionate to the amount of damages")]

b. Adjustment of Lodestar

Although the "lodestar" can be adjusted upward or downward in unusual cases, it should not ordinarily be adjusted for such factors as exceptional success, novelty, or complexity of the claim. No upward adjustment is permitted merely because the plaintiff's attorney is working on a contingency fee basis and would get nothing if the case were lost. [**City of Burlington v. Dague,** 502 U.S. 1071 (1992)]

Chapter Seven
Scope of Judicial Review

CONTENTS	PAGE
Key Exam Issues	144
A. Introduction	145
B. Scope of Review of Questions of Fact	146
C. Scope of Review of Legal Interpretations	150
D. Scope of Review of Application of Law to Fact (a/k/a "Mixed Questions")	160
E. Scope of Review of Exercises of Discretion	162

Key Exam Issues

Exam questions involving judicial review usually require an analysis of the scope of review—the degree to which a court has power to substitute its judgment for that of the agency. To analyze this issue, it is necessary to analyze precisely what sort of agency determination is challenged on review.

1. **Fact**

    In administrative law, findings of "fact" are typically reviewed either under the *substantial evidence* test or under the *arbitrary and capricious* test. There is a longstanding debate as to whether the former is a bit stricter than the latter. Both are, however, supposed to be very deferential, requiring a court *affirm if the finding was reasonable*, even if the court disagrees with it. Note, however, that where an agency adopts a finding on a credibility issue that contradicts the finding of the ALJ who heard the case below, this disagreement detracts from the substantiality of evidence in support of the agency's decision.

2. **Conclusions of Law**

    The body of law governing scope of review for agency conclusions of law is regrettably complex, but a simple idea underlies it: Notwithstanding *Marbury*, courts should, under some circumstances, defer to an agency's reasonable construction of a law that the agency is in charge of administering.

    - Judicial review of an agency's construction of *a statute it administers*:

        o Either of two standards of review can apply to an agency's construction of a statute it administers. Simplifying, ***Chevron* deference** requires a court to defer to an agency's reasonable construction of a statute it administers. A weaker form of deference, ***Skidmore* deference (or *Skidmore* respect)**, requires a court to consider the agency's construction and accept it insofar as the court finds it persuasive.

        o The framework for choosing between these two standards is unsettled. According to the ***Mead* doctrine**, *Chevron* deference applies where: (a) Congress delegated to the agency the power to give its statutory construction the force of law; and (b) the agency applied this power to the statutory construction under review. Otherwise, apply *Skidmore*.

    - Judicial review of an agency's construction of *its own regulation*. Subject to some limitations discussed below, courts should defer to an agency's reasonable construction of its own regulation. This doctrine is called ***Auer* deference** or sometimes by an older name, ***Seminole Rock* deference.**

3. **Application of Law to Fact**

    Courts sometimes distinguish between issues of "basic" or "evidentiary" fact and legally significant inferences drawn from these facts. Suppose, for instance, that a plaintiff brings a negligence case based on the claim that he slipped on a banana peel dropped by the defendant. The jury would need to determine the basic fact of whether the defendant dropped the banana peel. If the jury determines the defendant did drop the banana peel, then the jury will need to press on to determine whether this action, along with any other pertinent facts, added up to "negligence."

    Sometimes, courts characterize this latter type of derivative finding as one of fact. Older cases refer to findings of "ultimate fact" or "material fact." In administrative law, such a characterization triggers application of one of the deferential standards of review of fact discussed above.

    In other cases, courts characterize these derivative findings as "mixed questions of law and fact" or as "applications of law to fact." Functionally, this shift in characterization has little real effect on scope of review. At least in contexts where Congress has granted formal adjudicative authority to an agency, the general rule is that the court **must accept the agency's reasonable application** of a broad legal term to the basic facts. For example, if the issue is whether, under specific facts, A was an "employee" of B, the court should accept the agency's reasonable application of the term "employee."

Courts are not always consistent in applying this principle. If, for instance, an application question does not depend on agency expertise, or if the facts are not complex or disputed, an aggressive court might well substitute its judgment for that of the agency.

4. **Exercise of Discretion**

Under the arbitrary-capricious test, courts determine whether the agency considered the *relevant factors* in exercising policy discretion and avoided any *clear error in judgment*. *Relevant factors* are those that Congress wanted the agency to consider as it exercised its discretion to make policy.

A. Introduction

1. Scope of Review—In General

A critical issue in determining the relationship between the judiciary and administrative agencies is the extent of a court's power to substitute its judgment for that of the agency. This issue is referred to as the *"scope"* of judicial review. Sometimes it is called the *"standard"* of judicial review. The scope of review must be determined every time a party seeks judicial review of an agency decision. The scope of review will vary, depending on whether the challenged agency decision is a question of *fact*, a question of *law*, a question of *application of law to facts*, or a question of *discretion.*

2. The APA's Scope-of-Review Provision, § 706(2)

For cases brought under the APA, 5 U.S.C. § 706(2) provides a default template for determining the scope of review. Courts are "to hold unlawful and set aside agency action, findings, and conclusions" that they determine are:

- Arbitrary, § 706(2)(A);
- Contrary to law, § 706(2)(B)–(D);
- Unsupported by "substantial evidence" in record proceedings (*e.g.*, "formal" proceedings under §§ 556–57);
- Unwarranted by the facts "to the extent that the facts are subject to trial de novo by the reviewing court," § 706(2)(F).

Applying these instructions to our categories of fact, law, and policy gives us the following:

- Facts.
    - Apply the "substantial evidence" standard where record proceedings are required by statute. § 706(2)(E).
    - Agencies need to determine facts for informal proceedings, too—*e.g.*, there have to be facts undergirding a legislative rule promulgated via notice-and-comment. Apply § 706's default standard of "arbitrariness" review to these factual determinations. § 706(2)(A).
    - You can pretty much ignore de novo review under § 706(2)(F)—courts have come close to writing it out of the law.
- Law. The APA tells the courts to set aside agency actions contrary to law. Note, however, that such review is frequently deferential under doctrines like ***Chevron*** and ***Auer*** deference.

- Policy discretion. Section 706(2)(A) tells courts to set aside agency actions that are "arbitrary, capricious, [or] an abuse of discretion." None of the more specific instructions in § 706(2) apply to displace this default approach. Therefore, policy determinations are subject to arbitrariness review.

3. Other Statutory Instructions

Congress sometimes trumps the APA's default instructions on scope of review, especially on issues of fact. For instance, Congress has sometimes instructed agencies to use notice-and-comment procedures to promulgate rules but also instructed courts to apply *substantial evidence* review to the facts underlying these rules. Under the APA's default standard, we would expect *arbitrariness* review to apply, as just discussed.

B. Scope of Review of Questions of Fact

1. Deferential Review by Various Names

In general, judicial review of agency findings of fact is supposed to be quite deferential—a form of rationality review. This makes sense insofar as: (a) Congress has put agencies in charge of determining facts; and (b) agencies are supposed to have greater subject-specific expertise than courts.

a. "Substantial Evidence"

The ***general rule*** is that a court will not set aside an agency finding that is supported by "*substantial evidence,*" meaning that the court must uphold reasonable findings even if the court disagrees with them. The substantial evidence standard is similar to the scope of appellate review of a *jury* determination, and is discussed in more detail below. [**Universal Camera Corp. v. NLRB,** 340 U.S. 474 (1951)]

b. "Arbitrary and Capricious"

As explained *supra* at p. 145, the arbitrariness standard of review applies in APA cases to findings of fact in non-record proceedings. More specifically, this means that arbitrariness review commonly applies to the factual underpinnings of informal rulemakings and informal adjudications. For further discussion of judicial review of the facts underlying rules, *see infra,* pp. 166–166.

(1) Distinction with a Difference?

Many courts take the view that *substantial evidence* review is a bit less deferential than *arbitrariness* review. [*See, e.g.,* **In re Gartside,** 203 F.3d 1305 (Fed. Cir. 2000); *cf. generally* **Universal Camera Corp. v. NLRB,** 340 U.S. 474 (1951) (explaining that Congress had expressed a "mood" in the APA to toughen the courts' application of substantial evidence review)]

Justice Scalia has long thought that this stance is nonsense—after all, substantial evidence review already requires a court to affirm any reasonable conclusion of fact. To be more deferential, arbitrariness review would require courts to affirm some *unreasonable* conclusions of fact—which doesn't make much sense. [**Assoc. of Data Processing Service Org., Inc. v. Bd. of Governors of the Federal Reserve System,** 745 F.2d 677 (D.C. Cir. 1984)]

c. "Clearly Erroneous"

Under the 1961 Model State APA and in many states, a court is empowered to set aside an agency finding of fact if it is "clearly erroneous." Here, an appellate court can reverse if it is *firmly convinced* that the agency's findings of fact were wrong. This is the standard generally used in the federal courts for appellate review of a trial judge's factual determinations. The "clearly erroneous" standard arguably gives the court more power to overturn agency fact-findings than does the substantial evidence test.

d. "Preponderance of the Evidence"

In rare cases, a court is required to reevaluate the evidence and decide which side preponderates. In California, for example, courts exercise independent judgment on the evidence if a vested, fundamental right is involved. [Cal. Civ. Proc. Code § 1094.5; **Frink v. Prod,** 31 Cal. 3d 166 (1982)]

e. Variations in Standards Maybe Not So Significant in Practice

In practice, the variations in these standards of review may not be terribly significant. If a court is convinced that an agency finding of fact is wrong, it will usually reverse no matter what standard it purports to apply. This does not stop litigants from arguing over the applicable standard of review, however. And you should be prepared to do so on your administrative law exam.

2. More About "Substantial Evidence"

As mentioned above, the substantial evidence test is the *prevailing test* in both federal and state administrative law, and may be applied where the statute is not clear as to the proper scope of judicial review. For example, the Supreme Court read a statute that required affirmance of findings "if supported by evidence" as requiring application of the "substantial evidence" standard. [**Universal Camera Corp. v. NLRB,** 340 U.S. 474 (1951)]

a. APA Provision

Under the APA, in cases where record proceedings are required by statute, a reviewing court must set aside agency fact determinations that the court determines are "unsupported by substantial evidence" on the "whole record." [APA § 706(2)(E)]

(1) "Substantial Evidence" as Rationality Review

Substantial evidence means relevant evidence that "a reasonable mind might accept as adequate to support a conclusion." [**Consolidated Edison Co. v. NLRB,** 305 U.S. 197 (1938)] Even if the court disagrees with the agency's findings, it *must affirm* them if they are *reasonable.*

(2) "Whole Record"

The phrase "whole record" means that the court must look at *both sides* of the record. It is not sufficient to merely look at the evidence that supports the agency's conclusion. [**Universal Camera Corp. v. NLRB,** 340 U.S. 474 (1951)] *Universal Camera* involved review of an agency's determination of credibility in a case decided by the National Labor Relations Board. The Court found that Congress had expressed a "mood" in the APA favoring *stricter* review of agency determinations of fact, especially in labor cases, than some lower courts had previously exercised.

(3) Inferences of Fact

The substantial evidence test also applies to *factual inferences* drawn from basic or evidentiary facts. For example, an agency might infer a person's motives from her conduct. A court should uphold this inferential finding of fact so long as it is reasonable. [**Radio Officers' Union v. NLRB,** 347 U.S. 17 (1954); **Universal Camera Corp. v. NLRB,** 190 F.2d 429 (2nd Cir. 1951) (Judge Frank's concurring opinion on remand) (discussing application of substantial evidence review to "secondary inferences" or "derivative inferences")]

b. Disagreement Between Agency and ALJ on Credibility

Here comes one of the classic chestnuts of administrative law:

How should courts address disagreement between an agency and an ALJ on a finding of fact? It is usually the ALJ's job to hear the evidence; the agency bases its decision on review of a record compiled below. You might think that the law would acknowledge this point by requiring agency heads to show deference to an ALJ's findings of fact—at least where those findings hinge on credibility determinations based on witness demeanor. The APA, however, provides that agencies have de novo control over ALJ initial decisions. [**APA § 557(b)**] Moreover, a reviewing court checks whether substantial evidence supported the *agency*'s finding—not whether substantial evidence supported the finding of the ALJ assisting the agency. These points suggest that courts should ignore contradictions between agencies, which are in charge, and ALJs, who are not.

Courts nonetheless give at least some weight to ALJ *credibility* determinations that have been overturned by agencies. The key here is to recognize, as the Supreme Court did, that an ALJ's disagreement with an agency's credibility determination *detracts from the substantiality* of the evidence supporting the agency finding. [**Universal Camera Corp. v. NLRB,** *supra*] How much does such conflict detract from the substantiality of the evidence? The ALJ's report should be given the weight it deserves "in reason and in the light of judicial experience." [*Id.*]

(1) The Classic Illustration—*Universal Camera*

In *Universal Camera*, an employee challenged his dismissal, alleging that he had been fired for testifying at an earlier NLRB proceeding, and not for reasons of discipline (as alleged by the employer). The ALJ believed the employer's witnesses, but the Board believed the employee and reversed, finding that the discharge was an unfair labor practice. The Supreme Court held that on issues of *credibility*, the ALJ's decision was part of the record and entitled to be considered by the reviewing court, along with other material in the record, in deciding whether substantial evidence supported the Board's decision.

(2) Findings Based on a Mix of Demeanor and Other Evidence

Often, an agency finding of fact will rest on a mix of evidence that does not implicate credibility (*e.g.*, undisputed evidence) and evidence that does implicate credibility. In such mixed cases, if the agency rejects the ALJ's credibility determination, the court will engage in fairly critical review. [**Penasquitos Village, Inc. v. NLRB,** 565 F.2d 1074 (9th Cir. 1977)]

Example: In *Penasquitos*, the issue was whether employees were discharged for union activity or for loafing on the job. Significant circumstantial evidence suggested the employees were discharged because of union activity, but the ALJ believed the employer's testimony that they were discharged for loafing. The NLRB agency heads disagreed and held the employees were discharged because of union activity. In large part because credibility played an important role in the case, the court determined that the NLRB's findings were not supported by substantial evidence.

(3) Reminder: Limited Scope of the *Universal Camera* Principle

The theory behind giving weight to an ALJ's fact finding is that the ALJ was able to hear and see the witnesses. Where the ALJ's findings do not turn on credibility—*e.g.*, inferences drawn from undisputed testimony, or matters involving the agency's expertise—this theory does not apply. Thus, where credibility is not at issue, a disagreement between agency and ALJ will not detract from the substantiality of the evidence supporting the agency.

(4) Duty to Explain Disagreement on Credibility

Courts expect an agency that disagrees with an ALJ's credibility determination to explain why. [**Aylett v. Secretary of Housing and Urban Development,** 54 F.3d 1560 (10th Cir. 1995) (where agency disagrees "with the ALJ's assessment of witness credibility," the agency should "fully articulate reasons for so doing, and then, with heightened scrutiny, we must decide whether such reasons find support in the record")]

c. General Duty to Explain Disagreement with ALJ

Even for issues that do not turn on credibility, an agency *should not totally ignore* the findings and conclusions of the administrative law judge. [**Cinderella Career & Finishing Schools, Inc. v. FTC,** 425 F.2d 583 (D.C. Cir. 1970)]

Example: In the *Cinderella* case, the ALJ found that certain advertisements were not misleading, after hearing detailed testimony from consumers. The FTC nevertheless held that the ads *were* misleading, ignoring the testimony relied upon by the ALJ. The court held that the agency was not free to disregard without an explanation the evidence taken and findings made by the ALJ—*even though the issues did not turn on credibility*.

3. Constitutional Facts

For many years, courts exercised stricter review where agency findings of fact affected a claimant's constitutional rights. [**Ohio Valley Water Co. v. Ben Avon Borough,** 253 U.S. 287 (1920); **Crowell v. Benson,** 285 U.S. 22 (1932)]

a. "*Ben Avon* Rule"

In 1920, the Supreme Court declared that a reviewing court must exercise *independent judgment* with respect to agency findings of "constitutional facts" in ratemaking cases. [**Ohio Valley Water Co. v. Ben Avon Borough,** 253 U.S. 287 (1920)] The "constitutional fact" in question was the valuation of a utility's property, which was the key to determining whether the rates set by an agency were reasonable.

b. Its Demise

For the most part, courts no longer follow *Ben Avon*'s approach. Independent judgment of constitutional facts persists only in a few contexts. [*See, e.g.*, **Bose Corp. v. Consumers Union,** 466 U.S. 485 (1984) (requiring independent review of finding of "actual malice" in defamation case due to First Amendment implications); **Ng Fung Ho v. White,** 259 U.S. 276 (1922) (independent review of citizenship in deportation case)]

4. Jurisdictional Facts

Similarly, courts for many years assumed a broader scope of review where the "facts" found by the agency were essential to its jurisdiction. [**Crowell v. Benson,** 285 U.S. 22 (1932)] *Crowell* involved a federal workers' compensation case and required the court to review an agency's findings regarding whether an employee was injured within the course of employment and whether the injury occurred in navigable waters. The Court exercised independent review over these "jurisdictional" facts. *Note: Crowell* is not followed today, but it has never been squarely overruled.

C. Scope of Review of Legal Interpretations

1. Agency Interpretations of Law and Judicial Deference Doctrines

Agencies frequently interpret the meaning of statutes, their own regulations, or other sources of law. The traditional view was that a court could, in good *Marbury* fashion, substitute its own legal interpretation for that of an agency. Several doctrines purport to constrain this judicial power in modern administrative law. They include, notably:

- *Chevron* **deference,** which, where it applies, instructs courts to affirm an agency's reasonable construction of a statute it administers. [**Chevron, USA v. Natural Resources Defense Council,** 467 U.S. 837 (1984)]

- *Skidmore* **deference (a/k/a** *Skidmore* **"respect"),** which, where it applies, instructs a court to pay due attention to an agency's construction of a statute it administers and to affirm if the court finds the agency's construction to be persuasive.

- *Auer* **deference (a/k/a** *Seminole Rock* **deference),** which instructs courts to affirm an agency's reasonable construction of its own regulation.

2. *Chevron*'s Strong Deference

a. Overview of *Chevron*'s Two (or Three) Steps

Chevron requires a court to affirm an agency's reasonable construction of a statute that the agency has been charged with administering. Thus, *Chevron* might apply to EPA's construction of the Clean Air Act, but not to EPA's construction of, say, the National Labor Relations Act.

It is common to speak of the "*Chevron* two-step." Step 1 inquires whether Congress has spoken directly to the precise issue of statutory construction in play. If Congress has done so, then courts (and agencies) should give effect to congressional intent. If Congress has not done so, then *Chevron* contemplates that agencies, rather than courts, should exercise primary control over the gap-filling function of resolving statutory ambiguity. Courts should therefore affirm an agency construction at step 2 so long as it is "permissible" or reasonable. [**Chevron, USA v. Natural Resources Defense Council,** 467 U.S. 837 (1984)]

As mentioned on p. 150, administrative law supplies not one but two deference doctrines potentially applicable to an agency's construction of a statute it administers—*Chevron* deference and *Skidmore* deference. The problem of choosing which to apply is sometimes called *Chevron* step 0.

Proceeding out of numerical order, we will first examine steps 1 and 2 §more detail, and then turn to step 0 and other issues relating to the scope of "*Chevron*'s domain."

b. **Very Short Summary of Facts of *Chevron***

In *Chevron*, EPA adopted a legislative rule that construed the statutory phrase "stationary source" for purposes of the permitting regime of the Clean Air Act Amendments of 1977. Under the EPA's interpretation, a "stationary source" could be an entire factory, not a particular polluting source in the plant. Under this "bubble approach," a manufacturer could, without permitting, install a new source of pollution in the plant if it removed another source of equal or greater pollution.

The D.C. Circuit held that the bubble approach was improper under the statute. The Supreme Court reversed, holding that "stationary source" was ambiguous. Congress had implicitly delegated to the EPA the power to construe the meaning of this phrase. The reviewing court should affirm the agency's construction so long as it was reasonable—a test that the EPA's construction of "stationary source" satisfied.

c. ***Chevron* Step One—Did Congress Speak Directly to the Precise Issue?**

At step one, a court checks whether Congress has clearly expressed its intent on the relevant question:

> First, always, is the question whether Congress *has directly spoken to the precise question at issue.* If the intent of Congress is clear, that is the end of the matter, for the court, as well as the agency, must give effect to the unambiguously expressed intent of Congress.

[**Chevron, USA v. Natural Resources Defense Council,** 467 U.S. 837 (1984)]

(1) Criteria for Identifying Clear Intent

In determining whether Congress has expressed a clear intent, a court should employ all "traditional tools of statutory construction." [**Chevron, USA v. Natural Resources Defense Council,** 467 U.S. 837 (1984)] For example:

- Courts examine dictionary definitions of disputed language. [*See, e.g.*, **MCI Telecommunications Corp. v. American Telephone & Telegraph Co.,** 512 U.S. 218 (1994) (extensive use of dictionaries to establish that the term "modify" means to change moderately or in minor fashion)]

- Courts sometimes use traditional "canons of construction." [*See, e.g.*, **INS v. St. Cyr,** 533 U.S. 289 (2001) (applying canon against retroactivity to determine that statute was unambiguously prospective, thus leaving, "for *Chevron* purposes, no ambiguity for an agency to resolve")]

- Courts examine related provisions of the statute in order to place the disputed provision in context and achieve a harmonious construction of the statute.

- Many judges examine a provision's legislative history to determine whether its meaning is clear. (Warning: Don't try this with Justice Scalia!) Legislative history includes such documents as committee reports and statements of legislators on the floor of Congress.

In short, all reasonable arguments on statutory construction are fair game at *Chevron* step one.

(2) Contrasting Judicial Approaches to the Toolkit

Chevron step one is really just a matter of applying a clear-statement rule to the regular toolkit of statutory interpretation. Judges' different attitudes toward this toolkit therefore naturally show up in *Chevron* analysis.

Some judges have a "textualist" bent. For these judges, the statutory text is the sole expression of congressional intent. They discount the use of legislative history to determine statutory meaning on the ground that Congress as a whole enacts statutes, not legislative history. On a related point, legislative history is subject to manipulation by individual members of Congress and staff. Justice Scalia is a prime example of a textualist.

Other judges follow more "purposive" or "intentionalist" approaches to statutory interpretation. They are willing to construe a statute so as to achieve the purposes of Congress in enacting a particular law (or a particular provision in the law) even when those purposes have not been spelled out. This approach often leads to a finding that a statute is not clear and requires the judge to proceed to *Chevron* step two.

Example: Step one in the big tobacco case: The Food and Drug Administration ("FDA") has statutory authority over "drug[s]" and "drug delivery devices." It invoked this authority to regulate tobacco products, reasoning that nicotine is a "drug" and cigarettes are "drug delivery devices." A person unscarred by law school might think that FDA was plainly correct. The Court nonetheless rejected FDA's claim of authority to regulate tobacco under *Chevron* step one in a 5–4 decision. The Court observed that FDA is required by statute to ban *unsafe* drugs. Tobacco products, however, cannot be made safe. Thus, if tobacco products fell within FDA's regulatory jurisdiction, FDA would have to ban them. Congress plainly did not contemplate that tobacco products would be banned entirely, given numerous subsequent statutes (such as cigarette labeling laws) that contemplate the sale of tobacco products. Moreover, the Court observed that it was unreasonable to think that Congress would delegate the extraordinary power to ban tobacco products implicitly. [**FDA v. Brown & Williamson Tobacco Corp.**, 529 U.S. 120 (2000)] [Justice Breyer wrote the 4-justice dissent. He argued that Congress had charged the FDA with broad, flexible authority to regulate in the interests of public health and safety and that the agency could, under the statute, regulate tobacco products without banning them entirely. He would have affirmed the agency's statutory construction as reasonable.]

Example: Step one and the big climate change case: The EPA rejected a petition for rulemaking requesting that it use its authority under the Clean Air Act to regulate greenhouse gas emissions, such as carbon dioxide, from new motor vehicles. The agency rejected the petition on the ground that greenhouse gases do not fall within its statutory authority to regulate "air pollutant[s]," a category that includes "any physical, chemical . . . substance or matter which is emitted into . . . the ambient air." The agency's reasons included: (a) Congress was aware of the global climate change problem when it last comprehensively amended the Clean Air Act in 1990, and it declined to adopt binding emissions limits on greenhouse gases at that time; (b) Congress has adopted "specifically tailored solutions to global atmosphere issues" in other contexts (such as regulating ozone-depleting chemicals); (c) the Clean Air Act was designed to address local air pollutants rather than gases evenly distributed across the globe, such as carbon dioxide; and (d) following *Brown & Williamson* (discussed in the previous example), climate change, like tobacco regulation, presented such an important issue that Congress would not have addressed it implicitly. The Court, in a 5–4 decision, held that the "statutory text forecloses EPA's reading." The CAA's definition of "air pollutant" was "sweeping." Congressional actions in 1990 said nothing about congressional intent when the pertinent language was amended in 1970 and 1977. The majority distinguished *Brown & Williamson*, observing:

(a) the conclusion that EPA has regulatory authority would not require it to ban greenhouse gas emissions; and (b) unlike FDA, EPA did not confront "an unbroken series of congressional enactments that made sense only if adopted against the backdrop" of the agency's "consistent and repeated statements" that it lacked the relevant regulatory authority. [**Massachusetts v. EPA,** 549 U.S. 497 (2007)]

d. *Chevron* Step Two—Was the Agency's Choice Reasonable?

Chevron instructs, "if the statute is silent or ambiguous with respect to the specific issue, the question for the court is whether the agency's answer is based on a permissible [*i.e.,* reasonable] construction of the statute." [**Chevron, USA v. Natural Resources Defense Council,** 467 U.S. 837 (1984)] Step two is generally considered to be very deferential. If the agency makes it to step two, it will very likely win its point.

(1) Wait a Second—What Is Step Two For?

Step one is not a free-floating inquiry into whether an agency's enabling act is ambiguous. Rather, it inquires whether Congress has spoken directly to the precise issue raised by the agency's statutory construction—*e.g.* Did Congress express a clear intent regarding application of the "bubble concept" to the statutory phrase "stationary source"? If an agency statutory construction gets past step one, then it follows that Congress did not clearly preclude it—and the statutory construction *must* fall within the zone of reasonable possibilities. But if the agency statutory construction must fall within the zone of reason to get past step one, what good is step two?

(2) One Possibility: Step Two Doesn't Do Much

It is probably fair to say that many courts don't give a lot of thought to the metaphysics of *Chevron*—which can have a how-many-angels-can-dance-on-the-head-of-a-pin quality. Such courts state the *Chevron* two-step but treat the second step as something of a formality. This treatment is consistent with the fact that if agencies get to step two, they generally win.

(3) Another Possibility: Step Two as Arbitrariness Review

Chevron teaches that the choice among reasonable statutory constructions implicates discretionary policymaking. Agency discretionary policy choices, as discussed below in this chapter, are reviewed for arbitrariness. Courts reviewing for arbitrariness check whether an agency has engaged in "reasoned decisionmaking." On this approach, it is not enough for an agency to make a choice for which a reasonable explanation *could be* given. Rather, the agency must have offered a reasoned explanation for its choice at the time it was made.

Some scholars and courts contend that step two should be regarded as this type of arbitrariness review. On this view, a court applying step two should check whether an agency supported its statutory construction with reasoned decisionmaking. [*See, e.g.,* **Judulang v. Holder,** 132 S.Ct. 476, 483 n. 7 (2011) (suggesting step two equates to arbitrariness review); Ronald A. Levin, *The Anatomy of* Chevron: *Step Two Reconsidered,* 72 Chi.-Kent L. Rev. 1253 (1997) (similar)]. A considerable body of D.C. Circuit case law states that the two tests "overlap."

e. *Chevron* Step 0—What Is *Chevron*'s "Domain"?

On the face of the matter, *Chevron* might seem like it cedes a lot of power to agencies from courts, depriving the latter of their *Marbury* power to say "what the law is." One might therefore think that agencies should earn such favorable treatment for their statutory constructions—maybe not all of them "deserve" rationality review rather than stricter review for correctness. Along these lines, the Supreme Court has developed a somewhat muddled body of law for determining whether a particular agency statutory construction merits *Chevron* deference. There are two cases in particular that you need to know about to apply this "step 0" of *Chevron*—**United States v. Mead Corp.,** 533 U.S. 218 (2001), and **Barnhart v. Walton,** 535 U.S. 212 (2002).

(1) The *Mead* Framework for *Chevron* Step 0

Mead's framework for determining the applicability of *Chevron* deference has its own two-step. It instructs courts to check: (a) "that Congress delegated authority to the agency generally to make rules carrying the force of law," and also (b) that the agency invoked this authority when it promulgated the statutory construction subject to review. [*Mead,* **533 U.S. at 226–27**] In short, courts check for delegation of authority and invocation of that delegated authority.

The Court advised that Congress can signal its delegation of *Chevron* authority to an agency by granting it the "power to engage in [relatively formal] adjudication or notice-and-comment rulemaking." [*Mead,* **533 U.S. at 227**] The underlying idea here is that it is sensible to think that Congress would expect agency interpretations developed through relatively open, deliberative procedures to enjoy the force of law. The Court was careful to note, however, that Congress could signal a delegation of *Chevron* authority by "other indication[s]" that the Court left unspecified.

(2) *Mead*'s Safe Harbors

One upshot of the *Mead* framework is that an agency can safely lay claim to *Chevron* deference where it promulgates a statutory construction through formal adjudication, formal rulemaking, or notice-and-comment rulemaking. Other relatively extensive, public procedures might do in a pinch. In such a context, we have a delegation of authority (*e.g.,* Congress granted the agency power to make rules via notice-and-comment) as well as an invocation of that authority (*e.g.,* the agency promulgated the rule using its delegated power).

(3) Application of the *Mead* Framework to *Mead*

Mead imported "day planners." The applicable tariff schedule required payment of a 4% duty for importation of "bound diaries." The Customs Service issued a "tariff classification ruling" that the day planners were "bound diaries" and thus subject to the tariff. Mead believed that its day planners did not qualify either as "diar[ies]" or as "bound."

Customs has authority to issue rules with the force of law. It did not, however, invoke its force-of-law power when it adjudicated the status of the day planners. The Court observed that Customs issues many thousands of tariff rulings every year from dozens of offices with little or no procedure. Customs itself advises third parties not to rely on its ruling letters, which are binding only in the individual case, and only until Customs gives advance notice of a change. The ruling letters did not function like generally applicable law, and the Court concluded that Customs had not invoked any power to imbue them with the force of law.

(4) Justice Scalia Wrote a Heckuva Dissent

Justice Scalia dissented in *Mead.* He contends that *any* agency legal interpretation issued by the highest level of the agency is deserving of *Chevron* deference. Because the ruling in *Mead* was issued by the highest level of the Customs Service, Scalia believed it should receive strong deference. His dissent is a tour de force of administrative law and a really good read—whether you find yourself agreeing with it or not.

(5) Reaching *Chevron* from Outside a *Mead* Safe Harbor—The *Barnhart* Approach

A lot of agency statutory constructions fall outside of the *Mead* safe harbors just discussed—*e.g.*, interpretive rules issued without notice-and-comment. Recall that *Mead*, however, conceded that extensive agency procedures are not always required for *Chevron* deference. Congress can signal the necessary delegation of force-of-law power by means "other" than granting authority to engage in formal proceedings or notice-and-comment rulemaking.

Shortly after *Mead* was issued, Justice Breyer went out of his way to exploit this "other" possibility in *Barnhart v. Walton*. This case turned on the Social Security Administration's longstanding construction of the statutory term "disability." The agency had adopted this construction in 1957 in an opinion letter. Decades later, the agency embedded this definition in a rule adopted via notice-and-comment. As such, all nine justices agreed that *Chevron* deference applied.

Justice Breyer, writing for eight justices, went a bit further. He explained that *Chevron* should have applied even if the definition had not been vetted through notice-and-comment. *Chevron* deference was warranted in light of the "interstitial nature of the legal question, the related expertise of the Agency, the importance of the question to administration of the statute, the complexity of that administration, and the careful consideration the Agency has given the question over a long period of time. . . ." [**Barnhart v. Walton,** 535 U.S. 212 (2002)]

The upshot of *Barnhart* is that, even where an agency statutory construction does not fall within a *Mead* safe harbor, *Chevron* deference might still apply depending on the court's application of Justice Breyer's indeterminate, multi-factor test.

f. *Chevron* and the Problem of Agency "Jurisdiction"—*City of Arlington*

The issue of whether *Chevron* should apply to an agency's interpretation of the scope of its "jurisdiction" has been percolating through the case law and law reviews for some time. The key rationale for refusing to apply *Chevron* in this context is to block agency power grabs.

In its most recent significant *Chevron* opinion, the Court, in an opinion authored by *Chevron* maximalist Justice Scalia, definitively rejected the idea that *Chevron* deference should not apply to "jurisdictional" determinations. He explained that the distinction between jurisdictional and non-jurisdictional decisions at the agency level is a "mirage." Any claim that an agency has exceeded its statutory authority can be characterized as a "jurisdictional" question—or not. As the jurisdictional inquiry can add nothing but confusion to review of agency action, federal judges should avoid it. [**City of Arlington v. FCC,** 133 S.Ct. 1863 (2013)]

g. *Chevron*'s Interaction with Stare Decisis—*Brand X*

As we have seen, an agency must "earn" *Chevron* deference for its statutory constructions. Suppose that a statutory construction is litigated before an agency has done so. Rather than apply *Chevron*'s rationality review, the court instead applies *Skidmore* deference, which requires the court to adopt the construction it deems most persuasive. Can the agency later adopt a different definition eligible for *Chevron* deference? Put another way, can an agency's *Chevron* authority trump a judicial precedent?

The answer is a qualified yes: "A court's prior judicial construction of a statute trumps an agency construction otherwise entitled to *Chevron* deference only if the prior court decision holds that its construction follows from the unambiguous terms of the statute and leaves no room for agency construction." [**National Cable & Telecommunications Association v. Brand X Internet Services,** 545 U.S. 967 (2005)] Put another way, if the judicial precedent was, in essence, a "step one" decision interpreting the statute in accord with the clear intent of Congress, then the agency can't adopt a contradictory construction later. If the judicial precedent leaves room for other reasonable constructions, then the agency can exploit its *Chevron* power to choose among them.

h. *Chevron* and Agency Flip-Flops

One might think that an agency's statutory construction should merit less deference if the agency can't make up its mind and keeps changing it. In theory, *Chevron* sees things a bit differently. In the *Chevron* case itself, EPA had, over time, adopted several different constructions of "stationary source." The Court advised that this was not problematic insofar "[a]s an initial agency interpretation is not instantly carved in stone." Indeed, an agency should "consider varying interpretations and the wisdom of its policy on a continuing basis." [**Chevron, USA v. Natural Resources Defense Council,** 467 U.S. 837 (1984)]

Nonetheless, an agency that changes interpretive course has an obligation to explain why it has done so rather than ignore prior precedents. [**FCC v. Fox Television Stations, Inc.,** 129 S.Ct. 1800 (2009); **Atchison, Topeka & Santa Fe Railway v. Wichita Board of Trade,** 412 U.S. 800 (1973)]

APPLICATION OF THE *CHEVRON* DOCTRINE

```
┌─────────────────────┐
│ Has the agency      │   No      ┌─────────────────┐         ┌──────────────────────┐
│ construed a statute │─────────▶ │ Chevron         │ ------▶ │ Comment: EPA would   │
│ it is charged with  │           │ deference       │         │ not, for example,    │
│ administering?      │           │ does not apply. │         │ get Chevron          │
└─────────────────────┘           └─────────────────┘         │ deference for its    │
           │                                                   │ construction of the  │
           │ Yes                                                │ OSH Act.             │
           ▼                                                   └──────────────────────┘
```

Step Zero: Has Congress delegated power to the agency to imbue its statutory construction with the force of law, and has the agency used this power?

— No → *Chevron* deference does not apply; apply *Skidmore*'s weak deference instead.

Comment: Under *Mead*, agency statutory constructions produced via relatively formal procedures (e.g., notice-and-comment; formal adjudication) met *Chevron* deference. Outside these safe harbors, apply *Barnhart*'s multi-factor inquiry.

↓ Yes

Step 1: Has Congress directly spoken to the precise issue?

— Yes → Congress's clear intent controls.

Comment: All "traditional tools of statutory construction" are fair game.

↓ No

Step 2: Has the agency given a reasoned explanation for its choice?

— No → Remand case to agency for proceedings consistent with court decision.

Comment: Some courts and scholars think Step 2 is arbitrariness review as applied to the policy choice of choosing among reasonable statutory constructions.

↓ Yes

Uphold agency statutory construction

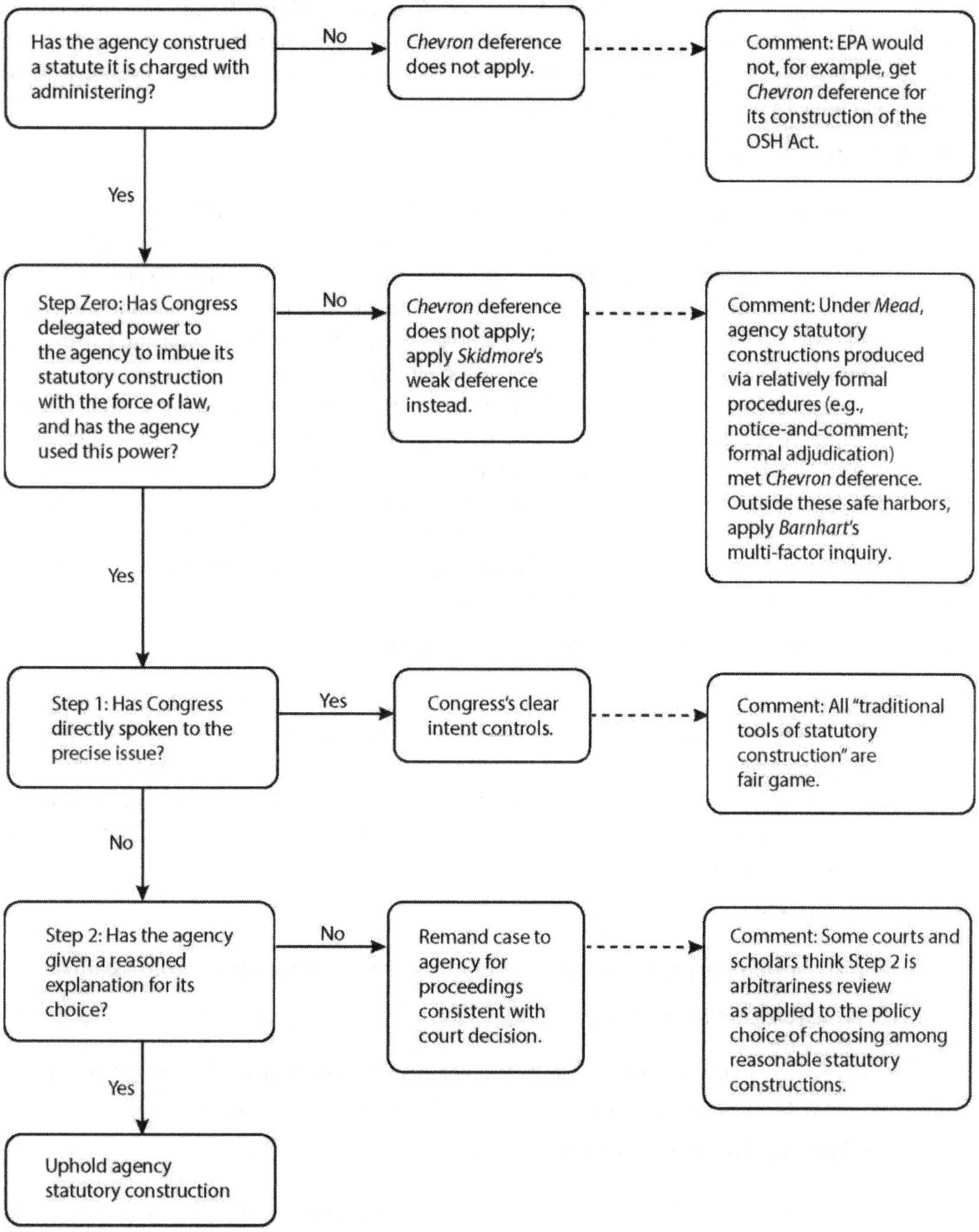

3. *Skidmore*'s Weak Deference

Suppose that an agency has produced a construction of a statute it administers, but the reviewing court determines that *Chevron* is inapplicable under the *Mead/Barnhart* step 0 framework. [*See supra,* pp. 153–155] In that case, the court should still accord *Skidmore* deference (or "*Skidmore* respect") to the agency's views. [*See* **Skidmore v. Swift & Co.**, 323 U.S. 134 (1944) ("We consider that the rulings, interpretations and opinions of the Administrator under this Act, while not controlling upon the courts by reason of their authority, do constitute a body of experience and informed judgment to which courts and litigants may properly resort for guidance.")]

a. Details from *Skidmore*

The plaintiffs spent their nights at the premises of their employer, Swift & Co. They were on-call to respond to fire alarms and the like. They were otherwise free to eat, sleep, play pool, etc. Plaintiffs sued to recover overtime under the Fair Labor Standards Act (FLSA) on the theory that their on-call time was work time. The FLSA does not create a structure for initial agency adjudication of such claims. The FLSA does, however, empower its administrator with authority to investigate industry conditions and to bring injunctive actions to stop violations. The Administrator had issued an interpretive bulletin expressing the agency's views on application of the FLSA to inactive duty. These views were not binding on the courts. They were, however, policies "made in pursuance of official duty, based upon more specialized experience and broader investigations and information than is likely to come to a judge in a particular case." The agency's standards for public enforcement and judicial standards for determining rights under the FLSA should "be at variance only where justified by very good reasons." Therefore, the agency's views were plainly "entitled to respect."

b. Factors Bearing on the "Power to Persuade"

The agency construction should get the weight that it deserves: "The weight of such a judgment in a particular case will depend upon the thoroughness evident in its consideration, the validity of its reasoning, its consistency with earlier and later pronouncements, and all those factors which give it power to persuade, if lacking power to control." [**Skidmore v. Swift & Co.,** *supra*] Any factor that tends to make the agency's construction more "persuasive" is fair game. Courts commonly mention the following:

(1) Consistency

The agency interpretation is more worthy of deference if maintained consistently.

(2) Contemporaneousness

The interpretation is more worthy of deference if adopted soon after the statute was passed, since the agency was probably familiar with the legislative purpose.

(3) Thoroughness of Consideration

An interpretation is more worthy of deference if the agency carefully considered it at a high level (as opposed to, *e.g.*, the unstudied response of a low-level staff member).

(4) Agency Expertise

The interpretation is more worthy of deference if it reflects agency expertise. In contrast, courts might be just as good or better than agencies at applying the common law or in construing nontechnical statutes.

| EXAM TIP |  |

Don't rush into *Chevron* analysis without considering the *Mead/Barnhart* framework for step 0. If step 0 does not have an obvious conclusion, then you should probably explain how either *Chevron*'s strong deference or *Skidmore*'s weak deference would apply on the facts.

4. *Auer* Deference to Agency Interpretations of Its Own Regulations

An agency's construction of its own regulation "is controlling unless plainly erroneous or inconsistent with the regulation." [**Auer v. Robbins,** 519 U.S. 452 (1997); **Bowles v. Seminole Rock Co.,** 325 U.S. 410 (1945)] One reason for such deference is that "requiring the Secretary to construe his own regulations narrowly would make little sense, since he is free to write the regulations as broadly as he wishes." [*Id.*] Broad deference "is all the more warranted when … the regulation concerns 'a complex and highly technical regulatory program,' in which the identification and classification of relevant 'criteria necessarily require significant expertise and entail the exercise of judgment grounded in policy concerns.'" [**Thomas Jefferson University v. Shalala,** 512 U.S. 504 (1994)]

a. No Step 0

Unlike *Chevron, Auer* deference does not come encrusted with a muddled step 0. Along these lines, *Auer* deference can apply even to an interpretation first offered in an *amicus* brief so long as it represents the agency's "fair and considered judgment" rather than a post hoc effort to justify an earlier agency action. [**Auer v. Robbins,** 519 U.S. 452 (1997)]

b. *Auer* Applies Only to "Fair and Considered Judgment"

In **Christopher v. SmithKline Beecham Corp.**, the Supreme Court declared that "deference is … unwarranted when there is reason to suspect that the agency's interpretation 'does not reflect the agency's fair and considered judgment on the matter in question.' " [132 S.Ct. 2156 (2012)]

Signs that this might be the case include: "when the agency's interpretation conflicts with a prior interpretation, or when it appears that the interpretation is nothing more than a 'convenient litigating position,' or a 'post hoc rationalizatio[n]' advanced by an agency seeking to defend past agency action against attack" [*Id.*]

c. *Auer* Doesn't Apply to Parroting Rules

One of the perceived dangers of *Auer* deference is that it offers a potential end run around the limitations on *Chevron* deference. Suppose an agency adopts a rule that pretty much repeats the language of a statute. The agency might later obtain *Auer* deference for its construction of this rule. As the rule added nothing to the statute, however, the agency would, in effect, being obtaining strong *Auer* deference for its statutory construction—without having to worry about the bother of *Chevron* step 0.

The Court has blocked this path by the simple expedient of ruling that *Auer* deference does not apply to rules that "parrot" statutes. [**Gonzales v. Oregon,** 546 U.S. 243 (2006) (refusing to give *Chevron* deference to an interpretation of a parroting rule)]

d. *Auer* Doesn't Apply to Unfair Surprises

The *SmithKline* case, *supra*, p. 159, revolved around whether pharmaceutical sales representatives ("detailers") were "outside salesmen" under the Fair Labor Standards Act. For many decades, pharmaceutical companies had treated detailers as "outside salesmen" with apparent acquiescence from the Department of Labor. DOL nonetheless submitted an amicus brief in which the agency set forth a regulatory interpretation that excluded detailers from the category of "outside salesmen."

Citing its concern that this interpretation exposed the industry to massive and unexpected liability, the Court denied *Auer* deference. It explained, "[t]o defer to the agency's interpretation in this circumstance would seriously undermine the principle that agencies should provide regulated parties 'fair warning of the conduct [a regulation] prohibits or requires.' Indeed, it would result in precisely the kind of 'unfair surprise' against which our cases have long warned." [**Christopher v. SmithKline Beecham Corp.**, 132 S.Ct. 2156 (2012)]

EXAM TIP

Kind of a ticky-tacky thing here—but remember on your exam that *Chevron* or *Skidmore* apply to agency statutory constructions, but *Auer* applies to agency regulatory constructions.

D. Scope of Review of Application of Law to Fact (a/k/a "Mixed Questions")

1. Overview

In virtually every case, the decisionmaker must determine whether some set of facts either do or do not satisfy a legal standard. For instance, suppose in a negligence case that the jury determines that the defendant did indeed drop the banana peel on which the plaintiff slipped. The jury would also have to determine whether this ***basic fact*** or ***evidentiary fact*** added up to "negligence."

This latter type of determination has gone by several different names in the law. Sometimes, courts refer to them as findings of "ultimate fact" or "material fact" that are derived from findings of evidentiary facts. In such cases, courts apply the deferential standards of review for agency fact-finding. [*See, e.g.,* **Penasquitos Village, Inc. v. NLRB**, 565 F.2d 1074 (9th Cir. 1977) (applying substantial evidence standard to NLRB determinations regarding whether employees had been subject to coercive interrogation or had been unlawfully discharged for union activity)]

In some cases, courts refer to such determinations as resolving "mixed questions of law and fact" or issues of "application of law to fact." For instance, in our negligence example, the decisionmaker needed to both find basic facts (*e.g.,* who dropped the banana peel) and determine the significance of these basic facts under a broad legal standard (*i.e.,* negligence).

Example: A statute gives benefits to an employee who quits a job for "good cause" but not to one who quits for other reasons. An employee resigns, claiming that the reason was sexual harassment. An agency first determines why the employee quit. These are ***basic fact*** determinations, to which the substantial evidence test (discussed above) applies. The agency must also define the term "good cause" in abstract ***legal terms*** (*i.e.,* did the legislature intend to allow an employee who quits for noneconomic reasons, such as sexual harassment, to get benefits?). Suppose the court determines that "good cause" does include "compelling" noneconomic reasons such as sexual harassment. Once the facts are found and the law is interpreted, the "ultimate" question is whether this particular employee quit for "good cause." Determining this issue requires *application of the law to the facts.*

2. Reasonableness Test—The *Hearst* Framework

Important rights under the National Labor Relations Act turn on whether a person is an "employee." In the *Hearst* case, the National Labor Relations Board conducted an adjudication in which it determined that "newboys" (grown men who distributed newspapers) were "employees."

Discussing the proper standard of review for applications of law to fact by agencies charged with their initial adjudication, the Court explained:

> [W]here the question is one of specific application of a broad statutory term in a proceeding in which the agency administering the statute must determine it initially, the reviewing court's function is limited.... [T]he Board's determination that specified persons are 'employees' under this Act is to be accepted if it has '*warrant in the record*' and a *reasonable basis in law*.

[**NLRB v. Hearst Publications, Inc.,** 322 U.S. 111 (1944) (emphasis added)]

Thus, at least in those cases where the agency has exercised delegated power to initially resolve an adjudicative matter, courts should affirm an agency's *reasonable* application of law to fact. Note that this same deferential approach should apply if the court characterizes an issue as one of "ultimate fact"—a possibility noted *supra,* p. 160.

a. *Hearst*'s Contrast Between Pure Issues of Law and Mixed Questions

Hearst actually presented two issues bearing on whether the newsboys were "employees." The first was whether Congress, when it adopted the NLRA, had intended for the term "employee" to incorporate by reference common law standards on the employment relation. This issue presented a pure question of law. No one needed to know anything at all about the working conditions of the plaintiff newsboys to resolve it—the issue did not depend on the factual particulars of the case. On a closely related point, as this issue did not turn on the facts of a given case, a ruling on this point would apply generally across cases—as one would expect of generally applicable "law."

The Court held that "[u]ndoubtedly [such] questions of statutory interpretation, especially when arising in the first instance in judicial proceedings, are for the courts to resolve, giving appropriate weight to the judgment of those whose special duty is to administer the questioned statute." In other words, courts are in charge of interpreting the law, offering only something like *Skidmore* deference to agency statutory constructions. *Chevron*, of course, adopted a different approach some years later.

The second issue in *Hearst* was whether, based on all the relevant factual circumstances, the newsboys were "employees." A decisionmaker necessarily has to know the facts of the particular case to make this type of determination. Thus, it makes sense to refer to such issues as "mixed questions of law and fact" or as "applications of law to fact." Here, *Hearst* explained that deferential rationality review should apply, as just explained, *supra,* p. 161.

b. *Hearst*'s Rationales for Deferential Review

Hearst's basic rationales for deferential review on mixed questions are what you should expect: delegation and expertise. Congress had delegated authority to the Board to make fact-specific determinations of who qualifies as an "employee" through the Board's adjudicative process. In exercising this authority in its "usual administrative routine," the Board developed pertinent expertise.

3. Judicial Inconsistency on Application Questions

Courts have not been consistent applying a *Hearst*-style deferential approach. In numerous cases involving judicial review of the applications of law to fact, courts have substituted their judgment rather than deferring to a reasonable agency application. Courts are more likely to substitute judgment on application questions where the issue does not hinge on sifting complex facts, where the agency appears to have no particular expertise, or the issue seems especially important. [*See, e.g.*, **Packard Motor Car Co. v. NLRB,** 330 U.S. 485 (1947)]

EXAM TIP

Do bear in mind that *Hearst's* approach of leaving courts in charge of pure issues of law has been abandoned by the *Chevron* doctrine, discussed *supra* pp. 150–156.

E. Scope of Review of Exercises of Discretion

1. Overview of the Problem

Many enabling acts give agencies broad discretion to make and implement policy. For example, an agency might have discretion regarding whether to adopt a strong or a weak rule, whether to address a particular problem, or how severely to punish a licensee who has violated the statute.

In a few important contexts, agency discretionary action is unreviewable. This issue is discussed *infra* at 187–188. Judicial review is, however, presumptively available for exercises of discretion that culminate in final agency action. This subsection explores how courts are supposed to deploy this power of reviewing agency discretionary action. Determining the limits of this power requires balancing the need for judicial control against the danger of allowing generalist, unelected judges to substitute their policy preferences for those of expert agencies exercising delegated power.

2. APA Standard—Arbitrariness Review

Under the APA, the court shall "hold unlawful and set aside agency action, findings, and conclusions found to be . . . arbitrary, capricious, an abuse of discretion or otherwise not in accordance with law. . . ." [APA § 706(2)(A)] All three terms—arbitrary, capricious, abuse of discretion—mean the same thing. Courts commonly refer to review for "arbitrariness" or to the "arbitrary and capricious" test.

3. The Meaning of Arbitrariness Review

Review for arbitrariness is supposed to be deferential yet meaningful: Agency determinations are entitled to a "presumption of regularity," and "[t]he court is not empowered to substitute its judgment for that of the agency." That said, agency decisions are subject to "thorough, probing, in-depth review." [**Citizens to Preserve Overton Park v. Volpe,** 401 U.S. 402 (1971)] Principles governing how the courts are to strike this balance follow:

a. Threshold Legal Questions

A discretionary act must, of course, comply with any law limiting the agency's power. Thus, discretionary acts are subject to review to determine whether they fell within the scope of an agency's delegated power and whether the agency complied with legally required procedures. [**Citizens to Preserve Overton Park v. Volpe,** 401 U.S. 402 (1971)]

b. Review for Reasoned Decisionmaking

You might recollect that a jury verdict should survive a motion for judgment as a matter of law so long as the reviewing judge can conceive of any reasonable justification for the verdict. Put another way, the judge tests whether the jury reached a reasonable result, not whether the jury itself had a reasonable justification for choosing this result.

Arbitrariness review, by contrast, demands that an agency demonstrate that it relied on a reasoned justification for its action at the time it was taken. Courts review such justifications for "reasoned decisionmaking," which involves checking whether "the decision was based on a consideration of the *relevant factors* and whether the agency avoided any *clear error in judgment.* [**Citizens to Preserve Overton Park v. Volpe,** 401 U.S. 402 (1971)] If the reviewing court determines that an agency failed this standard, the court should not substitute its own judgment for that of the agency. Instead, the usual practice is to vacate the action and remand to the agency, which may attempt to fix its explanatory defects and repeat the action. [**Camp v. Pitts,** 411 U.S. 138 (1973)]

(1) The *State Farm* Gloss

The Supreme Court offered a slightly more detailed gloss on the arbitrary-capricious test in the canonical case, **Motor Vehicle Manufacturers Association v. State Farm Mutual Auto Insurance Co.,** 463 U.S. 29 (1983) (vacating rescission of a rule requiring passive restraints in automobiles). The Court explained:

> Normally, an agency rule would be arbitrary and capricious if the agency has relied on factors Congress has not intended it to consider, entirely failed to consider an important aspect of the problem, offered an explanation for its decision that runs counter to the evidence before the agency, or is so implausible that it could not be ascribed to a difference in view or the product of agency expertise.

(2) "Hard Look" Review

The relatively intense scrutiny of the agency's reasoning process and conclusions that occurred in the *State Farm* is sometimes referred to as "hard look review." One well-known description of hard-look review explained it as follows:

> Its supervisory function calls on the court to intervene not merely in case of procedural inadequacies, or bypassing of the mandate in the legislative charter, but more broadly if the court becomes aware, especially from a combination of danger signals, that the agency has not really taken a "hard look" at the salient problems, and has not genuinely engaged in reasoned decisionmaking. If the agency has not shirked this fundamental task, however, the court exercises restraint and affirms the agency's action, even though the court would on its own account have made different findings or adopted different standards. [**Greater Boston Television Corp. v. FCC,** 444 F.2d 841 (D.C. Cir. 1970), *cert. denied,* 403 U.S. 923 (1971)]

c. Relevant Factors

The "relevant factors" are the considerations that Congress wished an agency to take into account when exercising its policymaking discretion. For example, § 109(b)(1) of the Clean Air Act tells EPA to set national "ambient air quality standards . . . [that] allowing an adequate margin of safety, are requisite to protect the public health." 42 U.S.C. § 7409(b)(1). EPA, unsurprisingly, is supposed to consider "public health" when limiting air pollution.

A statute might also forbid consideration of some factors. For instance, EPA is forbidden from considering costs when it sets NAAQS pursuant to the Clean Air Act. [**Whitman v. American Trucking Ass'n,** 531 U.S. 457 (2001)].

The agency's contemporaneous justification for its discretionary action must demonstrate that it gave sufficient attention to the "relevant factors" (the stuff Congress wanted the agency to consider) and did not rely upon forbidden factors.

(1) Agencies Don't Have to Consider Other Agencies' Relevant Factors

Note that an agency need not consider the policies and goals of ***all*** federal statutes as relevant factors in making a complex economic decision. In general, the agency should consider only the policies and goals of the statute it is charged with enforcing. It lacks expertise in other statutory areas and such a requirement would render a very large number of agency decisions of questionable validity. [**Pension Benefit Guaranty Corp. v. LTV Corp.,** 496 U.S. 633 (1990)]

d. Reasonableness of Agency Action

Even if the agency exercised discretion within statutory bounds and considered all the relevant factors, the court should reverse if the agency made a *"clear error of judgment."* [**Citizens to Preserve Overton Park v. Volpe,** 401 U.S. 402 (1971)]

It is probably fair to say that courts prefer to throw out agency discretionary actions on the quasi-procedural ground that an agency failed to consider the relevant factors rather than on the substantive ground that the agency was grossly mistaken in its judgment. Rhetorically, it is not so easy for a generalist court to say that the "expert" agency is flat out wrong.

Example—*State Farm*: In 1977, the National Highway Traffic Safety Administration ("NHTSA") adopted a rule requiring all new cars produced after September 1982 to use air bags or automatic seat belts (*i.e.,* seat belts that restrain the occupant without buckling up). In 1981, however, NHTSA rescinded the rule. Its main rationales for doing so included: (a) it had learned that manufacturers would rely almost entirely on the seatbelt option for compliance rather than install airbags; and (b) it could not predict that usage of seat belts would increase enough to justify the costs of the new rule.

The Supreme Court held that rescission of the rule was arbitrary and capricious. The most obvious problem was that the agency's own documents had concluded that airbags, if installed, would save thousands of lives a year. By a 9–0 vote, the justices agreed that the agency's failure to explain why it had not modified the rule to require airbags was arbitrary.

By a 5–4 vote, the Court also held that the agency's decision was arbitrary because it had not adequately explained its stance on automatic safety belts. Regarding detachable belts, the Court accepted the agency's assessment that studies demonstrating their efficacy were flawed—it was up to the expert agency to make such determinations. The agency had failed, however, to address the issue of *inertia*. It makes sense to think that inertia keeps people from strapping on manual belts; by the same token, inertia may discourage people from unhooking detachable belts. The agency should have discussed this possibility. (If you are thinking this analysis sounds kind of thin, well, so did the four dissenters.) The Court also held that the agency had arbitrarily failed to give due and separate consideration to continuous passive belts. This was particularly problematic because the agency had approved GM's use of such belts several years before. The agency was free to change its views, but it had to explain why.

Example: *Massachusetts v. EPA*: A statute required the EPA to limit new car tailpipe emissions of air pollutants "which in the [Administrator's] judgment cause, or contribute to, air pollution which may reasonably be anticipated to endanger public health or welfare." The EPA declined to reach a judgment regarding whether greenhouse gases endanger public health—*i.e.*, an "endangerment finding." Its justifications included, *inter alia*: (a) adoption of a regulation might impair the President's ability to negotiate with developing countries to reduce their greenhouse gas emissions; and (b) deploying this authority would lead to an "inefficient, piecemeal approach to address[ing] the climate change issue." The Court held that these were not permissible factors for the EPA to consider in determining whether to make an endangerment finding. The statute required the EPA to adopt emission control rules if it concluded that greenhouse gases, such as carbon dioxide, contributed to global warming and that global warming endangered public health. [**Massachusetts v. EPA,** 549 U.S. 497 (2007)]

e. Mixed Messages on the Duty to Explain Policy Changes

Should agencies have a heightened duty to explain their decisions to abandon old policies and adopt new ones? The Court confronted this problem in **FCC v. Fox Television Stations, Inc.**, but failed to give an entirely clear answer. [129 S.Ct. 1800 (2009)]

The FCC has a statutory duty to police against "indecent" broadcasts. As you can imagine, this has created problems over the years figuring out what "indecent" means. For many years, the agency took the position that it would not hold broadcasters liable for "fleeting expletives" that a person might blurt out during a broadcast. After some incidents involving Cher, Nicole Ritchie, and U-2 singer Bono, the agency changed course, abandoning the exemption for fleeting expletives.

By a 5–4 vote, the Court upheld the FCC's explanation for its decision against the charge of arbitrariness. Writing for the five, Justice Scalia acknowledged that an agency changing policy course must advert to the change, explain any rejection of factual determinations underlying the old policy, and give due consideration to reliance issues. The agency must also, of course, have good reasons for the change, but it need not demonstrate "the reasons for the new policy are *better* than the reasons for the old one; it suffices that the new policy is permissible under the statute."

Writing for a four-justice dissent, Justice Breyer contended that an agency must also answer the question, "Why change?" He added that "a rational answer to this question typically requires a more complete explanation than would prove satisfactory were change itself not the issue." For instance, FCC had explained its policy shift in part by observing that viewers should not be subjected to the "first blow" of a fleeting expletive. Justice Breyer pointed out, however, that the FCC had been aware of this problem for decades, and it therefore did not give a good answer to "why change?"

Muddying the waters, Justice Kennedy authored a solo concurrence. In it, he joined the portion of Justice Scalia's opinion that rejected heightened scrutiny. He also, however, seemed to agree with Justice Breyer's basic point that an agency should answer "why change?" He observed that "[t]he question in each case is whether the agency's reasons for the change ... suffice to demonstrate that the new policy rests upon principles that are rational, neutral, and in accord with the agency's proper understanding of its authority."

4. Review of Facts Underlying Rules

Agencies, of course, need factual bases for the rules they promulgate. Review of such facts is discussed here in the policy section because: (a) a form of the arbitrariness standard generally applies; and (b) these fact determinations are closely intertwined with the policy judgments informing rulemaking.

a. Old Fashioned Arbitrariness Review of Facts

Under the traditional approach, a reviewing court would assume the existence of facts sufficient to support a rule "if any [such] state of facts reasonably can be conceived." [**Pacific States Box & Basket Co. v. White,** 296 U.S. 176 (1935)] This *Pacific States Box* approach is still applied in some states. [**Borden, Inc. v. Commissioner of Public Health,** 448 N.E.2d 367 (Mass. 1983)]

b. Modern Arbitrariness Review of Facts

As discussed above, *supra,* p. 163, modern review for arbitrariness requires an agency to demonstrate that it had a reasoned justification for its action at the time it was taken. [*See* **Motor Vehicle Manufacturers Association v. State Farm Mutual Auto Insurance Co.,** 463 U.S. 29 (1983)] Part of offering a reasoned justification for a policy choice is demonstrating that it has sufficient factual support.

Under the APA, an agency's factual determinations derived through non-record proceedings are subject to review for arbitrariness. [**APA § 706(2)(A),** *discussed supra* at p. 145] Review of facts for arbitrariness checks for rationality—*i.e.*, courts are supposed to defer to reasonable agency findings.

(1) Duty to Respond to Criticism

The agency must respond to critical comments about the factual basis of its proposed rule, and the methodology on which it is based, if those comments step over a threshold requirement of materiality. [**Portland Cement Association v. Ruckelshaus,** 486 F.2d 375 (D.C. Cir. 1973)]

(2) Scientific Frontiers

The Court has cautioned that reviewing courts must be unusually deferential when reviewing rules based on predictions within the agency's area of expertise that are at the frontiers of scientific knowledge. [**Baltimore Gas & Electric Co. v. Natural Resources Defense Council,** 462 U.S. 87 (1983)]

(3) Substantial Evidence Standard

Several statutes require reviewing courts to use the "substantial evidence" standard in assessing facts underlying legislative rules. As noted above, *supra,* p. 146, there is some debate over whether "substantial evidence" review is in theory or in practice somewhat tougher on agencies than review for arbitrariness.

(4) Actual Mileage Varies

Although review for arbitrariness is in theory deferential, the actual level of scrutiny naturally varies depending on the judges, facts, and agencies involved.

5. Limited Review of Administrative Remedy

Choice of a remedy is freighted with policy judgments. Accordingly, judicial review of an agency choice of remedy is highly deferential; the court should not substitute its own judgment for that of the agency. [**ABF Freight Lines, Inc. v. NLRB,** 510 U.S. 317 (1994) (upholding remedy where Board ordered employee reinstated even though he had committed perjury in the hearing)]

Example: The USDA issued a cease-and-desist order against a packinghouse for short-weighting cattle, and suspended its operations for 20 days. The court of appeals set aside the suspension as being more severe than previous USDA action in similar cases. The Supreme Court held that the agency's remedy must be upheld unless it was *"without warrant in law or justification in fact."* The mere fact that the remedy was unusually severe did *not* necessarily indicate that the suspension violated this standard. [**Bute v. Glover Livestock Co. of Texas,** 411 U.S. 182 (1973)] However, note that where an agency fails to explain why a particular remedy used in recent, similar cases was not employed, the matter may be remanded to the agency to clarify its rationale. [**NLRB v. Food Store Employees Union,** 417 U.S. 1 (1974)]

a. Abuse of Discretion

Despite cases like *Glover Livestock, supra,* an occasional case finds that an agency's particularly harsh choice of remedy was an abuse of discretion. [**Corder v. United States,** 107 F.3d 595 (8th Cir. 1997) (holding that formula for computing monetary penalties against grocery stores that violate the food stamp rules failed to take account of relevant factors such as whether violation was first offense, culpability of the owner, loss to the government, and owner's ability to pay)]

b. Scope of Remedy Within Agency Discretion

The agency's decision to proceed against an entire industry, or merely to attack a problem on a company-by-company basis, is within its discretion. A strong showing of abuse of discretion is required to overturn an agency's judgment on such matters. [**FTC v. Universal-Rundle Corp.,** 387 U.S. 244 (1967)] Also, an agency's order to cease and desist from illegal conduct may, if appropriate, go *beyond* the specific conduct proved in the hearing. Otherwise, the respondent might seek alternative means to circumvent the decision. [**FTC v. Mandel Brothers, Inc.,** 359 U.S. 385 (1959)]

Chapter Eight
Access to the Courts: Types of Review, Immunities, Tort Liability, Reviewability

CONTENTS	PAGE
Key Exam Issues	170
A. **Types of "Review" Available**	171
B. **Sovereign Immunity**	176
C. **Tort Liability of Government**	178
D. **Tort Liability of Government Officials**	181
E. **Statutory Preclusion of Judicial Review**	185
F. **Commitment to Agency Discretion**	187
G. **Threshold Requirements of "Agency Action" by an "Agency"**	189

Key Exam Issues

Keep in mind the following:

1. **"Types" of Review Available**

    Many agency organic statutes include provisions governing judicial review proceedings. These agency specific schemes are referred to as *special statutory review.* Where special statutory review is unavailable or otherwise inadequate, the APA authorizes judicial review of final agency action. This default APA cause of action is referred to as *general statutory review.* Where neither of these types of review is available or adequate, a claimant can sometimes invoke *nonstatutory review*. This residuary category includes injunctive relief, mandamus, and damages actions, among various possibilities.

2. **Sovereign Immunity**

    You only get to sue the government in the government's courts if the government lets you. So, to sue the government, you need a waiver of sovereign immunity.

    The federal government has waived its sovereign immunity for suits that do not seek money damages at *§ 702 of the APA.* For many suits seeking money damages, the *Federal Torts Claims Act* and the *Tucker Act(s)* waive sovereign immunity. Some enabling acts also waive sovereign immunity for specific agencies (*e.g.*, with "sue and be sued clauses").

    Sovereign immunity also applies at the state level. State sovereign immunity in federal court implicates a convoluted body of law growing out of the Eleventh Amendment.

    Historically, litigants have often dodged sovereign immunity by suing government *officials* rather than the government itself. These officials may, however, be cloaked by either qualified or absolute immunity.

3. **Tort Liability of Government or its Officials**

    Government agencies are frequently liable in tort for actions of their officials. The federal government is liable under the *Federal Tort Claims Act,* but FTCA liability is limited by many procedural requirements and exceptions. Notably, the FTCA waiver is subject to an exception for *discretionary functions* and does not apply to *constitutional torts.*

    Plaintiffs can sue government officials in their personal capacities for damages. For instance, a plaintiff might bring a *Bivens* action against a federal official for violation of certain constitutional rights. State and local officials are subject to liability under 42 U.S.C. § 1983 for violations of federal rights. Doctrines of qualified and absolute immunity protect government officials from liability.

4. **Statutory Preclusion of Judicial Review**

    Courts, you may not be surprised to learn, generally think of judicial review as a good thing. Accordingly, there is a general *presumption* that agency action is *reviewable.*

    Congress can nonetheless *preclude review by statute*, see **5 U.S.C. § 701(a)(1).** Courts often aggressively construe statutes to avoid finding that Congress intended to preclude review. This judicial inclination is especially strong for constitutional claims and for claims that challenge broadly applicable law.

5. **Agency Discretion as Bar to Judicial Review**

    Section 701(a)(2) of the APA instructs that judicial review is not available for agency actions "*committed to agency discretion by law.*" Section 706(2)(A), however, instructs courts to review agency action for arbitrariness or "abuse of discretion." Courts have squared this apparent contradiction by identifying contexts in which agency "discretion" is so broad or important as to preclude judicial review. For instance, the Supreme Court has held that agency decisions declining to bring enforcement actions are presumptively unreviewable. Courts sometimes declare that agency action is unreviewable where agency discretion is so broad that there is "no law to apply." (Take this formulation with a grain of salt—there is always at least a bit of law to apply.)

6. **"Agency Action" as Prerequisite to Review under the APA**

To be reviewable under the APA, the agency conduct in question must meet the definition of "agency action." *Section 551(13)* of the APA broadly defines "agency action" to include "the whole or a part of an agency rule, order, license, sanction, relief, or the equivalent or denial thereof, or failure to act."

The last phrase of this definition, "failure to act," raises a problem—all agencies are at all times failing to take an infinite number of actions. It would not make much sense to interpret this definition as authorizing review of all things an agency is not doing. To avoid this problem, the Supreme Court has held that "failure to act" amounts to reviewable "agency action" only where an agency has "failed to take a discrete agency action that it is required to take." [**Norton v. Southern Utah Wilderness Alliance**, 542 U.S. 55 (2004)]

A. Types of "Review" Available

A party seeking to challenge agency action in court needs a cause of action. Administrative law categorizes the various options into three types: special statutory review, general statutory review, and non-statutory review.

1. Special Statutory Review

Many agency enabling acts grant a cause of action for judicial review of agency action. These statutes commonly specify which courts have subject matter jurisdiction, deadlines for filing, proper plaintiffs, etc. Often, review is channeled to the D.C. Circuit Court of Appeals. This court's control over many important administrative matters bolsters its power and reputation as the second-most important court in the United States.

2. Introduction to General Statutory Review Under the APA

"General statutory review" refers to the default cause of action created by the APA itself at §§ 701–706. The details of this cause of action unfold over the next two chapters, but here are some high points:

a. Section 704—Review Available for "Final Agency Action"

APA § 704 (first sentence) provides: "Agency action made reviewable by statute and ***final agency action for which there is no adequate remedy in a court*** are subject to judicial review."

The first part of this sentence merely reiterates the obvious point that a petitioner can use an available special statutory review scheme. The second, bolded part allows for review of "final agency action" where an adequate remedy in court would be otherwise unavailable.

(1) State Analogues

In many states, a single statute sets forth general procedures for review of decisions made by state agencies. [*See, e.g.*, 1961 Model State APA § 15; N.Y. Civ. Prac. L., art. 78; Cal. Code of Civ. Proc. § 1094.5]

b. Section 703—Available "Forms" of Review

Section 703 uses somewhat intimidating language to convey a simple message: the APA values function over form. It states, "[t]he form of proceeding for judicial review is . . . any applicable form of legal action, including actions for declaratory judgments or writs of prohibitory or mandatory injunction or habeas corpus, in a court of competent jurisdiction" and that "the action for judicial review may be brought against the United States, the agency by its official title, or the appropriate officer."

What this boils down to in practice is that a party challenging agency action via the APA will typically seek injunctive and/or declaratory relief to vacate the action—and the APA is just fine by that.

c. Section 702—Statutory Standing

Section 702 specifies "statutory standing," *i.e.*, which parties can invoke the APA's cause of action. It states, "A person suffering legal wrong because of agency action, or adversely affected or aggrieved by agency action within the meaning of the relevant statute, is entitled to judicial review thereof." As will be developed below in Chapter 9, this provision, as construed by the Supreme Court, casts a very wide net.

d. More from § 702—Partial Waiver of Sovereign Immunity

Under the doctrine of sovereign immunity, you can only use the government's courts to sue the government if the government lets you. As it evolved over the years, this doctrine became very complex, filled with fictions, and generally quite awful. To lessen this problem, in 1976, Congress amended § 702 to waive the federal government's sovereign immunity from claims that do not seek "money damages." Moreover, the "APA's waiver of sovereign immunity applies to any suit whether under the APA or not." [**Trudeau v. FTC,** 456 F.3d 178 (D.C. Cir. 2006)]

(1) Note: "Money Damages" as Compensatory Relief

Section 702's exclusion of actions for "money damages" tracks the distinction between specific and compensatory relief. [**Dept. of Army v. Blue Fox, Inc.,** 525 U.S. 255 (1999) (scope of § 702 waiver "hinged on the distinction between specific relief and substitute relief, not between equitable and nonequitable categories of remedies")]

Thus, § 702's waiver does not cover actions that seek *compensatory* damages, *i.e.*, relief "intended to provide a victim with monetary compensation for an injury to his person, property, or reputation." [**Bowen v. Massachusetts,** 487 U.S. 879 (1988)] The waiver does, however, apply to actions seeking *specific* monetary relief. [*Id.* (holding state's claim to recover expenses owed under Medicaid fell within the scope of § 702's waiver)]

e. Jurisdiction for General Statutory Review

Special statutory review schemes will generally specify which courts have subject matter jurisdiction. Often, they choose the courts of appeals, in part because the agency will already have handled the job of developing a factual record.

Section 702, however, does not grant subject matter jurisdiction, nor does any other part of the APA. [**Califano v. Sanders,** 430 U.S. 99 (1977)] This gap does not pose much of a problem for general statutory review because petitioners can, as a default, claim jurisdiction via the general federal-question statute, 28 U.S.C. § 1331, which no longer imposes any amount-in-controversy requirement. Note that this statute lodges subject matter jurisdiction in the *district courts*.

(1) Some Additional Jurisdictional Statutes

Additional statutory provisions granting jurisdiction include 28 U.S.C. § 1337 (involving an act of Congress regulating commerce), § 1343 (deprivation of constitutional rights by state officials), and § 1361 (action in nature of mandamus).

3. "Nonstatutory" Review

Sometimes, neither special statutory review nor general statutory review may be available. For instance, general statutory review may be unavailable because the claimant wishes to challenge non-final action. [**Trudeau v. FTC,** 456 F.3d 178 (D.C. 2006)] Or the claimant may seek monetary damages for a constitutional violation. In such contexts, review is sometimes available through a residuary category that administrative law refers to as "nonstatutory review." (This name is a bit misleading as many of the "nonstatutory" possibilities have been codified.)

Nonstatutory review grew out of a practice of evading sovereign immunity by suing *officials* rather than the government itself. An underlying idea here is that, where an official acts beyond his authority (*ultra vires*), that official is "stripped of his official or representative character." [**Ex parte Young,** 209 U.S. 123 (1908); *see also* **Chamber of Commerce v. Reich,** 74 F.3d 1322 (D.C. Cir. 1996) (discussing history of nonstatutory review); *see generally* Jonathan R. Seigel, Suing the President: Nonstatutory Review Revisited, 97 Colum. L. Rev. 1612 (1997) (offering detailed exploration of history and modern deployment of nonstatutory review)]

a. Injunctive and Declaratory Relief

The Supreme Court has authorized injunctive relief against both federal and state officials to block actions that exceed their authority. The seminal cases include: **American School of Magnetic Healing v. McAnnulty,** 187 U.S. 94 (1902) (granting injunction to block subordinate postal official from carrying out Postmaster General's order barring plaintiff from advertising); **Ex parte Young,** 209 U.S. 123 (1908) (authorizing injunctive relief against state Attorney General to block enforcement of unconstitutional law). It is common to combine requests for injunctive relief with requests for declaratory relief.

b. Mandamus

The common law writ of mandamus is available in most states, and in federal courts under 28 U.S.C. section 1361. Section 1361 gives district courts jurisdiction over any mandamus-type action to compel a federal officer, employee, or agency to perform a duty owed to the plaintiff. However, mandamus is discretionary and requires that the plaintiff establish a "clear right" to relief. [**Norton v. Southern Utah Wilderness Alliance,** 542 S.Ct. 55 (2004) (observing that mandamus "was normally limited . . . to the ordering of a precise, definite act . . . about which [an official] had no discretion whatever") (quotation marks omitted); *In re* **Cheney,** 406 F.3d 723 (D.C. Cir. 2005) (observing that "mandamus is drastic; it is available only in extraordinary situations")]

c. Certiorari

In many states, the common law writ of certiorari is used to review a "judicial" or "quasi-judicial" action if there is a ***record*** available. However, certiorari is ***not available in the federal courts*** to review administrative decisions because of an early Supreme Court decision. [**Degge v. Hitchcock,** 229 U.S. 162 (1913)]

d. Habeas Corpus

Habeas corpus is available to contest *restrictions on individual freedom.* Various statutory provisions bear on this writ. [*See, e.g.*, 28 U.S.C. § 2241] The Constitution provides that this writ "shall not be suspended, unless when in Cases of Rebellion or Invasion the public Safety may require it." [**U.S. Const., § 9, cl. 2**]

e.g. Example: A statute provided for a limited form of judicial review of the decisions of Combatant Status Review Tribunals in lieu of habeas for alleged enemy alien combatants at Guantanamo Bay. The Supreme Court held that this review was inadequate in light of, inter alia, severe limitations on the detainees' access to evidence that would allow them to rebut the government's case. [**Boumediene v. Bush,** 128 S.Ct. 2229 (2008)]

e. Damages Actions

Suppose a government official breaks down your door. Under early practice, you might sue that official for trespass, damage to your property, etc. In the subsequent litigation, the official would rely on legal authority and official immunity.

The federal system now largely handles common-law-style claims through the Federal Tort Claims Act (FTCA) and the Tucker Act, discussed below at pp. 178–180. The FTCA does not, however, cover "constitutional torts," which, in a very limited class of cases, plaintiffs can pursue by means of a *Bivens* action, discussed below at pp. 183–184.

4. Review During Enforcement Actions

APA § 703 provides: "Except to the extent that prior, adequate, and exclusive opportunity for judicial review is provided by law, agency action is subject to judicial review in civil or criminal proceedings for judicial enforcement." Thus, generally speaking, a party can defend against an enforcement action based on a rule on the ground that the rule is illegal. [*See, e.g.*, **United States v. Nova Scotia Food Products Corp.,** 568 F.2d 240 (2d Cir. 1977) (court reviewed validity of rule when it was used as the basis for an enforcement action against a fish processor)]

a. Preclusion of Review by a Statutory Deadline

Special statutory review procedures often include relatively short deadlines for seeking judicial review of a rule. An enforcement action may, of course, commence long after such a deadline has passed. In such cases, the issue arises whether a party can still challenge the validity of a rule as a defense to its enforcement. The answer to this question is a qualified "yes."

(1) Challenge Precluded by Deadline—*Yakus*

The Emergency Price Control Act granted the government authority to set price controls during World War II. By statute, challenges to price controls had to be filed with the Administrator within 60 days of promulgation; a person aggrieved by a denial of a protest had 30 days to seek review by an Emergency Court of Appeals. Yakus challenged a criminal conviction for violating a price control on the sale of meat. The Supreme Court held that statutory preclusion of challenges to a price control in an enforcement proceeding did not violate due process. The Court was plainly influenced by the exigencies of the war. [**Yakus v. United States,** 321 U.S. 414 (1944); *cf.* **Adamo Wrecking Co. v. United States,** 434 U.S. 275 (1978) (casting doubt on *Yakus*)]

(2) Substantive Challenges Allowed After Deadline

Blocking review of a rule during enforcement proceedings creates an obvious potential for unfairness and *ultra vires* action. In light of such concerns, the D.C. Circuit has held that, where a statutory deadline does not expressly block all later review, the court will hear *substantive* challenges to a rule during post-deadline enforcement proceedings. It will not, however, hear procedural challenges. [**Independent Community Bankers of America v. Board of Governors of the Federal Reserve System,** 195 F.3d 28 (D.C. Cir. 1999)]

b. Right to Jury Trial

A defendant has a Seventh Amendment right to jury trial on the issue of liability when the government asserts in court a claim of civil penalties for violation of a regulatory statute. [**Tull v. United States,** 481 U.S. 412 (1987) (civil penalties for dumping into navigable waters)] However, Congress can reserve the determination of the *amount* of the penalty to the trial judge; only the issue of liability for the penalty must go to the jury. [**Tull v. United States,** *supra* (statute allowed penalties "not to exceed" $10,000 per day; no right to jury trial on setting amount of penalty)]

(1) No Jury Trial in Agency Enforcement

However, if the agency is empowered to assess a civil penalty in an *administrative* proceeding, there is no right to a jury trial. [**Atlas Roofing Co. v. Occupational Safety & Health Review Commission,** 430 U.S. 442, 450 (1977) ("At least in cases in which 'public rights' are being litigated, . . . the Seventh Amendment does not prohibit Congress from assigning the factfinding function and initial adjudication to an administrative forum with which the jury would be incompatible.")]

MEANS OF OBTAINING JUDICIAL REVIEW	AVAILABLE IN FEDERAL COURT?	AVAILABLE IN STATE COURT?	RESULT OF REVIEW
STATUTORY PROCEDURES (*E.G.*, APPEAL TO COURT OF APPEAL IF PROVIDED BY STATUTE)	Yes	Yes	Dependent on statute
INJUNCTION AND DECLARATORY JUDGMENT	Yes, but court must have jurisdiction	Yes	Court declares agency action invalid and enjoins agency from taking such action
MANDAMUS	Yes	Yes, in most states	District court can compel a federal officer, employee, or agency to perform a duty owed to plaintiff

CERTIORARI	No	Yes, where a record is available	Court reviews "judicial" or "quasi-judicial" action
HABEAS CORPUS	Yes	Yes	Plaintiff is granted relief from the restriction on his individual freedom

B. Sovereign Immunity

1. In General

The doctrine of sovereign immunity stems from the ancient rule that "the King can do no wrong." In essence, this doctrine provides that government action is not subject to judicial review by individual suit unless the *government has consented* to be sued.

a. Waivers to Be "Strictly Construed"

"We have frequently held . . . that a waiver of sovereign immunity is to be strictly construed, in terms of its scope, in favor of the sovereign." [**Dept. of Army v. Blue Fox, Inc.,** 525 U.S. 255 (1999)]

2. Waivers by the Federal Government

a. Waiver for Actions That Do Not Seek Money Damages

As discussed *supra* at p. 172, the federal government has waived sovereign immunity for actions that do not seek "money damages." [**5 U.S.C. § 702**] Sovereign immunity thus does not pose an obstacle to, for example, challenging a rule or the results of an adjudication.

b. Cross-Cutting Statutes That Waive as to Money Damages

Several important, cross-cutting statutes waive the federal government's immunity for various claims for money damages. The most prominent examples are:

The ***Federal Tort Claims Act,*** which permits plaintiffs to sue the federal government to obtain compensation for torts committed by its employees. For more on the FTCA, see generally §§ 698–705.

The **Tucker Act**, which grants jurisdiction "to render judgment upon any claim against the United States founded either upon the Constitution, or any Act of Congress or any regulation of an executive department, or upon any express or implied contract with the United States, or for liquidated or unliquidated damages in cases not sounding in tort." [**28 U.S.C. § 1491(a)(1)**] The Tucker Act does not create substantive rights against the United States, which must be found in some other source of law. Plaintiffs commonly rely on the Tucker Act for contract and takings claims.

c. Agency-Specific Statutes

Congress sometimes waives sovereign immunity in an agency's enabling act. For instance, a provision authorizing an agency "to sue and be sued" effects a broad waiver of sovereign immunity for that agency. [**Federal Deposit Ins. Corp. v. Meyer,** 510 U.S. 471 (1994)]

3. Overview of the Eleventh Amendment and Related Law

This subsection offers a brief overview of the federal constitutional protections of state sovereign immunity growing out of or related to the 11th Amendment.

The 11th Amendment provides:

> The Judicial power of the United States shall not be construed to extend to any suit in law or equity, commenced or prosecuted against one of the United States by Citizens of another State, or by Citizens or Subjects of any Foreign State.

On its face, this language is quite narrow. It would, for instance, block a citizen of Texas from suing the state of New York in federal court. It would not block a citizen of Texas from suing the state of Texas in federal court.

The Supreme Court has, however, read the 11th Amendment as one aspect of broader concepts of state sovereign immunity embedded in the Constitution. The Constitution's protections of state sovereign immunity are thus broader than the text of the 11th Amendment might suggest. They are also subject to a complex set of limitation.

a. Citizens Can't Sue Their Own States

Notwithstanding the limited text of the Eleventh Amendment, sovereign immunity protects a state from suits in federal court brought by its own citizens. [**Hans v. Louisiana,** 134 U.S. 1 (1890)]

b. Bar on Private Actions Against States in State Courts

Congress cannot abrogate a state's sovereign immunity by adopting a law that allows suit to be brought against a state in *state* (as opposed to federal) court. [**Alden v. Maine,** 527 U.S. 706 (1999)]

c. Bar on Private Actions in Administrative Courts

Congress cannot authorize private action against states in administrative adjudication under its Commerce Clause power. [**FMC v. South Carolina State Ports Authority,** 535 U.S. 743 (2002)]

d. Congressional Abrogation Through the Fourteenth Amendment

Congress can authorize actions against states in federal courts when it is implementing the Fourteenth Amendment, on the theory that the Fourteenth Amendment overrides the Eleventh Amendment. [**Fitzpatrick v. Bitzer,** 427 U.S. 445 (1976)] However, Congress must make its intention to abrogate unmistakably clear. [**Dellmuth v. Muth,** 491 U.S. 223 (1989)]

The Court reviews exercise of this abrogation power to ensure that Congress uses it only to remedy and deter violations of rights guaranteed by court decisions under the Fourteenth Amendment. [**Kimel v. Florida Board of Regents,** 528 U.S. 62 (2000) (declaring, "[t]here must be a congruence and proportionality between the injury to be prevented or remedied and the means adopted to that end"; holding that Congress could not subject states to liability for violations of the Age Discrimination in Employment Act)]

e. Congress Cannot Use Article I Powers to Abrogate

Congress lacks power to abrogate the Eleventh Amendment under the authority of the Commerce Clause or its other Article I powers. [**Seminole Tribe of Florida v. Florida,** 517 U.S. 44 (1996)]

f. Federal Government as Plaintiff

The Eleventh Amendment bars private suits against states. It does not prohibit the *federal government* from suing a state in federal court. [**Seminole Tribe of Florida v. Florida,** 517 U.S. 44 (1996)]

g. Suing a State Official for Injunctive Relief as a Work Around

The Eleventh Amendment does not block a plaintiff from suing a state official for injunctive relief to forbid actions alleged to be unconstitutional or in violation of a federal statute. [***Ex parte* Young,** 209 U.S. 123 (1908)] The *Ex parte Young* doctrine indulges the fiction that a suit seeking to affect an official's discharge of her duties is not really against the state because the state would not authorize illegal action.

Nor does the Eleventh Amendment prevent a court from awarding *attorney's fees* to the plaintiff who successfully obtains such an injunction. [**Hutto v. Finney,** 437 U.S. 678 (1978)]

h. Limits on Suing State Officials for Damages

A plaintiff may sue individual state officials for damages that will *not have to be paid by the state.* (Note, however, that such actions may be barred by official immunity *see infra,* p. 184.) [**Scheuer v. Rhodes,** 416 U.S. 232 (1974)] However, the Eleventh Amendment forbids an action in federal court for damages if, even though suit is filed *against a state official,* the damages would in fact be *paid by the state.* [**Edelman v. Jordan,** 415 U.S. 651 (1974)]

Example: *Edelman* involved an action against a state officer for retroactive welfare benefits that had been denied by the state under an unlawful regulation. Since liability would fall on the state treasury, the action was barred. (The Court also held that state participation in a federal-state welfare program did not constitute consent to be sued.)

C. Tort Liability of Government

1. In General

An action in tort can provide an effective form of judicial review of government activities. However, the doctrine of sovereign immunity will preclude tort liability unless the government has *waived* its immunity.

2. Introduction to the Federal Tort Claims Act

a. Federal Government Liability for Negligent Torts

Tort actions against the federal government have been authorized since 1946 under the Federal Tort Claims Act ("FTCA"). [28 U.S.C. §§ 1346(b), 2671 *et seq.*]

Subject to various procedural limitations and substantive exceptions, the FTCA allows:

> [C]ivil actions on claims against the United States, for money damages ... for injury or loss of property, or personal injury or death caused by the negligent or wrongful act

or omission of any employee of the Government while acting within the scope of his office or employment, under circumstances where the United States, if a private person, would be liable to the claimant in accordance with the law of the place where the act or omission occurred.

28 U.S.C. § 1346(b)(1).

b. Strict Liability Torts

The FTCA has not been applied to *strict liability* torts. For example, the United States is not liable where the plaintiff claims injury from an ultrahazardous activity carried on by government employees, unless negligence can be shown. [**Laird v. Nelms,** 406 U.S. 797 (1972) (damage from sonic boom)]

c. Intentional Torts

The FTCA expressly *exempts* the government from liability for many intentional torts caused by federal employees, such as defamation or misrepresentation. [**28 U.S.C. § 2680(h)**]

The FTCA also, however, largely exempts federal investigative and law enforcement officers from the protection of this exemption. [*Id.* (preserving the FTCA waiver for torts such as assault, battery, and false imprisonment by investigative and law enforcement officers)]

d. Discretionary Functions

The government is immune from tort liability for damages "based on the exercise or performance of or the failure to exercise or perform a discretionary function or duty" even if the discretion is abused. [28 U.S.C. § 2680(a)]

"[T]he purpose of the exception is to prevent judicial second-guessing of legislative and administrative decisions grounded in social, economic, and political policy through the medium of an action in tort." [**United States v. Gaubert,** 499 U.S. 315 (1991) (quotation marks omitted)]

This exemption can be difficult to apply in practice.

(1) High-Level Decisions

High-level policy decisions about how to implement a regulatory program are within the discretionary function exception. [**United States v. Varig Airlines,** 467 U.S. 797 (1984) (the decision to approve manufacturers' designs for new commercial aircraft by spot-checking the designs, rather than by checking every detail, is immune under the discretionary function exception)]

(2) Lower Level Implementation Decisions

Lower-level actions may or may not be covered by the discretionary function exception. An action cannot be discretionary where it violates a statute or regulation. Where an action falls within the discretion left by a statute, regulation, or guideline, there is a presumption that the action was grounded in policy concerns and thus involved a discretionary function. [**United States v. Gaubert,** 499 U.S. 315 (1991)] "For a complaint to survive a motion to dismiss, it must allege facts which would support a finding that the challenged actions are not the kind of conduct that can be said to be grounded in the policy of the regulatory regime." [*Id.*]

 Example—bank supervision: Agency employees closely supervised the management of a bank. Their discretion to recommend managerial changes reflected agency policy. Therefore the government was immune from negligence liability under the discretionary function exception. [**United States v. Gaubert,** *supra*]

Example—driving: Driving a car involves discretionary decisions, but that discretion is not grounded in regulatory policy. Consequently, negligent driving is *not* within the discretionary function exception. [**United States v. Gaubert,** *supra*]

Example—scientific judgment: If approval of a new polio vaccine violated clearly established objective scientific standards, it would not be a discretionary function, but if the approval process required the exercise of policy judgment, it would be a discretionary function. [**Berkovitz v. United States,** 486 U.S. 531 (1988)]

e. FTCA Excludes Constitutional Torts

The FTCA subjects the government to liability under circumstances where, if it were a private person, it "would be liable to the claimant in accordance with the *law of the place* where the act or omission occurred." [28 U.S.C. § 1346(b)(1)] The Supreme Court has held that "law of the place" refers to state law. The FTCA therefore does not waive sovereign immunity for constitutional torts committed by federal officials. [**FDIC v. Meyer,** 510 U.S. 471 (1994)]

In very limited contexts, a plaintiff can use a *Bivens* action to sue a federal official for damages for violation of a constitutional right. [*See infra,* pp. 183–184, discussing *Bivens* actions].

f. FTCA Expands *Official* Immunity

In 1988, Congress amended the FTCA in the Federal Employees Liability Reform and Tort Compensation Act, commonly known as the Westfall Act. The Westfall Act provides that, where the FTCA applies, its remedy against the government is exclusive, precluding liability against the government employee. [**28 U.S.C. § 2679(b)(1)**] This result holds even if an exception in the FTCA itself blocks the government from being liable. [**United States v. Smith,** 499 U.S. 160 (1991); **Levin v. United States,** 133 S.Ct. 1224 (2013)]

3. Liability of State Government

a. Traditional Rule and Its "Proprietary" Exception

Under the traditional rule, state and local governments were not liable for the torts of agents. However, this rule was subject to an exception that the government could be held liable if the agent was engaged in a *"proprietary"* rather than a *"governmental"* function. This distinction created a great deal of confusion in classifying agents' activities.

b. Modern Trend—Immunity Limited or Abolished

Today, many states have abolished or limited governmental immunity by statute or judicial decision. [*See, e.g.,* **Muskopf v. Corning Hospital District,** 55 Cal. 2d 211 (1961); **Jones v. State Highway Comm'n,** 557 S.W.2d 225 (Mo. 1977) (noting that nearly 30 states had abolished or limited state governmental immunity by judicial decision or statute); *and see* Torts Summary]

c. Governmental Liability Under § 1983—Local vs. State

Under 42 U.S.C. § 1983, plaintiffs can sue local government entities for damages for violations of federal rights. Local government entities are not subject to liability for an employee's violation based on simple application of respondeat superior, however. Rather, for liability to extend to the local government, the employee must have been carrying out an official policy or custom. [**Monell v. Department of Social Services,** 436 U.S. 658 (1978)]

Note that § 1983 does not permit damage actions against *states or state agencies* because states are not "persons" under section 1983. [**Will v. Michigan Department of State Police,** 491 U.S. 58 (1989)] This immunity extends to state officials sued in their "official" capacities because such suits are really directed against the state itself. [*Id.*]

D. Tort Liability of Government Officials

1. In General

Government officials frequently enjoy official immunity from tort claims or claims based on violations of constitutional rights, which arise from their activities in the line of duty. The default rule is qualified immunity, which protects officials from liability for damages where they do not "violate *clearly established* statutory or constitutional rights of which a *reasonable* person would have known." Some officials, however, enjoy absolute immunity.

2. Modern Law—Immunities for Officials

a. Absolute Immunity Based on Official Position

Certain officials are *absolutely immune* from liability for damages for actions taken pursuant to their official functions, even though their conduct is tortious or violates constitutional or statutory rights.

(1) The President

The President (or a former President) of the United States is absolutely immune from damage actions for official conduct occurring during his term of office. [**Nixon v. Fitzgerald,** 457 U.S. 731 (1982)] However, the President can be made to disclose documents needed for a criminal case [**United States v. Nixon,** 418 U.S. 683 (1974)] and is not immune from liability arising out of acts occurring before he assumed office [**Clinton v. Jones,** 520 U.S. 681 (1997) (President not entitled to deferral of discovery until after he leaves office for claims arising out of alleged sexual harassment occurring before he became President)].

(2) Presidential Aides

A presidential aide has absolute immunity from liability if engaged in discharging a special function so sensitive as to require a total shield. For example, conducting diplomatic relations probably would fall within this area. However, other functions give rise only to qualified immunity (*see infra* at p. 183). [**Harlow v. Fitzgerald,** 457 U.S. 800 (1982)]

(3) Judges

State and federal judges are absolutely immune from liability for actions taken in the line of duty. The theory is that a judge could not carry out judicial duties under the threat of possible liability. [**Stump v. Sparkman,** 435 U.S. 349 (1978)]

Example: A trial judge ordered a child to be sterilized without even holding a hearing. Despite the fact that this decision was blatantly wrong, the judge was not held liable because he had acted under a statute granting him broad general jurisdiction. [**Stump v. Sparkman,** *supra*]

 Compare: If the judge had acted in the clear absence of any jurisdiction, he would not be immune from suit. [**Bradley v. Fisher,** 80 U.S. (13 Wall.) 335 (1871)]

(a) Injunctive Relief and Attorneys' Fees

While a judge cannot be sued for damages, a judge may be *enjoined* under 42 U.S.C. § 1983 from acting in an unconstitutional manner (such as by setting bail for offenses for which a person cannot be imprisoned). Moreover, a judge who has been subject to such an injunction is liable for a plaintiff's attorney's fees under 42 U.S.C. § 1988. [**Pulliam v. Allen,** 466 U.S. 522 (1984)]

(4) Others Engaged in Adjudicative Process

Prosecutors, agency officials who present evidence, witnesses, and administrative law judges all enjoy absolute immunity. [**Butz v. Economou,** 438 U.S. 478 (1978); **Imbler v. Pachtman,** 424 U.S. 409 (1976)]

However, state public defenders are not absolutely immune from liability for intentional torts. [**Tower v. Glover,** 467 U.S. 914 (1984) (alleged conspiracy between public defender, judge, and prosecutor to convict plaintiff)] Similarly, the members of a prison disciplinary committee who adjudicate prisoner misconduct cases have qualified, not absolute, liability. [**Cleavinger v. Saxner,** 474 U.S. 193 (1986)]

(5) Legislators

Both federal and state legislators enjoy absolute immunity from liability for actions taken as legislators.

(a) Congress

Members of Congress are protected by the Speech or Debate Clause of the Constitution. [U.S. Const. Art. 1, § 6; **Gravel v. United States,** 408 U.S. 606 (1972)]

(b) State Legislators

State legislators and rulemakers enjoy absolute immunity from civil liability (both from damages *and* equitable relief) for conduct in enacting laws, adopting rules, or otherwise serving in a legislative capacity.

 Example: The chairman of a state legislative committee was immune from civil liability where he was charged with conspiring to "smear" a candidate by summoning him to a hearing. [**Tenney v. Brandhove,** 341 U.S. 367 (1951)]

b. Absolute Immunity Under the Westfall Act/FTCA

As noted above, § 705, the Westfall Act provides that the FTCA's remedy against the government, where applicable, is exclusive. The Westfall Act thus provides absolute immunity to government employees for tort claims cognizable under the FTCA. This immunity holds even where the FTCA itself applies an exception that blocks the government itself from being held liable. [**28 U.S.C. § 2679(b)(1); United States v. Smith,** 499 U.S. 160 (1991) (government doctor negligently delivered a child at Army hospital in Italy but FTCA excluded recovery for injuries sustained outside the country); **Levin v. United States,** 133 S.Ct. 1224 (2013)]

(1) Common Law Immunity

In a decision of uncertain scope that preceded enactment of § 2679(b), the Court held that a high government official was immune from tort liability for actions within the scope of his discretionary authority. [**Barr v. Matteo,** 360 U.S. 564 (1959) (issuance of defamatory press release is within scope of department head's discretionary authority)]

c. Qualified Immunity

The default rule is that government officials enjoy only *qualified immunity* from claims for civil damages.

Under this standard, "government officials performing discretionary functions generally are shielded from liability for civil damages insofar as their conduct does not violate *clearly established* statutory or constitutional rights of which a *reasonable* person would have known." [**Harlow v. Fitzgerald,** 457 U.S. 800 (1982)]

(1) An Objective Test That Is Fact Sensitive

Qualified immunity requires assessment of whether the law at issue was "clearly established." The Supreme Court has stressed that this issue is fact sensitive: "The relevant, dispositive inquiry in determining whether a right is clearly established is whether it would be clear to a reasonable officer that his conduct was unlawful in the situation he confronted." [**Brosseau v. Haugen,** 543 U.S. 194 (2004)]

Thus, the question is not whether a given law is "clear" in the abstract (*e.g.*, Is the 4th Amendment "clear"?) Rather, the proper question is whether "a reasonable official would understand that what he is doing violates that right." [*Id.*]

3. Legal Basis for Damage Actions

a. Federal Officials—Common Law Torts

A federal official *not performing duties within the scope of authority* can be sued in tort under state law. (This was the plaintiff's theory in **Barr v. Matteo,** *supra*, which was rejected because the issuance of press releases was found to be within the official's authority.)

b. Federal Officials—*Bivens* Actions for Constitutional Violations

In limited contexts, the Supreme Court has determined that a plaintiff can sue to recover monetary damages from a federal official for violation of federal constitutional rights. [**Bivens v. Six Unknown Named Agents of the Federal Bureau of Narcotics,** 403 U.S. 388 (1971)] Such *Bivens* actions provide a judicially-crafted remedy analogous to the remedy Congress created for deployment against state officials in 42 U.S.C. § 1983.

In *Bivens* itself, the plaintiff claimed that agents of the Federal Bureau of Narcotics had violated his Fourth Amendment rights by an unconstitutional search and seizure. The Court recognized that "the Fourth Amendment does not in so many words provide for its enforcement by an award of money damages." Reasoning that infringements to legal rights should have remedies, the Court held that a damages remedy should be available in part because "no special factors counsel[ed] hesitation" and there had been no "affirmative action by Congress." [*Id.*]

Soon after *Bivens,* the Court extended the reach of its remedy to certain 8th Amendment and 5th Amendment claims. [**Carlson v. Green,** 446 U.S. 14 (1980) (holding prison officials could be sued for damages for violating a prisoner's Eighth Amendment rights by denying medical care); **Davis v. Passman,** 442 U.S. 228 (1979) (holding that damages action could lie against congressman for sex discrimination in violation of employee's Fifth Amendment right to due process).

(1) Three Decades of Refusing to Expand *Bivens*' Reach

The Supreme Court has in recent decades consistently refused to expand the reach of *Bivens* actions. [*See* **Correctional Services Corp. v. Malesko,** 534 U.S. 61 (2001) (noting that since 1980, "we have consistently refused to extend *Bivens* liability to any new context or new category of defendants")]

(2) The Two-Step Inquiry

The Supreme Court has explained that determining whether to expand the reach of *Bivens* depends on a two-step inquiry:

(1) Courts should check "whether any alternative, existing process for protecting the interest amounts to a convincing reason for the Judicial Branch to refrain from providing a new and freestanding remedy in damages"; and

(2) Where no alternative process displaces *Bivens,* courts should "pay[ ] particular heed ... to any special factors counseling hesitation before authorizing a new kind of federal litigation."

[**Wilkie v. Robbins,** 551 U.S. 357 (2007) (plaintiff relied on *Bivens* to seek damages based on claim that government officials had improperly retaliated against him for invoking his property right to exclude; Court refused to extend *Bivens* in part because of "difficulty of devising a workable cause of action" that could identify "illegitimate pressure" that would rise to level of illegality); **Minneci v. Pollard,** 132 S.Ct. 617 (2012) (refusing to extend *Bivens* to apply to Eighth Amendment claim brought by prisoner against employees of private company that operated federal prison; Court observed that prisoner could invoke state tort law remedies)]

(3) *Bivens* Limited to Actions Against Officials

A *Bivens* claim can be brought only against the official who allegedly violated the plaintiff's constitutional rights, not against the agency for which the official is working. [**FDIC v. Meyer,** 510 U.S. 471 (1994)]

c. State Officials—Liability Under § 1983 for Violations of Federal Law

One of the most famous provisions of the U.S. Code, 42 U.S.C. § 1983, provides:

Every person who, under color of any statute, ordinance, regulation, custom, or usage, of any State or Territory, subjects, or causes to be subjected, any citizen of the United States or other person within the jurisdiction thereof to the deprivation of any rights, privileges, or immunities secured by the Constitution and laws shall be liable to the party injured in an action at law, suit in equity, or other proper proceeding for redress.

Summarizing the immense amount of law that has grown up around § 1983 is beyond the scope of this outline. Note, however:

(1) Official Immunities Apply

The official immunities discussed *supra* at pp. 181 *et seq.* apply to § 1983 actions for damages against officials.

(2) Section 1983 Extends to Some Statutory Violations

On its face, § 1983 covers violations of rights guaranteed not just by the Constitution but also by federal "laws." The Supreme Court has explained that whether a violation of a statute falls within § 1983's reach depends on:

> whether the statute, by its terms or as interpreted, creates obligations "sufficiently specific and definite" to be within "the competence of the judiciary to enforce," is intended to benefit the putative plaintiff, and is not foreclosed "by express provision or other specific evidence from the statute itself."

[**Golden State Transit Corp. v. City of Los Angeles,** 493 U.S. 103 (1989) (citations omitted)]

E. Statutory Preclusion of Judicial Review

1. In General

Section 701(a)(1) of the APA provides that agency decisions are reviewable "except to the extent that . . . statutes preclude judicial review."

Section 701(a)(2)'s use of the phrase, "to the extent that" indicates that statutory preclusion can be complete or partial. A decision might be reviewable as to certain issues but not others, or review might be available to certain parties but not others.

2. Background Presumption of Reviewability

Case law has established a ***presumption of reviewability.*** Courts find review foreclosed by statute only where there is "clear and convincing evidence" that Congress so intended. [**Abbott Laboratories v. Gardner,** 387 U.S. 136 (1967); **Bowen v. Michigan Academy of Family Physicians,** 476 U.S. 667 (1986)]

As explained in the next subsection, the Court often sets a very high bar for interpreting a statute as precluding judicial review. Nonetheless, on rare occasions, the Court has found statutory preclusion in the absence of express statutory direction. For discussion of "implied preclusion," *see infra,* p. 186.

3. Interpretation to Avoid Preclusion

Consistent with the presumption of reviewability, courts often interpret statutes that might seem to preclude judicial review as allowing at least limited review.

To simplify a bit, the more important the underlying issue at stake, the more likely a court is to find a way to interpret its way around statutory preclusion. Along these lines, Professor Ronald Levin has observed that, as practical matter, "the presumption against preclusion of constitutional grievances is almost irrebuttable." The Court is likewise disinclined to find that statutory preclusion blocks litigation of the validity of a law or rule of general applicability. Conversely, the Court is much more tolerant of statutory preclusion where it will block judicial resolution only of case-specific issues of fact or of application of law to fact. [Ronald M. Levin, Understanding Unreviewability in Administrative Law, 74 Minn. L. Rev. 689, 739–40 (1990)]

a. Illustration—Preclusion of Review of Factual Determinations

A benefits statute provided that decisions of the agency "are final and conclusive and not subject to review." The Court interpreted this to mean that review of *factual* determinations was precluded but relief was available where "there has been a substantial departure from important procedural rights, a misconstruction of the governing legislation, or some like error going to the heart of the administrative determination." [**Lindahl v. Office of Personnel Management,** 470 U.S. 768 (1985)]

b. Illustration—Avoiding Preclusion of Review of Rules

A statute provided amnesty for alien farm workers illegally in this country and for an administrative process for determining their applications. The statute barred judicial review of "a determination respecting an application" except in the context of review in the Court of Appeals of a deportation order. A class action alleged that INS procedural rules violated both constitutional and statutory provisions. The Court held that Congress had not precluded this form of review because the suit attacked the entire system of hearings, not merely a particular "determination respecting an application." The plaintiffs did not seek to have an application approved; rather they wished to insure fair procedures for determining applications. The fact that serious constitutional issues were raised was certainly a factor in the Court's decision to hear the case. [**McNary v. Haitian Refugee Center,** 498 U.S. 479 (1991); **Bowen v. Michigan Academy of Family Physicians,** 476 U.S. 667 (1986) (permitting judicial review of a regulation denying benefits despite preclusion of review of the denial of individual applications)]

c. Illustration—Construing to Avoid Preclusion of a Constitutional Issue

A statute allowed the Director of the CIA to discharge any CIA employee "whenever he shall deem such termination necessary or advisable in the interests of the United States." The Director discharged a homosexual employee, Doe, without stating any reason. The government argued that the statute precluded review of Doe's constitutional claims. Although the statute plainly concedes broad discretion to the Director in a highly sensitive context, the Court rejected this argument. The Court explained, "where Congress intends to preclude judicial review of constitutional claims its intent to do so must be clear." To justify this clear-statement rule, the Court added that "[w]e require this heightened showing in part to avoid the 'serious constitutional question' that would arise if a federal statute were construed to deny any judicial forum for a colorable constitutional claim." [**Webster v. Doe,** 486 U.S. 592 (1988)]

4. Implied Preclusion

As we have just seen, the Court often construes *express* statutory provisions quite narrowly to avoid finding preclusion. Given this habit, one might be forgiven for thinking that the Court would never *imply* preclusion absent an express instruction from Congress. The Court has nonetheless declared that the presumption in favor of review "may be overcome by inferences of intent drawn from the statutory scheme as a whole." [**Block v. Community Nutrition Institute,** 467 U.S. 340, 345 (1984)] In keeping with the strong presumption of reviewability, however, the mere fact that Congress has expressly authorized one limited form of review of an agency action does not, without more, raise an inference that it has precluded other means. [**Sackett v. EPA,** 132 S.Ct. 1367 (2012)]

e.g. **Illustration: Block v. Community Nutrition Institute** provides the most prominent example of implied preclusion. This case raised the question of whether consumers of dairy products could obtain judicial review of "milk market orders" issued by the Secretary of Agriculture under the Agricultural Marketing Agreement Act of 1937. Milk market orders are the product of a complex regulatory scheme designed to support milk prices payable to producers. In other words, these orders make milk products more expensive to consumers on purpose. Under the statute, both milk producers and milk "handlers" (who process milk into products for consumers) had the right to participate in agency proceedings that produce the market orders. They might also seek judicial review but only after exhausting their administrative remedies. The Court determined that this scheme, by implication, precluded judicial review of milk market orders at the behest of consumers. Allowing consumers to sue would "severely disrupt this complex and delicate administrative scheme." In particular, it would allow handlers to evade the exhaustion requirement by suing as consumers (or finding a cooperative consumer to bring suit for them). It would also enable them to make an end run around sharp limitations on injunctive relief. [**Block v. Community Nutrition Institute,** 467 U.S. 340 (1984)]

F. Commitment to Agency Discretion

1. The Apparent Contradiction

The APA states that agency action is not reviewable "to the extent that agency action is *committed to agency discretion by law*." [APA § 701(a)(2)] The APA also, however, provides that agency actions should be set aside for "*abuse of discretion*." [APA § 706(2)(A)] Thus, the APA seems to say that agency discretionary action is both reviewable and unreviewable.

2. "No Law to Apply"

The Supreme Court has resolved this conflict by construing § 701(a)(2) to block review only where agencies for some reason should enjoy an especially high level of discretion.

One of the Court's favored formulations for this heightened discretion is that § 701(a)(2) blocks review only in those "rare instances where statutes are drawn in such broad terms that in a given case there is no law to apply." [**Citizens to Preserve Overton Park v. Volpe,** 401 U.S. 402 (1971) (quotation marks and citation omitted)] There is no law to apply where the statute provides no judicially manageable standards to detect abuse. [**Heckler v. Cheney,** 470 U.S. 821 (1985)]

This "no law to apply" formulation should be taken with a grain of salt as there is *always* some law to apply, "beginning with the fundamental constraint that the decision must be taken in order to further a public purpose rather than a purely private interest." [**Webster v. Doe,** 486 U.S. 592 (1988) (Scalia, J., dissenting)]

a. Illustration: Finding Some Law to Apply in *Overton Park*

In *Citizens to Preserve Overton Park, supra,* a statute provided that no funds could be granted to construct a highway through a public park if there was a "feasible and prudent" alternate route. The Secretary of Transportation nevertheless approved funding of such a highway, without stating a reason for doing so. The Secretary contended that the word "prudent" in the statute conveyed wide-ranging discretion that blocked review under § 701(a)(2). The Court disagreed, noting that Congress plainly meant for the Secretary to emphasize the factor of protecting parkland and give less weight to cost considerations. Thus, the Secretary's action was constrained by "law to apply."

b. Illustration: "High Quality and Cost-Effective" Is Law

Courts generally construe statutes that appear to provide for broad discretion to include a standard sufficient for judicial review for abuse of discretion. For example, a statute called for "high quality and cost-effective" health care. One might plausibly think that this phrase is so vacuous as to leave "no law to apply." The D.C. Circuit nonetheless concluded that this language did not trigger preclusion under § 701(a)(2). [**Cody v. Cox,** 509 F.3d 606 (D.C. Cir. 2007) (noting that "[w]e have regularly found Congress has not committed decisions to agency discretion under far more permissive and indeterminate language")]

3. What Is "Committed to Agency Discretion"

Insofar as there is always some law to apply if a court looks hard enough for it, other factors must contribute to determining whether § 701(a)(2) precludes review. Accordingly, the Court has held agency action unreviewable in several contexts where judicial review would be counterproductive or contrary to long practice.

a. Decisions Not to Enforce or Prosecute

Decisions declining to prosecute or enforce a statute are *presumptively unreviewable*. In general, judicial review of such decisions would be a bad idea because: (a) they implicate a "complex balancing" of agency resources and priorities; (b) where an agency declines to enforce, it does not deploy coercive force against individuals; (c) where an agency does not bring an enforcement action, it does not create a record that can "focus" judicial review; and (d) agency decisions to decline to enforce are analogous to prosecutors' decisions not to indict, which have "long been regarded as the special province of the Executive Branch." [**Heckler v. Cheney,** 470 U.S. 821 (1985) (holding unreviewable FDA's decision not to initiate enforcement action regarding drugs used for state executions)]

Note, however, that this presumption is rebuttable. If Congress provides instructions to an agency regarding when to bring an enforcement action, § 701(a)(2) will not block judicial review of compliance. [**Cook v. FDA,** 733 F.3d 1 (2103) (holding that death row inmates could obtain review of FDA's failure to comply with a statute providing that the agency "shall" sample and examine drugs imported from unregistered establishments; noting "ample support" from case law for the idea that "shall" means "must")]

b. Dismissal of Intelligence Officers

Section 102(c) of the National Security Act of 1947 allowed the Director of the CIA to discharge any CIA employee "whenever he shall deem such termination necessary or advisable in the interests of the United States." The Director discharged a homosexual employee without stating any reason.

The Court held that § 701(a)(2) blocked review of whether the Director had complied with § 102(c). Along the way, the Court invoked the "no law to apply" principle and observed that the statute, which merely requires the Director to "deem" a person a security threat "fairly exudes deference."

The Court also, however, rested its decision on security concerns, observing "the Agency's efficacy, and the Nation's security, depend in large measure on the reliability and trustworthiness of the Agency's employees." [**Webster v. Doe,** 486 U.S. 592 (1988)]

Note, however, that the Court did not deploy § 701(a)(2) to block review of Doe's *constitutional* claims—where the Constitution itself would provide "law to apply." Moreover, it declined to read § 102(c) as precluding review by statute under § 701(a)(1), as discussed at *supra,* p. 186.

c. Agency Allocations of Lump-Sum Appropriations

Congress has, under the Snyder Act, authorized the Indian Health Service to "expend such moneys as Congress may from time to time appropriate, for the benefit, care, and assistance of the Indians" for the "relief of distress and conservation of health." The Service shifted resources from a program that provided medical clinical services to handicapped children in the Southwest to a national program.

The Court held that this allocation decision was unreviewable under § 701(a)(2). Justifying this conclusion, the Court noted: (a) allocation of lump-sum funds has "traditionally" been regarded as committed to agency discretion; (b) the point of lump-sum allocations is to grant agencies flexibility; and (c) allocation involves a "complicated balancing" of factors regarding agency resources and priorities. [**Lincoln v. Vigil,** 508 U.S. 182 (1993)]

G. Threshold Requirements of "Agency Action" by an "Agency"

The APA's template for general statutory review, §§ 701–706, applies to "agency action[s]." [APA §§ 701, 702, 704] Thus, the APA's template does not apply either: (a) to actions by entities other than "agencies"; or (b) to agency determinations that do not amount to "agency action."

Both "agency" and "agency action" are defined terms in the APA. [APA §§ 551(1), (13)]

1. "Agency"—A Broad Definition That Excludes the President

a. APA Definition of "Agency"

The APA's definition of "*agency*" is extremely broad and vague:

Agency means each authority of the Government of the United States, whether or not it is within or subject to review by another agency. [APA § 551(1)]

This definition goes on to enumerate specific exceptions, including, among others, Congress, federal courts, territorial governments, and the government of the District of Columbia.

b. The President Is Not an "Agency"

Even though the President is not listed among the exceptions to the APA's definition of "agency," the Supreme Court held that the President is not considered an "agency" except where Congress explicitly so states. The Court was concerned with issues of separation of powers and undue judicial interference with presidential functions. As a result, the President's decisions are not reviewable under the APA for abuse of discretion; they are, however, subject to review for violation of provisions of the Constitution. [**Franklin v. Massachusetts,** 505 U.S. 788 (1992) (holding that President's decision to allocate overseas military personnel to states for apportioning congressional seats was not reviewable under the APA for abuse of discretion but that "the President's actions may still be reviewed for constitutionality")]

2. "Agency Action" Under the APA

a. APA Definition of "Agency Action

"*Agency action*" includes the whole or a part of an agency rule, order, license, sanction, relief, or the equivalent or denial thereof, or failure to act." [APA § 551(13)]

This definition can be divided into three subcategories. First, it lists various types of affirmative acts an agency might take—*e.g.*, rules, orders, etc. Note that these affirmative acts have their own definitions in § 551. The "equivalent[s]" of these acts also fall within the definition of "agency action." Thus, a "rule" by any other name remains a "rule."

Second, the definition of "agency action" includes "denial[s]" of requests for previously listed affirmative acts. Thus, a denial of a petition for a rule would constitute "agency action." Note that "denial" in this context means an active refusal rather than, for instance, a failure to make a determination.

Third comes the most problematic bit—"agency action" includes "failure[s] to act." Viewed one way, agencies are at all times failing to take an infinite number of actions. Moreover, it is child's play to re-characterize any given action as a failure to act. Adopting this broad interpretation of "failure to act" would prevent the definition of "agency action" from imposing a meaningful limit on the availability of judicial review. The Supreme Court avoided this result in **Norton v. Southern Utah Wilderness Assoc.**, 542 U.S. 55 (2004), discussed below at p. 190.

b. "Programmatic" Attacks

A plaintiff cannot invoke the APA's scheme of general statutory review to mount a "kind of broad programmatic attack" that piles up a large amount of agency activity without focusing on one or more particular "agency actions." [**SUWA**, *supra*]

For instance, in **Lujan v. National Wildlife Federation**, the Court rejected a challenge to the Bureau of Land Management's "land withdrawal program" in part because it did not amount to a discrete "agency action":

> The term "land withdrawal review program" (which as far as we know is not derived from any authoritative text) does not refer to a single BLM order or regulation, or even to a completed universe of particular BLM orders and regulations. It is simply the name by which petitioners have occasionally referred to the continuing (and thus constantly changing) operations of the BLM in reviewing withdrawal revocation applications and the classifications of public lands and developing land use plans as required by the FLPMA.

[497 U.S. 871 (1990) (observing that the BLM's "land withdrawal program "is no more an identifiable 'agency action' . . . than a "weapons procurement program" of the Department of Defense or a "drug interdiction program" of the Drug Enforcement Administration")]

c. Limiting Judicial Power to Fix "Failure[s] to Act"

The APA template for general statutory review applies to "agency action[s]." [APA §§ 701 *et seq.*] The category of "agency action," however, includes "failure to act." [APA § 551(13)] Also, §706(1)instructs courts to "compel agency action unlawfully withheld or unreasonably delayed."

Together, these provisions implicate the problem of determining the scope of judicial power to force agencies to act. In **Norton v. Southern Utah Wilderness Assoc.**, 542 U.S. 55 (2004), the Court hemmed in this power by: (a) narrowly construing the meaning of "failure to act" as a form of "agency action"; and (b) construing judicial remedial authority under § 706(1) as extending only to agency actions that are legally required rather than discretionary.

(1) The Court's Narrow Construction of "Failure to Act"

> The Court defined "failure to act" as used in the APA's definition of "agency action" as limited to a "failure to take one of the agency actions (including their equivalents) earlier defined in § 551(13)." [**Norton v. Southern Utah Wilderness Association** 542 U.S. 55 (2004)] Thus, "agency action" includes failure to adopt a rule, or an order, or another listed element of the definition of "agency action."
>
> To help justify this conclusion, the Court observed that all the other types of "agency action" listed in § 551(13) shared the attribute of discreteness—*i.e.*, they are focused

activities rather than broad programs. The canon of construction *ejusdem generis* suggested that the final element in the list of agency actions, "failure to act," should share this quality.

(2) Remedy Extends to Compelling Actions "Unlawfully Withheld or Unreasonably Delayed"

A court's remedial power under § 706(1) extends only to compelling agency action that is "unlawfully withheld or unreasonably delayed." In *Norton v. SUWA,* the Court declared, "a delay cannot be unreasonable with respect to action that is not required." Thus, a court can fix a failure to act by compelling action only if the action was "legally required."

Note well: This limitation to actions that are "legally required" blocks a court from using its remedial power to tell an agency how it must exercise its discretion. [*Id.*]

For discussion of the standard for determining if agency action has been "unreasonably withheld," *see infra,* p. 211.

(3) The Combined Force of These Requirements

Application of the principles of *Norton* to the facts of that case reveals its true power to curb judicial control of agency inaction. SUWA contended that the Bureau of Land Management (BLM) had failed to carry out its statutory mission of preventing impairment of the wilderness qualities of wilderness study areas. More particularly, SUWA was upset by damage caused by the use of off-road vehicles (ORVs).

Under *Norton*, an entity such as SUWA cannot seek relief that is not "required by law." By hypothesis, within an agency's zone of discretion, the law does not require a particular result. Thus, a court could not, consistent with *Norton*, order the BLM to implement its non-impairment duty in any particular way—e.g., by banning ORV use.

You might think that SUWA could get around this problem by seeking a more general order requiring BLM to comply with its statutory mission to prevent impairment. The court order would tell the agency to do its job without telling it how. This move cannot work, however, because of the Court's narrow construction of the APA's definition of "failure to act." This definition captures an agency's failure to adopt a particular rule or order. It does not capture an agency's programmatic failure to do a better job carrying out a broad statutory mission.

In sum, a petitioner who is unhappy with an agency's failure to implement a broad statutory mission cannot use § 706(1) either: (a) to obtain a court order telling the agency how to exercise its discretion to implement its mission; or (b) to obtain a more general court order telling the agency to do its job without telling it how to do so.

Chapter Nine
Access to the Courts: Standing and Timing

CONTENTS	PAGE
Key Exam Issues	194
A. Standing to Seek Judicial Review in Federal Court	195
B. The Timing of Judicial Review	208

Key Exam Issues

Exam questions involving judicial review typically involve questions of both standing and timing. Standing refers to whether *a particular plaintiff is* entitled to seek review. Timing doctrines may block a plaintiff from challenging an agency action either too early or too late.

1. **Standing**

    One of reasons that "standing" doctrine is confusing is that the term actually refers to three distinct doctrines—constitutional standing, statutory standing, and prudential standing.

    a. **Constitutional standing**

        A plaintiff must have suffered an ***injury in fact*** that was ***caused by*** the conduct that the plaintiff challenges. Also, it must be likely as opposed to speculative that a favorable decision for the plaintiff will ***redress*** the injury. As you will see, the meaning of "injury in fact" is not clear. Also, courts have not been consistent on the strength of the causal link needed for constitutional standing nor on the likelihood that a favorable judicial order would remedy the plaintiff's injury.

    b. **Statutory standing**

        The issue of statutory standing speaks to whether Congress (or some other legislature) has granted a particular plaintiff a statutory right to sue for some violation of law. The most important grant of statutory standing you will encounter in your Administrative Law class is **5 U.S.C. § 702** of the APA. This statutory provision authorizes suit by persons "adversely affected or aggrieved within the meaning of the relevant statute." A generous judicial gloss on this language provides that a plaintiff can sue to enforce a statutory requirement so long as the plaintiff seeks to protect an interest that "arguably" falls within the "zone of interests" to be protected by that statute.

    c. **Prudential standing**

        Courts purport that constitutional limits on standing are required by Article III of the Constitution—perhaps with some help from Article II. By contrast, courts freely admit that they developed prudential limits on standing. The most prominent example of a prudential limitation is the doctrine of ***third party standing***, which limits the ability of a plaintiff to vindicate the legal interests of somebody else. As, by hypothesis, prudential limits are not constitutionally required, Congress can trump them with a grant of statutory standing.

2. **Timing**

    A court may reject a petition for review for any of the following reasons:

    a. **Finality**

        Administrative law generally requires that agency action be ***final*** before it is susceptible to judicial review. According to the black letter, an agency action is final if it is: (a) consummated; and (b) determines legal rights and obligations or otherwise creates legal consequences.

    b. **Ripeness**

        Parties frequently challenge agency rules before they are applied in specific cases. Whether such a pre-enforcement challenge is ***ripe*** for immediate review depends broadly on two factors. The first is "fitness" for review. This inquiry generally turns on whether a case would benefit from further factual development by administrative authorities before proceedings in court. A purely legal challenge that does not depend on case-specific facts will generally satisfy this fitness prong. The second factor involves judicial assessment of the hardship a plaintiff will suffer if judicial review is delayed.

c. **Exhaustion of administrative remedies**

In some contexts, administrative law regards an agency action as final even though a party might seek review of that action within the agency itself. Where parties skip intra-agency remedies, their suits are vulnerable to dismissal for *failure to exhaust*.

Exhaustion doctrine has both statutory and common-law forms. The most important statutory exhaustion requirement for your administrative law class is at **5 U.S.C. § 704** of the APA, but various agency enabling acts contain their own exhaustion provisions.

Where no statutory exhaustion requirement applies, courts apply a common-law form of the doctrine. Common-law exhaustion applies a balancing test that weighs a party's interest in immediate judicial review against institutional interests favoring further review by the agency. The default balance favors requiring exhaustion. Circumstances where courts depart from this balance include: (a) where requiring exhaustion would cause *undue prejudice* to a party; (b) where an agency *lacks authority* to grant relief; and (c) where intra-agency appeal would be *futile* because the agency is *biased* or has otherwise predetermined the outcome.

A. Standing to Seek Judicial Review in Federal Court

1. Introduction—One Word; Three Doctrines

A party who wishes to obtain judicial review of an administrative decision must have "standing" to do so. In federal courts, the term "standing" refers to three distinct doctrines.

First, there is constitutional standing, which courts generally attribute to the Article III of the Constitution, which limits judicial authority to resolution of "cases or controversies." The Supreme Court has also suggested that constitutional standing limitations block courts from infringing on the President's constitutional authority under Article II, § 3 to "take Care that the laws be faithfully executed." [**Lujan v. Defenders of Wildlife,** 504 U.S. 555 (1992). *But see* **Steel Co. v. Citizens for a Better Environment,** 523 U.S. 83, 102 n. 4 (1998) (explaining that "standing jurisprudence . . . may sometimes have an impact on Presidential powers, [but it] derives from Article III and not Article II)"]

Second, there is statutory standing. This doctrine examines whether Congress has authorized a plaintiff to sue to enforce a given statutory provision. The most important grant of statutory standing is **5 U.S.C. § 702** of the APA, which provides a that "a person suffering legal wrong because of agency action, or adversely affected or aggrieved by agency action within the meaning of the relevant statute, is entitled to judicial review thereof."

Third, there is prudential standing. This doctrine is composed of a set of limitations on standing that courts admit to having fashioned themselves—rather than claiming to find them somewhere in the Constitution.

a. Flexibility on Order of Decision

The Supreme Court has held that a federal court must resolve jurisdictional issues before it may address the merits of a case. Thus, a federal court must address questions of standing before deciding the merits. [**Steel Co. v. Citizens for a Better Environment,** 523 U.S. 83 (1998)] A court may, however, choose the order in which it decides non-merits issues. For instance, it "may dispose of an action by a *forum non conveniens* dismissal, bypassing questions of subject-matter and personal jurisdiction, when considerations of convenience, fairness, and judicial economy so warrant." [**Simochem Intern. Co. Ltd. v. Malaysia Intern. Shipping Co.,** 549 U.S. 422 (2007)]

2. Constitutional Standing

a. The Injury/Causation/Redressability Test

The Supreme Court has interpreted the "case or controversy" requirement of Article III as requiring the following for constitutional standing:

> First, the plaintiff must have suffered an ***"injury in fact"***—an invasion of a legally protected interest which is (a) concrete and particularized, and (b) "actual or imminent, not 'conjectural' or 'hypothetical[.]' "
>
> Second, there must be a ***causal connection*** between the injury and the conduct complained of—the injury has to be "fairly . . . trace[able] to the challenged action of the defendant, and not . . . th[e] result [of] the independent action of some third party not before the court."
>
> Third, it must be "likely," as opposed to merely "speculative," that the injury will be "*redressed*" by a favorable decision.

[**Lujan v. Defenders of Wildlife,** 504 U.S. 555 (1992) (many citations omitted; bold added)].

(1) A Test That Is Easy to Memorize but Hard to Apply

The law of constitutional standing is famously messy. The concept of "injury in fact" is not well-defined, and justices and judges frequently disagree on its application. The requirements of causation and redressability are, to put the matter charitably, elastic. A cynic might be inclined to say that the Supreme Court tightens and loosens these requirements as the occasion demands. Results tend to be ideologically charged, with conservatives and liberals on the Court casting their votes in predictable ways.

The upshot of these problems for you in your Administrative Law course is that there is no substitute for careful reading and analysis of the standing cases your professor chooses to assign. The "easy" three-part test of injury/causation/redressability hides as much as it illuminates.

(2) Disagreement over Purpose

Generalizations about constitutional standing doctrine should be regarded carefully given its messy state. That said, its ideological charge is reflected in the differing purposes of constitutional standing that conservatives and liberals tend to stress. The conservative wing frequently stresses its importance as a bulwark against courts usurping the powers of the majoritarian, political branches. [**Clapper v. Amnesty Intern. USA,** 133 S.Ct. 1138 (2013) (Alito, J.) ("The law of Article III standing, which is built on separation-of-powers principles, serves to prevent the judicial process from being used to usurp the powers of the political branches.")]

The liberal wing tends to emphasize the role of standing as ensuring that plaintiffs have the type of personal stake in litigation necessary to generate the adversarial clash needed for effective judicial decisionmaking. [**Id.** (Breyer, J. dissenting) (explaining that the case-or-controversy requirement "helps to ensure that . . . questions will be presented "in a concrete factual context conducive to a realistic appreciation of the consequences of judicial action"); **Massachusetts v. EPA,** 549 U.S. 497 (2007) (explaining that "the gist of the question of standing is whether petitioners have such a personal stake . . . as to assure . . . concrete adverseness")].

b. Injury-in-Fact—Principles, Dichotomies, Pressure Points

(1) Injury Need Not Be Economic

Injury in fact does ***not require*** a showing of ***economic*** harm. Harm to a person's ***aesthetic or recreational interests is sufficient.*** [**Summers v. Earth Island Inst.**, 555 U.S. 488, 494 (2009) ("While generalized harm to the forest or the environment will not alone support standing, if that harm in fact affects the recreational or even the mere esthetic interests of the plaintiff, that will suffice.")]

(2) But the Injury Can't Be Solely "Ideological"

In *Sierra Club v. Morton,* the plaintiff Sierra Club sought to block construction of a proposed ski resort in a national forest. It claimed standing based on its longstanding interest in environmental protection. The Court rejected this effort in part due to a slippery slope concern that everyone can claim a "special interest." [**Sierra Club v. Morton**, 405 U.S. 727 (1972)]

EXAM TIP

Watch out for mere "ideological" injuries. Suppose you are an environmentalist, and you are upset that an agency has taken some action that you believe threatens the "Puce Bandicoot" with extinction. Your outrage might be genuine, but the Court will regard it, by itself, as ideological and insufficient for standing. To obtain standing, you will have to allege an injury that is "concrete," "particularized," and "actual or imminent." (More on all these requirements follows below.) It might be enough for a cognizable aesthetic injury if you allege that you have watched the Puce Bandicoot in the past, have specific plans to travel to its habitat, and will be deprived of the pleasure of watching the animal in the future if the agency action is allowed to stand. (If this all seems a trifle strange and strained to you, then it is a sign that you are paying attention.)

---

(3) The Injury Must Be "Concrete" Rather than "Abstract"

To count for standing, an injury must be "concrete" rather than "abstract." The justices agree that damage to a generalized interest in seeing the law obeyed is on the "abstract" side of this line. [*See, e.g.,* **Federal Election Comm'n v. Akins**, 524 U.S. 11, 23–24 (1998)]

The very abstractness of the distinction between "concrete" and "abstract" injuries leaves room for the justices to disagree over its application. For instance, in *FEC v. Akins,* the plaintiffs challenged the FEC's refusal to categorize the American Israel Public Affairs Committee ("AIPAC") as a "political committee," which would have subjected AIPAC to various disclosure requirements. The plaintiffs claimed injury because they wanted information from these disclosures to guide their voting. The government sought dismissal, arguing that the plaintiffs' claimed injury amounted to a generalized grievance that could not support standing. Justice Breyer, writing for the majority over Justice Scalia's vigorous dissent, rejected the government's argument. Justice Breyer explained that the "informational injury" the plaintiffs claimed, which was "directly related to voting," was "sufficiently concrete and specific" to count as an injury-in-fact. [*Id.*; *see also* **Hein v. Freedom from Religion Foundation, Inc.**, 551 U.S. 587 (2007) (Souter, J., dissenting) (explaining that "intangible harms must be evaluated case by case" to determine if they are "too abstract" to support standing; contending that the injury of "seeing one's tax dollars spent on religion" in alleged violation of the Establishment Clause was concrete enough for standing)]

(4) The Injury Must Be "Particularized" Rather than a "Generalized Grievance"

Many Supreme Court cases state that a "generalized grievance" cannot amount to an injury-in-fact for constitutional standing. The Court has sometimes justified this stance on the ground that widely-shared, generalized grievances are best left to the majoritarian, political branches to resolve.

Note well: the bar on generalized grievances does not stand for the proposition that an action that harms many people cannot cause cognizable injuries for the purpose of standing. As Justice Scalia explained in his dissent in *FEC v. Akins, supra*, in a mass tort, "[o]ne tort victim suffers a burnt leg, another a burnt arm—or even if both suffer burnt arms, they are different arms." [**Federal Election Comm'n v. Akins**, 524 U.S. 11 (1998) (Scalia, J. dissenting)] Rather, the bar on generalized grievances blocks claims based on undifferentiated injuries—where the harm suffered by the plaintiff is no different than the harm suffered by the group.

The justices agree that harm to the shared interest in seeing the law obeyed for its own sake is an example of a forbidden generalized grievance. [**Lance v. Coffman**, 549 U.S. 437, 439–42 (2007) (per curiam) (reviewing cases); **Lujan v. Defenders of Wildlife**, 504 U.S. 555, 573–74 (1992) ("We have consistently held that a plaintiff raising only a generally available grievance about government—claiming only harm to his and every citizen's interest in proper application of the Constitution and laws, and seeking relief that no more directly and tangibly benefits him than it does the public at large—does not state an Article III case or controversy.")]

For a notable application of the generalized grievance requirement, albeit in a 4-justice dissent, consider Chief Justice Roberts' opinion in *Massachusetts v. EPA.* In this case, a five-justice majority held that Massachusetts had established in injury-in-fact on the theory that EPA's failure to regulate greenhouse gases meant that the state would lose coastal property due to rising sea levels. In his dissent, the Chief Justice explained that Massachusetts' claimed injury faced insurmountable causation and redressability problems. As for other harms caused by global warming, he opined that

> The very concept of global warming seems inconsistent with this particularization requirement. Global warming is a phenomenon harmful to humanity at large, and the redress petitioners seek is focused no more on them than on the public generally—it is literally to change the atmosphere around the world.

[**Massachusetts v. EPA**, 549 U.S. 497 (2007) (Roberts, C.J., dissenting) (citation and quotation marks omitted)]

(5) The Injury, If Not "Actual," Must Be "Imminent" Rather than "Conjectural" or "Speculative"

An injury need not be presently occurring to qualify for constitutional standing—a future injury can do the trick provided it is "imminent." [**Lujan v. Defenders of Wildlife,** 540 U.S. 555 (1992) (Plaintiffs were interested in protection of endangered species in foreign countries. They alleged that they had once visited the habitat of the species and planned to do so again at some point. Because their "some day" plans to return were not specific enough, they had not shown "imminent" harm)]

The Court has conceded that "imminence" is an "elastic" concept that must be understood in light of its purpose of ensuring that an injury is not too "speculative" to qualify for standing. [**Id.**]

(a) Probabilistic Injury at the Supreme Court

Suppose that you learn today that there is a ten percent probability that a meteor will strike you dead one year from now. Learning this fact will likely ruin your day. Should this chance, however, qualify as an "imminent" injury, or is the risk so low that the injury is too "speculative" or "conjectural" to qualify for standing?

The Supreme Court's most recent discussion of this problem of probabilistic injury sent very mixed signals. In *Clapper v. Amnesty International USA*, the plaintiffs challenged a provision of the FISA Amendments of 2008, which authorized surveillance of individuals who are not "United States persons" and are reasonably believed to be outside the United States. The plaintiffs included attorneys and human rights organizations. They claimed injury-in-fact based on the "objectively reasonable likelihood" that authorized surveillance would compromise their communications with foreign contacts.

The Supreme Court rejected this claim of injury. The main text of its opinion insisted that a "threatened injury must be *certainly impending* to constitute injury in fact." (Emphasis added.) The Court then explained that the plaintiffs' theory of injury depended on a highly attenuated chain of speculative events (*e.g.*, that the government would target a plaintiff's particular contacts, that it would use its new authorities to justify surveillance, etc.). As such, the claimed injury was too speculative. [**Clapper v. Amnesty Intern. USA**, 133 S.Ct. 1138 (2013)]

Clapper does not provide clear guidance on the standard for probabilistic injury going forward, however, because the Court also conceded in a footnote that it has sometimes "found standing based on a 'substantial risk' that the harm will occur." The Court did not square these two seemingly disparate standards. [**Id.**; *cf.* **Monsanto Co. v. Geertson Seed Farms**, 130 S.Ct. 2743, 2754–55 (2010) (holding that "reasonable probability" that genetically engineered alfalfa would infect respondents' crops provided injury for constitutional standing)]

(b) Probabilistic Injury at the D.C. Circuit

The D.C. Circuit has declared that an increased risk of harm can qualify as an injury-in-fact for constitutional standing where there is: "(i) a substantially increased risk of harm and (ii) a substantial probability of harm with that increase taken into account." The court has also advised that the Supreme Court's "imminence" requirement imposes "a very strict understanding of what increases in risk and overall risk levels can count as 'substantial.' " [**Public Citizen, Inc. v. Nat'l Highway Traffic Safety Admin.,** 489 F.3d 1279 (D.C. Cir. 2007)]

(6) Procedural Injuries

As has been mentioned several times above, the bar on generalized grievances blocks a plaintiff from basing standing on damage to a shared, generalized interest in ensuring that the government obeys the law for its own sake. A plaintiff thus cannot challenge an agency procedural violation simply because the plaintiff really hates it when the government does not follow legally required procedures. [**Lujan v. Defenders of Wildlife,** 540 U.S. 555 (1992)] Instead, a plaintiff seeking to challenge a procedural violation must allege that the procedure in question is designed to protect a concrete interest of the plaintiff. [*Id.* (noting that a plaintiff who lives next to the site of a proposed dam would have standing to contest an agency's failure to prepare an Environmental Impact Statement assessing the dam's impacts)]

(7) Associational Standing

Recall from above, *supra,* p. 173, that purely "ideological" injuries do not suffice for standing. Thus, a voluntary organization cannot bring suit to challenge a government action merely because that action implicates values that are important to the association's mission. [**Sierra Club v. Morton,** 405 U.S. 727 (1972) (plaintiff association could not base standing on its longstanding interest in protecting the environment)]

A voluntary organization can usually get around this problem by claiming *associational standing,* a derivative form based on the standing of one or more of its members. An association can invoke the standing of one or more of its members where: (i) those members would have standing in their own right; (ii) the suit seeks to protect interests bearing on the association's mission; and (iii) participation by individual members is not required to determine either the claim or the relief. [**Hunt v. Washington Apple Advertising Comm'n,** 432 U.S. 333 (1977)]

As a practical matter, a voluntary organization typically tries to demonstrate associational standing by submitting affidavits from one or more members explaining why they have standing. [*See, e.g.,* **Lujan v. Defenders of Wildlife,** 540 U.S. 555 (1992) (discussing affidavits submitted by members of Defenders of Wildlife describing plans to visit the habitats of the Nile crocodile, Asian elephant, and leopard)]

(8) Do States Sometimes Get "Special Solicitude" on Standing?

As discussed above, in *Massachusetts v. EPA,* a five-justice majority held that Massachusetts had standing to contest EPA's failure to regulate greenhouse gas emissions from new motor vehicles. The majority based this conclusion in large part on evidence that global warming would cause Massachusetts to lose coastal property to rising seas. The Court boosted Massachusetts' claim to standing, at least to some indeterminate degree, by citing an obscure, hundred-year-old precedent for the proposition that states have a special claim to standing in the federal courts to protect their "quasi-sovereign" interests that extend to "all the earth and air within [their] domains." [**Massachusetts v. EPA,** 549 U.S. 497 (2007) (quoting **Georgia v. Tennessee Copper Co.,** 206 U.S. 230 (1907)] Chief Justice Roberts, writing for a four-justice dissent, insisted that *Tennessee Copper* does not entitle states to "special solicitude" for standing. States will no doubt invoke this "special solicitude" in the future where their standing is in doubt. It is far from clear, however, how much this factor will affect judicial decisions.

(9) Taxpayer Standing

(a) General Rule

Ever get really mad because the government is spending tax dollars—some of which you paid—on conduct you think is illegal? If so, have you suffered an injury sufficient for constitutional standing in federal court?

At least for federal and state-level taxes, the answer, subject to a very narrow exception, is no. The annoyance you feel at the perceived misuse of your tax dollars is a generalized grievance that cannot support standing. [**Frothingham v. Mellon,** 262 U.S. 447 (1923) (seminal case barring claims based on federal taxpayer status); **DaimlerChrysler Corp. v. Cuno,** 547 U.S. 332 (2006) (("[S]tate taxpayers have no standing under Article III to challenge state tax or spending decisions simply by virtue of their status as taxpayers.")]

(b) The *Flast v. Cohen* Exception

The taxpayer in *Flast* challenged a federal program granting benefits to parochial schools for violating the Establishment Clause. Rather than dismiss this challenge as a generalized grievance, the Court carved an exception to the bar on taxpayer standing. This exception allows the plaintiff to proceed where she alleges: (a) a violation by Congress of its authority to tax and spend under Art. I, § 8 of the Constitution; and (b) that this violation "exceeds specific constitutional limitations imposed upon the exercise of the congressional taxing and spending power." [**Flast v. Cohen,** 392 U.S. 83 (1968)] This test was satisfied in *Flast* itself as the plaintiff had challenged taxing and spending that violated the Establishment Clause.

(c) Distinguishing *Flast* Nearly Out of Existence

In part due to its obvious tension with the bar on generalized grievances, the Court has applied *Flast* very narrowly, limiting its reach to challenges to *legislative enactments* that exercise *taxing and spending power* in violation of the *Establishment Clause*. [*See, e.g.,* **Hein v. Freedom From Religion Foundation, Inc.,** 551 U.S. 587 (2007) (plurality) (refusing to apply *Flast* where spending was not specifically authorized by Congress but was instead allocated by the executive from general appropriations); **Arizona Christian School Tuition Organization v. Winn,** 131 S.Ct. 1436 (2011) (refusing to apply *Flast* exception to a state law that allowed persons donating to sectarian schools to take an equivalent state tax credit; according to plurality, granting a tax credit to a donor does not *extract* taxes from an objecting plaintiff, who thus suffers no cognizable harm)]

Two members of the current Court, Justices Scalia and Thomas, insist that *Flast* should be overruled as an unprincipled exception to the bar on generalized grievances. [**Hein v. Freedom From Religion Foundation, Inc.,** 551 U.S. 587 (2007) (Scalia, J., concurring)]

EXAM TIP

When tackling the problem of determining whether an alleged injury satisfies the requirements for constitutional standing, bear strongly in mind that the law, such as it is, sets up several important dichotomies—*e.g.*, an injury must be **concrete** rather than **abstract**; it must be **particularized** rather than a **generalized grievance**; it must be **actual or imminent** and not *speculative or conjectural*. The Supreme Court justices often sharply disagree on how to apply these dichotomies in marginal cases. You therefore should not be surprised to find good arguments either way on whether the injury requirement has been satisfied. Seeing both sides may in fact be a sign that you have given a good answer.

c. Causation and Redressability

Recall the second and third prongs of the black letter of constitutional standing, which require:

> "a *causal connection* between the injury and the conduct complained of—the injury has to be fairly . . . trace[able] to the challenged action of the defendant," and

> "it must be *likely*, as opposed to merely *speculative*, that the injury will be *redressed* by a favorable decision."

[Lujan v. Defenders of Wildlife, 504 U.S. 555 (1992) (quotation marks and citations omitted)]

These two requirements commonly overlap. For instance, if an agency action caused an injury, then vacating that action will in many circumstances redress the injury. If the plaintiff's injury has other causes than the agency action, then ordering the agency to change its action might not remediate the injury.

(1) Vagueness and, ahem, Room for Judgment

The causation and redressability requirements are quite vague and leave a lot of room for judicial judgment. In some cases, the Court seems to have demanded quite a tight causal connection between an injury and agency action and a strong showing that a favorable judicial order will redress the plaintiff's injury. In others, the Court has tolerated far more attenuated connections.

(2) Tough Applications of Causation/Redressability

(a) Tax Exemptions and Hospitals

Plaintiff challenged an IRS ruling that hospitals could claim tax-exempt status even though they did not supply free medical services to the poor. Plaintiff's claimed injury was that he was denied free medical services. Plaintiff lacked standing since the denial of services might not have been *caused* by the IRS's ruling. Moreover, a change in IRS tax treatment of hospitals would not necessarily *remedy* the harm by guaranteeing the plaintiff free medical services (*i.e.*, the hospital might simply forgo its tax-exempt status). This case illustrates the overlap between causation and redressability and that a court's decision can often be stated under either heading. **[Simon v. Eastern Kentucky Welfare Rights Organization,** 426 U.S. 26 (1976)]

(b) Tax Exemptions and Desegregation

Plaintiffs were parents of children attending public schools that were under court orders to desegregate. They alleged that the IRS had improperly granted tax exemptions to segregated private schools. These exemptions encouraged the private schools to open and expand and thus tended to thwart the desegregation of public schools. *Held:* Plaintiffs failed the causation test. It was not known what would happen if the exemptions were withdrawn (the schools might not change their policy, or the parents might not withdraw their children), nor was it sufficiently clear that the presence of the private schools made much difference to desegregation where the plaintiffs lived. [**Allen v. Wright,** 468 U.S. 737 (1984)]

(c) Endangered Species

Plaintiffs complained that Agency B failed to consult with Agency A about funding projects abroad that might jeopardize an endangered species. However, Agency B was not a party to the suit and denied that Agency A had any authority over its actions. *Held:* Because Agency B would not be bound by a judgment against Agency A, the plaintiffs failed to establish redressability. Moreover, Agency B played only a minor role in funding the projects. The project might go ahead even without its funding or approval. [**Lujan v. Defenders of Wildlife,** 504 U.S. 555 (1992) (plurality)]

(d) Violation of Reporting Rules for Past Conduct

Defendant failed to file various reporting forms about its toxic chemical storage and discharges, which violated a federal statute. Plaintiff sued under a citizen suit provision in the statute, claiming that its injury in fact was that its members had been denied information they needed to improve the local environment. However, Defendant brought its filings up to date before the action commenced; thus the violations in the case all had happened in the past. The Court held that none of the remedies plaintiff sought would redress the harms caused by the late reporting. For example, plaintiff sought civil penalties for the violation. However, because these would be paid to the United States Treasury, not to Plaintiff, the penalties would not remedy the members' injury in fact. [**Steel Co. v. Citizens for a Better Environment,** 523 U.S. 83 (1998)]

(3) More Relaxed Applications of Causation/Redressability

(a) Civil Penalties to Deter Future Misconduct

In the example just above, ***Steel Co.***, the plaintiffs lacked standing to seek civil penalties payable to the government because they could not redress the plaintiffs' injuries stemming from past misconduct. Contrast this result with the Court's assessment of standing in *Friends of the Earth v. Laidlaw Environmental Services, Inc.* In this case, the plaintiffs claimed injury in fact from mercury discharges into a river. As in ***Steel Co.***, they sought civil penalties which would be payable to the government. Unlike ***Steel Co.***, however, the Supreme Court held that the plaintiffs had standing. The difference was that the plaintiffs in ***FOE*** sought to deter *future* misconduct, and the Court determined that payment of civil penalties was likely enough to deter future violations to satisfy redressability. [**Friends of the Earth v. Laidlaw Environmental Services, Inc.,** 528 U.S. 167 (2000)]

(b) Regulating One Source of Greenhouse Gas Emissions

In ***Massachusetts v. EPA,*** the state sought review of EPA's refusal to regulate greenhouse gas emissions from new motor vehicles. Massachusetts claimed injury based on evidence that global warming would cause it to lose coastal property. EPA argued that the state could not satisfy the requirements of causation and redressability. Regulating one source of emissions in one country would do little or nothing to save Massachusetts' coastal property from rising seas given the global nature of the problem. The Court rejected this argument, adopting an every-little-bit-helps approach. Restrictions on new car emissions would at least slow the process of global warming. [**Massachusetts v. EPA,** 549 U.S. 497 (2007)]

(4) Relaxed Redressability for Procedural Claims

Suppose that you successfully sue an agency for failure to follow notice-and-comment procedures for a rule that caused you a cognizable concrete injury. The agency might respond by using notice-and-comment to adopt the very same rule. In that case, ordering the agency to follow legal procedures would not redress your injury—in which case maybe you should not have had standing to press your claim in the first place.

Of course, adopting this line of reasoning would largely immunize agencies from challenges to their failures to follow legally required procedures—which cannot be right. The Supreme Court, recognizing this problem, has stated that a "person who has been accorded a procedural right to protect his concrete interests can assert that right without meeting all the normal standards for redressability and causation." [**Lujan v. Defenders of Wildlife,** 504 U.S. 555 (1992)]

Example—environmental impact statement: A statute requires that Agency A file an environmental impact statement before taking action (such as building a dam). The agency fails to file the required statement. Plaintiff would be harmed by construction of the proposed dam (*e.g.,* because it would inundate her farm). Plaintiff has standing to raise the claim that Agency A failed to prepare and file the required environmental impact statement. In reality, it is quite likely that Agency A will build the dam even after filing the required statement. Therefore, it would be difficult to argue that failure to file the statement was the cause of Plaintiff's injury or that filing the statement would remedy the harm. Nevertheless, Plaintiff has standing to contest violation of a procedure designed to protect her concrete interests. [**Id.**]

3. Statutory Standing

The concept of statutory standing speaks to whether a legislature has authorized a class of plaintiffs to bring suit to challenge violations of a given law. Some statutes include provisions identifying plaintiffs who can sue for their enforcement. For instance, the Endangered Species Act contains a "citizen suit" provision that authorizes "any person" to "commence a civil suit . . . to enjoin any person . . . who is alleged to be in violation of any provision of this chapter or regulation." [**16 U.S.C. § 1540(g)(1)(A);** *but see* **Lujan v. Defenders of Wildlife,** 504 U.S. 555 (1992) (holding that the ESA's citizen suit provision cannot authorize suit by persons lacking constitutional standing)]

The most important provision of statutory standing you will encounter in your Administrative Law course is **5 U.S.C. § 702** of the APA. This provision states, "[a] person suffering *legal wrong* because of agency action, or *adversely affected or aggrieved* within the meaning of a relevant statute, is entitled to judicial review thereof." Courts have interpreted this language very broadly to authorize a plaintiff to bring suit so long as the interests she seeks to protect are "arguably within the zone of interests" of the law that the plaintiff claims the agency has violated. More on what this means follows.

a. Historical Development

(1) The Old "Legal Interest" Test

Not everybody gets to sue to contest every legal violation. For instance, suppose that there is a minor car accident in your law school parking lot that you did not witness and that did not involve any of your property. You cannot bring suit for negligence because the event did not implicate your legal interests—you have not suffered any "legal wrong" cognizable by the courts. Put another way, you lack a common-law cause of action.

Under a now outdated approach, a party challenging a government action would need to demonstrate that it had caused her a cognizable "legal wrong." This requirement is not problematic where the action implicates a recognized common-law action. If government agents break down your door, a tort claim is a plausible response. It was, however, problematic where a plaintiff was injured by a government action that did not implicate rights recognized by common law or created by positive law. For instance, in **Alabama Power Co. v. Ickes,** a utility challenged the legality of federal loans to municipalities to build electricity-distribution systems. The Supreme Court rejected this claim on the ground that, even if the loans were illegal, the utility had no legal right to be free from lawful competition. [302 U.S. 464 (1938)]

(2) Congress Expands Standing to "Aggrieved Persons"

Section 402(b) of the Communications Act of 1934 authorized judicial challenges by "*any ... person aggrieved* or whose interests are adversely affected by any decision of the [Federal Communications] Commission granting or refusing any such application" for a broadcast license. The Supreme Court held that this "aggrieved persons" standard authorized persons suffering economic harm to seek review even if they could not have satisfied the "legal rights" test. **[FCC v. Sanders Bros. Radio Station,** 309 U.S. 470 (1940)]

Example—standing of competitors: The Federal Communications Commission ("FCC") licensed A to construct a broadcasting station in an area in which B was already broadcasting. B sought judicial review of the decision under a statute that allowed standing to anyone "aggrieved" by an FCC decision. Even though B would have had no cause of action at common law, the Court held that "aggrieved persons" included those who would suffer economic injury as a result of the agency's decision. The Court observed that Congress might have expanded standing to persons who have suffered financial harm from the FCC's issuance of a license because such persons might be the only ones sufficiently interested to bring an action contesting the legality of the FCC's order. [**Id.**] Where Congress authorizes a private party to sue to protect the public interest, it has, in essence, authorized that party to function as a "private attorney general." [**Associated Industries of New York v. Ickes,** 134 F.2d 694 (2d Cir. 1943) vacated as moot, 320 U.S. 707 (1943)]

Example—unhappy listeners aggrieved: Petitioners sought to intervene in proceedings for renewal of a broadcast license to present evidence of discrimination and over-commercialization. FCC dismissed the petition and renewed the license. Petitioners appealed. The D.C. Circuit rejected FCC's effort to limit the reach of "persons aggrieved" to persons suffering economic harm or electrical interference. Responsible members of the listening public, too, can be "persons aggrieved" with standing to represent the public interest. [**Office of Communications of United Church of Christ v. FCC,** 359 F.2d 994 (D.C. Cir. 1966)]

b. Section 702 and the Zone of Interests Test

Section 702 of the APA, on its face, looks like a combination of the old "legal interest" test along with the statutory "person aggrieved" test. It states:

> A person suffering *legal wrong* because of agency action, or *adversely affected or aggrieved* by agency action within the meaning of a relevant statute, is entitled to judicial review thereof.

The Supreme Court has construed this language as a very broad grant of statutory standing. A plaintiff seeking standing under the APA merely needs to show that the interests she seek to protect are "arguably within the zone of interests to be protected or regulated by the [relevant] statute." [**Association of Data Processing Service Organizations, Inc. v. Camp,** 397 U.S. 150 (1970)]

Stressing the laxity of this test, the Court later added that it blocks statutory standing only where "the plaintiff's interests are so marginally related to or inconsistent with the purposes implicit in the statute that it cannot reasonably be assumed that Congress intended to permit the suit." [**Clarke v. Securities Industry Ass'n,** 479 U.S. 388 (1987)] Moreover, "there need be no indication of congressional purpose to benefit the would-be plaintiff." [**Id.**]

Example: Petitioners, in the data processing business, challenged a ruling by the Comptroller of the Currency allowing national banks to provide data processing services (*i.e.*, plaintiffs claimed competitive injury). The Supreme Court held that the plaintiffs' interests arguably fell within the zone of interests protected by § 4 of the Bank Service Corporation Act, which limited the activities of bank service corporations to the "performance of bank services for banks." [**Association of Data Processing Service Organizations, Inc. v. Camp,** 397 U.S. 150 (1970)]

Example: Banks challenged a rule adopted by the National Credit Union Administration that allowed federal credit unions to be composed of multiple, unrelated employer groups. The banks claimed that this rule violated § 109 of the Federal Credit Union Act (FCUA), which provides that "[f]ederal credit union membership shall be limited to groups having a common bond of occupation or association." The Supreme Court held that the banks had statutory standing to bring this claim. The Court reiterated, "in applying the 'zone of interests' test, we do not ask whether, in enacting the statutory provision at issue, Congress specifically intended to benefit the plaintiff. Instead, we first discern the interests 'arguably . . . to be protected' by the statutory provision at issue; we then inquire whether the plaintiff's interests affected by the agency action in question are among them." Even if Congress did not specifically intend for § 109 to protect the interests of banks, the banks' interest in limiting the reach of credit unions arguably fell within the zone of interests to be protected. [**National Credit Union Association v. First National Bank and Trust Co.,** 522 U.S. 479 (1998)]

Example: Petitioner ranchers had statutory standing under the Endangered Species Act to challenge an agency action designed to protect fish. Fish & Wildlife Service (FWS) issued a Biological Opinion that minimum lake levels should be maintained to protect sucker fish. Ranchers challenged the Biological Opinion for violating § 7 of the ESA, which requires agencies to "use the best scientific and commercial data available." Although the ESA is, as a whole, obviously designed to preserve species, § 7 is intended "at least in part, to prevent uneconomic (because erroneous) jeopardy determinations." As such, "[p]etitioners' claim that they are victims of such a mistake is plainly within the zone of interests that the provision protects." [**Bennett v. Spear,** 520 U.S. 154 (1997)]

(Most Recent) Example: 25 U.S.C. § 465, a provision of the Indian Reorganization Act (IRA), authorizes the Secretary to acquire property "for the purpose of providing land for Indians." The Secretary used this authority to acquire land intended for development as a casino. Patchak, the owner of nearby land, brought suit under the APA, claiming that the purchase exceeded the Secretary's authority because the band was not recognized by the Federal Government at the time of the IRA's enactment. The government and the tribe argued that

Patchak lacked standing because § 465 focuses on land acquisition rather than land use. The Supreme Court emphasized that the zone-of-interest test for standing "is not meant to be especially demanding," and is to be applied "in keeping with Congress's evident intent when enacting the APA to make agency action presumptively reviewable." Moreover, this test does not require that the plaintiff be a member of a class that Congress sought to benefit in the statute that the plaintiff seeks to enforce. Realistically, land acquisition decisions implicate expected land use. As such, "the interests Patchak raises—at least arguably—fall within the zone . . . protected or regulated by the statute." [**Match-E-Be-Nash-She-Wish Band of Pottawatomi Indians v. Patchak,** 132 S.Ct. 2199 (2012)]

(An Outlier) Example: A statute gave the Postal Service a monopoly on carrying the mail. A postal workers union complained that the Postal Service had allowed a new form of competition, which would cost postal jobs. The Court held that the purpose of the monopoly statute was to give an economic advantage to the Postal Service to protect its revenue and allow it to serve all customers. Because Congress had not intended to protect postal *jobs,* the union was outside the zone and could not sue. This decision seems far stricter than the cases discussed above. [**Air Courier Conference v. American Postal Workers Union,** 498 U.S. 517 (1991)]

4. Prudential Standing

In addition to constitutional limits on standing, courts also impose ***prudential*** limits. Courts admit to having made up these limits themselves rather than purporting to locate them in Article III's "case or controversy" limitation.

The line between constitutional and prudential limits has not always been clear, in part due to disagreement among the justices and in part due to evolution of standing doctrine. For instance, the Court has sometimes characterized the bar on "generalized grievances" as prudential, but in recent years has characterized it as constitutional. [*Compare* **Allen v. Wright,** 468 U.S. 737 (1984) (describing this bar as a "judicially self-imposed limit") *with* **Hollingsworth v. Perry,** 133 S.Ct. 2652 (2013) (holding that plaintiffs' interest in vindicating California law barring gay marriage amounted to a "generalized grievance" that could not support constitutional standing)]

a. Third Party Standing (or Jus Tertii)

Suppose that the government takes an action that infringes the legal rights of *A,* and that *A* is therefore not able to purchase some product from *B*. On the face of the matter, *B* might have suffered an injury due to the government action sufficient for ***constitutional standing.*** If *B* sues to undo the government action, however, *B* will be seeking to vindicate *A*'s legal rights. Courts are generally hostile to this practice, commonly barring it under the prudential doctrine of ***third party standing.*** [**Warth v. Seldin,** 422 U.S. 490 (1975) (observing that a plaintiff "generally must assert his own legal rights and interests, and cannot rest his claim to relief on the legal rights or interests of third parties")] Courts justify this hostility in part on the ground that persons who have suffered injury to their legal rights should generally have the "appropriate incentive to challenge (or not challenge) governmental action and to do so with the necessary zeal and appropriate presentation." [**Kowalski v. Tesmer,** 543 U.S. 125 (2004)]

To leap the hurdle of third party standing, a plaintiff seeking to vindicate the legal rights of another must demonstrate: (1) that she has a "'close' relationship with the person who possesses the right"; and (2) that "there is a 'hindrance' to the possessor's ability to protect his own interests." [**Id.**] The Court characterizes itself as "quite forgiving" in applying these standards to First Amendment claims and where "enforcement of the challenged restriction *against the litigant* would result indirectly in the violation of third parties' rights." [**Id.** (citing, *inter alia,* **Griswold v. Connecticut,** 381 U.S. 479 (1965) (holding that defendant physicians convicted of violating Connecticut contraception law had standing to assert constitutional rights of married couples)]

Example: Criminal defense attorneys brought § 1983 suit to challenge Michigan's practice of denying appointed appellate counsel to indigent defendants convicted after a guilty plea. The Supreme Court accepted, *arguendo*, that the attorneys had constitutional standing because the practice at issue caused them to lose appointments and payments. Still, the attorneys were not seeking to protect their legal right to serve as appointed counsel—they had no such right. Instead, they sought to vindicate the rights of prisoners to have counsel. The Court held that the plaintiff attorneys satisfied neither prong of the test for third party standing. They had no relationship, much less a "close" one, with defendants who were not yet their clients. Regarding "hindrance," the plaintiff attorneys had argued, with some logic, that criminal defendants needed their counsel to press constitutional claims effectively. The Court conceded "an attorney would be valuable to a criminal defendant challenging the constitutionality of the scheme." It added, however, "we do not think that the lack of an attorney here is the type of hindrance necessary to allow another to assert the indigent defendants' rights." This conclusion was motivated in part by a concern to avoid granting lawyers generally "third-party standing to bring in court the claims of future unascertained clients." [**Kowalski v. Tesmer,** 543 U.S. 125 (2004)]

b. The Zone-of-Interests in Non-APA Cases

The Supreme Court has declared that the "zone of interests" test, required by 5 U.S.C. § 702 for APA cases, also applies as a prudential limitation in non-APA cases. [**Bennett v. Spear,** 520 U.S. 154 (1997)] For discussion of the "zone of interests" test, *see supra,* p. 205.

c. Congress Can Trump Prudential Standing

Given that courts concede that prudential standing doctrine is not constitutionally required, it follows that Congress can, when it wishes, displace these limitations with broad grants of statutory standing. [**Bennett v. Spear,** 520 U.S. 154 (1997) (holding that "citizen suit" provision in the Endangered Species Act, which authorizes "any person" commence suit, displaces the prudential "zone of interests" requirement)]

B. The Timing of Judicial Review

1. In General

Even if a plaintiff has standing to seek review of administrative action, the case must be brought to court at the right time. Generally speaking, the action challenged must be *final,* the case must be *ripe,* and the plaintiff must have *exhausted administrative remedies.* In addition, the plaintiff must avoid the *doctrine of primary jurisdiction,* which may route the case to an agency rather than to court. Finally, whether the reviewing court will grant a *stay* of agency action pending review may be critical to protecting the plaintiff's interests.

2. Final Order Rule

A court normally declines to review agency rulings unless they are *final.* The finality requirement contains two elements:

(a) the action must mark the *consummation* of the agency's decisionmaking process (rather than being merely tentative or interlocutory); and

(b) the action must be one by which ***legal rights or obligations have been determined*** or from which ***legal consequences will flow***. [**Bennett v. Spear,** 520 U.S. 154 (1997)]

a. Statutory Requirements

The final order rule is frequently set forth in agency enabling statutes that provide for judicial review, and also in both state and federal APAs. Of most importance for your Administrative Law class, 5 U.S.C. § 704 of the APA provides, most relevant part:

> Agency action made reviewable by statute and *final agency action* for which there is no other adequate remedy in a court are subject to judicial review. A preliminary, procedural, or intermediate agency action or ruling not directly reviewable is subject to review on the review of the final agency action.

The first part of this provision acknowledges the obvious point that, where Congress has set up a particular scheme for judicial review in an agency's enabling act, this scheme controls. Where Congress has not done so, the APA establishes a default cause of action that is generally limited to *final agency actions.*

b. Some Leading Cases

(1) Decision to Issue a Complaint Was Not Final

The FTC issued a complaint against Oil Co. because the FTC "had reason to believe" that the statute had been violated. Oil Co. sought interlocutory review in court of the FTC's decision that it had "reason to believe" the statute had been violated. The Court held that review was barred by the final order rule of § 704. [**FTC v. Standard Oil Co. of California,** 449 U.S. 232 (1980)] The Court indicated that intervention at this stage would deny the FTC a chance to correct its own mistakes and apply its expertise. It would lead to inefficient and perhaps unnecessary piecemeal review. It would delay ultimate resolution of the controversy. Finally, it would allow every respondent to turn the FTC from prosecutor into defendant before adjudication concludes.

(2) Biological Opinion with Legal Consequences Was Final

Under the Endangered Species Act, if an agency determines that a proposed action may adversely affect a threatened or endangered species or its habitat, the agency must consult with the Fish & Wildlife Service (FWS), which will issue a Biological Opinion assessing the proposed action's effects and, as needed, identifying "reasonable and prudent alternatives" for minimizing them. An agency that follows the terms of the Biological Opinion cannot be held liable for "taking" an endangered or threatened species in violation of the ESA.

Ranchers challenged a Biological Opinion that advised the Bureau of Reclamation to maintain higher reservoir levels to protect fish. The government contended that the Biological Opinion was not final but instead merely advisory as it did not formally bind the Bureau. The Supreme Court rejected this argument, noting that a "Biological Opinion of the sort rendered here alters the legal regime to which the action agency is subject." In essence, the Biological Opinion functions as a permit that authorizes limited taking of a species. An agency may be "technically free to disregard the Biological Opinion and proceed with its proposed action, but it does so at its own peril (and that of its employees)." [**Bennett v. Spear,** 520 U.S. 154 (1997)]

(3) Administrative Compliance Order Held Final

Under the Clean Water Act, EPA may bring a civil enforcement action in court against persons who have "discharge[d] any pollutant" into "navigable waters" without a permit. The daily penalty for violation may not exceed $37,500. Alternatively, the agency can, on its own authority, issue an administrative compliance order (ACO). If a party does not comply with the ACO, then the agency might at that point bring a civil enforcement action in court. EPA has taken the position that failure to comply with an ACO doubles the potential penalty in the civil enforcement action to $75,000 per day.

EPA issued an ACO against the Sacketts for filling wetlands on their property without a permit. The Sacketts sought a hearing before the agency to contend that the wetlands were not "navigable waters" within the CWA. EPA denied this request. The Sacketts then sought declaratory and injunctive relief in district court.

The Supreme Court held that the ACO was final and subject to review in court. Regarding *consummation*, the Court concluded that the denial of the Sacketts' request for a hearing showed that the agency had reached a definitive conclusion. EPA tried to avoid this result by noting a portion of the ACO that invited the Sacketts to discuss its terms informally. The Court rejected this argument, stating "[t]he mere possibility that an agency might reconsider in light of 'informal discussion' . . . does not suffice to make an otherwise final agency action nonfinal." Regarding *legal consequences,* the Court observed that the ACO required the Sacketts to restore the land, grant the agency access for inspections, and, according to the government's litigating position, exposed the Sacketts to double penalties. [**Sackett v. EPA,** 132 S.Ct. 1367 (2012)]

c. Finality and the Problem of Guidance Documents

You will recall from discussion of interpretive rules and general statements of policy that these types of rules are supposed to lack the "force of law." [*See supra,* p. 100] This might lead one to think that these guidance documents cannot be "final" because they cannot satisfy the requirement of determining legal rights and obligations. Guidance documents, however, often have major impacts on regulated parties, which suggests that they should not be immunized from judicial review. Responding to this dilemma, courts have held that guidance documents can under some circumstances amount to final agency action.

Example: Under Title V of the 1990 Amendments to the Clean Air Act, stationary sources of air pollution must obtain operating permits from state authorities that administer permitting programs approved by EPA. If EPA disapproves a permitting program, then EPA takes it over, and the state loses highway funds. Plaintiffs challenged a document entitled "Periodic Monitoring Guidance for Title V Permitting Programs," which detailed EPA's understanding of a rule requiring monitoring of pollutant emissions.

EPA argued that this "guidance" could not amount to final agency action because it was not technically "binding." The D.C. Circuit responded that the guidance was "practically binding," a category that applies where an agency *treats* a document as "a legislative rule, . . . bases enforcement actions [on it, and] leads private parties or State permitting authorities to believe that it will declare permits invalid unless they comply with the terms of the document."

Turning to the two-prong test for finality, the court concluded that the "guidance" document amounted to *consummated* agency action. It had been signed by two high-ranking EPA officials, was the product of an extensive four-year drafting process, and EPA agreed with petitioners that the underlying policy position at issue was "settled."

The document created *legal obligations* because it read like a "ukase," mandating that "State permitting authorities . . . search for deficiencies in existing monitoring regulations and replace them through terms and conditions of a permit." EPA had tacked on language at the end of the document claiming that it was "intended solely as guidance" and was not "final agency action." This bit of business was standard boilerplate that should be ignored. [**Appalachian Power Co. v. EPA,** 208 F.3d 1015 (D.C. Cir. 2000); *cf.* **Center for Auto Safety v. NHTSA,** 452 F.3d 798 (D.C. Cir. 2006) (holding that agency policy statement that did not eliminate the discretion of agency officials and read as "guidelines, not binding regulations" was not final agency action)]

Example: A trade association sent a letter to the Administrator of the Wage and Hour Division of the Department of Labor, inquiring whether the association's members were subject to regulation. The Administrator sent a letter back saying that they were. The association sought judicial review to challenge the letter's conclusion. The D.C. Circuit held that the letter constituted final agency action. It stated:

> When a published interpretation represents the initial views of an agency, approved by the [agency head], when it is the product of the process provided by the agency for taking into account the position of agency staff as well as [outsiders], when the interpretation is not labeled as tentative or otherwise qualified by arrangement for reconsideration, it has the feature of "expected conformity". . . . This embraces conformity not only by the businessman affected but by the agency personnel. And we see no basis for saying that this interpretative "agency action" is not "final" for purposes of the APA and judicial review.

[**National Automatic Laundry & Cleaning Council v. Schulz,** 443 F.3d 689 (D.C. Cir. 1971)]

d. Exception—Violation of Clear Right

Courts have noted the existence of a narrow exception to the requirement of finality "in a case of 'clear right' such as outright violation of a clear statutory provision. . . ." [**Association of National Advertisers, Inc. v. FTC,** 627 F.2d 1151 (D.C.Cir.1979) (Leventhal, J., concurring) (citing **Leedom v. Kyne,** 358 U.S. 184 (1958), *cert. denied,* 447 U.S. 921 (1980); *see also* **Ticor Title Ins. Co. v. FTC,** 814 F.2d 731, 749–50 (D.C. Cir. 1987) (William, J.) (discussing the scope of the "clear right" exception to finality)]

e. Exception—Unreasonable Delay

"Where a federal court has jurisdiction to hear challenges to an agency action it also has jurisdiction over claims of unreasonable delay." [**Cobell v. Norton,** 240 F.3d 1081 (D.C. Cir. 2001)]

(1) APA Provisions

APA § 555(b) provides: "With due regard for the convenience and necessity of the parties and their representatives, and within a reasonable time, each agency shall proceed to conclude a matter presented to it." And § 706(1) provides that a reviewing court shall "compel agency action unlawfully withheld or unreasonably delayed."

(2) *TRAC* Factors

Courts are leery of granting relief for claims of unreasonable delay in part because they do not wish to distort agency priorities or misallocate constrained resources. On the other hand, if no judicial review is available for claims of delay, agencies could avoid complying with their statutory mandates entirely. To balance these concerns, the D.C. Circuit has prescribed consideration of the following influential set of factors (commonly called the *TRAC* **factors**):

(1) the time agencies take to make decisions must be governed by a "rule of reason,"; (2) where Congress has provided a timetable or other indication of the speed with which it expects the agency to proceed in the enabling statute, that statutory scheme may supply content for this rule of reason; (3) delays that might be reasonable in the sphere of economic regulation are less tolerable when human health and welfare are at stake; (4) the court should consider the effect of expediting delayed action on agency activities of a higher or competing priority; (5) the court should also take into account the nature and extent of the interests prejudiced by delay; and (6) the court need not "find any impropriety lurking behind agency lassitude in order to hold that agency action is 'unreasonably delayed.' "

[**Telecommunications Research & Action Center v. FCC,** 750 F.2d 70 (D.C. Cir. 1984) (citations omitted)]

(3) Violation of Statutory Deadlines and Claims of Delay

Sometimes, Congress imposes a statutory deadline for agency action, and the agency fails to meet it. In these situations, a plaintiff might well sue the agency to compel agency action unreasonably delayed. Courts have split on treatment of such claims.

The D.C. Circuit has held that violation of a congressional deadline does not settle the issue of whether a court should order agency action. Out of "respect for the autonomy and comparative institutional advantage of the executive branch," courts should still consider the *TRAC* **factors** to determine whether "to assume command over an "agency's choice of priorities." [*In re* **Barr Laboratories, Inc.,** 930 F.2d 72 (D.C. Cir. 1991) (denying drug manufacturer's petition for a writ of mandamus to force FDA to expedite processing of an application for approval of a generic drug after the statutory deadline had passed; court observed that granting such an order would simply allow plaintiff to jump over other drug manufacturers in line)]

By contrast, the Tenth Circuit has declared:

> [W]hen Congress by organic statute sets a specific deadline for agency action, neither the agency nor any court has discretion. The agency must act by the deadline. If it withholds such timely action, a reviewing court must compel the action unlawfully withheld. To hold otherwise would be an affront to our tradition of legislative supremacy and constitutionally separated powers.

[**Forest Guardians v. Babbitt,** 174 F.3d 1178 (10th Cir. 1998) (holding that court must order Secretary to comply with "statutory duty to designate the critical habitat for the silvery minnow without regard to his preferred priorities"; remanding to district court to determine "what work is necessary to complete the designation" and to order designation "as soon as possible.")]

3. Ripeness

The court will not review agency action unless it is "ripe" for review. The typical ripeness case involves agency action, such as a rule, that has ***not yet been specifically applied*** to the plaintiff. Nevertheless, the action is causing immediate problems for the plaintiff, who therefore seeks ***pre-enforcement review.***

a. Purposes of Requirement

The ripeness doctrine is designed to prevent courts "from entangling themselves in abstract disagreements over administrative policies, and also to protect the agencies from judicial interference until an administrative decision has been formalized and its effects felt in a concrete way by the challenging parties." [**Abbott Laboratories v. Gardner**, 387 U.S. 136 (1967)]

b. Ripeness as Constitutional and Prudential Limitation

The ripeness doctrine has constitutional dimensions as part of the requirement that federal courts may hear only cases or controversies—not abstract or hypothetical matters. [**Reno v. Catholic Social Services, Inc.,** 509 U.S. 43 (1993)] It also has prudential roots in judicial discretion to decline to issue injunctive or declaratory relief. [**Abbott Laboratories v. Gardner**, 387 U.S. 136 (1967)] Even where ripeness concerns are solely prudential, a court can raise them sua sponte. [**Reno,** *supra*]

c. Test for Ripeness

The court must consider two factors in determining whether an administrative decision is ripe for review: (i) the *"fitness of the issues"* for immediate review and (ii) the *"hardship to the parties"* that would result if the court withheld review. [**Abbott Laboratories v. Gardner,** 387 U.S. 136 (1967)]

(1) Fitness for Review

The fitness inquiry asks whether judicial review would benefit from information that could be generated by agency enforcement proceedings. Issues that are purely legal and do not depend in any way on case-specific facts therefore are typically fit for review.

(The Supreme Court in *Abbott Labs* also identified finality as an element of fitness. Finality is itself a prerequisite for judicial review, however, and must be considered regardless of whether ripeness is implicated.)

Example: Pursuant to its statutory authority to adopt rules "for the efficient enforcement of the Act," FDA promulgated a rule authorizing suspension of "certification service" of manufacturers of color additives that denied access to agency inspectors. Uncertified color additives are considered "unsafe" and banned from interstate commerce.

The Court found that the rule was not fit for pre-enforcement review even though the petitioners' challenge focused on the legal issue of whether the agency had exceeded its legal authority. The Court observed that it had no idea how and when FDA would deploy its authority under the rule or what enforcement problems it would encounter. Waiting for the agency to apply the regulation would provide such information, which would aid judicial determination of whether the rule aided efficient enforcement of the FDA's enabling act. [**Toilet Goods Association v. Gardner,** 387 U.S. 167 (1967)]

Example: The Sierra Club challenged a "forest plan" for a large forest that would permit clear-cutting of trees. Before the plan could be implemented, however, the Forest Service had to propose a specific site plan and allow a public hearing. The Court held that the forest plan was not ripe for review because both the court and the agency would benefit from postponement. The agency could refine the forest service plan in the context of considering a specific site plan, and the court could better consider the challenge by ruling on the legality of a specific site plan. [**Ohio Forestry Association v. Sierra Club,** 523 U.S. 726 (1998)]

(2) Hardship to the Parties

Plaintiffs must demonstrate hardship from a deferral of judicial review. Normally, that hardship comes in the form of a dilemma: The plaintiff must decide whether to comply with the rule in question and alter its primary, day-to-day conduct, or to defy the rule. Either decision carries serious risk of harm. The plaintiff needs immediate judicial review of the disputed rule so as to avoid the need to choose between compliance and defiance.

Example: An FDA rule required that every time a drug manufacturer used a brand name on a prescription drug label, it also include the generic name. Plaintiff drug manufacturers sought pre-enforcement judicial review. The Court held that they had demonstrated the required hardship. They either had to take expensive steps to alter their primary, day-to-day conduct by destroying labels and printing new ones, or they had to risk confiscation of their products, potential civil and criminal penalties, and grave danger to their reputations in an industry in which "public confidence . . . is especially important." [**Abbott Laboratories v. Gardner,** 387 U.S. 136 (1967)]

Counterexample: Recall from a few examples ago the facts of *Toilet Goods*, in which petitioners challenged a rule providing that FDA could stop certification services for manufacturers of color additives that denied inspectors' access to their facilities. In addition to finding this rule unfit for pre-enforcement review, the Court also downplayed the hardship it would cause. It observed that, unlike the pharmaceutical manufacturers of *Abbott Labs*, the color additives manufacturers were not required to alter their "primary" conduct—*i.e.*, the rule did not affect "when contracts must be negotiated, ingredients tested or substituted, or special records compiled." In addition, the Court noted that the consequences of suspension of certification were not as severe as in *Abbott Labs*, where violators faced civil and criminal sanctions for misbranding. [**Toilet Goods Association v. Gardner,** 387 U.S. 167 (1967)]

(a) Benefit-Creating Programs

The Court's focus in its hardship inquiry on forced changes in primary conduct creates a problem for plaintiffs seeking pre-enforcement review of programs that confer benefits rather than impose obligations. In **Reno v. Catholic Social Services, Inc.,** plaintiffs challenged regulations adopted by the Immigration and Naturalization Service (INS) on the ground that these regulations construed statutory criteria for legalization too narrowly. Pre-enforcement review was not available as the rules did not require applicants to do anything immediately—they limited access to a benefit rather than imposing new restrictions. Also, an applicant might be rejected by the agency for reasons other than application of the contested rules. [**Reno v. Catholic Social Services, Inc.,** 509 U.S. 43 (1993)]

d. Review of Informal Administrative Action

One of the Court's more recent discussions of the ripeness doctrine, *National Park Hospitality Ass'n v. Department of the Interior*, indicates that at least some informal agency actions cannot cause the hardship necessary for ripeness. The exact implications of this case for this point are not clear, however.

The National Park Service (NPS) adopted a rule, after notice-and-comment, declaring that the Contract Disputes Act (CDA), which creates special procedures for disputes over government contracts, does not cover concession contracts. The National Park Hospitality Association objected to this rule. The Court ruled this dispute unripe in large part because it did not create sufficient hardship. It noted that the NPS is not the agency charged with administering the CDA. This agency's conclusion that the CDA did not cover concession contracts was thus "no more than a general statement of policy designed to inform the public of the NPS's views on the proper application of the CDA." As such, the rule in question did "not create adverse effect of a strictly legal kind," and "it create[d] no legal rights or obligations." Moreover, the rule did not affect the concessioners' "primary conduct," leaving them free to conduct their day-to-day businesses as they wished. Also, "[m]ere uncertainty over the validity of a legal rule" does not "constitute hardship for the purposes of ripeness analysis." [**National Park Hospitality Ass'n v. Department of the Interior,** 538 U.S. 803 (2003)]

Thus, under *NPHA,* one can argue that an agency's construction of a statute *that it is not charged with administering* cannot cause sufficient hardship for ripeness.

e. Statutory Time Limits for Review

A number of statutes require that rules be reviewed within a short period (*e.g.,* 90 days) after adoption and ***preclude any review at a later time.*** These time limits do not begin to run, however, until the rule is ripe for review. [**Louisiana Environmental Action Network v. Browner,** 87 F.3d 1379, 1385 (D.C. Cir. 1996)] A party should not, however, count on this rule to save a post-deadline filing. [*See* **Eagle-Picher Industries v. EPA,** 759 F.3d 905 (D.C. Cir. 1985)] (declaring that the court "will be very reluctant . . . to save a late petitioner from the strictures of a timeliness requirement" unless the claim at issue was "*indisputably* not ripe")]

f. Statutory Preclusion of Pre-Enforcement Review

Congress can, of course, preclude pre-enforcement review. The Court has stated, "we shall find that Congress has allocated initial review to an administrative body where such intent is fairly discernible in the statutory scheme." [**Thunder Basin Coal Co. v. Reich,** 510 U.S. 200 (1994) (citation marks and quotations omitted)] Where judicial review is delayed rather than precluded, "the strong presumption that Congress did not mean to prohibit all judicial review" does not come into play. [**Id.**]

> **Example:** A statute provides that miners can name representatives to participate in safety inspections. The nonunion miners at Coal Co. named union officials to represent them, as permitted by an agency rule. Coal Co. challenged the legality of the rule before it had been applied. The Mine Act was silent with regard to the availability of pre-enforcement review, but it also contained comprehensive provisions channeling challenges to enforcement actions to the Federal Mine Safety and Health Review Commission and the Courts of Appeals. The Court held that pre-enforcement review was precluded because the "Mine Act's comprehensive enforcement structure, combined with the legislative history's clear concern with channeling and streamlining the enforcement process, establishes a 'fairly discernible' intent to preclude district court review in the present case." [**Thunder Basin Coal Co. v. Reich,** *supra*]

> **Counterexample:** In **Free Enterprise Fund v. Public Company Accounting Oversight Bd.,** the plaintiffs contended that the Public Company Accounting Oversight Board (PCAOB) violated separation-of-powers principles. The Sarbanes-Oxley Act provides that actions by the PCAOB are subject to extensive review and control by the SEC. Parties aggrieved by a final order or rule issued by the SEC can seek review in a court of appeals pursuant to 15 U.S.C. § 78y. Rather than seek judicial review by this circuitous path, the plaintiffs ran straight to court to challenge the Board's legality. The government contended that the case should be thrown out because the path for review laid out by § 78y is exclusive.

The Supreme Court disagreed. It noted that, generally, where Congress creates procedures "designed to permit agency expertise to be brought to bear on particular problems," those procedures "are to be exclusive." The Court will presume, however, that Congress

> does not intend to limit jurisdiction [a] if a finding of preclusion could foreclose all meaningful judicial review; [b] if the suit is wholly collateral to a statute's review provisions; and [c] if the claims are outside the agency's expertise.

Applying these principles, the Court observed, *inter alia,* that (a) the plaintiffs' constitutional challenge was "collateral" to any agency action that could be subject to review; (b) the Court would not force the plaintiffs to "bet the farm" by contesting the PCAOB's constitutionality as a defense to a Board sanction; and (c) the constitutional claims at issue fell within judicial rather than agency competence and expertise. [**Free Enterprise Fund v. Public Company Accounting Oversight Bd.**, 130 S.Ct. 3138 (2010)]

EXAM TIP

When addressing a *ripeness* question on an exam, remember that you have to look at both the fitness and hardship prongs. For *fitness,* consider whether the questions presented are purely legal or instead depend to some degree on issues of fact or discretion that might be determined in further agency enforcement proceedings. For *hardship*, be sure to discuss whether the agency's rule affects the petitioner's day-to-day, primary conduct.

---

4. Exhaustion of Administrative Remedies

Administrative law accepts that an agency action can be "final" even though opportunities within the agency remain for review. Administrative law also, however, commonly insists that a party *exhaust* such intra-agency possibilities for review before seeking help from the courts. In many contexts, Congress has specified exhaustion requirements by statute. In contexts where Congress has not spoken to this issue, courts apply a common-law form of the exhaustion doctrine. [**Myers v. Bethlehem Shipbuilding Corp.**, 303 U.S. 41 (1938) (discussing general rule requiring exhaustion of administrative remedies)]

a. Purposes of Exhaustion Rule

The exhaustion requirement has two broad purposes: protecting agency autonomy and promoting judicial efficiency. [**McCarthy v. Madigan,** 503 U.S. 140 (1992)]

(1) Agency Autonomy

The exhaustion requirement: (a) respects congressional delegations of authority to agencies rather than courts; (b) is especially important "when the action under review involves exercise of the agency's discretionary power or when the agency proceedings in question allow the agency to apply its special expertise"; (c) accords with the common sense notion that agencies should get the first chance to fix their mistakes; and (d) applies "with special force when frequent and deliberate flouting of administrative processes could weaken an agency's effectiveness." [**Id.**]

(2) Judicial Efficiency

The exhaustion requirement promotes judicial efficiency by: (a) mooting some issues before they ever arrive at court; and (b) creating administrative records that are useful to the courts, "especially in a complex or technical factual context." [**Id.**]

b. Common Law Exhaustion Doctrine

Courts apply a balancing test to determine whether to excuse the common-law exhaustion requirement. In general,

> [A]dministrative remedies need not be pursued if the litigant's interests in immediate judicial review outweigh the government's interests in the efficiency or administrative

autonomy that the exhaustion doctrine is designed to further. Application of this balancing principle is intensely practical . . . because attention is directed to both the nature of the claim presented and the characteristics of the particular administrative procedure provided. [**Id.**]

To give this balancing test some operative meaning, courts have identified several recurring situations in which they will excuse exhaustion: where requiring exhaustion would cause undue prejudice to the plaintiff; where doubt exists as to whether the agency can grant effective relief; and where exhaustion is futile due to agency bias or because the outcome has otherwise been clearly predetermined. [**Id.**]

(1) Undue Prejudice

Courts have excused exhaustion where the delay associated with administrative review would be excessive or otherwise cause irreparable harm. [**Gibson v. Berryhill,** 411 U.S. 564 (1973) (agency delays most frequent ground for finding administrative remedies inadequate); **Bowen v. City of New York,** 476 U.S. 467 (1986) (disability claimants would suffer irreparable harm if required to exhaust administrative remedies; district court had noted that the "ordeal of having to go through the administrative appeal process may trigger a severe medical setback").

Example: Prisoner brought a *Bivens* action against prison officials for violation of his Eighth Amendment rights by their deliberate indifference to his medical condition. The Supreme Court excused exhaustion in part because administrative rules on grievances "impose[d] short, successive filing deadlines that create[d] a high risk of forfeiture of a claim for failure to comply." [**McCarthy v. Madigan,** 503 U.S. 140 (1992)]

(2) Inadequate Agency Authority to Remediate

Exhaustion of remedies may be excused where there is "some doubt as to whether the agency was empowered to grant effective relief." An agency might lack "institutional competence" to resolve an issue, "such as the constitutionality of a statute." Alternatively, it might lack authority to order the requested relief. [**Id.**]

In a closely related vein, courts have excused exhaustion where "the challenge is to the adequacy of the agency procedure itself," a situation in which the adequacy of the remedy "is for all practical purposes identical with the merits of the plaintiff's lawsuit." [**Id.**]

Example: In the *McCarthy* case just discussed, the plaintiff, perhaps with an eye on exhaustion doctrine, was careful to make clear that he sought only money damages. The administrative grievance procedure did not authorize monetary relief. The Court cited "the absence of any monetary remedy in the grievance procedure" as "weigh[ing] heavily against imposing an exhaustion requirement." [**Id.**]

(a) More on Constitutional Claims

One might think that exhaustion should always be excused for constitutional claims that an agency is not competent or lacks authority to resolve (*e.g.*, one based on an argument that a statute is facially unconstitutional). This view, however, ignores that an agency might dispose of a case on other grounds or resolve it in a manner that sheds useful light on the constitutional claim. Thus, even for such constitutional claims, the touchstone for determining whether to require exhaustion remains a balancing test that weighs institutional interests against harm to the plaintiff. [**Rafeedie v. INS,** 880 F.2d 506, 513–17 (D.C.Cir.1989) (excusing exhaustion of a due process claim that the agency could not resolve, where agency stance was clearly settled, agency proceeding clearly would not alter outcome, and agency expertise was not implicated)]

Example: The Federal Trade Commission ("FTC") issued a complaint against Ticor charging antitrust violations. Ticor denied these charges and also challenged the constitutionality of the FTC, claiming that independent agencies violate separation of powers. It sought an immediate judicial decision on the constitutional issue before exhausting its remedies before the FTC. The author of the lead opinion, Judge Edwards, deployed exhaustion to dispose of the case. He ruled that Ticor had to exhaust its remedies on the nonconstitutional issues before securing a judicial decision on the constitutional claim—even though the FTC lacks authority to decide the constitutional claim. Among the factors that influenced him were that the constitutional claim was unlikely to succeed and Ticor had no irreparable injury from delaying consideration of that issue. [**Ticor Title Insurance Co. v. FTC,** 814 F.2d 731 (D.C. Cir. 1987)]

Example: A nonprofit organization, Marine Mammal Conservancy, Inc. ("MMC"), struck a deal to obtain ownership and possession of dolphins from owner. The Department of Agriculture brought proceedings under the Animal Welfare Act that led to a consent decree transferring ownership to the DOA. MMC had petitioned to intervene in the proceedings and sought review of the consent decree; the ALJ denied these requests. Rather than appeal within the agency, MMC sought judicial review, arguing that denial of the chance to participate in the proceedings had deprived it of due process. The D.C. Circuit rejected MMC's argument that exhaustion was excused for this constitutional claim. Exhaustion of constitutional claims can promote the policies underlying exhaustion doctrine, "giving agencies the opportunity to correct their own errors, affording parties and courts the benefits of agencies' expertise, compiling a record adequate for judicial review, promoting judicial efficiency." These policies supported requiring exhaustion as: (a) agency review would shed light on the meaning of the agency rules that MMC had challenged, and (b) the agency might resolve the case on different grounds, eliminating the need for a court to reach the constitutional issue. [**Marine Mammal Conservancy, Inc. v. Department of Agriculture,** 134 F.3d 409 (D.C. Cir. 1998)]

(3) Bias or Otherwise Predetermined Result

Exhaustion will not be required if the plaintiff can establish that the agency is certain to reject its claims whether due to bias or otherwise. Courts, as you might expect, require a strong demonstration of such bias. [**Marine Mammal Conservancy, Inc. v. Department of Agriculture,** 134 F.3d 409 (D.C. Cir. 1998) ("Doubt about the success of prosecuting an administrative appeal is no reason to excuse a litigant's failure to make the attempt.")]

Example: The Selective Service System ("SSS") revoked deferments of students engaged in a constitutionally protected demonstration. The students did not exhaust remedies, but it would have been futile to do so because the head of the SSS had already declared that there would be no reversals. Also, irreparable injury was involved: The SSS's reclassifications chilled free speech. Exhaustion was not required. [**Wolff v. Selective Service Board No. 16,** 372 F.2d 817 (2d Cir. 1967)]

c. Exhaustion Under the APA

5 U.S.C. § 704 of the APA provides in part:

> Except as otherwise expressly required by statute, agency action otherwise final is final for the purposes of this section whether or not there has been presented or determined an application for a declaratory order, for any form of reconsideration, or, ***unless the agency otherwise requires by rule and provides that the action meanwhile is inoperative***, for an appeal to superior agency authority.

Okay, you might need to read this sentence a couple of times to get it down. What it boils down to for our purpose is that, absent a contrary statutory command, a party seeking review ***pursuant to the APA cause of action***, need not exhaust opportunities for intra-agency appeal ***unless*** two conditions are satisfied: (a) the agency must demand exhaustion by rule; and (b) the agency must provide that the action is inoperative during the pendency of the intra-agency appeal. [**Darby v. Cisneros,** 509 U.S. 137 (1993)]

d. Exhaustion as Preclusion of Judicial Review

The exhaustion rule ordinarily has the effect of ***delaying*** judicial review because the court orders the appellant to return to the agency and attempt to obtain relief there first. However, when the petitioner can no longer obtain the administrative remedy (*e.g.,* because the time to do so has run out), application of the exhaustion rule may ***preclude*** judicial review entirely.

(1) Review in Criminal Case

In Selective Service cases, a draftee could get judicial review of his classification only by refusing induction and being criminally prosecuted. If courts insisted on exhaustion of administrative remedies, then a draftee's failure to exhaust would result in loss of a defense in the criminal proceedings. In one case, the defendant's argument that he was protected from the draft depended on a strictly legal argument of statutory interpretation. The Court excused exhaustion and allowed the defendant to raise this defense. In support of this conclusion, the Court observed that resolution of the legal issue did not depend on agency expertise or require development of an administrative record. In addition, the consequences to the defendant of requiring exhaustion would be very severe. [**McKart v. United States,** 395 U.S. 185 (1969)]

In a later case, however, the Court refused to excuse exhaustion for a defendant whose defense rested on a fact-sensitive determination of conscientious objector status. Under these circumstances, agency fact-finding, agency expertise, and an agency record would all be useful. It was important to respect Congress's delegation of the fact-finding task to the Selective Service System. Also, allowing draftees to bypass the draft board with respect to factual claims would encourage widespread flouting of the administrative process. [**McGee v. United States,** 402 U.S. 479 (1971)]

e. Civil Rights Statute

Under 42 U.S.C. § 1983, a federal court has authority to remedy violations of federal rights by state and local officials or by subsidiary governmental entities (*e.g.*, municipalities). The plaintiff in a § 1983 action is not required to exhaust state administrative or judicial remedies before bringing suit. [**Patsy v. Board of Regents,** 454 U.S. 813 (1982) (victim of discrimination on basis of age and sex by state university need not exhaust state antidiscrimination remedy or university grievance procedure)]

f. Issue Exhaustion

Normally a court will review only issues that the petitioner has first raised before the agency. Issue exhaustion makes sense because it allows the agency to consider the issue first, perhaps granting relief to the litigant and thus rendering judicial review unnecessary. The requirement also compels a litigant to raise an issue before the agency rather than holding it back and presenting it to a possibly more sympathetic court in the first instance. Even if the agency does not grant relief, the agency's consideration of the issue will inform the court's subsequent decision. In many situations, courts defer to agency legal interpretations, so issue exhaustion is needed to ensure that the court will have an agency decision to review.

(1) Application—Social Security Cases

Claimant's application for Social Security disability benefits was denied, and she exhausted all administrative remedies. On judicial review, she pressed arguments that had not been raised before the agency. The Supreme Court ruled that issue exhaustion was not required. The Court noted that, in the absence of a controlling statute or regulation, courts have imposed issue exhaustion based on "an analogy to the rule that appellate courts will not consider arguments not raised before trial courts." The premise of this rule is that parties should bring all available evidence to a trial court with authority to determine facts and that the parties should not use appellate proceedings as a chance for post-trial sandbagging. This premise does not apply where agency adjudication does not depend on an adversarial process. In Social Security cases, private parties are often unrepresented by counsel and may be unsophisticated. The ALJ is supposed to develop the record and raise appropriate issues in a nonadversarial setting. Given these circumstances, requiring issue exhaustion was unwarranted. [**Sims v. Apfel,** 530 U.S. 103 (2000); *cf.* **id.** (O'Connor, J., concurring in part and concurring in the judgment) (warning prospective plaintiffs that "[i]n most cases, an issue not presented to an administrative decisionmaker cannot be argued for the first time in federal court. On this underlying principle of administrative law, the Court is unanimous."]

(2) Application to Rulemaking

The case law on whether issue exhaustion applies to rulemaking is mixed. Some cases indicate that a person challenging a rule promulgated through notice-and-comment cannot raise an objection during judicial review that was never made during the notice-and-comment process. [*See* **Koretoff v. Vilsack,** 707 F.3d 394 (D.C. Cir. 2013) (holding that almond producers could not press challenges to a rule based on arguments that had not been raised during the notice-and-comment process). *But see* **American Forest & Paper Association v. EPA,** 137 F.3d 291 (5th Cir. 1998) (stating, "we have never held that failure to raise an objection during the public notice and comment period estops a petitioner from raising it on appeal"); *but then also see* **BCCA Appeal Group v. U.S. E.P.A.,** 355 F.3d 817 (5th Cir. 2004) (stating "only in exceptional circumstances should a court review for the first time on appeal a particular challenge to the EPA's approval of a state implementation plan that was not raised during the agency proceedings)]

EXAM TIP

If you face an exhaustion problem on your exam, first consider whether common-law or statutory exhaustion is in play. If a statute controls, such as 5 U.S.C. § 704, follow its commands. If the common law doctrine controls, then you must balance the institutional benefits of requiring exhaustion, promoting agency autonomy and judicial efficiency, against the harm to the plaintiff of delaying review. Consider, *inter alia*, whether requiring exhaustion would cause undue prejudice to the plaintiff, would be pointless due to lack of agency authority, or would be futile due to clear agency bias or other strong evidence of a predetermined outcome.

5. Primary Jurisdiction

Primary jurisdiction comes into play where both a court and an agency have concurrent original jurisdiction to determine a dispute. The plaintiff initiates proceedings in its favored venue, the court. The court, however, can invoke *primary jurisdiction* to refer the case (or select issues raised in it) to the agency for initial resolution if the court determines that the agency should have first crack. "No fixed formula exists for applying the doctrine of primary jurisdiction. In every case the question is whether the reasons for the existence of the doctrine are present and whether the purposes it serves will be aided by its application in the particular litigation." [**United States v. Western Pacific R. Co.,** 352 U.S. 59 (1956)]

a. Factors Favoring Application of Primary Jurisdiction

The doctrine of primary jurisdiction "seeks to produce better informed and uniform legal rulings by allowing courts to take advantage of an agency's specialized knowledge, expertise, and central position within a regulatory regime." [**Pharmaceutical Research and Mfrs. of America v. Walsh,** 538 U.S. 644 (2003) (Breyer, J., concurring)]

Example—uniformity: Shipper sues railroad to recover "excessive charges." A statute appeared to give shipper the choice of suing in court or before the ICC. The Court nonetheless referred the matter to the ICC. Otherwise different courts would produce different decisions about the fairness of a single railroad rate. [**Texas & Pacific Railway v. Abilene Cotton Oil Co.,** 204 U.S. 426 (1907)]

Example—agency expertise: Shipper sues railroad to find out whether bomb casings fit the high tariff rate for bombs or the lower rate for gasoline-filled drums. The Court held that the ICC must decide the case because it involves expert knowledge about the safety procedures necessary for transporting each product. [**United States v. Western Pacific Railroad,** 352 U.S. 59 (1956)]

b. Factors Weighing Against Application of Primary Jurisdiction

If a court properly has jurisdiction of the case, and if sending it to the agency will substantially prolong the dispute, the presumption is against applying the doctrine of primary jurisdiction. A court is particularly likely to reject the claim that an agency has primary jurisdiction of the case when the case seems *traditionally judicial* or *nontechnical* in nature, or where the agency fails to provide an adequate remedy.

Example—traditional judicial case: A plaintiff who was "bumped" from an airline flight because of overbooking sued the airline in a common law fraud action. Although an agency—the Civil Aeronautics Board ("CAB")—had power to order airlines to cease unfair and deceptive practices, the Court refused to apply the primary jurisdiction rule and permitted the court action to continue. The plaintiff's fraud theory is a traditional common law claim that courts are accustomed to handling. Moreover, the CAB had no power to award damages to the plaintiff. [**Nader v. Allegheny Airlines,** 426 U.S. 290 (1976)]

 **Example—nontechnical issue:** A dispute between shipper and carrier turned upon the interpretation of provisions in the carrier's rate schedule, which had been approved by the ICC. The Supreme Court held that the district court could retain jurisdiction because the provisions were *nontechnical.* [**Great Northern Railway v. Merchants Elevator Co.,** 259 U.S. 285 (1922)] *But note:* The Court added that if the tariff could not be construed without extensive evidence on railroad practices or reasonableness of rates, the matter would have to be referred to the ICC.

c. Judicial Disposition of Matters Subject to Primary Jurisdiction

A court may raise the issue of primary jurisdiction sua sponte. [**Pharmaceutical Research and Mfrs. of America v. Walsh,** 538 U.S. 644 (2003) (Breyer, J., concurring)] Where a court applies the doctrine of primary jurisdiction, it should retain the case on its docket if there are remaining issues that the agency cannot resolve. If the court determines that primary jurisdiction applies to all issues in the case, then the court should dismiss. In either event, the agency decision remains subject to judicial review. [**Best v. Humboldt Mining Co.,** 371 U.S. 334 (1963)]

EXAM TIP

When answering a question dealing with primary jurisdiction, be sure to look at what type of action is at issue. *A traditionally judicial issue* (*e.g.,* a contract claim) or a *nontechnical issue* can often be tried in a court rather than heard by the agency, especially if deferring to the agency will result in prolonging the dispute. However, if the agency can *immunize* private conduct from federal regulatory law (e.g., antitrust cases), the agency should get first crack at the case. If the agency has *exclusive* jurisdiction, the agency must get first crack at the case.

6. Stays Pending Judicial Review

Once a court has determined that an administrative decision is reviewable, it may grant a stay to *postpone agency action pending the outcome* of its review.

a. APA Provisions

Federal and state APAs recognize that both agencies and courts have power to order stays. APA § 705 provides:

> When an agency finds that justice so requires, it may postpone the effective date of action taken by it, pending judicial review. On such conditions as may be required, and to the extent necessary to prevent irreparable injury, the reviewing court . . . may issue all necessary and appropriate process to postpone the effective date of an agency action, or to preserve status or rights pending conclusion of the review proceedings.

b. Factors Considered in Granting Stay

In deciding whether to grant a stay pending judicial review, a court will consider the following familiar criteria:

(1) Likelihood of Prevailing on the Merits

"Has the petitioner made a strong showing that it is likely to prevail on the merits of its appeal? Without such a substantial indication of probable success, there would be no justification for the court's intrusion into the ordinary processes of administration and judicial review." [**Virginia Petroleum Jobbers Association v. FPC,** 259 F.2d 921 (D.C. Cir. 1958)]

(2) Irreparable Injury

"Has the petitioner shown that without such relief, it will be irreparably injured? The key word in this consideration is irreparable. Mere injuries, however substantial, in terms of money, time and energy necessarily expended in the absence of a stay, are not enough. The possibility that adequate compensatory or other corrective relief will be available at a later date, in the ordinary course of litigation, weighs heavily against a claim of irreparable harm." [**Id.**]

(3) Effect of Stay on Other Interested Parties

"Would the issuance of a stay substantially harm other parties interested in the proceedings? . . . Relief saving one claimant from irreparable injury, at the expense of similar harm caused another, might not qualify as the equitable judgment that a stay represents." [**Id.**]

(4) Public Interest

"Where lies the public interest? In litigation involving the administration of regulatory statutes designed to promote the public interest, this factor necessarily becomes crucial. The interests of private litigants must give way to the realization of public purposes." [**Id.**]

c. Illustration—Stay Denied

Blue Ridge Gas applied to the FPC for authorization to distribute natural gas in Virginia. A competitor, Virginia Petroleum, sought to intervene in the FPC hearing, but its request was denied. Virginia Petroleum sought judicial review of the denial, and a stay of the FPC hearing pending review. The court denied the motion to stay. Although Virginia Petroleum was likely to prevail, it would suffer no irreparable harm. Also, the question of public interest was found to be within the agency's expertise. [**Virginia Petroleum Jobbers Association v. FPC,** 259 F.2d 921 (D.C. Cir. 1958)]

d. Illustration—Stay Granted

Upon reenlistment in the Army, a sergeant was investigated as to possible homosexuality. At the conclusion of hearings, the Army recommended discharge. The sergeant requested a stay of proceedings pending judicial review of the validity of the Army's evidence. The motion to stay was granted. Petitioner would suffer irreparable harm to his reputation if discharged, and he appeared to have a good chance of success on appeal. [**Schwartz v. Covington,** 341 F.2d 537 (9th Cir. 1965)]

REQUIREMENTS FOR JUDICIAL REVIEW—AN APPROACH

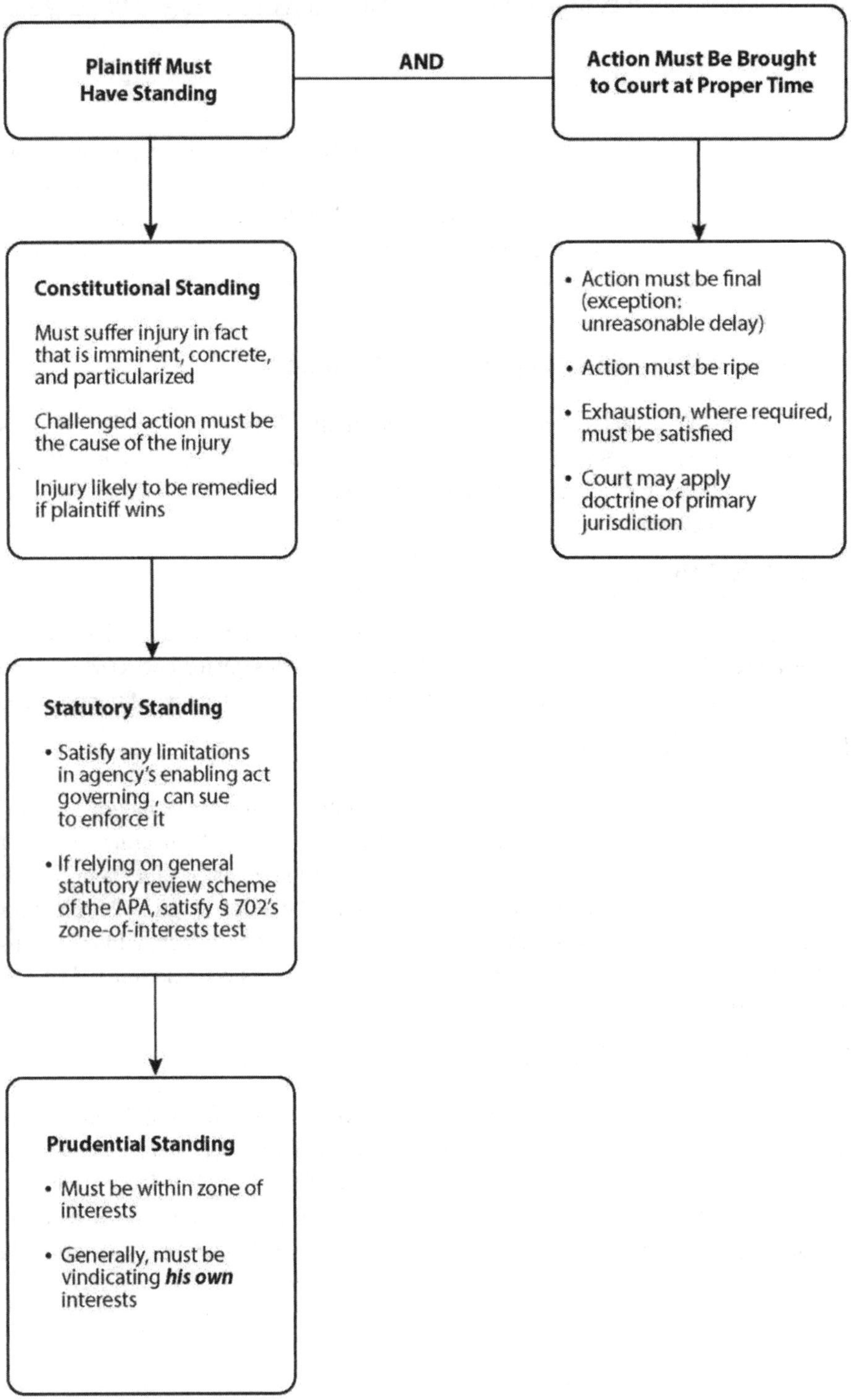

Plaintiff Must Have Standing AND **Action Must Be Brought to Court at Proper Time**

Constitutional Standing

Must suffer injury in fact that is imminent, concrete, and particularized

Challenged action must be the cause of the injury

Injury likely to be remedied if plaintiff wins

Statutory Standing

- Satisfy any limitations in agency's enabling act governing , can sue to enforce it
- If relying on general statutory review scheme of the APA, satisfy § 702's zone-of-interests test

Prudential Standing

- Must be within zone of interests
- Generally, must be vindicating *his own* interests

Action Must Be Brought to Court at Proper Time

- Action must be final (exception: unreasonable delay)
- Action must be ripe
- Exhaustion, where required, must be satisfied
- Court may apply doctrine of primary jurisdiction

224 | Administrative Law

Review Questions and Answers

Review Questions

Fill In Answer

1. A congressional statute gives the Department of the Interior the power to allow or to curtail mining within the national forests "as the best interests of all users of the national forest shall dictate." Is this an invalid delegation of legislative power?

2. A statute gives a state health department the power to make rules safeguarding public health. The department adopted a rule requiring bicycle riders to wear helmets. At a previous session, the legislature had considered such a measure, but it had not passed. Is the rule valid?

3. A federal statute provides that the Librarian of Congress can adopt regulations for the proper operation of the Library. The Librarian adopts a regulation stating that the names of borrowers of books from the library will be available for sale to purchasers of lists for advertising purposes. Is the rule valid?

4. A statute gives the Immigration and Naturalization Service the power to adjudicate cases involving illegal aliens. The statute goes on to provide that if, after a trial-type hearing, the agency finds that the individual is illegally in the country, it can impose a range of sanctions including imprisonment. Is the statute valid?

5. A statute provides that the Federal Aviation Administration can assess a penalty of from $100 to $1,000 per violation for failure to adhere to federal standards for airplane maintenance. After a hearing, the agency assesses Nocturnal Airlines a $600 penalty. Is this penalty valid?

6. A federal statute provides for a new office to investigate and prosecute banking fraud. The Chief Justice of the Supreme Court will appoint the director, who can be removed by the President for good cause, but the Senate must approve the discharge by a two-thirds vote. Finally, the Senate can veto any regulations adopted by the director.

    a. Is the provision allowing the Chief Justice to choose the director constitutional?

    b. Is the provision for Senate approval of removal of the director constitutional?

    c. Is the provision for veto of the director's rules constitutional?

7. A federal statute provides that the President can remove certain officers only for good cause. The President removes such an officer without stating any cause. The officer sues for her salary. Will the officer win if she was:

    a. The Secretary of the Treasury?

b. A member of the Securities and Exchange Commission (an agency that engages in rulemaking and adjudication)?

c. A member of the agency that operates federal prisons?

8. Ted is a clerk at the Library of Congress. His contract of employment provides no protection and he could be fired at any time. The Library proposes to fire Ted for the reason that he has been stealing books. Ted says this is not true. The government asserts that there is no right to a hearing in this situation. Is the government correct?

9. By statute, aliens are entitled to visas to work in the United States if they establish that there is a need for persons having their skills. Assume that the statute provides for no rights to a hearing. Norm wants to come to the United States to work as an engineering professor; however, his request for a visa is denied without a hearing. Is Norm entitled to a hearing?

10. A regulation of Nevada state prisons provides that a prisoner may be transferred between less secure and more secure prisons. Bob is transferred from a minimum security prison to solitary confinement for an indefinite term in a maximum security prison after a violent gang incident. Does this transfer implicate Bob's liberty interest?

11. Mel, a junior high school student, is suspended from school for five days for fighting on the playground. He is not given any chance to explain his side of the story. Is the suspension valid?

12. A State X statute grants tenure to college professors but provides that they can be discharged for good cause. It also provides that they are entitled to no hearing upon discharge, merely an opportunity to examine their file and discuss the discharge with the dean. Karen has tenure. She is discharged for plagiarism in her research, after complaints by a fellow English professor. Karen denies that she is guilty of plagiarism.

a. Assume Karen is given no hearing but is allowed to examine her file and discuss the discharge with her dean. Is the discharge valid?

b. Assume Karen is suspended after being allowed to examine her file and discuss the discharge with her dean. Twenty days after her suspension, she is given a trial-type hearing in which she is allowed to cross-examine her accuser. Is the discharge valid?

13. City provides housing vouchers to all homeless people so they can stay in shelters; however, vouchers will be terminated if the recipient engages in criminal activity. Suspecting Laura of selling drugs in the shelter, City cuts off her vouchers. It promises to give her a hearing within 15 days. Laura denies selling drugs. Is City's action valid?

14. Jed operates a draw poker parlor in a town where gambling is legal. However, one must have a license to operate a gambling facility, and the license must be renewed each year.

a. Jed's license is not renewed because the gambling board declares that he was using shills in violation of regulations. It denies a hearing. Is Jed entitled to a hearing?

b. The board adopts a new rule that no poker parlor will be licensed if it is within 100 feet of a school. Jed's parlor is next to a junior high school, so his license is not renewed. Is he entitled to a hearing?

15. Town adopts a land use plan under which all land in the Brentwood neighborhood is zoned agricultural. Pam, one of the 400 people who own property in Brentwood, wants to build a shopping center on her land.

   a. Is she entitled to a hearing?

   b. Town's charter provides for petitions for variance from land use plans in the case of extreme hardship. Pam requests a variance from the land use plan, arguing that her particular parcel is completely unsuited for agriculture, so that the zoning plan would work an extreme hardship on her. The Town Council rejects her petition without a hearing. Is she entitled to a hearing?

16. State X operates public housing for poor people. Occasionally, the department will order a tenant shifted from one apartment to another if it is determined that the tenant has an apartment that is larger than his family needs. Does such an order implicate the due process rights of a tenant told to move?

17. Federal regulations require a trucker to receive a certificate of convenience and necessity before transporting goods by truck in interstate commerce. The United States Department of Transportation requires a hearing by the Surface Transportation Board before denial of such a certificate. The agency's regulations require that the trucker show, by written application, that he already owns (or has a binding contract to purchase) adequate equipment for the carriage of such goods. No oral hearing will be granted unless the written showing is made. Ken wishes to transport fertilizer between El Paso, Texas and Oklahoma City, Oklahoma. However, he does not yet own any adequate equipment, nor has he contracted to purchase any. The Board refuses to grant him a hearing and denies his application for a certificate. Must the hearing be granted?

18. A statute gives the Nuclear Regulatory Commission ("NRC") power to license new nuclear reactors. A hearing must be granted before such a license is denied. At the hearing, the private party has the burden of proof to show that its plan for a reactor is safe within NRC guidelines. Even before a hearing will be granted, the NRC requires submission of elaborate written data containing extensive scientific studies concerning safety. Idaho Power Co. wishes to build a nuclear reactor, but its application is denied without a hearing since it has failed to submit the written studies. Is the NRC's action valid?

19. The application packet for the Law Review at State Law School states that spots on the review will be granted to persons who submit the 20 best "write-on" packages. Student X does not make the cut. Have his due process rights been implicated?

20. A federal statute provides that an agency can adopt safety standards but only "after providing for a fair hearing." The Safety Agency adopts standards for computer screens after validly following the APA provisions for informal rulemaking. Y Co., whose business will be wiped out by the new rules, requests a hearing at which it can cross-examine agency experts to show that the rule is far more drastic than needed. Is Y Co. entitled to a hearing?

21. A federal statute provides that the Environmental Protection Agency ("EPA") can grant a variance from water pollution standards to an applicant upon a showing that the applicant cannot meet the standard under existing technology. The statute provides that the applicant is entitled to a "hearing" on its application. The EPA refuses to provide for a formal hearing under the APA. Is it required to provide such a hearing?

22. A federal statute allows the Farm Mortgage Agency ("FMA") to grant extensions of time to farm debtors who cannot make payments on their mortgage because of a natural disaster. The statute explicitly makes the decision to grant such extensions discretionary with the agency, and it says nothing about procedures that the FMA should follow in granting or denying relief. Betsy is turned down when she asks for an extension of time and the FMA refuses to grant her an oral hearing or provide an explanation of its decision. Can a court properly require the FMA to provide Betsy with a hearing or other procedure?

23. PhoneHome, a cell phone company, is uncertain how the Federal Communications Commission ("FCC") will treat text messaging. If text messaging is found to be a "commercial mobile service," telephone carriers would be prohibited from censoring text messages based on the content of the message. Although it has yet to receive a request to send a text message from a controversial group, PhoneHome is concerned about being "caught between a rock and a hard place"–either facing possible penalties for violating the provision or the wrath of a majority of its customer base for providing services to a controversial group. Therefore, it petitions the FCC for a decision as to whether text messaging is a commercial mobile service. The FCC refuses to consider the case because there is no current dispute. Is the position well taken?

24. For many years, the National Labor Relations Board ("NLRB") had decided in its adjudications that certain conduct by an employee in organizing a union was not protected by the National Labor Relations Act, and that the employer could rightfully discharge an employee who engaged in such conduct. In reliance on this policy, Big Steel Co. discharges Mel. Mel files charges that an unfair labor practice has occurred. In the adjudication of the charges, the NLRB changes its policy and declares that the previous rule was wrong.

Furthermore, it awards back pay to Mel in the amount of $6,000. Big Steel Co. seeks judicial review, arguing that the change is invalid. Will the order for back pay be reversed?

25. The Securities and Exchange Commission ("SEC") filed a complaint against Sam, saying that he should lose his license as a stockbroker because he was negligent in giving investment advice to Mabel, a widow. Sam pointed out that the SEC had never done this before. Consequently, in Sam's case, the SEC held that a stock brokerage license could be revoked because of negligent advice but that this new rule would be prospective only; *i.e.*, it would not be applied to Sam. Later, the SEC filed a complaint against Fred for the same thing and revoked his license, citing the Sam case. Should a court reverse the decision in Fred's case?

26. The Nuclear Regulatory Commission ("NRC") is considering whether to license the construction of a new nuclear reactor. The Sierra Club seeks to intervene in the proceedings to take the position that the reactor will cause extensive thermal pollution in the ocean. The NRC statute says nothing about intervention nor does it provide for taking thermal pollution into account in deciding whether to grant a license. The NRC denies the Sierra Club the right to intervene and the Club appeals. Will the NRC be upheld on judicial review?

27. The Medical Board in State X brings a proceeding to revoke Dr. Joe's license because he prescribed excessive amounts of barbiturates. The only evidence against Dr. Joe is offered by Mary, who said that Stella had told her that Dr. Joe would prescribe any amount of phenobarbital whenever she asked for it. Stella died as a result of an overdose of phenobarbital. Assume that Mary's statement does not meet any state law hearsay exception. The ALJ revoked Dr. Joe's license and the Medical Board adopted the ALJ's opinion.

    a. Should the ALJ have admitted Mary's evidence?

    b. State X follows the residuum rule. Should the court affirm the Medical Board's decision?

    c. Assume State X does not follow the residuum rule. Can Dr. Joe argue that the proceedings violated his constitutional right to confront the witnesses against him?

28. The Nuclear Regulatory Commission ("NRC") is considering whether to license a new nuclear reactor and is thus conducting formal adjudicatory proceedings under the APA. During the proceedings, the NRC administrative law judge referred to a new book on radiation safety procedures. Relying on what she had learned in this book, she rejected the application and the full agency affirmed.

    a. Assuming that the company was not given warning that the book would be relied upon, and thus had no opportunity to contradict the information in the book, would evidence taken from the book be acceptable?

b. Assuming that the ALJ told the company that she planned to refer to the book and take official notice of the discussion on nuclear safety therein, and the company offered no rebuttal, would evidence taken from the book be acceptable?

29. The Department of Transportation's Surface Transportation Board is considering an application by King Truck Lines to carry fertilizer between Atlanta and Miami. The price at which King wishes to carry the fertilizer is much lower than the rate now charged by railroads for the same service.

a. The Board states that a great deal of business would be diverted to the trucking line from the railroads, and this would have a destructive effect on the finances of the competing railroads. However, no actual evidence is presented of the economic effect that the new service would have. Is the Board's conclusion supported by substantial evidence?

b. Suppose in this case that the trucking firm introduces evidence of three expert transportation economists to the effect that relatively little trade would be diverted from the railroads to the trucks. The evidence shows that the effect on the railroads would be insignificant, while the effect on the trucking company would be to change a failing company into a relatively successful competitor. The agency states that it does not accept the financial analysis of these economists. Is the agency's decision still supported by substantial evidence?

30. The Federal Aviation Administration issues licenses for pilots. The APA's formal adjudication provisions apply to the agency's decisionmaking. The pilot must establish that he has the requisite training and experience. Luigi applies to be a pilot but a factual issue has arisen concerning whether he has the necessary experience. His case is heard by an ALJ, but the agency instructs the ALJ not to make any report. Instead, the agency tells Luigi that it proposes to deny the license because it finds that he has lied about his experience. After the decision becomes final, Luigi argues that he has been denied his rights under the APA since the ALJ did not write a report. Is he correct?

31. A federal agency charged with monitoring coal mine safety brings charges against Acme Coal Co. for permitting illegally high concentrations of methane gas in its mine. The APA's formal adjudication provisions apply to the agency's decisionmaking. The ultimate decisionmaker is a three-person board. The organization chart of the agency indicates that Wiley Coyote, the director of compliance, supervises a staff of investigators. Wiley is also in charge of the ALJs who hear cases. Acme contends that this organization is invalid.

a. Is Acme correct?

b. Would the results in this case change if Wiley were one of the agency heads?

32. The Federal Communications Commission ("FCC") charged television station KISS with fraud in its license application and proposes to revoke its broadcasting license. The APA's formal adjudication provisions apply to the agency's decisionmaking. Ian was the FCC's investigator. Ian met with the FCC Commissioners, who decided there was probable cause to proceed against KISS. Paul prosecuted the case before Alex, the ALJ. Alex decided that KISS did not commit fraud and that its license should not be revoked. However, the FCC Commissioners reversed Alex's decision and decided to revoke the license. Are the following incidents reversible error?

   a. The meeting between Ian and the FCC Commissioners, who ultimately decided the case.

   b. Alex did not understand some testimony about complex engineering matters and asked Sam to help him figure out what it meant. Sam works in the FCC's engineering department and had not previously been involved in the case.

   c. While the FCC commissioners considered the case, Ian met with Carla, the FCC chair, and told her that the ALJ's decision was completely off base.

   d. Rex, who managed another TV station, had lunch with Carla, an FCC Commissioner, while the case was under submission, and told her that KISS was a rotten broadcaster and deserved to lose its license.

33. State University brings a proceeding to expel Roy, who took part in a demonstration against the school. According to the rules of the university, a hearing board consisting of three faculty members is to hear the case, decide what happened, and fix an appropriate penalty.

   a. Roy proves that the faculty members on the board are philosophically in favor of law and order and are opposed to various sorts of radical activities and disruptions. Does this establish that they are biased?

   b. One of the faculty members on the hearing board was overheard making a statement prior to the hearing to the effect that Roy was a well-known troublemaker who should be gotten rid of. If Roy proves this, has he established bias?

   c. Assuming that the facts given in paragraph b. represent bias, can the university take the position that under the rule of necessity the board of faculty members must hear the case?

   d. Assume that at the hearing another member asks questions of Roy that are obviously very hostile. During the hearing, the board member makes the statement, "Frankly, I think that you are lying." Do these facts indicate that this fact finder was biased?

34. By statute, the State Board of Dental Examiners must pass upon the education and moral caliber of persons applying for licenses as dentists in State X. The Board finds that Martha is of poor moral character and refuses to grant her a license. Martha takes the position that the Board is unconstitutionally made up exclusively of dentists, who have a pecuniary interest against licensing her. Will this position prevail?

35. The Secretary of the Interior has the power to permit or curtail mining on public lands. He announces that development of oil shale resources on public lands will be permitted. A hearing will be held to decide which of various applicants will be allowed to make the development. The winning company will be chosen on the basis of its financial resources, technological skills, and environmental responsibility. The rights are very valuable, and there is a heated competition among a number of oil companies to get the award. Prior to the hearing, the president of Nevada Oil Co. took the official responsible for making the decision to dinner. Afterwards, there was some discussion about the pending case and the president of Nevada Oil talked about the fine environmental record of his company. Ultimately, Nevada Oil received the award. Can a disappointed applicant have the award reversed?

36. The Federal Communications Commission ("FCC") declined to renew the license of television station WXYZ on the basis that WXYZ had persistently and deliberately engaged in racist programming. The ALJ recommended that the license be terminated, and WXYZ appealed to the full Commission. Oral argument was made before the Commission. Of the seven Commissioners, two were unavoidably absent on the day of the oral argument. Before the decision was reached, two more members resigned and their replacements were appointed. The decision to terminate the license was four votes to three. Of the four votes in the majority, two came from newly appointed Commissioners and the other two from the Commissioners who had been unavoidably absent. Is this decision valid?

37 By statute, the Director of Immigration and Naturalization Service ("INS") has power to grant discretionary relief to persons who are otherwise deportable but who face political punishment in their home country. Tashi, who is deportable, argues that he would be subject to political persecution if he had to return to Tibet. After a hearing and the filing of briefs, the matter is ready for decision. The actual decision was reached by Ralph, one of the attorneys on the staff of the Director. However, the Director signed the decision. Is this procedure acceptable?

38. Assume now that the facts stated in the previous problem are not admitted to by the INS. They are merely Tashi's contentions, which he wishes to prove. Is he entitled to take the deposition of the

Director in order to establish that the Director was not familiar with the case when he made the decision?

39. Turnco was criminally convicted of fraud in connection with an Air Force contract. Later, the Air Force held a hearing to decide whether Turnco should be permanently barred from bidding on Air Force contracts. At the hearing, can Turnco argue that it had never committed government contract fraud (because it should have been acquitted during the criminal case)?

40. Reverse the sequence of proceedings from the previous problem. The Air Force held a hearing and barred Turnco from bidding on future contracts due to fraud. Then Turnco was criminally prosecuted. At the criminal trial, can Turnco deny that it defrauded the government?

41. The Securities and Exchange Commission ("SEC") ordered revocation of Dennis's stock brokerage license because he had negligently advised a customer. Dennis appealed to the Court of Appeals for the Tenth Circuit, which reversed, holding the SEC had no power to revoke a license for this reason. The SEC decided this decision was wrong, and it hopes to persuade both the Tenth Circuit and other circuits of its position in future cases. In a subsequent case, Paula, also a stockbroker, negligently advised one of her customers.

    a. Can the SEC attempt to revoke Paula's brokerage license if Paula could appeal her case to the Tenth Circuit?

    b. Can the SEC attempt to revoke Paula's brokerage license if Paula could appeal her case to the Ninth Circuit?

42. John wishes to graze sheep on an Indian reservation. He telephones the Bureau of Indian Affairs in Washington and speaks to one of the attorneys, who assures him that no permit is needed if he grazes the sheep less than six months a year. This advice is wrong and the Bureau seeks to evict John from Indian lands. Will it be estopped from doing so?

43. A federal statute empowers the Health Agency to adopt regulations concerning reimbursement of hospitals for kidney dialysis procedures performed under Medicare. After an appropriate notice and comment procedure, the Health Agency publishes a regulation on February 20, 2014, that sets reimbursement rates for services performed after January 1, 2011. Under the rule, Downey Hospital is reimbursed only $80 for a procedure that it thought would produce a reimbursement of $120. Is this regulation valid?

44. The Securities and Exchange Commission ("SEC") adopts a rule giving respondents in administrative cases the right to take depositions before hearings. Dean, a stockbroker accused of fraud, seeks to take the deposition of the persons accusing him but the ALJ refuses to order a deposition. Is Dean entitled to take the deposition?

45. A section of the Federal Trade Commission Act gives the Federal Trade Commission ("FTC") power to make trade regulation rules. By a validly adopted rule, the FTC declares that all claims of product efficiency made in television commercials must be backed by adequate scientific studies, conducted according to prevailing scientific standards. In a television commercial, Flashy Toothpaste advertises that it will augment the user's sex appeal. There is no adequate scientific study that this will occur. The FTC brings an order against Flashy to cease and desist, claiming a violation of the rule. Flashy argues that it cannot be guilty of violating the rule, only of violating the statute, and that the FTC must consider again whether commercials must really be backed by scientific studies. Is Flashy's position well taken?

46. A statute allows the Federal Reserve Board to adopt rules setting the capital requirements for banks. On February 1, the Board published a notice in the Federal Register of a proposed rule raising capital requirements for banks. It invited written comments to be submitted by February 6. Bank Two submitted 50 pages of critical comments on February 5. The Board held no oral proceedings of any kind. The final rule was published in the Federal Register on February 12, and was effective on February 13. The final rule was accompanied by a two-line statement of basis and purpose that said the rules were necessary to assure the solvency of banks. But the statement did not respond to any of Bank Two's arguments. Bank Two seeks judicial review. Decide whether the court should overturn the rule based on the following arguments:

   a. The notice gave insufficient time for the public to submit comments.

   b. The APA requires agencies to hold oral argument before adopting rules.

   c. The court should order the agency to reconsider the rule and allow cross-examination of key witnesses with respect to critical factual assumptions.

   d. The rule could not be made effective on February 13.

   e. The explanatory statement failed to respond to Bank Two's arguments.

47. Water pollution by chemicals produced in the manufacture of chrome-plated products poses a serious problem. The Environmental Protection Agency ("EPA") proposes a rule that allows manufacturers to discharge not more than five parts per million (ppm) of chemical XYZ into navigable waters. During the rulemaking process, public comments persuaded the EPA that the standard was too lenient. In addition, the comments indicated that chemical ABC also posed health hazards. The final rule allows only one ppm of XYZ and ABC to be discharged. You can assume these rules are substantively valid. Decide whether a court will uphold the procedural validity of the rule in cases brought by the following

plaintiffs, both of which make chrome-plated products:

    a.   Company D produces XYZ in its process. It could have met the five ppm standard of the proposed rule but believes it will have to go out of business because it cannot meet the one ppm standard.

    b.   Company E discharges only ABC but not XYZ. It also believes that the standard for ABC will drive it out of business.

48. The FTC adopts a rule requiring disclosure of whether any parts of a product were made from imported materials. The publication of the final rule in the Federal Register announces that the FTC dispensed with notice and comment procedure because the public interest required that the rule be adopted immediately without any delays. Is this rule valid?

49. The Immigration and Naturalization Service ("INS") has power to allow deportable aliens to remain in the United States if they would be subject to extreme financial hardship as the result of deportation. It publishes the following documents, in each case without any prior notice and comment. Is the document procedurally invalid?

    a.   The INS publishes a document called "guidelines" instructing personnel in the field to disregard evidence that the alien has a business in the United States that would be destroyed by deportation.

    b.   The INS publishes a document called a "ruling" in which it states that the meaning of the term "hardship" in the statute is that the alien would be reduced to extreme poverty in his native country if he is deported.

    c.   The INS publishes a document stating that persons claiming relief under the statute must file a petition within five days after a final order of deportation.

50. The Securities and Exchange Commission ("SEC") proposes a new rule increasing the amount of disclosure of environmental problems that must be contained in a proxy statement. The rule is highly controversial.

    a.   During and after the comment period, numerous lawyers and lobbyists visited the SEC commissioners in their offices and tried to persuade the SEC to water down the new rule. The SEC did not disclose these contacts. The final rule is much less demanding than the proposed rule. Assuming environmentalists have standing to challenge the rule on judicial review, can they argue that it is procedurally invalid?

    b.   After the new rule was proposed, the chair of the SEC resigned and the President appointed Gus, a new chair. During his confirmation hearings, Gus stated that the proposed rule was very poorly considered and that he believed that companies should be able to keep embarrassing material about environmental problems confidential. Can environmentalists argue that the final rule is procedurally invalid?

51. The Nuclear Regulatory Commission ("NRC") operates a licensing scheme whereby certain laboratories having need for radioactive materials are permitted to use them under strictly limited conditions. The NRC reserves the right to inspect, at any time and without a warrant, the premises where the materials are being used. It makes such an inspection, discovers unauthorized uses of the material, and seeks to bar the laboratory from any further access to radioactive materials. Can the laboratory assert that the search was invalid?

52. The Securities and Exchange Commission ("SEC") suspects that Smith Co. (a stock brokerage corporation) has been selling unregistered stock. It issues a subpoena calling for the production of all records of stock sales during 2012. The corporation resists on the following grounds. Should any of them be accepted by the court as grounds for quashing the subpoena?

    a. It violates the privilege against self-incrimination.

    b. There has been no showing of probable cause that a violation has occurred.

    c. The burden of complying with the subpoena is too great.

53. The rules of the Small Business Administration ("SBA") require that anyone receiving an SBA loan preserve particular financial documents, in order that compliance with the loan restrictions may be ascertained. Beth is an individual who received an SBA loan for use in her business. The SBA believes that Beth spent part of the money on a personal yacht. This would be a violation of the SBA statute and also a criminal offense. The SBA orders Beth to produce particular financial records by which it can trace the use of the funds. Can Beth use her privilege against self-incrimination to avoid producing the records?

54. A federal statute sets up a panel to investigate malnutrition in the United States. The committee has subpoena power, and it subpoenas Zeke to testify at public hearings. It wishes to show that Zeke has been selling unfit meat and produce, contrary to state and federal criminal laws. Zeke wishes to resist the subpoena on the ground that he will be unconstitutionally deprived of the right to confront and cross-examine the informants against him.

    a. Should the subpoena be quashed?

    b. The rules of the malnutrition commission preclude persons appearing before it from having counsel with them. Is this restriction valid?

55. The Secretary of the Interior is empowered to allow or curtail mining in national forest areas and adopts a new set of regulations setting forth the procedure for applying for renewals of leases

already held for mining in the forests.

   a. The Secretary fails to give any public notice or to permit any public participation in the making of the new rules. Are the rules for that reason invalid?

   b. The Secretary fails to publish the new rules in the Federal Register. Sam, a tungsten miner, had no actual notice of the rules. He failed to file the necessary papers and his lease is declared terminated. Is the termination of Sam's lease valid?

56. The Civil Service Commission ("CSC") gives advice on whether political activities by federal employees would violate the Hatch Act. It sends out several hundred such letters per year. Bob is writing a book on the Hatch Act and wants copies of the letters. The Commission refuses to produce them.

   a. Is there a judicial remedy by which Bob can test the legality of the CSC's refusal to give him the documents?

   b. Is the CSC obligated to make public all of its private rulings?

   c. Can the government resist disclosure of the private rulings on the ground that they contain confidential material about federal employees submitted in confidence?

57. Clyde wishes to inspect a report prepared by the Department of Defense concerning Middle East policy. This report has been classified "Secret" under the government's classification procedure. Clyde asserts that the material should not be secret since there is nothing in it that would jeopardize foreign policy. In an action brought to compel disclosure of the document, will Clyde prevail?

58. The Comptroller of the Currency requires banks to submit a large volume of confidential financial information. Jake would like to inspect the filings made by the First National Bank. Can he do so under the Freedom of Information Act if the Comptroller refuses to release them?

59. The Secretary of the Interior is authorized to permit or curtail mining in the national forests. His deputy for environmental protection prepares a detailed report on the effect of strip mining in the national forests, including a great deal of factual material as well as recommendations for changes in policy.

   a. The Rex Coal Co. wishes to see the report. Is it entitled to see the entire report?

   b. Suppose the report rejected environmental complaints about a proposed mineral lease and had the effect of ending the administrative process and authorizing the lease. Must the report be disclosed?

60. A rule of the Environmental Protection Agency ("EPA") establishes the amount of chemical XYZ that can be discharged into rivers. Meadow, an environmentalist, persuaded an appellate court to

invalidate the rule because it was not supported by the rulemaking record. Meadow paid $100,000 in attorney's fees to obtain this result. Her attorney charged $300 per hour, but other environmental attorneys charge only $200 per hour.

 a. Is Meadow entitled to recover attorney's fees?

 b. The EPA statute provides that a court can order the agency to pay the attorney's fees of a prevailing party "if appropriate." Is Meadow entitled to recover any part of her attorney's fees?

 c. Under the facts given in paragraph b., is Meadow entitled to recover all of the attorney's fees?

 d. Assume that before the appellate court rendered its decision, the EPA settled the case by agreeing to rescind the rule. Is Meadow entitled to recover her attorney's fees?

61. The Securities and Exchange Commission ("SEC") seeks to revoke the license of Barney, a stockbroker, alleging that he cheated his customers. The SEC's hearing is formal adjudication under the APA. However, the ALJ rejects these charges and the SEC affirmed the ALJ's decision. Barney seeks to recover attorney's fees. Barney's attorney's fees were $100,000, based on charges of $300 per hour. Is Barney entitled to recover attorney's fees?

62. Rex alleges that he is completely disabled and is entitled to Social Security disability benefits. The government has taken the position that Rex is faking. A hearing is held before an ALJ in the Social Security Administration. Various doctors are called to testify on the question of disability. Rex's witnesses contend that he is truly and completely disabled, but the government's witnesses testify that he is faking. The ALJ states that he believes Rex and finds him to be truthful. On review by the appellate board, which is ultimately responsible for the decision in the case, the decision is reversed. The board states that based on its examination of the record, Rex's testimony was not convincing. On judicial review, Rex contends that there is no substantial evidence supporting the board's decision. Is Rex correct?

63. The Food and Drug Administration ("FDA") is conducting a study of the effectiveness of vitamins. It alleges that Megavite is ineffective for curing problems of iron deficiency and lack of energy. There is a full hearing before an ALJ. Considerable scientific evidence has been presented on both sides. The ALJ resolves the question in favor of Megavite. The Food and Drug Administration reverses, finding that on its analysis of the scientific evidence, Megavite is ineffective. Its drug certification is therefore revoked. On appeal, Megavite contends that there is not substantial evidence supporting the FDA decision. Is the decision apt to be reversed?

64. The Securities and Exchange Commission ("SEC") revoked the license of Morgan as a broker-dealer on the grounds that he had participated in securities fraud. By statute, judicial review is

obtained in the court of appeals.

a. In its review of the record of the SEC proceeding, is the court authorized to reweigh the evidence and find that the preponderance of the evidence is in favor of Morgan rather than the SEC?

b. In its proceeding, the SEC staff presented evidence of statements that Morgan had made in selling the stock of a particular company. These statements were clearly not correct in every detail, and if this had been the only evidence, a reasonable person could have come to the conclusion that Morgan had engaged in securities fraud. However, Morgan introduced considerable evidence to the effect that the errors in his statements were accidental, not deliberate, and that he had reasonable cause for believing in the statements that he had made. Further witnesses indicated that the persons to whom Morgan spoke did not consider these details important in their decision to invest in the stock. In deciding whether the SEC's decision is supported by substantial evidence, can the decision be upheld by looking to the SEC staff's evidence alone?

65. The Immigration and Naturalization Service ("INS") seeks to deport Sinead on the ground that she is not a citizen and that she does not qualify for any other statutory protection. Sinead contends that she is a citizen, but in an administrative proceeding the INS decides that this is not true. Would the federal district court be bound by the findings of the INS on appeal or in a habeas corpus action?

66. A statute authorizes the Securities and Exchange Commission ("SEC") to adopt rules relating to disclosures in proxy statements. There is a statutory exception providing that no such rules shall relate to matters of "internal business." The SEC adopts a rule through notice-and-comment that requires disclosure of environmental problems. As part of its statement of basis and purpose, the SEC interpreted the words "internal business" and said that those words do not describe environmental problems since such problems have a substantial impact on the community. On judicial review, assume the court does not agree with this interpretation. Does it have power to overturn the rule?

67. A statute provides that the SEC can revoke the licenses of stockbrokers for intentionally cheating customers. The SEC brings a proceeding to revoke Jake's broker's license. It found that Jake had negligently described a certain investment to a customer who had lost money as a result, and held that the statute is intended to cover negligence. There is substantial evidence supporting these findings. Must the court affirm?

68. The Federal Health Agency reimburses hospitals for outlays for Medicare patients. By regulation, it will pay $300 per session of kidney dialysis. Zeke, an auditor for the Health Agency in Dubuque, wrote a letter to Hospital X stating that the agency would

not reimburse for kidney dialysis unless three doctors first certified the need for the procedure. This is a new interpretation of the regulation and is contrary to prior agency procedure. On judicial review, must the court follow Zeke's interpretation of the regulation if it disagrees with it?

69. The Federal Highway Administrator is given statutory power to determine the routes of new highways. He is to consider such factors as cost, traffic movement, traffic safety, and minimization of the destruction of neighborhoods. The administrator approves the decision to construct an interstate highway that passes through a certain neighborhood of Acme City. The people in the neighborhood believe that a different route would have avoided disruption of their area, but the different route would be considerably more expensive and lengthier. Is it likely that the court will set aside the administrator's decision?

70. The Bureau of Indian Affairs is given the power to approve or disapprove proposals for leases of Indian lands. It is instructed to consider the best interests of the Indian tribe in its decision. The Bureau approves a proposed lease, over the opposition of the tribe, to coal mining companies that wish to perform strip mining on the Indian lands. The stated reason is the nation's need for additional coal.

   a. Is it likely that the Bureau's decision will be upheld?

   b. Assume that the Secretary approves the lease in the preceding paragraph without any discussion at all of the reasons. When the tribe seeks judicial review, the Secretary's attorney attempts to supply a list of reasons that relate to the best interests of the tribe. Is this an acceptable method of making a record?

71. The Securities and Exchange Commission ("SEC") has power to suspend the license of broker-dealers who are engaged in various sorts of securities fraud. Traditionally, in cases involving a particular violation, the agency would issue a reprimand against the broker-dealer on a first offense. However, in Tina's case, it terminated her license for exactly the same conduct.

   a. Is it likely that the reviewing court will set aside the penalty?

   b. Assume that hundreds of different broker-dealers were doing exactly the same thing as Tina. However, the SEC singled her out for sanction and so far has not gone after anyone else. Will this decision be set aside by a reviewing court?

72. The Iowa Encyclopedia Co. has a door-to-door selling scheme in which it tells customers that encyclopedias can be placed in their home for free. All they have to do is agree to buy the yearly supplements. However, the yearly supplements are so expensive that in fact the customer ends up paying more than the regular

amount for the set of encyclopedias and supplements. The Federal Trade Commission ("FTC") issues an order against Iowa Encyclopedia Co. to refrain from this practice. In addition, the FTC requires that in future sales, the company must charge the full value of its encyclopedias and must permit their purchase even if no supplement service is ordered at all. The company protests that the FTC order has gone far beyond the particular unlawful conduct originally alleged against it. Will the FTC's order withstand judicial review?

73. A statute gives the Department of the Interior power to permit or curtail mining in the national forests. The Department proposes to halt the mining of magnesium in a national forest. Clearfield Mining Co. believes that this action is an abuse of discretion since the proposal resulted from congressional pressure. The statute says nothing about judicial review. Can Clearfield go to the United States Court of Appeals for judicial review?

74. If Clearfield Mining Co. (in the previous question) goes into federal district court, must it allege that more than $75,000 is in controversy?

75. Bob wants to get a job with the Postal Service. Unfortunately, someone else was selected for the position even though Bob feels he was better qualified. The statute appears to give the Postal Service discretion to hire the person that it feels is best qualified.

   a. Bob would like to seek a writ of mandamus against the Postmaster. Can such a writ be obtained in the federal courts?

   b. Is this an appropriate case for mandamus?

   c. Suppose, instead, the statute provided that the Postmaster must hire the person who scores highest on a competitive exam. Bob has the highest score but the Postmaster hires someone else. Is this an appropriate case for mandamus?

76. The Milk Regulatory Board of Michigan passes a regulation that raises the minimum price for milk in the state to 70¢ per half gallon. A consumer seeks judicial review of this action. Can he obtain a writ of certiorari?

77. A statute permits the government to sue polluters in federal court for civil penalties. The statute allows the court to impose penalties of $10 to $1,000 per day for water pollution. The judge held that Blackwater Co. was liable for polluting a river and imposed the maximum penalty. Blackwater Co. asserts that it has a right to a jury trial on both issues but the judge refuses to put the issues to the jury. Should the decision be affirmed?

78. The law in State X prohibits suits for damages against the state for injuries caused by state employees. Liz, who was injured in an accident involving a truck operated by an employee of State X, believes that the statute is unconstitutional as a violation of due process of law. She brings an action in federal court for damages.

Assume that her constitutional argument is well-founded. Can the federal court hear the case?

79. Joe, a ranger working for the National Park Service, drove a jeep negligently while on duty and injured Anne. Joe was on duty at the time. Can Anne sue the United States?

80. Suppose that Anne claims that Joe violated her Fourth Amendment rights when searching the campground at which she was staying. Can Anne sue the United States for this violation?

81. The Immigration and Naturalization Service ("INS") conducts border searches. When Luisa sought to enter the country, she was negligently mistaken for a wanted criminal and detained for six hours by officials of the INS. Can Luisa sue the United States for damages for false imprisonment?

82. The Secretary of the Interior has authority over the control of predators on public lands. In response to complaints by environmentalists, the Secretary terminated the trapping and poisoning of coyotes on public lands. Ned is a sheep farmer who is entitled to graze sheep on public lands. After the Secretary's decision, several of Ned's sheep were eaten by coyotes. Ned brings a lawsuit based on a tort theory for damages against the Secretary of the Interior personally and against the United States.

    a. The Secretary moves to dismiss Ned's suit against him for damages on the ground that he is immune from suit. Should the court dismiss the action?

    b. The United States moves to dismiss the damage action against it on grounds of sovereign immunity. Should this action be dismissed?

83. A federal statute granting benefits to injured or disabled employees of the federal government, or to their families, provides that illegitimate children can receive no benefits. The statute provides that determinations of disability and damages shall be "final and unreviewable by any court." Fred is the illegitimate child of George, a federal employee who is injured. Fred wishes to attack the statutory denial of benefits to illegitimate children as an equal protection violation. May he do so?

84. The Federal Trade Commission ("FTC") has the power to restrain corporations from unfair methods of competition. Sweetbite Corp. sells sugary breakfast foods and advertises them heavily on television. Sweetbite gives many free trinkets to children who purchase the cereal. Goodenbland Corp. is a producer of healthy breakfast cereals. Goodenbland feels that Sweetbite's method of advertising is unfair since it preys so heavily on the susceptibility of children. However, the FTC has refused to take any action against Sweetbite. Assuming that Goodenbland has standing, can it get judicial review of the FTC's refusal to prosecute?

85. A statute gives the Federal Health Agency power, "in its discretion," to grant funds for the purpose of research in curing

Alzheimer's Disease. The agency head decided not to grant any funds for this purpose, because he felt that such research is a waste of money. Is the decision reviewable?

86. Dorothy objects to the Public Relations Department of the Pentagon. She feels that the daily handouts of news to reporters tend to devitalize independent investigations. Consequently, she alleges that they violate the freedom of the press under the First Amendment.

   a. Does Dorothy have standing to bring this action as a "citizen"?

   b. Does Dorothy have standing as a "taxpayer" since public money is expended in operating the Public Relations Department?

   c. Can Dorothy base her standing on the theory that she is "injured in fact"?

87. A statute empowers the Department of the Interior to either permit or curtail mining in the national forests "as the best interests of all users of the forest shall dictate." There is no provision concerning judicial review in the statute. Deepwell Corp. has been drilling for oil in a national forest under a previous Interior Department grant. The Department of the Interior now proposes to permit Evendeeper Corp. to drill for oil in the same forest. Does Deepwell have standing to complain?

88. A statute requires competitive bidding for government contracts and requires the government to give the contract to the "lowest responsible bidder." Both Seaworthy Corp. and Dolphin Corp. bid on a Navy contract. Seaworthy is the low bidder, but its bid is disqualified–the government feels that Seaworthy is not responsible since it went bankrupt two years ago. Instead, the contract is given to Dolphin, which had made a higher bid. Does Seaworthy have standing to complain of this decision?

89. A federal statute permits the expenditure of federal money for the construction of monuments, as the Secretary of the Interior shall decide. The Secretary proposes to construct a monument on a particular parcel of federal property in San Francisco in honor of a composer who lived nearby.

   a. Ed, who lives across the street from the site of the monument, opposes the construction. He feels that the design of the monument will be ugly and will blight the neighborhood. His complaint is that the Secretary has failed to file an environmental impact statement, which is required before the federal government takes action having a significant effect on the environment. Does Ed have standing?

   b. Assume the plaintiff in this case was instead an association formed by persons living near the park to resist construction of the monument. Would the association have standing to protest if an individual would have had standing?

90. The Department of Transportation allows the Surface Transportation Board to adopt regulations under which interstate trucking will be deregulated. The Surface Transportation Board adopts rules permitting trucks to carry any product they wish on the way back to their home after delivering a load that they were licensed to carry. All parties agree that these rules will make trucking more efficient by avoiding the need to return with an empty truck. However, it will undoubtedly reduce the number of persons employed as truck drivers. Can the truck drivers' union secure judicial review of this rule?

91. A federal agency adopts rules providing that magazines can receive reduced postal rates even though they contain solely advertising. The previous rules required the magazines to contain some editorial content. The authors' union attacks these rules, complaining that they will reduce employment opportunities for authors. Does the union have standing?

92. Norma applies for a license as a pilot. The license application remains with the Federal Aviation Administration ("FAA") for two years and they refuse to act upon it, repeatedly stating that a hearing will be scheduled in the near future but never scheduling one. Can Norma go to court to force the FAA to act?

93. The Surface Transportation Board adopts a new regulation stating that railroads that retain boxcars belonging to other railroads for an unreasonable time must pay a penalty of $100 per day. The Nevada Railroad seeks to enjoin the new regulation on the theory that it is not authorized by statute. Will the court hear this attack now?

94. Nell is a stockbroker who has made a contract with Paul. Paul's job is to get business for Nell by joining various organizations, talking about Nell's brilliant investment advice, and signing up clients for Nell. Paul gets a commission based on a percentage of Nell's sales to clients whom Paul has found. The Securities and Exchange Commission ("SEC") adopts a new regulation stating that broker-dealers may not make contracts with outsiders to get business for them and share their commissions with the outsiders. Nell tells Paul that they must cancel their contract. Can Paul get judicial review of the validity of the SEC's new regulation?

95. Large Corp. and Small Corp. want to merge but fear the application of the antitrust laws. They submit an application to the Antitrust Division of the Justice Department, which, under an established procedure, will review the facts and issue a ruling about the proposed merger. The subordinate official in the Antitrust Division who is charged with making these reviews informs the corporations by letter that the merger would violate the antitrust laws and that the Attorney General might well seek to attack it. Can the corporations obtain judicial review of this ruling?

96. The Securities and Exchange Commission ("SEC") served notice on Stanley that it was about to begin proceedings to revoke his

license as a broker-dealer, which would prohibit him from trading on behalf of others in the stock market. This action was taken as a result of certain securities frauds Stanley allegedly committed. Stanley feels that the particular conduct the SEC seeks to punish is beyond its regulatory jurisdiction. Stanley therefore goes into federal district court, seeking an injunction against the SEC to block the hearings. Should the court hear this case?

97. Under the Postal Obscenity Statute, the Postal Service has the power to seize and impound obscene matter sent through the mails. It can also prohibit persons found to have used the mails for such purposes from sending or receiving mail in the future. The Director of the Postal Service Obscenity Section states in a press release that a particular movie is certainly obscene and the Post Office plans to seize it if it goes through the mails. A print of the movie is seized in Florida. An administrative appeal procedure is provided for judging obscenity after the seizure occurs. Mel, the producer of the movie, seeks to enjoin the Postal Service to return the movie. He has not used the administrative appeal. Can this suit for injunction be heard?

98. Larry is a student at the Air Force Academy. He is suspected of cheating. The applicable regulations of the Academy provide that he can be given a hearing, but that he is not entitled to confront the witnesses against him. Before the hearing begins, Larry goes into federal district court, seeking to enjoin continuation of the hearing. Should the court hear this case?

99. A statute gives the Federal Highway Safety Agency the power to order the recall of motor vehicles for the correction by the manufacturer of safety defects. There is a hearing procedure for the purpose of making these determinations. In several cases, the exhaust systems on the 2008 Belchfires have leaked into the car and caused deaths by carbon monoxide poisoning. Roy brings a class action suit in federal district court on behalf of all purchasers of the 2008 Belchfires, in which the relief sought is that the manufacturer repair the defect free of charge. The automaker moves to dismiss the action on the ground that the Federal Highway Safety Agency should decide this issue. Should the court dismiss?

100. The legal services agency makes a grant of $5 million to a legal aid office in Portland, Oregon, for legal services to the poor. However, there are many restrictions in the grant, including some that prevent the attorneys from taking criminal cases or from participating in political activity. During the term of the grant, the government learns that the attorneys have been taking criminal cases and participating in politics. Following a hearing that substantiates these charges, the grant is terminated. The office is seeking judicial review, arguing that the various restrictions imposed are unconstitutional and that there was no substantial evidence that the attorneys were in fact engaging in prohibited conduct. Will the court grant a stay of the agency's determination pending judicial review?

Answers to Review Questions

1. **NO** — Although extremely vague, the standard used here brings the case within prior Supreme Court precedent, which upholds such delegations. If Congress can give the FCC power to regulate television and radio as "public convenience, interest or necessity" dictates, the delegation in the problem should clearly be upheld. [pp. 6, 8]

2. **POSSIBLY NOT** — Under *Boreali v. Axelrod*, this rule might be held ultra vires. The statute is vague, and it is unclear whether this sort of a measure is a proper public health measure. The legislature's failure to deal with the problem might also suggest that it did not intend the agency to adopt a rule on the subject. And state courts apply the ultra vires doctrine more strictly than do federal courts. [pp. 9–10]

3. **POSSIBLY NOT** — The rule raises questions about the privacy rights of the users of the library and, at least, has constitutional dimensions. Under cases like *Kent v. Dulles,* a court might hold the rule ultra vires (beyond the Librarian's power under the statute) because it does not concern the proper operation of the library. The court prefers this approach rather than invalidating the statute on constitutional grounds. In effect, it forces Congress to make the ultimate decision whether it really wants the agency to have this particular power. In *Rust v. Sullivan,* however, the Court ignored this approach and held a constitutionally questionable regulation was not ultra vires; then it went ahead and rejected the constitutional attack on the rule. [pp. 9–10]

4. **NO** — The courts have held that imprisonment can be imposed only by a court, not an agency. [p. 14]

5. **YES** — Federal agencies have the power to assess civil penalties, including a decision on the amount thereof within a statutory range. [pp. 14–15]

6.a. **PROBABLY NOT** — The Constitution allows Congress to adopt statutes providing that "inferior officers" can be appointed by the courts of law. An "inferior officer" is one "whose work is directed and supervised at some level by other officers appointed by the President with the Senate's consent." *Free Enter. Fund.* [p. 16] The question does not indicate that the director is subject to such control. It may be tempting to conclude that the director is an inferior officer by analogy to *Morrison,* in which the Court concluded that independent counsel (special prosecutors) were inferior officers. *Morrison* is somewhat dubious in this regard as a precedent as the Court was leaning over backwards to uphold a congressional effort to control executive criminal activity in the aftermath of Watergate. *Morrison* is also distinguishable insofar as the Court's conclusion depended on

		the factors that independent counsels had temporary positions limited to investigation of particular persons and allegations. [p. 16]
b.	NO	*Bowsher* prohibits Congress from having any role in the removal process of an officer engaged in executive functions other than by impeachment. [p. 19]
c.	NO	*Chadha* struck down all forms of legislative veto over executive action, including rulemaking, as forbidden attempts by Congress to legislate without submission to the presidential-veto. This provision also violates the requirement of bicameralism—both houses of Congress must act to adopt legislation. [p. 21]
7.a.	NO	Under *Morrison,* the President must have unrestricted power to remove certain officers where otherwise his ability to discharge constitutional duties would be impeded. A member of the cabinet who carries out fundamental presidential policy decisions is clearly in that category. [p. 18]
b.	YES	*Humphrey's Executor* established the validity of protecting the heads of independent agencies with "good cause" restrictions on removal. *Morrison* established a new, broader framework for determining the validity of these restrictions, but it cast no doubt on the result in *Humphrey's Executor*. [p. 18]
c.	PROBABLY YES	*Morrison* establishes that Congress can protect the jobs of most federal employees unless to do so would impede the President in carrying out constitutional functions. Probably the inability to fire a person engaged in managing prisons would not undermine the integrity of the executive branch by interfering with the President's ability to carry out constitutional functions. [p. 18]
8.	PROBABLY NOT	The government is correct that Ted has no "property" in his job since the contract confers no protection. This is like the position of an untenured teacher, who has no legitimate expectation in post-contractual employment sufficient to support a property interest. [p. 31] However, Ted's "liberty" interest will be implicated, and he will have a right to a "name-clearing" hearing if the reasons for discharge are seriously damaging to his reputation or employment prospects, the agency makes these reasons public, and Ted contests them. [p. 27]
9.	NO	There are no due process rights for an alien seeking to enter the country. [p. 28]
10.	YES	In *Sandin,* the Court held that a state regulation may implicate a prisoner's liberty interest where a restraint "imposes atypical and significant hardship on the inmate in relation to the ordinary incidents of prison life." [p. 29] The Court held in a later case, *Wilkinson,* that transfer to "Supermax" with solitary confinement for an indefinite period triggered due process. [p. 29]
11.	PROBABLY NOT	*Goss v. Lopez* held that a suspension of 10 days or less from high school was a deprivation of liberty and entitled the student

		to a conference with the disciplinarian and opportunity to state his side of the case. This case involves only a five-day suspension, but *Goss* probably would be followed in this situation. [p. 30]
12.a.	**NO**	Under *Loudermill,* if the state creates a tenured position, it cannot define the procedural protection for that position. Due process standards apply. In this situation, an oral trial-type hearing would be required, not merely a conference. [p. 31]
b.	**YES**	*Loudermill* established that the hearing can be given after suspension if there is an adequate opportunity before suspension to show that the state had no probable cause for its action and if a full hearing is provided promptly after the suspension. [p. 31]
13.	**PROBABLY NOT**	*Mathews* requires a three-factor balancing test to decide timing questions. Clearly Laura has a property interest; under *Goldberg* there is a property interest in welfare programs, at least as long as they are not discretionary. *Goldberg* requires a pretermination hearing before a person is terminated from welfare because of the brutal need of the recipient. Unlike *Mathews,* which upheld post-termination hearings for disability benefit recipients, homeless persons are likely to be much needier than disability recipients. Also, the decision turns much more on credibility problems than disability cases, which are decided mostly on written medical reports. However, the city's need for immediate action is greater here than in *Goldberg* or *Mathews*—it is not just a matter of saving money, but of removing somebody who might be selling drugs in shelters. This calls for immediate action. This is a close call and City's procedure might be upheld if there is an adequate pretermination procedure to determine probable cause. [p. 34]
14.a.	**PROBABLY YES**	Although there is some authority to the effect that no due process rights attach to licenses relating to such trades as gambling or selling liquor, this is probably no longer true. Nonrenewal of a license to operate a business without a hearing denies due process. [p. 32]
b.	**NO**	There are no facts to be determined—the rule prevents a license from being issued, and the location of the facility is not in dispute. Moreover, Jed would not have a right to a hearing to challenge the rule itself as it falls on the "legislative" side of *Londoner/Bi-Metallic*'s adjudicative-legislative dichotomy. [pp. 39–40]
15.a.	**NO**	No hearing is required even though Pam is deprived of a potential use of her property. Under *Bi-Metallic,* no individualized (or "adjudicative") facts need to be resolved, and the proceeding involves many landowners, not just Pam. Town obviously found generalized (or "legislative") facts about the Brentwood neighborhood, but this does not trigger due process. [pp. 38–40]
b.	**YES**	Here, as in *Londoner,* the proceeding is individualized, and individualized facts about Pam's property must be resolved.

		Moreover, the town charter appears to create an entitlement to a variance upon a showing of extreme hardship, so a denial of the petition is a deprivation of property. Consequently, due process would require a trial-type hearing. [pp. 39–40]
16.	**PROBABLY YES**	Since the department is bound by a standard ("larger than his family needs"), an undesired transfer will probably be treated as a deprivation of property. Probably a transfer of living quarters is significant enough so that it cannot be considered de minimis. And it would appear that issues of fact must be resolved (involving family needs) so a hearing should be required. [pp. 31, 40]
17.	**NO**	Although the statute requires a hearing before denial of a certificate, the agency can, by regulations, condition the hearing upon satisfaction of certain prerequisites. If the needed preliminary showing is not made, the hearing required by statute can be denied via the equivalent of administrative summary judgment. [p. 42]
18.	**YES**	This is a form of administrative summary judgment. The agency is entitled to ask for a written showing of scientific material so that it can determine whether there is any real issue of fact to be handled at the hearing. In the absence of such a submission, the hearing can be denied even though one is generally required by statute. This was established in the *Hynson, Westcott & Dunning* case. [p. 42]
19.	**PROBABLY YES**	Grading of the law review applications involves "adjudicative" facts; the Law Review is part of State Law School, plainly a state actor; the Law Review rules frame obtaining a spot as an "entitlement"; the weight of lower court authority holds that the entitlement approach applies to applications. [pp. 31, 33, 40, 42]
20.	**NO**	Y Co. is not entitled to a hearing under due process because the standard is generalized, not individualized. Nor is it entitled to an APA hearing; under *Florida East Coast Railway,* the statute calls for informal, not formal, rulemaking, so no trial-type procedure is necessary. In order to require formal rulemaking, the statute must explicitly call for a hearing "on the record." Courts generally defer to agency interpretations of the meaning of ambiguous terms like "fair hearing." [pp. 95–96]
21.	**PROBABLY NOT**	The application is adjudication under the APA since it is a request for a license. However, the APA does not apply unless a hearing is required by an external source such as a statute requiring a hearing "on the record." [p. 50] Under the leading approach of *Dominion,* the court will defer to an agency's interpretation of the word "hearing." If the agency determines that the word does not mean "hearing on the record," the court will probably accept that interpretation. [p. 51]
22.	**YES**	The weight of lower court authority indicates that the entitlement approach to "property" for due process applies to applications. Application of the *Mathews* framework to applications generally yields very little required process, given

the need for streamlined procedures at that stage. Absent due process constraints, a court is not at liberty to impose procedures on an agency that go beyond what the APA (or the agency's enabling act) would require. *See Pension Benefit Guaranty Corp. v. LTV Corp.* As there is no statutory requirement of a hearing, formal adjudication cannot be triggered. Informal adjudication is, however, subject to the general provisions of § 555. APA section 555(e) requires an explanation even though it requires no hearing. It could be that due process would not require more in this context. [pp. 33, 50, 66, 67]

23. **NO**

The FCC could issue a declaratory order under APA section 554(e), which authorizes such orders to terminate a controversy or remove uncertainty. Like a judicial declaratory judgment, no current dispute is necessary for a declaratory order to be a proper remedy. [p. 67]

24. **POSSIBLY YES**

Generally, the agency has the discretion to decide whether to implement a new policy by rulemaking or by adjudication. However, if the hardship caused by the retroactive effect of the decision is out of proportion to its public importance, the court will protect the employer from the consequences of the retroactive decision. This may be the case here, since the employer appears to have relied on the previous Board interpretations. There is no reason why the Board could not have changed its policy by means of a rule, rather than by adjudication; therefore, the court might reverse the back pay order. [p. 69]

25. **NO**

In *Wyman-Gordon,* the Court held that the NLRB violated proper procedure when it adopted a purely prospective holding in adjudication. It had engaged in rulemaking, not adjudication, but had failed to follow APA rulemaking procedures. However, ironically the Court allowed the NLRB to rely on the earlier invalid case in a subsequent case, holding that the later case was an independently valid adjudication. [pp. 68–69]

26. **DEPENDS**

Under APA section 555(b), intervenors have a qualified right, "so far the orderly conduct of public business permits . . . [to] appear before an agency. . . ." In *Envirocare of Utah, Inc.,* the court held that a petition to intervene may be denied where intervention would unduly complicate the proceeding or otherwise violate the agency's own rules, issues about which we lack sufficient facts. Thus, the answer probably depends on a determination of whether intervention would be disruptive. For example, are there other intervenors? Would Sierra Club's participation prolong or complicate the proceeding? Are the existing parties making the same arguments Sierra Club plans to make? [p. 54]

27.a. **YES**

The general rule in administrative law is that ALJs need not follow the rules of evidence and can admit whatever evidence they wish if it is of the sort that reasonable persons rely on in the conduct of serious affairs. This evidence clearly meets that

		standard. (Note, however, that an agency might exercise its discretion to adopt stricter evidentiary standards by procedural rule.) [p. 57]
b.	**NO**	The residuum rule requires that the decision be reversed because the only evidence in support of the critical finding is hearsay not admissible in a trial. Some states have rejected the residuum rule, and some that still follow it will allow a decision supported by hearsay alone to stand if the other circumstances are consistent with the hearsay. Under the latter standard, the decision might be affirmed. [pp. 57–57]
c.	**PROBABLY NOT**	Although reliance on hearsay does deprive the opponent of the right to confront the declarant, and the evidence in this case was critical to the result, it is unlikely that the decision would be set aside on this ground since the declarant was unavailable. [p. 58]
28.a.	**PROBABLY NOT**	Although an agency is free to take official notice—even of facts that are not indisputable—it must generally provide the parties with an opportunity to prove the contrary. [pp. 59–59]
b.	**YES**	This seems to be within APA § 556(e) and therefore would be acceptable since there was reasonable opportunity to contradict the material in the book. [p. 59]
29.a.	**PROBABLY YES**	In an area such as this, the Surface Transportation Board's expertise will certainly be considered in deciding whether there is evidence to support the decision. This is an area in which the Board specializes and in which it has technical knowledge. There is a certain degree of guesswork involved in predicting the economic effect of any change, and yet this is exactly what the Board was set up to do. Direct evidence of the effect that a rate change will have is hard to come by. For these reasons, it seems that this is an acceptable use of expertise. [pp. 60–60]
b.	**DEPENDS**	This is an area where the result is very hard to predict. Although the agency can reject the evidence of expert witnesses, it takes a substantial risk of reversal when it does so. According to *Davis & Randall,* such agency action should be upheld only if (i) the agency's criticisms of the expert are so compelling that the court feels the agency would not have been affected by anything the witness could say had he known of the agency's criticisms; and (ii) even assuming a hypothetical rebuttal by the witness, the court would have upheld the agency out of deference to its expertise. Based on the facts given in the problem, it does not appear that the agency's uncommunicated criticisms of the experts are that compelling—although it is likely that the court would defer to the agency if the experts had a chance to rebut the agency's point of view. Therefore, the outcome is hard to predict, but because the agency's rejection of the experts' opinion lacks any analysis or reasoning, it is possible that the agency decision would not be upheld. [p. 60]
30.	**NO**	In initial license proceedings, § 557 of the APA permits the agency to dispense with the usual requirement of either a recommended or initial decision. It can issue a tentative

decision itself. [p. 62]

31.a.	**YES**	Section 554(d) of the APA provides that the administrative law judge may not be subject to the supervision of an employee who is engaged in performing investigative or prosecutorial functions. [p. 76]
b.	**YES**	The rule of section 554(d) does not apply "to the agency or a member of the body comprising the agency." [pp. 76–77]
32.a.	**NO**	Agency heads are permitted to meet with investigators at the preliminary stage to decide whether to go forward with the case. [p. 77]
b.	**PROBABLY**	ALJs, like judges, are entitled to the assistance of law clerks and other staff members to help them understand evidence, find testimony in the record, and write decisions. APA § 554(d)(1), however, bars consultation with "a person or party on a fact in issue, unless on notice and opportunity for all parties to participate." The question here is ambiguous, but the communication probably involved forbidden consultation about adjudicative facts. Regardless of whether the communication was technically illegal, it was certainly unwise. [pp. 58, 83]
c.	**YES**	This is a violation of section 554(d), which prohibits employees who have engaged in prosecution or investigation in a case from participating in agency review of the decision. Carla is exempted from this provision, but Ian is not. [p. 76]
d.	**YES**	This is an outsider ex parte contact that violates APA section 557(d). Rex is an "interested person" and the communication is "relevant to the merits." [pp. 82–82]
33.a.	**NO**	Philosophical bias in favor of the law being enforced is not a ground for disqualification. (*See* the *Cement Institute* case.) [pp. 78–79]
b.	**YES**	Animus against a person or prejudgment of the facts disqualifies a fact finder. [p. 80]
c.	**NO**	There appears to be no reason why the university could not name other faculty members to the board in order to hear this case. Consequently, the rule of necessity seems not to be a barrier to correction of the bias. [p. 80]
d.	**NO**	A fact finder is entitled to develop attitudes during the hearing about the credibility of witnesses. Even if these are very unfavorable, it does not demonstrate bias—it merely shows that the fact finder is trying to evaluate the evidence presented. [p. 80]
34.	**NO**	A board made up of professionals is not presumed to be biased. Only a very strong showing of actual bias, such as was made in *Gibson v. Berryhill,* would suffice. *Friedman v. Rogers* makes it clear that a facial attack will not succeed. [p. 80]
35.	**YES**	If the hearing on the record was required by statute, APA § 557(d) applies and the ex parte contact was clearly improper. Even if the hearing was not required by statute, it is likely that

		the *Sangamon* principle would apply, since the hearing determined which of several applicants would receive valuable rights. *Sangamon* prohibited ex parte contacts in this situation under due process. [pp. 82, 116]
36.	**YES**	Oral argument is not a constitutional prerequisite. Assuming that all the members read, or at least familiarized themselves with, the transcript of the oral argument, it was not necessary that they actually be present. Consequently, the decision is valid. [p. 85]
37.	**NO**	This appears to be a violation of *Morgan I,* which requires that he who has the statutory responsibility for decisions must hear the case, at least in the sense of being familiar with the evidence and argument. Ad hoc delegations are not permitted. *(See KFC National Management Corp.)* [pp. 84–85]
38.	**NO**	This would be a violation of *Morgan IV,* which prevents the court from investigating the process by which the decisionmaker reached his decision. In the absence of some objectively determinable evidence that Tashi is correct, it is likely that he would receive no relief. [pp. 85–86]
39.	**NO**	Principles of res judicata and collateral estoppel apply generally in administrative law. Turnco should be precluded by collateral estoppel from relitigating the criminal case in the later administrative case. [p. 86]
40.	**YES**	Collateral estoppel should not apply here because the government's burden of proof in the administrative hearing was merely to prove its case by a preponderance. In the criminal case, it must prove its case beyond a reasonable doubt. This difference precludes application of collateral estoppel. [p. 87]
41.a.	**PROBABLY NOT**	Although not settled, it is likely that the SEC cannot relitigate the issue in the same circuit. It must acquiesce in the prior decision. [p. 88]
b.	**YES**	The government is not bound by nonmutual collateral estoppel and can relitigate the issue in another circuit in hopes of producing a conflict that will enable it to get to the Supreme Court. [p. 88]
42.	**NO**	The Supreme Court has never accepted a claim that the government can be estopped. Although a few lower court cases hold the government bound by estoppel, this is a weak case. For one thing, the advice was informal; well-founded claims of estoppel usually arise from formal written advice rather than telephone conversations. Furthermore, the use of estoppel here would prejudice the rights of the Indians. In cases where the government has been estopped, no particular individuals or groups have been harmed by the estoppel. Also, it is not clear that John has detrimentally relied on the advice. There is no showing that he will lose any investment by denial of future grazing rights. [pp. 88, 89]
43.	**NO**	Absent explicit statutory authorization, legislative regulations

		cannot be retroactive under the *Georgetown* case. In addition, it can be argued that the regulation violates the 30-day pre-effective date provision of section 553(d). [pp. 98, 105]
44.	**YES**	Agencies are bound by their own procedural rules, even though these rules were not required by any statute, unless the rule was adopted for agency convenience rather than the protection of outsiders. [p. 100]
45.	**NO**	If we take as given that the rule was a valid exercise of the FTC's legislative rulemaking authority, then the rule has the force of law. The FTC can therefore proceed directly under the rule rather than the statute. [p. 100]
46.a.	**YES**	The APA does not state how long the comment period must be, but it must be sufficient for people to prepare comments and participate in the process. Five days is too short, even though Bank Two was able to prepare comments during that period. [p. 103]
b.	**NO**	The APA does not require any oral proceedings in notice-and-comment rulemaking. [p. 103]
c.	**NO**	*Vermont Yankee* precludes courts from adding any new procedural requirements to those set forth in the APA. [p. 98]
d.	**YES**	APA § 553(d) requires a 30-day grace period before rules become effective absent a finding of good cause for a shorter period. There was no such finding here. [pp. 105–105]
e.	**YES**	Court decisions construe the APA to require the agency to respond in its statement of basis and purpose to material arguments made by the public in comments submitted during rulemaking. [p. 104]
47.a.	**PROBABLY NOT**	The final rule is probably a logical outgrowth of the proposed rule. A final rule does not have to be the same as the proposed rule. The agency is entitled to change it based upon the comments submitted by the public. The final rule can be either more or less restrictive as long as it is a logical outgrowth of the proposed rule, so that commenters would be placed on notice that such an outcome could occur. However, it can be argued that the final rule is so much more severe than the proposed one that Company D could not possibly have anticipated it. [p. 103]
b.	**PROBABLY YES**	Again the logical outgrowth test would suggest that Company E could not anticipate that the EPA would adopt a rule relating to its pollution problem when ABC was not even mentioned in the proposed rule. Yet the EPA was addressing the general problem of pollution from chromium manufacturing and perhaps E should have realized that all chemicals produced in manufacturing that product were up for review. [p. 103]
48.	**NO**	An agency can dispense with public proceedings only upon a finding that such proceedings would be impracticable, unnecessary, or contrary to the public interest. Generally, this requires a real emergency and the court carefully scrutinizes the agency's explanation. Here, the FTC failed to explain what sort

		of emergency required its shortcuts. Moreover, this is not a situation that appears to be a true emergency; the public could wait a little longer for disclosure to occur in order that people affected would have the right to comment on the rule. [pp. 110–111]
49.a.	**PERHAPS**	The document might fall under the policy statement exception to the APA, which allows the guidelines to be adopted without any prior procedures. A policy statement constrains the agency's discretion, but is tentative rather than definitive. These guidelines do affect a discretionary power, but they seem inflexible; field personnel are instructed to disregard certain evidence without any exceptions. Although courts often defer to the labels placed on rules by agencies, and this one is called a guideline rather than a rule, it may be too definitive to meet the policy statement exception. [pp. 114–115]
b.	**PROBABLY NOT**	This rule seems to fall under the interpretive rule exception to the APA. Courts usually follow the label placed on the rule by the agency and this is called a "ruling" rather than a "rule," which does suggest it is interpretive. It explains the meaning of a word in the statute and thus could well be interpretive. It does not appear to be legislative in either its purpose or its effect. [pp. 111–112]
c.	**NO**	This rule seems to fall under the procedural rule exception to the APA. It does not modify substantive rights but merely explains what procedures the public must follow to take advantage of certain legal rights. [p. 109]
50.a.	**PROBABLY NOT**	Although § 553 of the APA does not limit ex parte contacts, *Home Box Office* held that undisclosed ex parte contacts in informal legislative rulemaking were prohibited. Later cases have limited *HBO* to matters where the agency "rulemaking" implicates due process, which occurs under *Sangamon Valley* where the rule will determine conflicting claims to a valuable privilege (*i.e.*, where the "rule" is, for due process purposes, really an "adjudication"). Without the aid of due process, a judicially-imposed bar on ex parte contacts in informal rulemaking would *Vermont Yankee*. [p. 116]
b.	**PROBABLY NOT**	Bias standards from adjudication do not apply in rulemaking. According to one case, to disqualify a rulemaker for bias, you must offer clear and convincing evidence that he has an unalterably closed mind on the subject. This standard is designed to be almost impossible to meet, and the evidence here is weaker than that found inadequate in the *Association of National Advertisers* case. [p. 117]
51.	**PROBABLY NOT**	Although the warrant requirements of the Fourth Amendment do apply to civil investigatory searches (as shown by *Barlow's*), it appears that this case falls closer to *New York v. Burger,* which allowed a warrantless search. Like *Burger,* the defendant had a license and therefore had "consented in advance" to the inspections. Also, the search was not accompanied by any

unauthorized force, and was limited only to specific items. It seems that it was essential to carry out an urgent federal purpose. On the other hand, it is not so clear that a requirement of obtaining a warrant would frustrate the search requirement. Additional facts are needed to know whether the unauthorized use of the materials could be quickly concealed. Also, a search appears to be authorized here during any hour of the day or night, which goes beyond *Burger*. [pp. 124–126]

52.a.	**NO**	Corporations do not have this privilege. [p. 126]
b.	**NO**	This is not adequate grounds for quashing an agency's subpoena under the *Endicott-Johnson* case. [p. 123]
c.	**PERHAPS**	It is possible that the vast amount of information required here by the SEC is excessive for its regulatory purposes and that the court would scale down the request to documents relating to sales of particular stocks or to particular customers. [p. 124]
53.	**PROBABLY NOT**	The SBA regulations specifically require that certain records be retained. The *Shapiro* case held that Fifth Amendment protection did not apply to such records. Although the *Shapiro* doctrine was later limited by the *Marchetti* case, it would appear that Beth could not rely upon *Marchetti* here: The records required by the SBA are similar to those kept by persons in business, and the recordkeeping requirements concern a primarily noncriminal regulated activity. [p. 127]
54.a.	**NO**	This appears to be within the authority of *Hannah v. Larche*, which stated that investigatory panels need not allow cross-examination or afford other due process requirements. The theory in *Hannah* was that the proceedings were simply investigatory, and that the commission could not impose any sanctions for criminal or other violations. Although the *Hannah* case was limited by *Jenkins v. McKeithen*, the latter case involved an investigatory panel that was part of the criminal process; such facts do not appear in our problem. [p. 128]
b.	**NO**	Although the Constitution does not require counsel at investigatory proceedings, APA § 555(b) provides for representation by counsel for anyone compelled to appear before an agency. [p. 128]
55.a.	**NO**	Under APA § 553(b)(A), public participation is not required in connection with adopting rules of agency organization, procedure, or practice. This exception should apply so long as the "procedural" rules at issue did not encode a "substantive value judgment." [p. 109]
b.	**NO**	The new rules cannot be applied against Sam because they were not published in the Federal Register as required by APA section 552(a)(1). Unless a person has actual notice of unpublished regulations, he cannot be adversely affected by them. [p. 104]
56.a.	**YES**	The Freedom of Information Act provides that an action can be brought in the federal district court for a mandatory injunction

		to require the disclosure of such materials. [p. 129]
b.	**YES**	These appear to be "interpretations" not published in the Federal Register. If so, the agency must make all such interpretations available for public inspection and copying under APA § 552(a)(2). [p. 130]
c.	**PROBABLY YES**	Under APA § 552(b)(6), the agency need not disclose personnel and similar files, the disclosure of which would work a clearly unwarranted invasion of personal privacy. Clearly, disclosure about political activities would be a substantial invasion of privacy. But perhaps the rulings should be released to Bob with all names and identifying details removed; this would probably solve the privacy problem. [pp. 130, 136–137]
57.	**DEPENDS**	Under the Freedom of Information Act, the court can review the classification to decide whether secrecy is really necessary. We do not have enough facts to predict what the judge will do. [p. 133]
58.	**PROBABLY NOT**	Exemption 4 comes into play here for commercial or financial information that is privileged or confidential. Given that the information was submitted under compulsion rather than voluntarily, the test is whether disclosure would cause substantial harm to the competitive position of the person from whom the information was obtained. It appears that this test could be met here. There may be material within the report that is not confidential, and Jake is entitled to see whether it is possible to release this much without making public the confidential part. Exemption 8, for banking information, might also apply. [pp. 134, 138]
59.a.	**NO**	This brings into play APA § 552(b)(5)—an exemption for inter-agency or intra-agency memoranda which would not be available by law to a party other than an agency in litigation with the agency. This exemption generally allows an agency to refuse to disclose pre-decisional advice from the staff to the agency heads. Nevertheless, the agency must disclose the factual material in the report, although the policy recommendations need not be made available. Consequently, the court will order production of part of the report. Even then, if the agency can show that disclosure of the factual material would produce an unwarranted interference in the agency's decisionmaking, possibly that material can be kept secret also; but this does not appear to be true in the instant case. [pp. 135–136]
b.	**YES**	This is a decision that terminates a case and, as such, is a final opinion that must be publicized and indexed. It does not fall within the exception for intra-agency memoranda under the *Sears, Roebuck* case. [p. 135]
60.a.	**NO**	Without more facts or law, under the "American rule," a party is not entitled to obtain attorney's fees from her opponent, absent some exception or a statutory rule so providing. [p. 141]
b.	**PROBABLY YES**	Meadow is a prevailing party and it is likely that her efforts

			served the public interest. [p. 141]
	c.	**PROBABLY NOT**	Meadow is entitled to a reasonable hourly fee. Without further facts to justify an unusual adjustment to the "lodestar," the reasonable rate appears to be $200, not $300. Moreover, the court must find that the number of hours spent by the attorney was reasonable. [pp. 142]
	d.	**PROBABLY NOT**	Under *Buckhannon,* fees can be recovered only if the party prevails as the result of a court decision or a consent decree, not a settlement. However, it might be argued that the *Buckhannon* rule should not apply under an "as appropriate" statute. [p. 141]
61.		**PROBABLY NOT**	Under the Equal Access to Justice Act, he can recover fees only if the SEC's position was not "substantially justified," meaning justified to a degree that could satisfy a reasonable person. The facts given here indicate the SEC was wrong, but fail to show that its position was not "substantially justified." [pp. 131, 132]
62.		**POSSIBLY YES**	Under the *Universal Camera* case, the administrative law judge's assessment of credibility questions is very important. The ultimate question for judicial review is whether "substantial evidence" supported the board's decision. The ALJ's contrary decision is a part of the record, and it detracts to some degree from the substantiality of evidence supporting the board's result. The board did not see Rex testify; the ALJ did. In a case as evenly balanced as this seems to be, a reviewing court might well conclude, in light of the ALJ's disagreement and superior opportunity to judge demeanor, that substantial evidence did not support the board. [pp. 148–149]
63.		**NO**	Here the fact that the administrative law judge has been reversed is of very little importance because questions of credibility are not involved. The FDA, not the ALJ, bears primary responsibility for resolving scientific questions presented. If a reasonable person could have come to the same conclusion, there is substantial evidence and the board's decision will stand. [p. 149]
64.a.		**NO**	An agency's findings of fact generally must be upheld on review if supported by *substantial evidence* on the whole record. This means that the SEC's fact findings have to be upheld if a reasonable person could have come to the same conclusion. The reviewing court is *not* allowed to reweigh the evidence and find that a preponderance of the evidence goes a different way. If a reasonable person could have come to the result reached by the agency, the court must uphold the agency even if it believes the result is wrong. [p. 146]
	b.	**NO**	The "whole record" requirement of the APA requires that the reviewing court look at both sides in deciding whether a reasonable person could have come to the conclusions that the SEC did. [p. 147]
65.		**NO**	Under the *Ng Fung Ho* case, an agency's findings concerning whether an alleged illegal alien is in fact a citizen may be reviewed independently. [p. 149]

66.	**PROBABLY NOT**	The scope of *Chevron* deference is not always clear, but *Mead* establishes a safe harbor that agency interpretations adopted through notice-and-comment should generally receive *Chevron* deference. Where this doctrine applies, courts should defer to an agency's reasonable construction of a statute it administers. This seems to be an ambiguous statute, and the SEC's interpretation, adopted after notice-and-comment, appears reasonable given the limited facts stated. [pp. 150, 154]
67.	NO	The SEC has erroneously interpreted the statute. It is limited to "intentionally cheating customers," yet the SEC has interpreted this to cover negligence. Under *Chevron* step one, the court is entitled to overturn an agency interpretation of the statute that is contrary to the plain meaning of the statute. [p. 151]
68.	NO	Under *Auer,* an agency's interpretation of its own regulation "is controlling unless plainly erroneous or inconsistent with the regulation." This standard, however, applies only to interpretations that represent the agency's "fair and considered judgment." Here, we have no explanation for the interpretation, no indication that it has been considered by high-level officials, and it represents a sudden change. These factors suggest that *Auer* should not apply. *Skidmore*'s weak deference might still apply, but this leaves the courts in charge of determining the most "persuasive" meaning. Here, we have no facts or argument explaining the new "interpretation," which should likely fail on judicial review. [pp. 158, 159]
69.	NO	Such decisions are reviewed under APA § 706(2)(A) to determine if they are "arbitrary, capricious, or abuse of discretion." Assuming that the Secretary has acted within his authority, the court is only permitted to set aside his decision if the administrator has failed to consider the relevant factors (or considered an irrelevant factor) or made a clear error of judgment. Since the facts do not suggest an arbitrary decision, it should be upheld. [pp. 162–164]
70.a.	NO	It should be set aside as an arbitrary. The only factor that the Secretary is instructed to take into account is the best interests of the tribe. The factor that he considered—the need of the nation for additional coal—is not such a factor. [p. 164]
b.	NO	There must be a record of some sort for the court to review in order to determine whether there has been an abuse of discretion. Post hoc rationalizations by agency attorneys are not sufficient. If the agency's explanation for its action is arbitrary, the preferred judicial approach is to remand to the Secretary, giving her a chance to make the necessary findings. The *Overton Park* case indicated that the court could conduct a trial to determine the Secretary's reasons, but it is unlikely that this case will be followed. [pp. 85, 163]
71.a.	NO	The courts have very narrow powers of review over the remedy chosen by the agency. It must be upheld unless it is "without warrant in law or justification in fact." In the *Glover Livestock*

		case, a penalty more severe than that previously meted out by the agency was upheld by the court. The agency should, however, acknowledge and explain its change in course. [pp. 165, 167]
b.	NO	Again, the courts have very narrow powers to act where the agency chooses to proceed against one person at a time rather than the entire industry. Absent additional facts showing a particular bias against Tina, the Court would probably uphold the SEC's determination as it did in the *Universal-Rundle* case. [p. 167]
72.	POSSIBLY YES	The mere fact that the Commission's order went beyond the specific wrongful conduct charged is not enough to render it defective. Otherwise, companies might easily circumvent the agency's orders. This is the teaching of the *Mandel Brothers* case. [p. 167]
73.	NO	Even though the agency's statute doesn't say so, judicial review is presumptively available under the APA's scheme for general statutory review. Jurisdiction would be based on 28 U.S.C. § 1331, and the case would proceed in district court. [pp. 171–173, 185]
74.	NO	There is no amount in controversy requirement in actions under section 1331. [p. 173]
75.a.	YES	Under 28 U.S.C. § 1361, a federal court may grant a writ of mandamus. Also, § 703 of the APA permits use of this form of action pursuant to general statutory review. [pp. 172, 173]
b.	NO	Mandamus only applies if the statute imposes a duty to act. It will not apply to merely discretionary determinations. [p. 173]
c.	YES	The statute appears to impose a clear legal duty; no discretion is involved. The court will grant a writ of mandamus requiring the Postmaster to hire Bob. [p. 173]
76.	NO	Certiorari is only available to review quasi-judicial action based on a record. Rulemaking cannot be reviewed in this manner. [p. 173]
77.	NO	*Tull* held that the issue of liability for civil penalties is a jury question; however, the trial judge can set the amount of penalties. Note that if the statute allows the agency to impose penalties directly, there is no right to a jury trial at all. [p. 175]
78.	NO	Under the Eleventh Amendment, the state is immune from actions for damages brought in the federal courts either by its own citizens or by citizens of a different state. [p. 177]
79.	YES	Subject to many caveats and procedural complications, the Federal Tort Claims Act waives sovereign immunity of the United States for the negligent acts of its employees acting in the scope of their employment. [p. 178]
80.	NO	The FTCA waiver of sovereign immunity does not apply to constitutional torts committed by federal officials. A *Bivens* action against the employee himself is a possibility, however.

[pp. 180–183]

81.	**YES**	The Federal Tort Claims Act does permit damage actions for false imprisonment by law enforcement officers. [p. 179]
82.a.	**YES**	Under the Federal Tort Claims Act, § 2679(b)(1), an action cannot be brought against a federal official for property damages (or personal injury) arising out of the official's negligent or wrongful act or omission while acting within the scope of employment. If the FTCA applies, its remedy against the United States is exclusive. [p. 180]
b.	**YES**	This action falls within the discretionary function exception of the Federal Tort Claims Act. This is a high-level policy decision about how to implement a specific program. [p. 179]
83.	**PROBABLY YES**	Cases frequently interpret preclusion statutes to apply only to denials of specific claims for benefits. However, attacks on the exclusion of groups of people from the benefits of the statute are often allowed despite preclusion statutes. [pp. 185–186]
84.	**NO**	Prosecutorial discretion is an area presumptively "committed to agency discretion by law" under APA § 701(a)(2) according to *Heckler v. Chaney*. The Court observed, among other factors, that it would be unwise to permit courts to interfere with the "complex balancing" of agency resources and priorities that go into determining whom to prosecute. [p. 188]
85.	**YES**	Under *Overton Park*, courts generally construe narrowly the reach of APA § 701(a)(2), which precludes judicial review of agency actions "committed to agency discretion by law." Here, it does not seem hard to find "law to apply." Congress intended to fund research on Alzheimer's. The agency's discretion concerns which proposals to fund, not to refuse to fund any at all. [pp. 187]
86.a.	**NO**	The Supreme Court has made it clear in several cases that one's interest as a citizen in preventing unconstitutional government actions is not sufficient for standing purposes. [p. 197]
b.	**NO**	Although it is possible to establish standing as a federal taxpayer, the requirements are very narrowly drawn. The challenged action must involve a legislative decision to spend for the general welfare, and the challenge must be based upon a specific constitutional limitation on the taxing and spending power. What this boils down to in practice is Establishment Clause violations. [p. 201]
c.	**NO**	The "injury in fact" test requires that the injury be: concrete rather than abstract; particularized rather than generalized; and actual or imminent rather than speculative or conjectural. The injury of being annoyed that the government isn't obeying the law is abstract. The injury of reducing Dorothy's access to high quality reporting is highly speculative and perhaps too generalized, to boot. [pp. 196, 197–199]
87.	**YES**	It can allege an "injury in fact" in the sense that its lease will be less valuable if others also have access to the same oil. It can

		also establish that it is within the zone of interest protected by the statute. Its interest is not inconsistent with the purposes of the statute. [pp. 197, 205]
88.	**YES**	Obviously, Seaworthy is injured in fact by having lost the contract. And the statute, which requires the contract to be awarded to the "lowest responsible" bidder, seems to place all of the bidders within the zone of interests protected by the statute. [pp. 197, 205]
89.a.	**PROBABLY YES**	The aesthetic injury is an injury in fact, under the *Lujan* and *Sierra Club* cases, as long as the plaintiff alleges that he in particular will be injured. The requirement of filing an environmental impact statement (under the National Environmental Policy Act) creates a zone of interest that protects those who might be harmed by specific federal developments. Because the injury claimed is procedural, Ed will not have to satisfy the causation and redressability requirements (meaning he does not have to show that, if the statement were filed, the project probably would be stopped). [pp. 197, 200, 204, 205]
b.	**YES**	Associations of persons harmed have generally been allowed standing to protect the interests of their members if specific members would have standing and the interests sought to be protected are germane to the association's purposes. [p. 200]
90.	**PROBABLY NOT**	The issue here is statutory standing under § 702 of the APA. On the one hand, the facts of the problem seem squarely on point with the *Air Courier* case, in which the Court rejected standing for unions to complain about a loss of postal service jobs because Congress did not intend for the statute to protect such jobs. On the other, *Air Courier* is an outlier in the Court's statutory standing jurisprudence. Other cases, including more recent ones, have stated that the plaintiff need not be a member of a class that Congress specifically intended to benefit in the statute at issue. Still, a court might conclude that the purpose of enhancing trucker employment is inconsistent with a deregulatory statute designed to increase competition—in which case the plaintiff union would fall outside the zone of interests arguably to be protected by the statute. [p. 205]
91.	**PROBABLY NOT**	The union probably lacks standing for two reasons. First, as in the previous problem, authors may not be within the zone of interests that the statute intended to protect or regulate. Second, there is a causation-remediability problem. Even if the magazines could not get reduced postal rates for all-advertising issues, they might still publish all-advertising issues and pay the higher rates. This case resembles *Allen v. Wright* and *Eastern Kentucky Welfare Rights,* which involved tax subsidies. The Court held that the challenged behavior might not change even if the tax subsidy were withdrawn. [p. 202]
92.	**POSSIBLY YES**	Under APA sections 555(b) and 706(1), the court has power to compel agency action that is unreasonably delayed. Courts use

this power very reluctantly, however, to avoid interfering with agency priorities and allocation of scarce resources. The problem provides no indication at all as to why the FAA is delaying what seems to be an ordinary licensing proceeding. So perhaps in this case, the court will order the agency to proceed on Norma's application. [p. 211]

93. **PROBABLY NOT** This is a "ripeness" problem—the agency has not yet sought to apply the regulation and the issue is whether the court should wait until the regulation is applied in a concrete case before giving judicial review. Although an issue of law is presented (whether this particular regulation is authorized by statute), the court might well be aided by seeing how the agency defines "unreasonable" in a particular case. The likelihood that the regulation will be clarified by its application suggests it is not yet ripe for review. [p. 213]

94. **PROBABLY YES** The case is ripe for review because Paul's business could be destroyed if Nell complies with the rule, as she is planning to do. This creates a serious hardship for Paul and the case will never become more ripe since Nell does not intend to contest the rule. [p. 213]

95. **PROBABLY NOT** This is an example of attempted judicial review of *informal* administrative action. The ruling is probably not "final agency action" because it does not represent the consummation of agency consideration and has no legal impact. In addition, informal action is less likely to be ripe for review than formal actions, such as the adoption of regulations. The showing of injury from delaying review is relatively weak. In fact it is not clear just what injury (apart from legal fees) would be incurred if the parties go ahead with their merger and then defend an attack by the government. Also, it is not even clear from the statement whether the Attorney General will prosecute at all. [pp. 208–209, 213]

96. **NO** This agency action is not "final" under the *Standard Oil of California* case; like that case, it only involves issuance of a complaint. [pp. 208–209]

97. **IT DEPENDS** If common-law exhaustion doctrine applies, this may be a case in which exhaustion of remedies would not be required. The Postal Service press release suggests that an appeal might be futile, civil liberties are involved, and a seizure of Mel's movies could do irreparable damage to his business. If the statutory exhaustion doctrine of § 704 applies, then it would seem that exhaustion should not be required as the agency action at issue is operative during the pendency of the intra-agency appeal. That is, the Postal Service has kept hold of the movie. [pp. 216–217, 218]

98. **POSSIBLY YES** Assuming the common-law doctrine applies, exhaustion of remedies might not be required because the hearing procedure of the Air Force Academy may be constitutionally defective in denying confrontation of adverse witnesses. The constitutional

| | | issue does not depend on knowing additional facts, and it is collateral to the other issues in the case. These points suggest that requiring exhaustion would not serve various purposes of the doctrine, including respecting agency expertise and building a helpful administrative record. Requiring exhaustion would, however, show respect for agency autonomy and possibly moot the matter. [pp. 216, 217] |

99. **PROBABLY YES**

First, there is probably no private right of action under this statute. The Supreme Court no longer implies such rights unless the statute actually creates them. Second, the doctrine of primary jurisdiction will probably apply in this case. The issue seems to be a technical one, more within the expertise of the agency than the district court. Furthermore, it seems that Congress has evidenced a desire to centralize the determination of this sort of issue within the agency. Also, there might be a danger of inconsistency if different courts decide this issue in different ways; however, this seems not to be a serious problem since Roy is bringing a class action, which would bind all purchasers. [p. 221]

100. **PROBABLY YES**

A stay seems appropriate. Irreparable injury is shown in the sense that without any money the office would have to close immediately, denying legal representation to many of its clients. Such an abrupt termination of legal services could well be contrary to the public interest. The government will argue that a stay will have the effect of forcing it to spend more money on a program that should be terminated, which is against its best interests. The court must also make a preliminary determination of the likelihood that the agency will prevail on the merits, something that is not possible from the sketchy facts given. On balance, and assuming that the office makes a reasonably good showing that it may prevail on the merits, a stay could well be granted. [pp. 222–223]

Exam Questions and Answers

Question I

A. Spray Corp. manufactures various aerosol products, one of which is Howl, a canned spray for driving away dogs. The United States Postal Service ("USPS") is a government corporation, which, for purposes of this question, is a federal agency and has the power to adopt legislative rules. The USPS purchases dog repellent on annual contracts won by competitive bidding under a federal statute. The statute requires that contracts for federal purchases of goods and services be awarded only after competitive bidding, and the "lowest responsible bidder" must receive the contract.

The contract for dog repellent for 2012 was won by Spray Corp., the lowest bidder and the maker of "Howl." However, during that year, a number of cans of Howl sold to the USPS apparently failed to work, and several mail carriers were severely mauled by large dogs. As a result, the USPS is refusing to pay for the Howl furnished under the contract. This dispute was set for hearing by the USPS Board of Contract Appeals in March 2013.

Spray Corp. had another difficulty with the government. The Environmental Protection Agency ("EPA") determined that Spray had violated water pollution laws. The EPA recommended that Spray Corp. buy new pollution control devices. Spray Corp. did so, and that matter is now closed.

In October of 2012, the USPS took several steps detrimental to Spray's interests. First, without any prior notice or hearing, it adopted a rule that would bar any private company that had been found in violation of water pollution laws from bidding on a USPS contract for five years. Secondly, the USPS announced that the bids for dog repellent needed in 2013 would be received on November 1, 2012. However, the announcement stated that Spray Corp. would not be allowed to bid on the 2013 contract because of the unsatisfactory performance of its products during the previous year. Spray admits its violation of pollution laws, but denies the power of the USPS to bar anyone from bidding on government contracts by reason of such violations. It also denies that Howl functioned inadequately during 2012.

Was Spray Corp. entitled to participate in administrative proceedings before the October 2012 actions? If so, how?

B. Assume that Spray obtained no relief and was barred from bidding on the 2013 contract. The hearing about breach of the 2012 contract occurred before an administrative law judge in March 2013.

Testimony was heard to the effect that Howl functioned effectively in many instances involving both big and small dogs, but did not function effectively in 11 cases, all of which involved big dogs. The USPS put on as witnesses some of the mail carriers who had been bitten. They testified that they used Howl on windless days, in the correct manner, but that it was not effective. However, Spray's witnesses testified that failures of this kind could be explained by adverse wind conditions, incorrect use of the device, or the fact that the mail carrier did not see the dog coming in time to spray it. Spray also put on as witnesses several mail carriers who had successfully used Howl against large dogs. The administrative law judge believed Spray's witnesses and found the government liable for the purchase price of all Howl purchased under the 2012 contract, in the amount of $96,000.

The USPS Board of Contract Appeals reversed the administrative law judge. It found that the mail carriers who had testified for the USPS had been truthful. It blamed the failures on the fact that Howl was simply not strong enough to stop a large dog unless used at exactly the correct range. Consequently, the appeals board found that Spray had breached its contractual warranty as to the effectiveness of its product. As a result, Spray became liable for the damages to the mail carriers that the USPS had previously paid in the amount of $83,000. In addition, the appeals board ordered Spray ineligible to bid on USPS contracts for the next five years upon its further findings that Spray was not "responsible" and thus not an eligible bidder.

Spray is now interested in the advisability of judicial review and wants to know what the scope of review will be and what its prospects of success are. Judicial review would be in the Court of Claims and pursuant to the Administrative Procedure Act.

Question II

A federal statute provides for the acquisition and preservation of historical monuments. The annual appropriation for the purpose is $5 million. The statute provides that the governor of each state shall appoint a historical monument board, which will select one or more historical sites in the state. These recommendations will be forwarded to the newly created National Historical Monuments Board ("NHMB"), which will select those most appropriate for inclusion under the act. However, at least one monument must be selected in each state.

The statute provides: "It is the intention of Congress that the funds appropriated under this act be used to acquire and preserve forever for the benefit and inspiration of the people of the United States those locations or structures at which occurred significant events in the history of the United States." However, the statute provides no rules of procedure for the state and federal boards and says nothing about judicial review.

The governor of Ohio selected three people for the Ohio monuments board. One of them was Art Ardmore, a real estate developer. The Ohio board met informally at Ardmore's home and picked as their only selection for inclusion in the monuments program the home of an amateur inventor who had discovered the pop-top beer can. This home is directly adjacent to land that Ardmore will develop as a real estate subdivision in the near future. This site selection was approved at an informal meeting of NHMB. Consequently, the purchase of the inventor's home by NHMB will be finalized in the next few months.

A group of Ohio citizens disagree with that decision. They wish to have a historical monument on the Kent State campus where several students were slain by the National Guard during a demonstration. From newspaper accounts, they learned of the selection of the inventor's home as a historical monument.

After unsuccessfully petitioning the state board and NHMB, the objecting Ohioans go into the federal district court in Ohio, seeking to enjoin the disbursement of federal funds for acquisition of the inventor's home and to require that federal funds be spent to acquire and maintain a site on the Kent State campus. What result and why?

Question III

KZXZ is a television licensee in Fresno, California. Its management likes to present X-rated movies in late-night time slots and has paid for exclusive Central California rights to a large film library of sexually oriented films. The FCC has taken no action against KZXZ although there have been a number of viewer complaints about its programming.

The FCC has had difficulties in deciding how to meet public complaints about pornographic material on television. There is a federal criminal statute against "uttering obscene, indecent or profane language" on radio or television; however, federal attorneys have declined so far to prosecute television stations for violations of the statute. The FCC has proceeded by way of forfeitures (*i.e.*, administratively imposed fines provided for by the Communications Act) in a few cases, but the licensees paid the fines rather than choosing to litigate them. Finally, the FCC has decided upon a tentative and voluntary system of prescreening of possibly objectionable material by its staff. If the staff finds the film satisfactory, the film can appear on TV without any concern for FCC sanctions. But if the staff thinks that the film is "obscene, indecent or profane," a station showing the film knows that it risks an FCC forfeiture, referral of the matter to the Justice Department for possible prosecution, or quite possibly nonrenewal of its broadcasting license.

This new practice of prescreening has become well known in the industry and was discussed in Broadcasting Magazine, a widely read trade periodical; however, it has not been officially announced by the FCC. Many films have already been prescreened by the staff and some have been approved, some disapproved. There has been no public announcement of these decisions. The industry believes that the

FCC is trying out the new scheme as a possible method of coping with the problem, to see whether it is feasible and how the industry and Congress will react to it.

KZXZ and its lawyers believe that the prescreening procedure is an illegal system of prior restraint, and that the procedure (or any other FCC regulation of sexually oriented programming) violates the First Amendment and is unauthorized under the Communications Act.

A. KZXZ wishes to find out what has been happening so far with the prescreenings—which films have been accepted, which ones rejected, and by what standards. It also wants to examine the communications that have passed between the staff and FCC commissioners in connection with adopting and operating the system. Can KZXZ obtain this information and, if so, how?

B. Assume KZXZ obtained no information about the prescreenings beyond what it already knew. KZXZ brings an action in the Federal District Court for the Central District of California, seeking to enjoin further operation of the prescreening system. The FCC moves to dismiss the complaint without reaching the merits. What are the grounds of the FCC's motion and how should it be decided? *(Please do not discuss the merits of the lawsuit—i.e., whether the prescreening system in fact violates the First Amendment or the Communications Act.)*

Question IV

The FCC has been concerned with violence on television for some time but has not developed any clear policy on the subject. Television station WVIO has offered some commercials advertising a new horror movie. The commercials contain explicit pictures of gory murders, screams of agony, cries for mercy, and the like. Paul Penny, WVIO's station manager, called Terry Tripp, the FCC's general counsel, and asked whether the FCC has any rules against violence on TV. Tripp said that this is a sensitive subject but that there are no definite rules. Tripp advised Penny that he need not be concerned about showing any commercials based on present law. WVIO ran the commercials, sometimes during the daytime.

When WVIO's license came up for renewal, several consumer groups requested the FCC to set the matter for a hearing because of the violent commercials, and the FCC did so. At the hearing, the commercial was screened. When the lights went on, the administrative law judge was visibly pale. She stated that the commercial was the most horrifying thing she had ever seen and that no station manager in his right mind would have broadcasted it, especially at a time when children might be watching. The judge recommended that the license not be renewed on the grounds of irresponsibility of the licensee in its choice of commercials. Under the Communications Act, broadcasting licenses are granted or renewed if this would serve the public interest, convenience, or necessity.

WVIO appealed to the full FCC, which affirmed the judge. Its opinion declared that station licenses would not be renewed if a licensee showed commercials with scenes of violence unrelated to the content of the message or excessive in relation to the content of the message, especially if children might be watching. Since it declared that the violence was excessive in relation to the content of the message, it declined to renew the license, stating that the public interest would not be served by allowing so irresponsible a licensee to broadcast.

WVIO has appealed. What arguments can it make in support of its appeal and how should they be resolved? (Please do *not* discuss whether the FCC's action violated the First Amendment or whether it is void for vagueness.)

Question V

A federal statute has created the National Institutes of Health ("NIH"), a federal agency placed in the Department of Human Resources. The agency exists for the purpose of making grants to researchers in the health sciences. The statute provides for a director of the agency, who is presently Theda Thomas. It says nothing about the procedures the agency should follow or about judicial review. The statute provides that "research funds shall be granted to those applicants whom the director decides can best contribute to the store of knowledge about the causes and cures of physical and mental disease." Every year the applications for grants far exceed the funds available to NIH.

NIH has published a booklet entitled "Guidelines for Grant Applications to NIH." The booklet states that grant applications must be submitted by February 1 and that the NIH's final decisions shall be announced on June 30. The booklet sets forth a model grant application, which requires information about the proposed project and the hoped-for results, a budget of how the money will be spent, and information on the qualifications of the principal investigator (that is, the person who applies for the grant and is in charge of the project). The booklet does not state that the criminal record of the principal investigator will be considered or must be disclosed. It suggests no procedures that a rejected applicant can follow.

Boris Barnes has a Ph.D. in psychology with a long record of important research and publications concerning the use of drugs for the control of certain psychotic behavior. He is a professor of psychology at Stanford University. He wishes to do a study that would yield information on the long-term results of treatment of mental patients with a particular drug. This will be an expensive project since it requires finding patients who received the drug several years ago and studying their present condition. Barnes believes that the particular drug has a very detrimental long-term effect on patients even though good short-term results are often obtained.

Barnes filed a lengthy application with NIH to receive funds for this project on January 15. He requested a $200,000 grant. However, NIH ran a routine check with the FBI that revealed that Barnes had been convicted of income tax evasion (a federal felony) 15 years before applying for the grant. He had served six months in prison and completed two years of probation. The tax evasion consisted of Barnes's claiming deductions on his tax return greatly in excess of what he was entitled to deduct.

Theda Thomas wrote a letter to Barnes on February 16 stating that his grant application would not be considered. The reason was "that your conviction for income tax evasion establishes to our satisfaction that there is a reasonable doubt about your integrity in financial matters; consequently, we feel that you are not qualified to administer a substantial grant. If you disagree with my conclusion, you are free to take the matter up with the Secretary of Human Resources." Thomas placed the letter to Barnes on the agency website; thus, it became a matter of public knowledge.

After receiving this letter, Barnes did not contact the Secretary of Human Resources. Instead, he filed an action against NIH and Thomas on March 1, in the Federal District Court of the Northern District of California, seeking a declaratory judgment that NIH must consider his application along with all others and that he is entitled to an administrative hearing.

A. NIH moves to dismiss the action. What are the grounds for NIH's motion and how should the district judge rule on each ground?

B. Assume the motion to dismiss is denied and the court decides to hear the case on the merits. How should the case be decided?

Question VI

A. On April 15, the FCC issued the following press release, which was well covered in all major newspapers in the country:

> As part of the government-wide campaign against misleading advertising in the mass media, the FCC announced today that it intends to utilize all available powers to inhibit and prevent misleading, distorted, and false advertising on radio and television. It announced that all licensees are responsible for reasonable verification of product claims made in commercials on radio and television. The FCC stated that it fully intended to use its powers to issue cease and desist orders, impose fines, and deny license renewals to enforce this policy.

The FCC's announcement caused considerable consternation and turmoil within the broadcasting business. Stations began to take steps to inform themselves about product claims made in commercial messages. As a result, station KASH-TV refused to accept for broadcasting several announcements advertising multiple vitamins manufactured by Wonka Vitamin Co. There had recently been publicity given to charges by a Ralph Nader task force that multiple vitamins were unsafe, ineffective, and ridiculously expensive. Consequently, KASH-TV felt that it did not wish to take the risk of running the ads.

Slick Co. is the advertising agency that produced the commercials in question for Wonka Vitamin Co. As counsel to Slick Co., advise the company about whether it could now seek a declaratory judgment to the effect that the FCC's new policy is invalid under the Constitution, the Communications Act, and the Administrative Procedure Act. (Do not consider at this stage of the question whether the FCC's policy is either properly adopted or substantively valid, merely whether Slick Co. could seek declaratory relief. Do not discuss which federal court is the appropriate one in which to bring the action.)

B. On May 10, a class action is filed in the Superior Court in Los Angeles. It is brought by Hank Harvey, on behalf of himself and all others similarly situated, in tort and contract against Wonka Vitamin Co. Harvey alleges that he has been injured by vitamin overdoses from taking the Wonka multiple vitamins. He also alleges that the vitamins have entirely failed to deal with the health problems (such as iron deficiency) for which they were advertised to be effective. He bases his class action on claims made in televised commercials.

Wonka Vitamin Co. moves to dismiss the action on the grounds that the case should be tried by the FCC under the authority of the April 15 press release. How should the court rule on this motion?

C. Station KADS ran the Wonka ad on June 6. The FCC notified KADS that it proposed to order KADS to cease and desist from running ads without conducting product verification. Its action was taken pursuant to a section of the Communications Act authorizing the FCC to issue cease and desist orders to licensees who violate any validly adopted rule.

At the hearing, the FCC provided evidence that KADS was aware of the press release, that the ads were misleading, that KADS had access to data that revealed that the ads were deceptive, and that the station had failed to try to ascertain the truthfulness of this or any other ad. The administrative law judge found in accordance with these charges and the FCC agreed. It cited the press release as its only authority. It claimed that the press release was a validly adopted rule that explained the meaning of "public interest, convenience, and necessity" (which is the statutory standard for FCC license decisions) and also that it was a policy statement explaining how the FCC would exercise discretion in the future. Will the FCC's order withstand judicial review? (Please assume that the FCC's policy concerning advertising is constitutional, and that the Communications Act would allow the FCC to impose sanctions by reason of unverified advertising if all procedural requirements were satisfied.)

Question VII

The Water Pollution Control Act provides that the Environmental Protection Agency ("EPA") can adopt rules setting limits on water pollution (including thermal pollution) for entire industries "after providing a fair hearing." The limits on pollution must be achievable through the "best available technology." On January 2, the EPA published in the Federal Register a proposed rule applicable to nuclear power plants that would limit the increase in the temperature of the water used to cool the reactor to not more than five degrees Fahrenheit. The EPA did not explain how it derived the five-degree standard. The notice stated that a public meeting would be convened on March 6 to consider the proposed rule and that comments would be welcome until April 1.

At the meeting on March 6, which was attended by representatives of dozens of nuclear power plants as well as many environmental groups, the staff member who presided (not an administrative law judge) said she would not permit any cross-examination of EPA staff members, and she would only listen to oral statements. The lawyer for Blue Demon Power Co. was among those who requested that staff members be cross-examined; he also spoke for 20 minutes explaining that Blue Demon's seven-year-old reactor presently heated the water by 36 degrees and could not possibly meet the five-degree limitation. Blue Demon submitted a lengthy written statement to this effect, accompanied by a scientific study showing that even with the application of the best available technology its cooling system would still heat the ocean water by 20 degrees.

On June 15, the EPA adopted a final rule that retained the five-degree test for new reactors, effective immediately. It adopted a 12-degree test for existing reactors and deferred the effective date for five years. It stated that there was no available technology that would permit such a reduction at the present time, but that research was actively continuing in the field and the various pollution control companies were rushing new models to market and that adequate equipment to meet the 12-degree standard would be available long before the effective date.

Blue Demon has discovered that the EPA relied on a staff study of the pollution control industry that stated that plenty of new equipment, suitable for limiting the heat increase to 12 degrees, would be available long before the effective date. Blue Demon believes this study is full of holes, that the proposed equipment will be unworkable for its type of reactor; will not meet the 12-degree standard for any type of reactor; and will not be ready by the effective date. It feels it could have demolished the study if cross-examination of its author had been allowed and if the study had been disclosed during the comment period.

Blue Demon has also discovered that representatives of an environmental group (Friends of the Earth) had many conversations with Sam Squid, the EPA Administrator, and the staff, both during the comment period and after it closed, urging the EPA to adopt extremely strict thermal pollution standards to preserve marine life. Blue Demon's lawyer had been unable to get an appointment with Squid or with the staff to discuss its point of view informally.

Blue Demon has also learned that Donna Flounder, an EPA staff member who worked for Friends of the Earth until November of last year, had been in charge of preparing the proposed rule and considering comments and was by far the most influential staff member on the subject. Flounder had many conversations with Squid urging him to adopt a strict limit on pollution and to disregard the critical comments submitted by Blue Demon and other operators. The EPA's final rule is an exact copy of Flounder's final memo to Squid.

Finally, Blue Demon discovered that Squid recently gave a speech to the Save the Whales Foundation in which he stated that thermal pollution from nuclear power plants was a grave threat to marine life and he intended to do all in his power to remedy the problem, consistent with economic and technological constraints.

Blue Demon properly seeks review of the rule in the appropriate United States Court of Appeals. What arguments should it raise and how should the court dispose of them?

Question VIII

Congress enacted a statute to deal with the critical problem of toxic waste dump sites. Thousands of these dump sites, in use for many years, are leaking toxic chemicals, endangering large numbers of people, and poisoning ground water. The statute creates a "superfund" to which all companies producing toxic wastes must contribute (in a total amount between $4 to $6 billion) to be matched by a contribution from the United States Treasury of $5 billion; the superfund will pay for cleaning up the most dangerous dump sites.

The statute creates the Federal Toxic Waste Agency ("FTWA"), headed by an Administrator, to administer the superfund and clean-up operations. The statute gives the FTWA five years to adopt rules to fix the amount each company must pay to the superfund. This amount depends on the toxicity of the chemical wastes the firm produces, the length of time it has been in operation, and its ability to pay. The statute provides that the rules fixing liability are to be adopted in conformity with section 553 of the Administrative Procedure Act and that the Administrator, in his discretion, may permit cross-examination on disputed issues of material fact. In the event a company fails to pay the amount set forth in the rules, this sum can be collected by an action in federal district court.

The FTWA decided to approach the rulemaking task in several phases. The first phase would establish which manufacturing processes produced sufficient toxic wastes so that such manufacturers would be forced to pay into the superfund. The second phase would fix the exact liabilities.

The rules recently adopted in this first phase list PFB as a chemical, the manufacture of which produces toxic wastes. They also list QRC as a chemical, the manufacture of which does not produce toxic wastes. Sniff Chemical Co. makes PFB exclusively and concedes that making it produces highly toxic wastes. However, Sniff believes that making QRC also produces toxic wastes. Sniff appeals to the District of Columbia Court of Appeals (the correct court) complaining of the omission of QRC from the list of chemicals whose manufacture produces toxic wastes. The Administrator moves the appeal be dismissed because Sniff lacks standing. How should the court rule on this motion?

Question IX

Assume the same facts as Question VIII. The FTWA undertook the second phase of rulemaking—assessing exact liabilities for superfund contributions. Along with the notice of proposed rulemaking published in the Federal Register, the Administrator included an announcement that no cross-examination would be permitted and only written comments would be considered. The Administrator observed that this limitation was appropriate because liability determinations would not depend on issues likely to raise credibility disputes (*i.e.,* the toxicity of chemicals; length of operations; ability to pay). Moreover, this limitation was necessary because of the enormous complexity of the problem, the thousands of firms affected, and the now-pressing time schedule (only about six months remained to do the job). Substantively, the proposed rules would impose liability of $22 million as applied to Sniff—about one-third of its entire net worth and much more than its available cash. One day after publication of the proposed rules, Sniff appeals to the District of Columbia Court of Appeals (again the correct court) arguing that the procedures to be used in the second phase of rulemaking are legally inadequate. Assuming the court reaches the merits of this claim, how should the court rule?

Answer to Question I

A. **Right to Participate in Administrative Proceedings**

To determine if Spray Corp. had a right to participate in administrative proceedings before the October 2012 actions, it is necessary to assess its due process rights as well as whether it had any participation rights created by statute or regulation. The problem provides no pertinent regulations, so the analysis below will focus on constitutional and statutory rights.

Rule barring bidding by pollution violators: Under the *Londoner/Bi-Metallic* doctrine, Spray had no constitutional right to a trial-type hearing on the issue of whether the United States Postal Service ("USPS") may properly bar violators of water-pollution laws from bidding. The action taken was *general* in nature, *not particularized.* One potential issue is whether the rule was aimed at only one specific bidder, which might make it adjudication rather than rulemaking. However, the rule is stated in a general rather than specific fashion and no doubt will be applied to other companies.

The question does not call for an analysis of the validity of the rule. If the issue were relevant, however, it could be questioned because it has a retroactive effect, in violation of the *Bowen v. Georgetown University Hospital* case because it increases the sanctions against a past violation of law by barring violators from bidding on government contracts. Normally, agencies lack power to adopt retroactive rules unless the statute specifically permits them to do so. Moreover, the rule is questionable from a rationality point of view. There is no logical connection between a water pollution violation and the company's ability to supply a good product to the USPS. The rule might also be ultra vires, because a company's environmental record is not a factor that the USPS can take into account in deciding whether it is the lowest responsible bidder.

Spray might argue that it had a right to participate in notice-and-comment proceedings under APA § 553. However, the USPS will argue that this particular rule falls under one of several possible exceptions. The most likely exception is that this rule relates to *public contracts* and therefore is entirely exempt under APA § 553(a)(2) from the requirements of notice and comment. A court might construe this exception narrowly, however, holding that the USPS rule relates to much more than public contracts; it actually represents an undertaking by the USPS to enforce the pollution laws. Therefore, it is not the simple sort of rule, merely regulating public contracts, that was contemplated by the § 553(a)(2) exception.

The USPS might also argue that this is an *interpretive rule* (interpreting the word "responsible") and thus exempt from the notice and comment procedures under APA § 553(b)(A). However, the USPS has not labeled the rule as interpretive, which suggests it intended to use its legislative rulemaking power, and any doubt should be resolved in favor of public participation. The rule seems to have an actual binding legal effect by barring Spray from bidding. Therefore, it may be argued that the rule is legislative rather than interpretive, and therefore requires a legislative-type hearing. If the notice and comment requirements of § 553 apply, the USPS must give prior notice and allow public comments before adopting the proposed rule and must publish the rule 30 days before its effective date. Although no oral hearing is required, the provision for public comments would permit Spray to make its position on the rule clear to the USPS.

Debarment of Spray from bidding due to unsatisfactory performance: This determination involves resolution of *individualized facts* (*i.e.*, did a particular product perform unsatisfactorily); thus, Spray's procedural due process rights could be implicated. It appears that due process has indeed been triggered because Spray has a right to receive the contract if it is the lowest responsible bidder—this is a *property interest* under the entitlement approach of *Board of Regents v. Roth.* Also, a *liberty interest* is arguably involved, because Spray's corporate good name has been maligned, with financial loss likely in terms of lost opportunities to sell to the government. The stigma-plus requirement is established by Spray's debarment from bidding.

If it is held that an administrative hearing is constitutionally required, the next issue is whether Spray is entitled to an ***immediate hearing***, or can the debarment from bidding be heard at the March 2013 hearing set for the 2012 contract dispute? Ordinarily, a hearing must occur ***before*** the relevant deprivation of liberty or property, unless there is good reason to delay it. Under the three-factor formula of *Mathews v. Eldridge,* Spray's interest in an immediate hearing is strong: It will miss out on the 2013 bidding unless the error is corrected now, the risk of error by the USPS is substantial (since there has been no proper hearing and the issue of breach is highly disputed), and the government has no apparent interest in delaying the hearing.

[For extra credit, the rights of Spray at a trial-type hearing might be discussed: confrontation of adverse witnesses, the right to present its own witnesses, the right to counsel, a decision based on the record, a statement of reasons, and an independent decisionmaker.]

[Another extra credit issue might be that the USPS could argue that Spray could sue the government in court for breach of contract and the resulting trial could provide the necessary hearing required by due process. [*See* Lujan v. G&G Sprinklers] However, this would not be correct, since such a trial could only concern issues relating to breach of the 2008 contract, not debarment from bidding on the 2009 contract.]

B. Judicial Review of the Agency Decision

Scope of review: Two decisions were reached by the USPS appeals board. The first decision—that Spray's product was not effective—seems like a pure question of fact (*i.e.,* what happened and why). The scope of review applicable to a pure question of fact determined through formal adjudication is "substantial evidence on the whole record" under APA § 706(2)(E).

The second decision was that, by reason of the failure of Howl, Spray was not a "responsible bidder." This involves the application of basic facts to a statutory term. The scope of review of a mixed question is sometimes treated as a review of fact, sometimes as a review of law. Here, the issue will probably be treated as one of fact and the substantial evidence rule would be applied to it as well. However, if it is treated as a question of law, *Chevron* would be applicable. Since the term "responsible" is obviously ambiguous, the court would have to accept a reasonable agency construction under Step 2. Thus the issue is one of reasonableness in either case and it seems to matter little whether the issue is classified as law or fact.

The appeals board decision concerning remedy—the five-year debarment from bidding—is a matter of agency discretion, and would be reviewed under the abuse of discretion standard.

Prospects for success: The strongest point in Spray's favor is the fact that the administrative law judge believed Spray's witnesses, not those of the USPS. Evidently, the administrative law judge decided that Howl was used on windy rather than windless days, or that the mail carriers did not see the dogs coming in time. When an agency reverses the administrative law judge on an issue of credibility, this undercuts the substantiality of evidence in favor of its decision. [Universal Camera Corp. v. NLRB] On the other hand, the issues may actually turn on technical chemical analysis, rather than credibility of witnesses, so the conclusion of the administrative law judge is entitled to no special deference. Even so, it could be argued that the USPS has no expertise in considering issues relating to chemistry.

Another point in Spray's favor is that apparently there was no evidence supporting the Board's finding that the chemical was not strong enough to stop a large dog unless used at exactly the correct range. Indeed, this could be a case in which the agency could be reversed for ignoring the approach taken by the administrative law judge. [Cinderella Career & Finishing Schools, Inc. v. FTC]

However, the standard for review of the Board's decision on product effectiveness is substantial evidence. The Board's finding here appears reasonable and should be affirmed. Similarly, its finding on the application question of whether Spray is "responsible" is reviewed under the substantial evidence test; that finding also appears reasonable. It is very unlikely that the Board's discretionary choice of remedy would be overturned since the agency apparently weighed the proper factors and reached a reasonable result.

Answer to Question II

Constitutional Standing: The Ohio citizens probably face insuperable problems with either the injury-in-fact requirement or redressability. The given facts do not suggest that making the inventor's home a monument will, in itself, cause them cognizable injury. Unhappiness at the choice would constitute an abstract and "generalized" injury insufficient to satisfy Article III. Minor supplementation of the facts, however, might create the possibility of claiming aesthetic or environmental injury (*e.g.*, if the proposed monument would be quite ugly and one or more of the plaintiffs uses the area).

Alternatively, the plaintiffs might characterize their injury as deprivation of the chance to enjoy a Kent State monument. We have no evidence to suggest, however, that a decree enjoining the NHMB from building the monument to the pop-top inventor would do much to increase the chances of a monument at Kent State.

It is not possible to base the plaintiffs' standing on the fact that they pay taxes; under *Flast v. Cohen,* as narrowed by later cases, taxpayer standing is appropriate only when contesting a legislative violation of the Establishment Clause via the taxing and spending power.

Statutory Standing: Plaintiffs would be proceeding under the APA's cause of action set forth at §§ 701-06. As such, for statutory standing under § 702, they would need to demonstrate that they seek to protect interests that arguably fall within the zone of interests to be protected by the statute at issue. This should be pretty easy to do because the statutory language suggests that the monuments are intended to inspire citizens, and anyone who might be inspired is within the zone of interests.

Sovereign immunity: Although once a serious problem, the government has now consented to be sued for nonmonetary relief for injuries caused by the actions of federal agencies. [APA § 702] Therefore, sovereign immunity would not bar an action by the Ohioans against the government.

Reviewability: There is no evidence that Congress intended to preclude judicial review of the selection of historical sites; therefore, the general presumption of reviewability prevails. However, the possibility remains that the decision is committed to agency discretion, and is thus unreviewable under APA § 701(a)(2).

It could well be argued that Congress meant to leave the funding decisions entirely to the discretion of the relevant state and federal agencies. Yet *Citizens to Preserve Overton Park v. Volpe* makes clear that the exemption from review of decisions committed to agency discretion is very narrow in scope. There is "law to apply" here—the sites have to "benefit and inspire" the people and have to be "locations at which occurred significant events" in United States history. This provides some framework of law—certainly as much as the "feasible and prudent" language found to be sufficient in *Overton Park*. Consequently, the decision is reviewable and is not one committed wholly to agency discretion.

Ripeness: It could be argued that the decision is not yet ripe for judicial review because the site has not yet been purchased. However, further delay in this case will not make the issues any more fit for review, and the remaining steps of actual purchase are merely mechanical. Thus, the decision does seem ripe for review.

Mandamus: Although it is possible that the court would enjoin the purchase of the pop-top site, it is most unlikely that it would issue a mandatory injunction to force acquisition of the Kent State site. This would be an unwarranted interference with the agency's discretion. Mandamus will not lie to compel an agency to take a particular discretionary action—only to compel the exercise of discretion or performance of a ministerial act. At best, therefore, the process would be started anew to choose a more favorable site.

Abuse of discretion: To demonstrate that the NHMB decision amounted to an abuse of discretion (or was arbitrary), the plaintiffs would need to show that the board had considered inappropriate factors, had failed to consider appropriate factors, or had made a clear error of judgment. Courts make these determinations based on the contemporaneous explanations that agencies offer for their actions. The facts of the problem do not offer an explanation for the board's choice. If it offered none, then the action should be vacated as arbitrary and remanded to the board for further proceedings. The balance of this analysis will assume, however, that the board gave some plausible sounding account of the historical significance of the pop-top beer can's invention and how inspiring it would be to preserve the garage where it occurred.

Courts are generally very reluctant to condemn agency decisions as "clear errors of judgment," and would likely not do so in this case. Surely there are people who would find the chosen site more beneficial and inspiring than Kent State, and surely people might find the invention of the pop-top beer can to be a significant historical event.

Perhaps the most plausible argument for finding an abuse of discretion is that the board improperly considered Ardmore's financial interest in choosing the pop-top beer can inventor's home. This argument, however, would need to overcome the presumption of honesty and integrity that attaches to administrative decisions. A strong showing of bad faith would be required to permit investigation of this point. Perhaps, however, a judge offended by the conflict-of-interest might stretch a point and vacate the choice as a clear error in judgment.

[It might bear noting that due process principles requiring recusal of biased decisionmakers are not applicable given that the agency action does not deprive anyone of property or liberty.]

Answer to Question III

A. Obtaining Information

Information as to prescreenings: Information about particular films could be subject to disclosure as "final opinions" or as "interpretations adopted by the agency" under section 552(a)(2) of the Freedom of Information Act (FOIA). Alternatively, they could be "identifiable records" that the agency must make available to the public under section 552(a)(3) of the FOIA. Therefore, KZXZ should first request the information from the FCC. If the request is denied, KZXZ should then seek a mandatory injunction from the federal district court in the district in which it resides to compel disclosure of this information.

The FCC could not prevent disclosure of the information regarding the films on the basis of the exemption for intra-agency memoranda under section 552(a)(5) of the APA, given that the results of the prescreenings were disclosed to those who submitted the films. Moreover, the results would be post-decisional, meaning they are final opinions (as opposed to pre-decisional memoranda designed to assist decisionmakers). [*See* NLRB v. Sears Roebuck] Conceivably, the information could be exempt from disclosure under section 552(a)(4) of the APA as commercial information obtained from a person that is privileged or confidential, but this seems unlikely because there was no expectation that the results of the prescreenings would be kept confidential.

Communications within FCC: The memoranda between the FCC commissioners and the staff fall within the exception for intra-agency memos under section 552(b)(5) of the FOIA. Such memos are not available by law to outsiders. Policymaking memoranda are exempt from disclosure because the agency cannot operate "in a fishbowl," and disclosure might inhibit candid comments. However, any *factual material* contained in these memos is ***not*** within the privilege, and disclosure can be compelled with appropriate deletions of protected material. Thus, at least some of the comments made by the staff on how the prescreening program is working probably would be subject to disclosure under the FOIA.

B. Motion to Dismiss:

The FCC can argue a number of grounds in support of its motion to dismiss KZXZ's complaint.

Agency action: In order to secure review under the APA, the plaintiff must establish that the conduct in question is "agency action" as that term is defined in APA section 551(13). [*See* Norton v. Southern Utah Wilderness Alliance] That means it has to be a rule, order, sanction, relief, or the equivalent thereof. The APA does not permit plaintiffs to cobble together disparate agency actions and subject them to a "broad, programmatic attack." The FCC might argue that KZXZ is improperly making a broad, programmatic attack on what are really a bunch of individual prescreening decisions. Insofar as FCC has adopted a coherent system for prescreening, however, it seems to have adopted a rule satisfying the "agency action" requirement.

Ripeness: The FCC will contend that litigation as to its prescreening procedures should not occur until it has formalized the process and applied it to KZXZ—in other words, until the suit is "ripe for review." To determine whether a regulation that has not yet been applied to a plaintiff is ripe for review, the susceptibility of the issues to immediate review must be weighed against the hardship to the parties from delaying review. [Abbott Laboratories v. Gardner]

The issues here may well be better suited to review in the context of actual facts—after it is seen precisely how the prescreening system is functioning, whether it is sensed as mandatory or voluntary, whether the staff has developed any standards, etc. At this point, the system is still very tentative and subject to change. Moreover, the FCC has not yet formally adopted it as a final decision. Thus, the issues are ***not*** well suited for immediate review.

Also, the hardship to KZXZ seems relatively modest. The prescreening system does not demand any immediate change to primary, day-to-day business conduct. The system is completely voluntary, so KZXZ is probably not taking any serious risks by screening a few films on TV that have not been prescreened. (However, an argument could be made that the present uncertainty is extremely damaging, and the KZXZ would not dare, as a practical matter, to defy the FCC staff by ignoring the procedure.) The suit could easily wait until the procedure is firmed up by formal adoption and actual application.

Finality: Under *Bennett v. Spear,* to be "final," an agency action must both: (a) be consummated; and (b) determine legal rights and obligations or otherwise have legal consequences. The facts of the problem state that the new prescreening system is "tentative," and there does not seem to be any reason for doubt on this point. Once the agency has completed its decisionmaking process, however, the legal consequences prong should be satisfied because the agency would have created a rule for obtaining a safe harbor from sanctions.

Exhaustion of remedies: The FCC might argue that KZXZ should exhaust its administrative remedies before seeking judicial review—*i.e.*, it must submit films for prescreening and appeal any adverse result first within the agency before seeking judicial review. After all, the FCC might approve the submitted films, eliminating any problem. The traditional rule is to give the agency a chance to complete its procedures, without interrupting them by premature review.

This argument, however, seems to be a ripeness argument in light disguise. KZXZ seeks to challenge the pre-screening "rule," not an application of that rule. The facts do not indicate that there is any available intra-agency process for challenging this rule. Moreover, even if there were, we appear to be dealing with a case brought pursuant to the APA's general cause of action. Under section 704, exhaustion of remedies, where not required by statute, may be required by a court or agency only where: (a) the agency has imposed this requirement by rule; and (b) the agency provides that its action is inoperative during intra-agency appeal. We have no facts suggesting that prong (a) is satisfied. As for prong (b), KZXZ's suit is based on the premise that the FCC is currently applying its pre-screening rule.

Assuming common-law exhaustion doctrine applies, KZXZ could argue that its requirements should be excused. Its objection is to the ***constitutionality*** of the procedure itself, and even if the films were approved, this objection would remain. Moreover, the issues are legal, not factual, and would not be clarified by having the agency screen any particular films. Because of the substantial constitutional questions here, and the great danger of chilling the First Amendment rights involved in media programming, it would seem that an exception to the common law exhaustion doctrine, assuming it applies, would be appropriate.

Commitment to agency discretion: The agency might argue that adoption of such procedures as prescreening, in order to enforce the federal statute prohibiting obscenity on TV, was committed to its discretion. But this argument is not persuasive, because the basis of KZXZ's attack is that the procedures are unlawful, and the agency would not have discretion to adopt an unconstitutional or illegal procedure.

Answer to Question IV

Adoption of new policy: It can be argued that the FCC's new policy on violence in commercials should have been adopted through rulemaking instead of adjudication. The main, and likely insuperable, obstacle to this argument is the *Chenery* principle that the choice between adjudication and rulemaking for policymaking lies in the informed discretion of the agency. Still, perhaps a case could be made that choosing adjudication amounted to an abuse of discretion. Choosing rulemaking would have eliminated the harsh and unjust result of adopting the policy in a way that retroactively punishes conduct that was arguably legal when it occurred. It also would have insured public participation so that all the pros and cons of a rule of far-reaching significance could have been explored. The problem obviously is not new and unexpected, and the harm from allowing renewal of WVIO's license is slight, based on the single nonrecurring instance of broadcasting the commercials.

Assuming that the choice of adjudication was otherwise proper, a good case can be made that the result should not have been retroactive based on the factors outlined in *Clark-Cowlitz* and *Retail, Wholesale, & Department Store Clerks*. Here, we have a very high burden on the regulated party (loss of an extremely valuable license), and the statutory interest in applying the new policy to the instant case is arguably low insofar as the agency can "send a message" regarding what it will tolerate without punishing the station. We do not have an abrupt departure from otherwise well-settled law or grounds for relying on that law. Still, the fact that the station was relying on advice from an agency staffer might help push a sympathetic court toward blocking retroactivity (even though the advice was not enough for estoppel, as discussed below).

Estoppel: A few cases suggest that the government can be estopped. However, it is unlikely that the FCC would be estopped by Tripp's advice to Penny. The United States Supreme Court cases have been very negative toward estoppel claims, but have not definitively precluded them. Most of the lower court cases arise in situations in which the government is acting in a proprietary character or engaged in programs like subsidies or insurance, not in standard regulatory programs where an estoppel would cause the agency to be prevented from implementing the public interest. Penny may well have detrimentally relied on Tripp's statement, but the case would be stronger if Penny had been advised by the FCC Commissioners in an advisory opinion or an interpretive regulation and if he had gotten the statement in writing. Also, Tripp made it clear that the area was sensitive and there was no definite rule, which suggests Penny was still assuming substantial risks. All in all, estoppel is unlikely.

Validity of new policy: Although you are instructed by the question not to discuss the First Amendment or the void for vagueness doctrine, it is apparent that the policy touches on sensitive First Amendment concerns and is suspiciously vague in an area in which clearcut rules are important (regulation of expression). Since the Communications Act standard itself is very vague (public interest, convenience, necessity), a court could certainly construe the statute to prohibit the FCC from regulating violence on television. In line with cases like *Kent v. Dulles,* statutes are often construed narrowly so that agency action touching on sensitive constitutional concerns is held ultra vires. *Rust v. Sullivan* is to the contrary, however. Although the FCC's statute has been upheld as a valid delegation of legislative authority, this does not mean that the FCC has carte blanche to suppress any form of expression because it decides that the public interest requires it; much clearer congressional approval might be needed for such a departure from present law.

Bias of judge: Although the judge made an unguarded comment about the case after seeing the commercial, this would not be considered a disqualifying personal bias since it arose from events at the hearing and simply was the judge's evaluation of the evidence she had seen and heard.

Remedy: It could certainly be argued that the FCC has committed a "clear error of judgment" by refusing to renew a license because of one isolated instance, particularly taking into account the harshness of forfeiting a license in which large economic investments have been made, the questionability of the new policy, the retroactive aspects of its adoption, and the Tripp advice. However, courts have a narrow scope of review and may not substitute their own judgment for that of an agency, even where the agency's remedy is unusually harsh or severe. Generally, an agency's remedy must be upheld unless it is without warrant in law or justification in fact, or amounts to an abuse of discretion. On the other hand, if the FCC failed to explain why its remedy was unusually harsh, WVIO may be able to have the case remanded so that the FCC can rationalize its decision.

Answer to Question V

A. **Motion to Dismiss**

Sovereign immunity: Previously this would have raised difficult questions of whether Thomas had acted beyond her powers—but it has now been waived in actions against the United States (except those for money damages) by APA § 702. Barnes need not seek money damages, but only a declaratory judgment that he is entitled to reconsideration of his application without considering the conviction; also, he might seek different administrative procedures. Neither is a claim for money damages.

Venue: Venue is appropriate under the federal statute. [28 U.S.C. § 1391(e)]

Exhaustion of remedies: We are told in the problem that the enabling act says nothing about agency procedures or judicial review. Judicial review of final agency action is nonetheless presumptively reviewable through the APA cause of action set forth at §§ 701-06. Section 704 addresses the problem of exhaustion. An agency (or court) can insist on exhaustion under § 704 only if the agency: (a) requires exhaustion by rule; and (b) provides that its action is inoperative during pendency of intra-agency review proceedings. Here, we have no indication that either prerequisite is satisfied—there is no NIH or DHR rule mentioned in the problem. Exhaustion is thus not required. [Darby v. Cisneros]

Ripeness: There should be no problem with ripeness since the agency has done all that it is ever going to do in Barnes's case. There is nothing tentative about its actions and nothing will be clarified by waiting for any other agency action.

Finality: The agency's action satisfies *Bennett v. Spear*'s two-prong test for finality that: (a) the agency has consummated its decisionmaking process; and (b) the action has legal consequences. Here, there was nothing tentative at all about the Director's decision, which has the legal effect of blocking Barnes from obtaining a grant (among other consequences). The possibility that review might be available by the Secretary speaks to the problem of exhaustion rather than finality.

Commitment to agency discretion: If the ultimate issue is simply whether Barnes's project should be funded as against another's project, and the decision turned on a scientific appraisal, the decision would probably be committed to agency discretion, but such is not the case. Under *Citizens to Preserve Overton Park v. Volpe*, the question of what factors an agency should consider when exercising statutory discretion presents a question of statutory interpretation and is not committed to agency discretion. In the instant case, whether Barnes's application should have been rejected because he was a convicted felon turns on whether the statute provides that a past criminal conviction is a relevant factor to consider.

Preclusion of review: This is not a problem because the statute does not implicitly or explicitly preclude review. Reviewability is presumed absent some strong reason for making decisions nonreviewable, and no such reason appears here.

B. Merits

Abuse of discretion: The scope of review here is whether the action is "arbitrary, capricious, or an abuse of discretion." An income tax conviction suggesting fraud in listing deductions is a relevant factor in consideration of a grant application. Giving a large federal grant certainly presupposes honesty in accounting for costs and funds; someone who greatly overstated deductions on a tax return quite possibly is not trustworthy in accounting matters. Perhaps Thomas overdid things by her decision that the grant application would not be considered at all—*i.e.,* that the tax conviction completely ruled out Barnes's application, as opposed to simply being taken into account as a negative factor. It might be reasonable to argue that a conviction over 10 years old could properly be considered, but not as a clear disqualifying factor, simply as a negative factor.

Right-privilege doctrine: In earlier days, Barnes's claim would undoubtedly have been denied because he was seeking a federal grant, which would amount to a privilege, not a right. Modern cases reject the distinction and enforce claims even for discretionary benefits if they have been wrongfully denied or denied without proper procedures.

Right to a hearing: Barnes should claim that he has a right to a hearing, although this claim is somewhat tainted by his failure to ask for one. The statute grants no right to a hearing so the APA is inapplicable, but Barnes can argue that he has been denied either liberty or property by the denial. The liberty argument is that rejection of the application for a government grant because he lacks financial integrity imposes a stigma that would prevent his getting any government grants in the future, and this would probably terminate his scientific career. Stigma isn't enough to implicate a liberty interest, but the denial of a government grant should likely move the case into the "stigma-plus" category. Moreover, Thomas made the letter public by posting it on the agency website, so that future grantors would be aware of it. Thus, the serious stigmatic effect of Thomas's determination should trigger a due process right to a name-clearing hearing.

Assuming the liberty argument is accepted, there are certainly adjudicatory facts at issue (financial integrity). Thomas might argue that the only issue is one of policy—does a prior tax conviction automatically debar an applicant for a grant—and not factual at all, which suggests no constitutional right to a hearing. Thus, the decision is wrapped up with the abuse of discretion issue already discussed—if Thomas is entitled to reject applicants who have tax convictions out of hand, there is obviously nothing to hold a hearing about. If she is entitled to treat convictions as a negative factor in considering financial integrity but not as a disqualifying factor, a hearing that explores all elements of Barnes's financial integrity would be appropriate.

Rulemaking-adjudication: It can be argued that the new policy—that tax convictions automatically debar an applicant—should have been adopted by rulemaking, not on a case-by-case basis. This would give the public an opportunity to have input in the decision and allow NIH to adopt a rule that would cover all crimes and thus give fair warning so that applicants would not suffer the stigma of rejection. But there is really no serious retroactive harm visited on grant applicants; their applications have simply been rejected. Moreover, NIH may not have anticipated the problem, and the problem of judging financial disqualifications may not be susceptible to codification in rule form. This argument should be rejected. Moreover, even if rulemaking were employed, the agency would not have to use public proceedings because rules relating to grants are excepted from the notice-comment rules [APA § 553(a)(2)].

Answer to Question VI

A. Slick's Action

Constitutional Standing: Slick has been "injured in fact" because its commissions depend on whether commercials are screened. There is a problem with causation and remediability; their commercial may not be screened even if the policy is struck down. This seems unduly speculative, however, since the commercials were rejected exclusively because of the FCC's policy.

Statutory Standing: Statutory standing under § 702 of the APA seems a bit more problematic. Under the strict approach of *Air Courier Conference v. American Postal Workers Union,* the court looks only to the particular statute under which the challenge is based (the Communications Act here) and looks for evidence that the statute was intended to protect or regulate the plaintiff. It seems unlikely that the act was specifically intended to protect advertising agencies; it is exclusively concerned with the interests of viewers and broadcasters. *Air Courier* was an exceptionally strict on statutory standing, however. More recent cases, such as *Match-E-Be-Nash-She-Wish Band of Pottawatomi Indians v. Patchak,* confirm an older view that statutory standing does not require that the plaintiff be a member of a class that Congress sought to benefit. This view is consistent with the general test stated in *Clarke v. Securities Indus. Ass'n*, which inquires whether "the plaintiff's interests are so marginally related to or inconsistent with the purposes implicit in the statute that it cannot reasonably be assumed that Congress intended to permit the suit." Here, an advertising agency might argue that, notwithstanding its obvious economic motivation, it seeks to protect values, such as freedom of expression and the sharing of commercial information, that are bound up with the public interest. On this view, Slick might satisfy the zone-of-interest test.

Finality: In order to secure review under the APA, the plaintiff must establish that the conduct in question is "final." To be final under *Bennett v. Spear,* the action must mark the consummation of the decisionmaking process and must have legal consequences. The press release is likely best regarded as a general statement of policy, informing the public and regulated parties how the agency intends to exercise its discretionary enforcement power. Although the press release was not promulgated through relatively formal means such as notice-and-comment, it was issued in the name of the FCC, and nothing suggests that its substance is in any way tentative. Still, the rationale behind exempting policy statements from notice-and-comment is that they do not have the "force of law," creating a problem at the second prong of the finality test. The press release might nonetheless be regarded as having the legal consequences needed for finality under the functional approach of *Appalachian Power v. EPA.* In that case, the D.C. Circuit declared that if a purported guidance document uses mandatory language that an agency treats as binding (*e.g.*, by basing enforcement actions upon it), then a reviewing court should regard the guidance as practically binding and creating legal consequences. Here, the FCC seems to have adopted a policy that it regards as binding on both its staff and regulated parties, and we may have legal consequences under *Appalachian Power*.

Agency Action: The APA authorizes review of "agency action," a term defined at APA § 551(13). *Norton v. Southern Utah Wilderness Alliance.* "Agency action" includes a rule, order, sanction, relief, or the equivalent thereof. (It also includes denials of agency action and failures to act, but these categories are not pertinent here.) The Court has held that plaintiffs cannot mount wholesale attacks on agency management by piling together disparate actions, calling them a "program," and attacking them all at once. *Id.* The FCC might argue that this is what the plaintiff is trying to do by challenging the press release rather than later enforcement actions. This line seems unpromising, however. The press release seems to be a "rule" as defined in the APA § 551(4)—a statement of general applicability and future effect designed to implement, interpret, or prescribe law or policy.

Ripeness: This issue arises because Slick seeks pre-enforcement review of a rule. Ripeness depends on the fitness of the issues for review and an assessment of the harm to the parties of delaying review. *Abbot Laboratories v. Gardner.* Fitness inquires whether judicial review would benefit from information that could be generated by administrative enforcement proceedings. (Finality is sometimes folded into the fitness inquiry, but finality is also an independent requirement discussed above.) Generally, purely legal issues are regarded as fit for review; cases that require development of facts are not. Here, it isn't clear from the problem whether any of Slick's claims would benefit from further factual development by the agency. Still, waiting for review might clarify the FCC's approach to "reasonable verification," which might bear on the legality of the press release.

Turning to hardship, assuming the press release amounts to a general statement of policy, there is the problem that, in *Nat'l Park Hospitality Ass'n,* the Court stated that a policy statement did not create "adverse effects of the strictly legal kind" needed for hardship. *NPHA* is distinguishable, however, as the policy statement in that case explained how the National Park Service thought the Contract Disputes Act should be implemented, but the NPS is not charged with administering the CDA. Here, the FCC is explaining how it intends to implement *its* statute, the Communications Act. This type of policy statement should be expected to enjoy far more practical force. Stepping beyond the *NPHA* issue, it seems reasonable to suppose that the FCC policy will cause Slick to suffer immediate harm, causing it to lose business and thus altering its primary, day-to-day conduct. The facts of the problem are sketchy on this point, however, and more investigation would be required.

In sum, based on the facts given, the ripeness inquiry is indeterminate. Slick can boost its chances of getting past this hurdle by confining its claims to those depending purely on issues of law (*e.g.*, procedural claims) and by making a strong factual case of hardship.

B. **Harvey's Action**

Primary jurisdiction: If primary jurisdiction is applicable, the initial proceedings should occur at the FCC, not in court. However, it seems clear that primary jurisdiction should not be applied here, simply because the FCC does not take cases brought by individuals and does not award damages to individuals. It does have powers to penalize broadcasters, for example, by cease and desist orders or civil penalties or license nonrenewals, but none of these would be very helpful to Harvey's class. In addition, the FCC has little or no expertise in considering tort or contract actions, and there is no problem of lack of uniformity from conflicting court decisions (the class action will definitively dispose of these claims). None of the reasons for primary jurisdiction are applicable.

C. **KADS's Action**

Rulemaking: The key issue on KADS's appeal is whether the press release qualifies as a validly adopted rule, because the Act only permits cease and desist orders for violation of a validly adopted rule. The question takes substantive validity off the table, which leaves us with the problem of determining whether the FCC followed the necessary procedures for rulemaking.

The press release does seem to state a rule as this term is defined in APA § 551(4)—a statement of general applicability and future effect designed to implement, interpret, or prescribe law or policy. However, was it "validly adopted"? Generally, APA § 553 requires prior notice, opportunity to comment, and a 30-day pre-publication period for a rule, and the FCC did none of this. But these requirements do not apply to interpretive rules or policy statements, and the FCC must be contending that the rule is interpretive (*i.e.*, it explains the meaning of "public interest", etc.) or a policy statement (*i.e.*, it explains how the FCC will exercise discretion).

Courts usually defer to agency descriptions that a rule is "interpretive," but the FCC never claimed this status for the rule at the time it was adopted. Nor does it really interpret the meaning of words of a vague statute.

It is more plausible to argue that the press release is a "policy statement," given that the press release described itself as a "policy" and announced how the FCC intends to deploy its enforcement discretion. However, a policy statement, to avoid the requirement of notice-and-comment, must be tentative. If it is a definitive statement of how the agency will exercise discretion, it must be adopted as a legislative rule. [Note that the Supreme Court in *Lincoln v. Vigil* may have undercut the tentativeness requirement for policy statements.] The language of the statement does appear to be very inflexible. Moreover, the action against KADS appears to confirm that the FCC treats the product-claim statement as a legislative rule, not a policy statement, given that the FCC is now seeking a sanction based directly on it and that KADS has not been given the opportunity to argue it is an improper policy.

In any event, it seems unlikely that the Communications Act requirement that a cease and desist order be based on a validly adopted rule means an interpretive rule or a policy statement. Surely the Act meant that cease and desist orders can only be based upon legislative rules, adopted after appropriate public input, stating a definite legal requirement that a broadcaster would understand is binding. An interpretive rule or policy statement could well be a valid way of warning the industry how the Commission will conduct its licensing operations, but would not be binding on the industry and thus not sufficient under the statute for a cease and desist order.

Adjudication: An agency can adopt a new "rule" through adjudication, as in *SEC v. Chenery* and *NLRB v. Bell Aerospace Co.,* and validly apply it to the parties to the adjudication, provided that the choice of adjudication rather than rulemaking was not an abuse of discretion. Here, the choice of adjudication would probably be upheld because there is no real hardship to KADS (it is ordered to cease and desist, not to pay a penalty) and no surprise (they had fair warning through the press release). Moreover, the problem is difficult and might well be susceptible to case-by-case development. However, the trouble is that cease and desist orders can only be imposed for violation of a rule, and this probably means a rule adopted through rulemaking, not a "rule" adopted as part of adjudication. However, this point is arguable and the FCC could contend that a rule adopted as part of adjudication could be the basis for a cease and desist order.

Even if the FCC could adopt its "rule" through adjudication, there is a possibility of applying the *Chenery* contemporaneous-explanation principle against it. The agency is changing its tune in the appellate court. Originally, it said it was relying solely on the rule adopted in the press release. Now, it is saying that it is adopting the new policy through adjudication. A court should not allow the agency to change its position during judicial review, but should remand for reconsideration of the basic policy decision.

In summary, even if the FCC did properly concoct its new principle through an adjudication, it probably could not issue a cease and desist order except in reliance upon a prior validly adopted legislative rule, and that does not exist here.

Answer to Question VII

Hearing: The key point in this question is whether a trial-type hearing is required. The Administrative Procedure Act ("APA") only requires a trial-type hearing in adjudication or rulemaking if the underlying statute requires one. Here, the statute calls for a "fair hearing." Under *United States v. Florida East Coast Railway*, this undoubtedly means only a legislative-type hearing, not a trial-type hearing. The magic words "on the record" are missing from the statute and, since the proceeding is undoubtedly general rulemaking and not adjudication, the statute would not be construed to require a trial-type hearing. In addition, *Dominion* establishes that *Chevron-type* deference should be given to an agency's interpretation of ambiguous terms like "fair hearing."

Consequently, only the requirements of APA § 553 are applicable here—meaning no administrative law judge has to be involved, and no cross-examination is required. (It is not clear whether the legislative-type hearing conducted by the EPA was required by the statute or whether even that could have been omitted—but this is irrelevant.) Even if the court thinks cross-examination would have been useful, *Vermont Yankee Nuclear Power Corp. v. Natural Resources Defense Council* prevents it from tampering with the agency's chosen procedure as long as the APA is satisfied.

Notice: The EPA's notice in the Federal Register was very sketchy. For example, the final rule that distinguishes between new and existing reactors was not foreshadowed in the notice. However, the final rule seems to meet the "logical outgrowth" test. It is close enough to the notice so that this variance would not invalidate the rule; only a radically different final product—as to which no reasonable warning was given to the industry—would induce a court to set the rule aside. However, the EPA also has to disclose important staff studies to the industry to permit comment under *Portland Cement Association v. Ruckelshaus*. The cases make clear that important factual data on which the agency relies must be disclosed to permit adversarial comment, and the EPA failed to do so. On this ground the court should invalidate the rule and require a new notice-and-comment cycle. Blue Demon will not be able to cross-examine the author (unless the EPA decides to allow cross-examination during the new comment period) but should be able effectively to criticize the study in writing.

Best available technology: Blue Demon argues the rule is substantively invalid because the statute requires that the limit be achievable through the best available technology, and the EPA has admitted that none is "available." However, the EPA interprets "available" to mean available before the rule goes into effect. It would seem that the court should not set aside the rule. Under *Mead*, the *Chevron* doctrine should apply to the interpretation as it is embedded in a rule made through notice-and-comment. Under *Chevron*, the EPA's reasonable statutory interpretation of an ambiguous provision should be sustained. Absent a strong reason to disagree with the agency (such as clear legislative history), the court must go along with the agency if it is a doubtful question.

Factual basis for the rule: The factual underpinnings of rules are generally reviewed under the arbitrary-capricious standard of APA § 706(2)(A), which requires the court to understand the agency's data base and methodology and make sure that all material comments were considered. The EPA has to explain its reasoning, the alternatives chosen and rejected, and generally indicate that it has taken a hard, thorough look at the problem. Although the EPA has disagreed with Blue Demon, this is not dispositive as long as the agency has adequately considered and responded to its objections. Here, the staff study on which the agency relies does adequately support the rule. So far as can be seen here, the EPA has considered all comments, and adjusted the final rule to deal with them together with the other information before it. It is not for the court to resolve conflicts in the evidence. However, the court cannot do its job adequately because the staff study was never made available to Blue Demon and other objectors to attack; perhaps their attacks would indeed have demolished the study and rendered it inadequate to support the rule. Thus, the court will not decide the issue of whether the rule is arbitrary and capricious for lack of factual support but will instead require a new notice-and-comment cycle in which the study can be attacked by objectors.

Ex parte contacts: Under the rule in *Home Box Office, Inc. v. FCC*, the contacts by Friends of the Earth with Squid would have been improper. That case would have required, at the very least, that Squid write memos about the conversations and place them in the record. However, later cases have disagreed with *Home Box Office* (or at least limited it to rules that involve conflicts between different segments of an industry for a valuable privilege), and ex parte contacts in informal rulemaking generally are now permissible. The *Home Box Office* principle also seems to contravene *Vermont Yankee* because *Home Box Office* seems to be a judicial decision that adds to the requirements of the APA. (Note that the ex parte rule of APA § 557(d) does not apply to informal rulemaking, but it does apply to formal rulemaking, so that the question of whether formal rulemaking was required, discussed above, is critical for this issue also.) Certainly, Squid's conduct in seeing environmentalists off the record but refusing to see reactor operators falls short of minimum standards of fairness, but it probably does not violate existing law unless *Home Box Office* makes a comeback. (Due process would preclude such ex parte contacts in adjudication but is inapplicable to the determination of legislative facts in general rulemaking.)

Flounder: The fact that Flounder worked for an environmental group before coming to the EPA raises no problem unless she has some more concrete conflict of interest than simply having worked for a group that desires strict environmental standards. She is entitled to have contacts with Squid off the record because the separation-of-functions provisions of APA § 554(d) do not apply in rulemaking. There is nothing inherently wrong with Squid having copied Flounder's final memo.

Squid's speech: Under *Association of National Advertisers v. FTC*, Squid is entitled to make speeches indicating a strong predisposition about legislative facts or policies. The bias cases like *Cinderella Career & Finishing Schools v. FTC* and *American Cyanamid Co. v. FTC* do not apply to rulemaking. As long as his speeches do not disclose an unalterably closed mind, they do not raise any statutory or constitutional issue. Squid's speech here does not show a closed mind—he says he is willing to consider economic and technical constraints—and the court will surely find that he is capable of considering the evidence and issues fairly.

Answer to Question VIII

Constitutional standing: Sniff needs to satisfy the canonical injury-causation-redressability test for constitutional standing in federal court. Clearing some underbrush, Sniff cannot base constitutional standing on its interest as a "citizen" in seeing the law obeyed. This type of injury is too abstract and generalized to count as an "injury in fact." Taxpayer standing won't work either as the Court has, in practice, limited its availability to plaintiffs alleging that taxing-and-spending decisions by a legislature have violated the Establishment Clause. *Flast v. Cohen* (as narrowed).

Sniff might try to satisfy the injury-in-fact requirement by claiming a competitive injury. This claim requires some imagination, for it is not apparent how Sniff is really injured by the FTWA's rule that QRC is not toxic. The problem does not say that QRC and PFB compete for the same markets. Perhaps Sniff is arguing that if QRC is classified as a toxic chemical, its own financial liability to contribute to the superfund as a PRC producer will be less because there will be more chemical producers who are required to contribute to the superfund. This claim, however, seems likely to run afoul of the requirement that an injury be "actual" or "imminent" rather than "conjectural" or "speculative." The Court has conceded that this distinction is "elastic." It has also sent mixed messages about whether the "imminence" standard for future injuries requires that the injury be "certainly impending" or merely that there be a "substantial risk" or "reasonable probability" of injury. *Clapper v. Amnesty International, Inc.* On its face, Sniff's competitive injury claim seems unlikely to satisfy either of these standards.

Sniff must also confront the causation and redressability components of the Article III standing test. The injury must be fairly traceable to the regulation and must likely be remedied by a favorable decision. *Simon v. Eastern Kentucky Welfare Rights Organization* held that indigent hospital users had no standing to challenge a regulation that removed the requirement that hospitals serve indigents in order to receive a tax exemption. Although plaintiffs had been denied service, the change in regulatory policy may not have caused this denial; similarly, a change in the regulation might not secure them service. Here it is equally arguable that adding QRC as a toxic might not make any difference at all in Sniff's ultimate contribution. However, since Sniff's injury in fact was based on the possibility that QRC's inclusion would decrease its own contribution, it would follow that adding QRC would remedy this injury. Thus as long as Sniff's rather speculative injury is considered an injury-in-fact, it would seem that Sniff can avoid the causation and redressability requirements. By definition, QRC's exclusion caused Sniff's injury, and QRC's inclusion would remedy that injury.

Statutory (or prudential) standing: In the bonus round, note that the agency's enabling act must part company from the APA's template for judicial review at §§ 701-06 because we are told that judicial review is proper in the D.C. Circuit rather than in district court, which would be the APA's default choice. Even where an enabling act displaces APA § 702, however, courts apply its "zone of interest" test as a prudential matter unless Congress clearly indicates otherwise (*e.g.*, with a "citizen suit" provision).

It seems likely that Sniff can meet the zone-of-interest test. This test merely requires that Sniff seek to protect an interest arguably within the zone of interests that the underlying statute seeks to protect. The statute seeks to protect the environment, but it also contemplates that contributions will be equitably apportioned among polluters. Sniff seeks to protect this latter interest, and thus should fall within the zone. *See, e.g., Bennett v. Spear*. (Note that in *Air Courier,* the Court required that a plaintiff show she is a member of a class that Congress intended to protect. Sniff might satisfy this tougher standard, too, but should not need to do so given that later cases have rejected this requirement, returning to a more relaxed approach to statutory standing. *Match-E-Be-Nash-She-Wish Band of Pottawatomi Indians, v. Patchak.*)

Answer to Question IX

As a threshold matter, note that the agency, when it declared that no cross-examination would be allowed, essentially promulgated a procedural rule to govern the rulemaking to determine the liabilities of individual firms. This procedural rule is probably fine as a statutory matter but raises more difficult constitutional concerns.

Statutory arguments: Sniff might object that the agency should have used notice-and-comment to promulgate the procedural rule barring cross-examination. This seems a non-starter, however, as the procedural rule applies to all interested parties equally and does not "encode a substantive value judgment." *Public Citizen v. Dept. of State*. The bar on cross-examination thus seems to fall safely within the exemption from notice-and-comment applicable to procedural rules in § 553.

Sniff might also object to the procedural rule on substantive grounds—*i.e.*, that it was arbitrary for the agency to categorically bar cross-examination given that it might be necessary in some instances to resolve fairly contested issues of material fact. Absent constitutional constraints, this argument is likely blocked by the Court's emphatic holding in *Vermont Yankee Nuclear Power Corp. v. Natural Resources Defense Council*, which instructed courts, in no uncertain terms, that they are not to second-guess agencies by requiring procedures (such as cross-examination) that the agency has decided not to employ. Otherwise, an agency would employ the most cumbersome procedures in every case to avoid the risk of being reversed on a procedural point.

Constitutional argument: Sniff might be able to make a constitutional argument based on the teaching of *Londoner-BiMetallic* that procedural due process protections are triggered when there is a deprivation of liberty or property turning upon an individualized determination of facts. Dictum in *Vermont Yankee* can also be cited to support this contention; the Court noted that additional procedures beyond those required by the APA or an agency can be required when "a very small number of persons are exceptionally affected, in each case upon individual grounds." Put another way, Sniff would be arguing that the rulemaking to determine liabilities is really, in a constitutional sense, an adjudication.

Sniff's ability to make this argument would depend on what, precisely, the rule purports to decide. We are told in the facts that the rule is to base liability on the toxicity of a firm's chemical wastes, the length of time it has produced them, and ability to pay. To the degree the rule is merely setting up a general schedule of how these factors should affect later liability determinations, it is determining legislative facts, which would not trigger procedural due process. For instance, putting PFB on a list of extremely toxic chemicals meriting higher liability would seem to be a matter of legislative fact.

The question, however, suggests that the agency did more than set up a general rule determining how to decide liability in particular cases—it also determined exact liabilities. Determining Sniff's exact liability presumably required resolution of adjudicative facts that are specific to Sniff—*e.g.*, which chemicals did it produce, for how long, what is its financial condition, etc. If this is so, then the "rule" is determining adjudicative facts, and Sniff has a basis for demanding additional due process protections applicable to this liability determination.

This demand for further process might not turn out as Sniff wants, however. The realities of the rulemaking proceeding (involving many companies, time pressure, and great complexity) suggest that procedural compromises are necessary. After all, the various facts relating to Sniff (such as ability to pay) can be determined from documents; confrontation of witnesses is not necessary, and, as far as we know, credibility is not at stake. Under *Mathews v. Eldridge*, Sniff's property interest in resisting the assessment is very substantial, the risk of error in dispensing with cross-examination seems relatively small, and the burden on the government from holding cross-examination (which presupposes some sort of trial-type proceeding) in a huge number of cases would be overwhelming. Thus, it is likely that the procedure actually provided met due process standards. Sniff's best hope to undermine this conclusion is to demonstrate that the nature of the underlying issues actually requires cross-examination for fair resolutions of liability.

Table of Cases

Abbott Laboratories v. Gardner 185, 213, 214
ABF Freight Lines, Inc. v. NLRB 167
Abraham Lincoln Memorial Hosp. v. Sebelius 113
Action for Children's Television v. FCC 117
Adamo Wrecking Co. v. United States 174
AEP Chapter Housing Ass'n v. City of Berkeley 79
Aetna Ins. Co. v. Lavoie 79
Air Courier Conference v. American Postal Workers
 Union 207
Air Traffic Controllers Org. v. Fed. Labor Relations
 Auth. 82
Air Transport Association of America, Inc. v.
 FAA 112
Alabama Power Co. v. Ickes 205
Alaska Professional Hunters Association v.
 FAA 113
Alden v. Maine 177
Allen v. Wright 203, 207
Almeida-Ameral v. Gonzales 128
Alyeska Pipeline Service Co. v. Wilderness
 Society 141
Amalgamated Meat Cutters v. Connally 7
American Bus Ass'n v. United States 114
American Cyanamid Co. v. FTC 78
American Farm Lines v. Black Ball Freight
 Service 100
American Forest & Paper Association v. EPA 220
American Hosp. Assoc. v. NLRB 41
American Mfrs. Mutual Ins. Co. v. Sullivan 33, 43
American Mining Congress v. MSHA 112, 113
American Radio Relay League, Inc. v. FCC 119
American School of Magnetic Healing v.
 McAnnulty 173
American Textile Manufacturers Inst. v. Donovan 8,
 10
American Trucking Ass'ns v. EPA 8
Amos Treat & Co. v. SEC 77
Anaconda Co. v. Ruckelshaus 93
Andresen v. Maryland 127
Appalachian Power Co. v. EPA 211
Arizona Christian School Tuition Organization v.
 Winn 201
Arizona Grocery Co. v. Santa Fe Railway 100
Arizona v. California 6
Arlington, City of v. FCC 155
Armstrong v. Commodity Futures Trading
 Comm'n 63
Arnett v. Kennedy 32
Arthur Young & Co., United States v. 127
Associated Industries of New York v. Ickes 205
Association of American Railroads v. U.S. Dep't of
 Trans. 9, 214
Association of Data Processing Service Org., Inc.
 v. Bd. of Governors of the Federal Reserve
 System 146
Association of Data Processing Service Organizations,
 Inc. v. Camp 206
Association of National Advertisers, Inc. v. FTC 96,
 118, 211

Atchison, Topeka & Santa Fe Ry. v. Wichita Bd. of
 Trade 88, 156
Atkins v. Parker 41
Atlas Roofing Co. v. Occupational Safety & Health
 Review Comm'n. 15, 175
ATX, Inc. v. Dep't of Transp. 82
Auer v. Robbins 106, 159
Automotive Parts & Accessories Association
 v. Boyd 104
Aylett v. Secretary of Housing and Urban
 Development 149
B.F. Goodrich Co. v. DOT 102
Bakalis v. Golembeski 79
Baltimore Gas & Electric Co. v. Natural Resources
 Defense Council 166
Barnhart v. Walton 154, 155
Barr Laboratories, Inc., In re 212
Barr v. Matteo 183
BCCA Appeal Group v. U.S. E.P.A. 220
Bell v. Burton 35
Bellis v. United States 126
Bennett v. Spear 206, 208, 209
Berger v. United States 80
Berkovitz v. United States 180
Best v. Humboldt Mining Co. 222
Bi-Metallic Investment Co. v. State Board of
 Equalization 40
Bishop v. Wood 27, 31
Biswell, United States v. 126
Bivens v. Six Unknown Named Agents of the
 Federal Bureau of Narcotics 183
Block v. Community Nutrition Institute 186, 187
Blum v. Stenson 142
Board of Pardons v. Allen 29
Board of Regents v. Roth 27
Borden, Inc. v. Commissioner of Public Health 166
Boreali v. Axelrod 10
Bose Corp. v. Consumers Union 149
Boumediene v. Bush 174
Bowen v. City of New York 217
Bowen v. Georgetown Univ. Hosp. 68, 98
Bowen v. Massachusetts 172
Bowen v. Michigan Academy of Family
 Physicians 185, 186
Bowles v. Seminole Rock Co. 159
Bowsher v. Synar 19
Bradley v. Fisher 182
Braswell v. United States 126
Brinkley v. Hassig 80
Brosseau v. Haugen 183
Buckhannon Board & Care Home, Inc. v. West
 Virginia Department of Health and Human
 Resources 141
Buckley v. Valeo 15
Burlington, City of v. Dague 142
Bute v. Glover Livestock Co. of Texas 167
Butz v. Economou 83, 182
C & W Fish Co. v. Fox 118
CAB v. Hermann 124
Califano v. Sanders 172
Camara v. Municipal Court 124
Camp v. Pitts 86, 163

Case	Page
Carlson v. Green	183
Carter v. Carter Coal Co.	9
Castillo-Villagra v. INS	59
Castle Rock, Town of v. Gonzales	33
Catholic Health Initiatives v. Sebelius	112
Center for Auto Safety v. NHTSA	211
Central Platte Natural Res. Dist. v. Wyoming	79
Chamber of Commerce v. Reich	173
Chamber of Commerce v. SEC	102
Checkosky v. SEC	105
Chemical Waste Mgmt., Inc. v. EPA	51
Chenery Corp.	64, 69
Cheney, In re	173
Chevron, USA, Inc. v. Natural Resources Defense Council	51, 150, 151, 153, 156
Chief Probation Officers v. Shalala	113
Chocolate Manufacturers Association v. Block	104
Christopher v. SmithKline Beecham Corp.	159, 160
Chrysler Corp. v. Brown	135
Cinderella Career & Finishing Schools, Inc. v. FTC	78, 149
Citizens Awareness Network, Inc. v. U.S.	50, 54, 61
Citizens for Responsibility & Ethics in Washington v. Office of Administration	129
Citizens to Preserve Overton Park v. Volpe	85, 118, 162, 163, 164, 187
Clapper v. Amnesty Intern. USA	196, 199
Clark-Cowlitz Joint Operating Agency v. FERC	69
Clarke v. Securities Industry Ass'n	206
Cleavinger v. Saxner	182
Cleveland Bd. of Educ. v. Loudermill	31
Clinton v. City of New York	3, 22
Clinton v. Jones	181
CNA Financial Corp. v. Donovan	135
Cobell v. Norton	211
Codd v. Velger	27
Cody v. Cox	188
Colonnade Catering Corp. v. United States	126
Commodity Futures Trading Comm'n v. Schor	4, 11
Community Nutrition Institute v. Young	115
Connecticut Dep't. of Pub. Safety v. Doe	41
Connecticut v. Doehr	36
Consolidated Edison Co. v. NLRB	147
Consumer Fed'n of Am. v. Dep't of Agric.	131, 132
Cook v. FDA	188
Corder v. United States	167
Correctional Services Corp. v. Malesko	184
County of Sacramento v. Lewis	27
Critical Mass Energy Project v. Nuclear Regulatory Commission	134
CropLife America v. EPA	114
Crowell v. Benson	14, 149, 150
D.C. Fed'n of Civic Ass'ns v. Volpe	81, 117
DaimlerChrysler Corp. v. Cuno	201
Darby v. Cisneros	219
Davis & Randall, Inc. v. United States	60
Davis v. Passman	184
DCP Farms v. Yeutter	81
Degge v. Hitchcock	173
Dellmuth v. Muth	177
Dept. of Army v. Blue Fox, Inc.	172, 176
DeRieux v. Five Smiths, Inc.	111
Dixon v. Love	35
Doe, United States v.	127
DOJ v. Tax Analysts	131
Dominion Energy Brayton Point, LLC v. Johnson	51
Donovan v. Dewey	126
Dunlop v. Bachowski	63
Dusenbery v. United States	37
Eagle-Picher Industries v. EPA	215
Edelman v. Jordan	178
Edmonds v. United States	16
Electric Power Supply Ass'n v. FERC	82
Electronic Privacy Information Ctr. v. U.S. Dept. of Homeland Sec.	109
Endicott Johnson Corp. v. Perkins	123
Env't Def. Fund v. EPA	77
Envirocare of Utah, Inc. v. Nuclear Regulatory Comm'n	54
EPA v. Mink	136
Epilepsy Found. of Ne. Ohio v. NLRB	70
Excelsior Underwear	68
Ezeagwuna v. Ashcroft	58
F.A. McDonald Co. v. Indus. Comm'n	60
Fahey v. Mallonee	34
FCC v. Fox Television Stations, Inc.	88, 156, 165
FCC v. ITT World Communications	140
FCC v. Sanders Bros. Radio Station	205
FCC v. Station WJR	85
FDA v. Brown & Williamson Tobacco Corp.	152
FDIC v. Mallen	35
Federal Crop Ins. Corp. v. Merrill	90
Federal Deposit Ins. Corp. v. Meyer	177, 180, 184
Federal Election Comm'n v. Akins	197, 198
Federal Radio Comm'n v. Nelson Brothers	6
Field v. Clark	4
Fisher v. United States	127
Fitzpatrick v. Bitzer	177
Flagstaff Broad. Fed'n v. FCC	88
Flast v. Cohen	201
Florida E. Coast Ry., United States v.	41, 47, 51, 96
Florida Power & Light Co. v. United States	103
Food Store Employees Union	167
Foote's Dixie Dandy, Inc. v. McHenry	89
Ford Motor Co. v. FTC	71
Forest Guardians v. Babbitt	212
Forsham v. Harris	131
Franklin v. Massachusetts	189
Franz v. Bd. of Med. Quality Assurance	59
Free Enter. Fund v. Pub. Co. Accounting Oversight Bd.	16, 17, 19, 215, 216
Friedman v. Rogers	80
Friends of the Earth v. Laidlaw Environmental Services, Inc.	203
Frink v. Prod	147
Frothingham v. Mellon	201
FTC v. Cement Inst.	79
FTC v. Cinderella Career & Finishing Schools, Inc.	79
FTC v. Grolier	136
FTC v. Mandel Brothers, Inc.	167
FTC v. Standard Oil Co. of California	209
FTC v. Texaco	86
FTC v. Universal-Rundle Corp.	167
Fuentes v. Shevin	35
Gagnon v. Scarpelli	39
Gamble-Skogmo, Inc. v. FTC	85
Gartside, In re	146
Gaubert, United States v.	179
Gehin v. Wis. Group Ins. Bd.	57
General Electric Co. v. EPA	37, 90, 114
General Motors Corp. v. Ruckelshaus	112
Georgia v. Tennessee Copper Co.	200
Gibson v. Berryhill	80, 217
Gideon v. Wainwright	38
Gilbert v. Homar	35
Goland v. CIA	132
Goldberg v. Kelly	31, 36, 63
Golden State Transit Corp. v. City of Los Angeles	185
Gonzales v. Oregon	159
Gonzalez-Rivera v. INS	128
Goss v. Lopez	30
Granfinanciera S.A. v. Nordberg	12
Gravel v. United States	182
Great Northern Railway v. Merchants Elevator Co.	222

Greater Boston Television Corp. v. FCC 163
Greene v. Babbitt 77
Greenholtz v. Nebraska Penal Inmates 29
Greenwood Manor v. Iowa Dep't of Pub. Health 52
Grimaud, United States v. 5, 14
Griswold v. Connecticut 207
Grolier, Inc. v. FTC 77
Guentchev v. INS 63
Hammer v. City of Osage Beach, Missouri...............27
Hannah v. Larche 128
Hans v. Louisiana 177
Hardt v. Reliance Standard Life Ins. Co. 141
Harlow v. Fitzgerald 181, 183
Heckler v. Campbell 41
Heckler v. Cheney 187, 188
Heckler v. Cmty. Health Servs....................................89
Hein v. Freedom from Religion Foundation,
  Inc. 198, 201
Hoctor v. United States Department of
  Agriculture 112
Hollingsworth v. Perry..207
Home Box Office, Inc. v. FCC 116
Hoska v. Dep't of the Army...58
Hudson v. Palmer..39
Hudson v. United States..15
Humana of South Carolina v. Califano 109
Humphrey's Executor v. United States.....................18
Hunt Foods & Industries, Inc. v. FTC.....................124
Hunt v. Washington Apple Advertising Comm'n...200
Hutto v. Finney 178
Idaho Farm Bureau Federation v. Babbitt...............102
Idaho Historic Pres. Council, Inc. v. City Council of
  Boise 84
Imbler v. Pachtman 182
IMS, P.C. v. Alvarez..119
Independent Community Bankers of America v. Board
  of Governors of the Federal Reserve System 175
Industrial Union Dep't v. American Petroleum
  Inst. 8, 10
Ingraham v. Wright..39
INS v. Chadha..3, 21, 22
INS v. Hibi...90
INS v. Lopez-Mendoza...128
INS v. St. Cyr...151
J.W. Hampton & Co. v. United States 5
Janis, United States v..128
JEM Broadcasting Co., Inc. v. FCC 109
Jenkins v. McKeithen..128
Jifry v. FAA 111
Jones v. Flowers..37
Jones v. State Highway Comm'n..............................180
Judicial Watch, Inc. v. United States Department
  of Justice 136
Judulang v. Holder..153
Kapps v. Wing 33
Kastigar v. United States...126
Kent v. Dulles 10
KFC Nat'l Mgmt. Corp. v. NLRB 85
Kimel v. Florida Board of Regents 177
Kissinger v. Reporters Committee for Freedom of the
  Press 129, 131
Koniag, Inc. v. Andrus...54, 81
Koretoff v. Vilsack 220
Kowalski v. Tesmer..207, 208
Laird v. Nelms 179
Lance v. Coffman 198
Landry v. FDIC...16
Lassiter v. Dep't. of Soc. Servs....................................38
Leedom v. Kyne...211
Levin v. United States..180, 183
Liberty Homes v. Department of Industry 119
Lincoln v. Vigil..189
Lindahl v. Office of Personnel Management 186

Londoner v. Denver 40
Long Island Care at Home, Ltd. v. Coke................104
Louisiana Ass'n of Indep. Producers v. Fed. Energy
  Regulatory Comm'n..83
Louisiana Environmental Action Network v.
  Browner...215
Lugar v. Edmonson Oil Co., Inc..................................42
Lujan v. Defenders of Wildlife........195, 196, 198, 199,
  202, 203, 204
Lujan v. G & G Fire Sprinklers 39
Lujan v. National Wildlife Federation....................190
Mackey v. Montrym..35
Major League Baseball v. Crist 124
Marathon Oil Co. v. EPA 52
Marchetti v. United States 127
Marcus v. Dir., Office of Workers' Comp.
  Programs 81
Marine Mammal Conservancy, Inc. v. Department of
  Agriculture 218
Market St. Ry. v. R.R. Comm'n..................................60
Marshall v. Barlow's Inc...125
Marshall v. Cuomo..76
Marshall v. Jerrico Inc..27, 80
Martin v. Occupational Safety and Health Review
  Comm'n 75
Massachusetts v. EPA 105, 153, 165, 197, 198, 200,
  203, 204
Massman Construction Co. v. TVA 83
Match-E-Be-Nash-She-Wish Band of Pottawatomi
  Indians v. Patchak 207
Mathews v. Eldridge 31, 34, 63
Mayberry v. Pennsylvania..80
McCarthy v. Madigan 216, 217
McCarthy v. Sawyer-Goodman Co. 60
McGee v. United States..219
McHugh v. Santa Monica Rent Control Bd.............15
McKart v. United States 219
McLaughlin v. Union Oil Co. 80
McNary v. Haitian Refugee Center 186
Mead Corp., United States v. 154
Mead v. Arnell 22
Megdal v. Oregon State Board of Dental
  Examiners 71
Memphis Light, Gas & Water Div. v. Craft 32, 36
Mendoza, United States v..87
MetWest Inc. v. Secretary of Labor 113, 118
Mid-Tex Electric Cooperative v. Federal Energy
  Regulatory Commission 111
Milner v. Dept. of the Navy 133
Milwaukee Metro. Sewerage Dist. v. Wis. Dep't of
  Nat. Res. 53
Minneci v. Pollard 184
Missouri Coal. for the Env't v. Joint Comm. on
  Admin. Rules..22
Mistretta v. United States 8
Mitchell v. W.T. Grant Co. 36
Mitchell, Helvering v. 14
Monell v. Department of Social Services 181
Monsanto Co. v. Geertson Seed Farms 199
Morgan v. United States 84
Morgan, United States v..85
Morrison v. Olson 4, 16, 18
Morton v. Ruiz 100, 130
Moser v. United States 90
Motor Vehicle Manufacturers Association v. State
  Farm Mutual Auto Insurance Co. 104, 163, 166
Mullane v. Central Hanover Bank 37
Multi Ag Media LLC v. USDA................................137
Muskopf v. Corning Hospital District 180
Myers v. Bethlehem Shipbuilding Corp. 216
Myers v. United States 18
Nader v. Allegheny Airlines...................................222
Nash v. Bowen 78

National Archives and Records Administration v. Favish 138
National Automatic Laundry & Cleaning Council v. Schulz 211
National Cable & Telecommunications Association v. Brand X Internet Services 156
National Credit Union Association v. First National Bank and Trust Co. 206
National Park Hospitality Ass'n v. Department of the Interior 215
National Petroleum Refiners Association v. FTC ... 100
Nat'l Parks and Conservation Ass'n v. Morton 134
Natural Resources Defense Council v. EPA 104
New York v. Burger 125
Ng Fung Ho v. White 149
Nielsen Lithographing Co. v. NLRB 88
Nightlife Partners v. City of Beverly Hills 75
Nixon v. Fitzgerald 181
Nixon, United States v. 181
NLRB v. Bell Aerospace Co. 71
NLRB v. Donnelly Garment Co. 79
NLRB v. Hearst Publications, Inc. 161
NLRB v. Ky. River Cmty. Care, Inc. 56
Noel Canning v. NRLB 17
North Amer. Cold Storage Co. V. Chicago 34
North Carolina v. Chas. Pfizer & Co. 87
Northern Arapahoe Tribe v. Hodel 111
Northern Pipeline Constr. Co. v. Marathon Pipe Line Co. 12
Norton v. Southern Utah Wilderness Alliance 171, 173, 190
Nova Scotia Food Products, United States v. 102, 103, 104, 174
NRDC v. Abraham 111
NRLB v. Wyman-Gordon Co. 68
O'Bannon v. Town Court Nursing Center 33
Office of Communications of the United Church of Christ v. FCC 54, 205
Office of Personnel Mgmt. v. Richmond 89
Office of Workers' Comp. v. Greenwich Collieries 56
Ohio Forestry Association v. Sierra Club 213
Ohio Valley Water Co. v. Ben Avon Borough 149
Oklahoma Press Publishing Co. v. Walling 124
Pacific States Box & Basket Co. v. White 166
Packard Motor Car Co. v. NLRB 162
Panama Refining Co. v. Ryan 5, 6
Papish v. Univ. of Missouri 30
Parham v. J.R. 37
Parklane Hosiery Co. v. Shore 86
Parratt v. Taylor 39
Passmore v. Astrue 58
Patsy v. Board of Regents 219
Paul v. Davis 28
Penasquitos Village, Inc. v. NLRB 148, 160
Pennsylvania Indus. Chem. Co., United States v. 90
Pension Benefit Guar. Corp. v. LTV Corp. 67, 164
Perry v. Sindermann 28
Petroleum Information Corp. v. Department of Interior 136
Pharmaceutical Research and Mfrs. of America v. Walsh 221, 222
Phillippi v. CIA 132
Pierce v. Underwood 142
Pillsbury Co. v. FTC 22, 81
Pittsburgh Steamship Co. 80
Portland Audubon Soc'y v. Endangered Species Comm. 82
Portland Cement Association v. Ruckelshaus 102, 166
Portmann v. United States 89
Professional Pilots Federation v. FAA 106
Public Citizen v. Dept. of State 109
Public Citizen, Inc. v. Nat'l Highway Traffic Safety Admin. 200
Public Citizens Health Research Group v. FDA 134
Pulliam v. Allen 182
Radio Officers' Union v. NLRB 148
Rafeedie v. INS 217
Red Lion Broad. Co. v. FCC 67
Reno v. Catholic Social Services, Inc. 213, 214
Retail, Wholesale 69
Rhoa-Zamora v. INS 59
Richardson v. Perales 57, 58
Riverside, City of v. Rivera 142
Rock Royal Coop., United States v. 9
Rodway v. USDA 104
Ruckelshaus v. Sierra Club 141
Rust v. Sullivan 10
Rybachek v. EPA 102
Sackett v. EPA 186, 210
San Luis Obispo Mothers for Peace v. Nuclear Regulatory Comm'n 86
Sandin v. Conner 29
Sangamon Valley Television Corp. v. United States 48, 95, 116
Schechter Poultry Corp. v. United States 6
Scheuer v. Rhodes 178
Schwartz v. Covington 223
Seacoast Anti-Pollution League v. Costle 52
Sealed Case, In re 136
Sears, Roebuck & Co. 135
SEC v. Jerry T. O'Brien, Inc. 124
See v. Seattle 125
Seminole Tribe of Florida v. Florida 178
Sepulveda v. Block 111
Shapiro v. United States 127
Shasta Minerals & Chemical Co. v. SEC 124
Shaughnessy, United States ex rel. Knauff v. 28
Shell Offshore Inc. v. Babbitt 113
Shively v. Stewart 54
Siegert v. Gilley 28
Sierra Club v. Costle 82, 84, 117
Sierra Club v. Morton 197, 200
Simochem Intern. Co. Ltd. v. Malaysia Intern. Shipping Co. 196
Simon v. Eastern Kentucky Welfare Rights Organization 202
Sims v. Apfel 220
Skidmore v. Swift & Co. 158
Smith, United States v. 180, 182
Sniadach v. Family Fin. Corp. 35
South Carolina State Ports Authority 177
Southwest Center for Biological Diversity v. U.S. Forest Service 119
Stauffer Chem. Co., United States v. 86
Steadman v. SEC 56
Steel Co. v. Citizens for a Better Environment 195, 203
Sterling Drug, Inc. v. FTC 130
Stern v. Marshall 11
Stivers v. Pierce 80
Storer Broad. Co., United States v. 41
Stump v. Sparkman 181
Sugar Cane Growers Cooperative of Florida v. Veneman 94, 105
Summers v. Earth Island Inst. 197
Syncor Internat'l Corp. v. Shalala 112
Tax Analysts & Advocates v. IRS 130
Telecommunications Research & Action Center v. FCC 212
Telephone & Telegraph Co. 151
Tenney v. Brandhove 182
Texas & Pacific Railway v. Abilene Cotton Oil Co. 221
Texas Boll Weevil Eradication Found., Inc. v. Lewellen 9

292 | Administrative Law

Thomas Jefferson University v. Shalala..................159
Thomas v. Union Carbide Agric. Prods. Co..............12
Thunder Basin Coal Co. v. Reich............................215
Ticor Title Ins. Co. v. FTC..............................211, 218
Todd & Co. v. SEC..9
Toilet Goods Association v. Gardner..............213, 214
Tower v. Glover..182
Trinity Broad. Co. v. FCC 37
Trudeau v. FTC...172, 173
Tull v. United States 175
Tumey v. Ohio..79
Turner v. Rogers 38
United States Department of Defense v. Federal
 Labor Relations Authority 137
United States Department of Justice v. Reporters
 Committee for Freedom of the Press..................136
United States Department of State v. Washington
 Post Co..136
United States Tel. Ass'n v. FCC 115
United Steelworkers of America v. Marshall..........118
Universal Camera Corp. v. NLRB 146, 147, 148
University of Missouri v. Horowitz 30
University of Tenn. v. Elliott 87
USA Group Services, Inc. v. Riley 107
Utah Constr. & Mining Co., United States v.............86
Utility Solid Waste Activities Group v. EPA..........110
Varig Airlines, United States v. 179
Vaughn v. Rosen...133
Vermont Yankee Nuclear Power Corp. v. NRDC....98,
 102, 106
Vietnam Veterans of America v. Secretary of the
 Navy..101
Virginia Petroleum Jobbers Association v. FPC 223
Vitarelli v. Seaton 100
Vitek v. Jones...29, 38
Walters v. Nat'l Assoc. of Radiation Survivors 38
Ward v. City of Monroeville....................................79
Warder v. Shalala..101
Warth v. Seldin 207
Washington v. Harper 29
Waukegan v. Pollution Control Bd. 14
Webster v. Doe 186, 187, 188
Weinberger v. Hynson, Westcott & Dunning, Inc. ...42
Weiner v. United States 19
West Chicago, City of v. NRC.................................52
Western Pacific R. Co., United States v..................221
Whitman v. American Trucking Associations 7, 164
Wilkie v. Robbins 184
Wilkinson v. Austin 28, 29, 30
Will v. Michigan Department of State Police 181
Wisconsin v. Constantineau......................................27
Withrow v. Larkin..74
Wolff v. McDonnell...29
Wolff v. Selective Service Board No. 16 218
Wong Wing v. United States....................................14
Wong Yang Sung v. McGrath..................................28
Wright v. Central DuPage Hosp. Ass'n. 13
WWHT, Inc. v. FCC 106
Yakus v. United States......................................6, 174
Yesler Terrace Community Council v. Cisneros......94
Yetman v. Garvey..42
Young, Ex parte 173, 178
Zemel v. Rusk..10

Table of Statutes

Administrative Procedure Act
§ 551	47
§ 551(1)	132, 189
§ 551(13)	189
§ 551(14)	83
§ 551(2)	132
§ 551(4)	48, 93, 99
§ 551(5)	48, 93
§ 551(6)	48
§ 551(7)	48
§ 552	129
§ 552(a)(1)	104, 105, 129
§ 552(a)(1)(D)	112, 114
§ 552(a)(2)	130, 136
§ 552(a)(3)(A)	130
§ 552(a)(4)(B)	133
§ 552(a)(4)(E)(i)	133
§ 552(a)(4)(E)(ii)(II)	141
§ 552(a)(6)(A)(i)–(ii)	132
§ 552(b)	133, 140
§ 552(b)(1)	133
§ 552(b)(2)	133
§ 552(b)(3)	134
§ 552(b)(4)	134
§ 552(b)(5)	135, 136
§ 552(b)(6)	136
§ 552(b)(7)	137
§ 552(b)(8)	138
§ 552(b)(9)	138
§ 552(c)	140
§ 552(c)(1)–(3)	140
§ 552(f)(1)	129
§ 552(f)(2)(A)	130, 131
§ 552(f)(2)(B)	131
§ 552b	140
§ 552b(a)(1)	140
§ 552b(a)(2)	140
§ 552b(c)(1)	140
§ 552b(c)(10)	141
§ 552b(c)(5)	141
§ 552b(c)(9)(B)	141
§ 552b(c)(10)	141
§ 553	47, 92
§ 553(3)(A)(i)	132
§ 553(3)(A)(ii)	132
§ 553(a)	109
§ 553(b)	102
§ 553(b)(A)	109, 112, 114
§ 553(b)(B)	110
§ 553(c)	51, 96, 103, 104, 109
§ 553(d)	103, 105
§ 553(d)(3)	110
§ 553(e)	105
§ 554	46, 47, 50
§ 554(a)	46
§ 554(b)	50, 53
§ 554(d)	50, 74, 75, 83
§ 554(d)(A)	76
§ 554(d)(B)	76
§ 554(d)(C)	76
§ 554(e)	67
§ 555	47
§ 555(b)	50, 54, 66, 128, 211
§ 555(c)	66, 123
§ 555(d)	55, 66, 123
§ 555(e)	63, 66, 105
§§ 556–57	46, 47, 92, 116
§ 556(b)	50, 53, 81
§ 556(c)(6)	55
§ 556(c)(7)	55
§ 556(c)(8)	55
§ 556(d)	50, 56, 57, 61
§ 556(e)	50, 58, 59, 118
§ 557	96
§ 557(b)	62, 85, 148
§ 557(b)(1)	62
§ 557(c)	63
§ 557(c)(3)(A)	50
§ 557(d)	82
§ 557(d)(1)	50, 82
§ 557(d)(1)(B)	83
§ 557(d)(1)(C)	83
§ 557(d)(1)(D)	83
§ 701	189
§§ 701–706	171, 189, 190
§ 701(a)(1)	170, 188
§ 701(a)(2)	185, 187, 188, 189
§ 702	176, 189, 194, 195, 204, 205, 208
§ 704	189, 195
§ 706	145
§ 706(1)	190, 191, 211
§ 706(2)	145, 146
§ 706(2)(A)	145, 146, 162, 166, 170, 187
§ 706(2)(B)–(D)	145
§ 706(2)(E)	145, 147
§ 706(2)(F)	145

Index

ABSOLUTE IMMUNITY
See Judicial Review—Tort Liability of Government and Officials

ADJUDICATION
  See also Adjudication—Formal, Adjudication—Informal, Adjudicative Integrity
adjudication distinguished from rulemaking (APA), 48
adjudication distinguished from rulemaking (Due Process), 48
adjudicative facts (determination of), 40
choice between adjudication and rulemaking to make policy, 70–71
declaratory orders, 67–68
definition under APA, 48
due process requirements for adjudicative hearing, 33–39
formal versus informal distinction, 47
retroactivity, 68–69
settlement and alternative dispute resolution, 55
sources of adjudicative procedure, 49

ADJUDICATION—FORMAL
adjudicators, 53
administrative law judges, 53, 77
burden of proof, 56
cross-examination, 61
discovery, 54–55
duty to explain (statutory), 62–63
evidentiary rules, 57
ex parte contacts, 82–83
formal versus informal distinction, 47
intervention, 54
notice, 53
official notice, 59
prehearing process, 53–56
record requirement, 58
residuum rule, 57–58
separation of functions, 76–77
settlement and alternative dispute resolution, 55
subpoena power, 55
summary of APA requirements, 50
triggering formal adjudication under APA, 51–52
types of decisions—initial, recommended, tentative, 62

ADJUDICATION—INFORMAL
APA's (very limited) requirements, 66
applicability of due process, 67
non-APA sources of procedural requirements, 67

ADJUDICATIVE INTEGRITY
agency head exception to separation of functions, 76–77
animus toward party, 80
APA provision on bias, 81
bias, 78–81
combination of adjudicative and enforcement functions, 75
consistency across cases—res judicata, 86–87
consistency across cases—stare decisis, 88
decisionmaker familiarity with case (*Morgan* principle), 84–86
estopping the government, 88–90
exceptions to separation of functions, 76–77
ex parte communications, due process limits, 84
ex parte communications, limits for formal adjudication (§ 554), 83
ex parte communications, limits for formal proceedings (§ 557), 82–83
financial bias, 79–80
impropriety of questioning decisionmaker as to mental processes, 85
legislative pressure, 81
necessity, 80
prejudgment of facts, 78–79
res judicata, 86–87
separation of functions (formal adjudication), 76–77
split-enforcement model, 75
stare decisis, 88

ADMINISTRATIVE LAW JUDGES
adjudicators for formal adjudication, 53
central panel alternative model, 78
statutory protections of independence, 77–78

ADMINISTRATIVE PROCEDURE ACT
  See also Adjudication—Formal, Adjudication—Informal, Adjudicative Integrity, Judicial Review (various), Rulemaking Procedures, Rules
overview of APA cause of action for judicial review, 171–73
overview of APA procedural template, 46–48
summary of APA requirements for formal adjudication, 50

AGENCY ACTION
See Judicial Review—Reviewability

ALTERNATIVE DISPUTE RESOLUTION
See Adjudication

APPOINTMENT POWER
congressional power (limits on), 15–16, 21
constitutional provision, 15
employees, 16
inferior officers, 16
officers of Congress, 15
officers of the United States, 15
recess appointments, 17

ARBITRARY, CAPRICIOUS, ABUSE OF DISCRETION
See Judicial Review—Scope

ASSOCIATIONAL STANDING
See Judicial Review—Standing

ATTORNEY'S FEES
Buckhannon limitation on fee-shifting, 141
Equal Access to Justice Act, 142
general rule of no fee-shifting, 141
FOIA, 133, 141
lodestar, 142
"prevailing parties" and statutory fee-shifting, 141

***AUER* DEFERENCE**
See Judicial Review—Scope

***BIVENS* ACTIONS**
See Judicial Review—Tort Liability of Government and Officials

***CHEVRON* DEFERENCE**
See Judicial Review—Scope

CONSTITUTIONAL STANDING
See Judicial Review—Standing

DECLARATORY ORDERS
See Adjudication

DELIBERATIVE PROCESS PRIVILEGE
See Obtaining Information

DUE PROCESS—ELEMENTS OF HEARING
balancing test (*Mathews*), 34–36
counsel, 38
ex parte contacts (due process limits), 84
findings and reasons, 38
impartiality, 37, 78–79
notice, 36–37
right to testify and confront, 37
state law remedies as sufficient due process, 39

DUE PROCESS—RIGHT TO A HEARING
adjudicative facts (determination of), 40
administrative summary judgment, 42
immaterial issues do not require hearing, 41
interests protected, 26–33
issues determined by agency rule, 41
liberty, 27–30
liberty, academic dismissals, 30
liberty, deprivation of constitutional rights, 28
liberty, prison, 28–29
liberty, stigma-plus, 27
Londoner/BiMetallic distinction, 39–40
"new" property, 30
property, 30–33
property, applications for benefits, 33
property, domestic violence restraining orders, 33
property, entitlement theory, 30
property, government employment, 31–32
property, licenses, 32
property, utilities, 32
rulemaking does not trigger right to hearing, 39–40
state action requirement, 42–43

DUE PROCESS—TIMING OF HEARING
balancing test (*Mathews*), 34
creditors' remedies, 36
government employment, 35
emergencies, 34
general rule—predeprivation, 33
licenses, 35
Social Security disability benefits, 34

ELEVENTH AMENDMENT
See Judicial Review—Sovereign Immunity

EQUAL ACCESS TO JUSTICE ACT
See Attorney's Fees

EXECUTIVE CONTROLS OVER ADMINISTRATIVE ACTION
appointment power, 15–17
centralized review of rulemaking, 20
cost-benefit analysis, 98
direction of agency heads by president, 20
Executive Order 12,866, pp. 20, 98
fiscal power, 19
inspectors general, 20
organizational power, 19
removal power, 18–19

EXHAUSTION
See Judicial Review—Timing

EX PARTE CONTACTS
See Adjudication—Formal, Adjudicative Integrity, Rulemaking Procedures

EX PARTE YOUNG
See Judicial Review—Sovereign Immunity

FEDERAL TORT CLAIMS ACT
See Judicial Review—Tort Liability of Government and Officials

FIFTH AMENDMENT
See Obtaining Information

FINALITY
See Judicial Review—Timing

FOURTH AMENDMENT
See Obtaining Information

FREEDOM OF INFORMATION ACT
See Obtaining Information

GOVERNMENT IN THE SUNSHINE ACT
See Obtaining Information

HARD LOOK REVIEW
See Judicial Review—Scope

IMMUNITIES
See Judicial Review—Tort Liability of Government and Officials, Judicial Review—Sovereign Immunity

INDEPENDENT AGENCIES
See Removal Power

INTERPRETIVE RULES
See Rules

ISSUE EXHAUSTION
See Judicial Review—Timing

JUDICIAL REVIEW—REVIEWABILITY
agency action as threshold requirement for review, 189–91
agency action, definition, 189–90
agency, definition, 189
commitment to agency discretion, 187–88
commitment to agency discretion, allocations of lump sums, 188–89
commitment to agency discretion, decisions not to enforce, 188
commitment to agency discretion, dismissal of intelligence officer, 188
commitment to agency discretion, "no law to apply," 187
failures to act, 190–91
presumption of reviewability, 185
statutory preclusion, 185–86
statutory preclusion, implied, 186–87
statutory preclusion, interpretation to avoid, 185–86

JUDICIAL REVIEW—SCOPE
APA scope-of-review provision, § 706, 145–46
arbitrariness review of discretion, 162–65
arbitrary, capricious, abuse of discretion, 162–65
Auer deference and interpretations of regulations, 159–60
Chevron deference, agency jurisdiction, 155
Chevron deference, generally, 150–57
Chevron deference, overview, 150
Chevron deference, stare decisis, interaction with, 155
Chevron deference, step 0 (*Mead* and *Barnhart*), 153–55
Chevron deference, step 1, 151–52
Chevron deference, step 2, 153
fact review, arbitrariness, 146, 166
fact review, constitutional or jurisdictional facts, 149–50
fact review, generally, 146–50
fact review, significance of agency—ALJ disagreement, 148–49
fact review, substantial evidence, 146–49
"hard look" review, 163
mixed questions—the *Hearst* framework, 160–62
petitions for rulemaking, review of, 106

post hoc rationalizations, 64, 163
reasoned decisionmaking, 163
remand without vacation, 105
Skidmore deference and statutory interpretations, 158
State Farm gloss on arbitrariness review, 163

JUDICIAL REVIEW—SOVEREIGN IMMUNITY
agency specific waivers, 177
APA waiver in § 702, 176
congressional power to abrogate state sovereign immunity, 177–78
Eleventh Amendment, overview, 177–78
Ex parte *Young*, 178
Federal Tort Claims Act, 176, 178–80
state governments, 180–81
strict construction of waivers, 176
Tucker Act, 176

JUDICIAL REVIEW—STANDING
associational standing, 200
constitutional standing, 196–204
constitutional standing, associational standing, 200
constitutional standing, injury, actual or imminent, 199
constitutional standing, injury—causation—redressability test, 196
constitutional standing, injury, concrete not abstract, 197
constitutional standing, injury, ideological, 197
constitutional standing, injury, particularized not generalized, 198
constitutional standing, injury, probabilistic, 199
constitutional standing, injury, procedural, 200
constitutional standing, injury requirement, 197–202
constitutional standing, injury, solicitude for states, 200
constitutional standing, injury, taxpayer standing, 201
constitutional standing, purpose, 196
prudential standing, 207–08
prudential standing, jus tertii, 207–08
prudential standing, third party standing, 207–08
statutory standing as cause of action, 204
statutory standing, § 702, 204–07
statutory standing, zone of interests, 205–07
taxpayer standing, 201
third party standing, 207–08

JUDICIAL REVIEW—TIMING
exhaustion, APA, § 704, 218–19
exhaustion, bias, 218
exhaustion, common law doctrine, 216–18
exhaustion, constitutional claims, 217
exhaustion, inadequate agency remedies, 217
exhaustion, purposes, 216
exhaustion, undue prejudice, 217
finality, 208–12
finality, APA, § 704, 209
finality, guidance documents, 210
finality, problem of unreasonable delay, 211–12
issue exhaustion, 219–20
primary jurisdiction, 221–22
ripeness, 212–15
ripeness, fitness for review, 213
ripeness, interaction with statutory time limits, 215
ripeness, hardship to parties, 213–14
ripeness, statutory preclusion of pre-enforcement review, 215
stays pending judicial review, 222–23
TRAC factors and unreasonable delay, 211–12
unreasonable delay, 211–12

JUDICIAL REVIEW—TORT LIABILITY OF GOVERNMENT AND OFFICIALS
absolute immunity, 181–83
Bivens actions, 183–84
common law torts and federal officials, 183
Federal Tort Claims Act, 176, 178–80
Federal Tort Claims Act, discretionary functions, 179

Federal Tort Claims Act, exclusion of constitutional torts, 180
Federal Tort Claims Act, expansion of official immunity, 180
qualified immunity, 183
section 1983, 180–81, 184
state governments, 180
Westfall Act, 180

JUDICIAL REVIEW—TYPES OF REVIEW AVAILABLE
Bivens actions, 183–84
general statutory review under the APA cause of action, 171–73
"nonstatutory" review, certiorari, 173
"nonstatutory" review, damages actions, 174
"nonstatutory" review, habeas corpus, 174
"nonstatutory" review, injunctive and declaratory relief, 173
"nonstatutory" review, mandamus, 173
review of rules during enforcement actions, 174
special statutory review, 171

LEGISLATIVE CONTROLS OVER ADMINISTRATIVE ACTION
appropriations, 21
committees, 21
Congressional Review Act, 22
investigations, 21
legislative veto (death of), 21
Senate confirmation of appointments, 21

LEGISLATIVE RULES
See Rules

LEGISLATIVE VETO
See Legislative Controls Over Administrative Action

LIBERTY
See Due Process—Right to a Hearing

***LONDONER/BIMETALLIC* DISTINCTION**
See Due Process—Right to a Hearing

MANDAMUS
See Judicial Review—Types of Review Available

***MATHEWS V. ELDRIDGE* BALANCING TEST**
See Due Process—Elements of Hearing, Due Process—Timing of Hearing

NEGOTIATED RULEMAKING ACT
See Rulemaking Procedures

NONDELEGATION DOCTRINE (JUDICIAL POWER)
adjunct theory, 14
criminal sanctions, 14
public/private rights distinction, 12
Schor framework, 11–13

NONDELEGATION DOCTRINE (LEGISLATIVE POWER)
canon of constitutional avoidance, 9–10
delegations to private parties, 9
early cases, 4
intelligible principles, 5
NIRA cases—*Schecter Poultry* and *Panama Refining*, 5–6
Whitman, 7–8

NOTICE-AND-COMMENT
See Rulemaking Procedures

POLICY STATEMENTS
See Rules

PRIMARY JURISDICTION
See Judicial Review—Timing

PROCEDURAL RULES
See Rules

PROPERTY
See Due Process—Right to a Hearing

PRUDENTIAL STANDING
See Judicial Review—Standing

OBTAINING INFORMATION
APA provisions on gathering information, 123
attorney-client privilege, 127
Fifth amendment limitations, 126–27
Fourth amendment limitations, 123–24
Freedom of Information Act, agencies covered, 129
Freedom of Information Act, "agency records," 130–32
Freedom of Information Act, attorney's fees, 133
Freedom of Information Act, deliberative process privilege, 135
Freedom of Information Act, exemption 5, inter/intra-agency memos, 135–36
Freedom of Information Act, exemptions, 133–39
Freedom of Information Act, generally, 129–40
Freedom of Information Act, procedures, 132–33
Freedom of Information Act, publication requirements, 129
Freedom of Information Act, records available for public inspection, 130
Freedom of Information Act, *Vaughn* index, 133
Government in the Sunshine Act, 140
home inspections, 124
physical inspections, 124–26
subpoena power, 123–24
use of information from unlawful searches, 128
warrantless inspections of pervasively regulated businesses, 125–26
warrants, 125

QUALIFIED IMMUNITIES
See Judicial Review—Tort Liability of Government and Officials

REASONED DECISIONMAKING
See Judicial Review—Scope

RECORD REQUIREMENTS
See Adjudication—Formal, Rulemaking Procedures

REMOVAL POWER
double good cause limits on removal (*Free Enterprise*), 19
good cause limits on removal, 18–19
independent agencies, 18
quasi-adjudicative/quasi-legislative (*Humphrey's Executor*), 18
undue interference test (*Morrison*), 18
unitary executive, 18

RES JUDICATA
See Adjudicative Integrity

RETROACTIVITY
See Adjudication, Rules

REVIEWABILITY
See Judicial Review—Reviewability

REVIEW OF AGENCY ACTION
See Judicial Review (various)

RIPENESS
See Judicial Review—Timing

RULEMAKING PROCEDURES
APA—informal versus formal rulemaking, 96
agency enabling acts as source of procedure, 96
bias, 117–18
comments, 103
congressional pressure, 117
cost-benefit analysis, 98
direct final rules, 110
electronic rulemaking, 103
exceptions to notice-and-comment requirements, 109–15
Executive Order 12,866, pp. 20, 98
ex parte contacts and formal rulemaking (APA, § 557), 82–83, 116
ex parte contacts and informal rulemaking, 116
formal rulemaking, 96, 109
generally applicable statutes other than APA as source of procedure, 96
good cause exception to notice-and-comment, 110–11
impartiality of rulemakers, 116–18
interim—final rules, 111
Negotiated Rulemaking Act, 106–07
notice-and-comment, 102–06
notice of proposed rulemaking, 102
notice, duty to disclose data, 102
petitions for rulemaking, 105
post hoc rationalizations, 64, 104
presidential influence, 20, 98, 117
procedural rules, 109–10
publication requirement, 104–05
record requirement, formal rulemaking, 118–19
record requirement, informal rulemaking, 118–19
revisions to proposed rules—logical outgrowth limit, 103
statement of basis and purpose, 104
statement of basis and purpose, duty to respond to comments, 104
statement of basis and purpose, bar on post hoc rationalizations, 64, 104
Vermont Yankee principle, 98, 102, 106

RULES
See also Rulemaking Procedures
advantages for policymaking, 98
characteristics of rules, 93
constitutional distinction between rulemaking and adjudication, 39–40, 95
definition of "rule" under APA, 93
direct final rules, 110
distinguishing interpretive from legislative rules, 112–13
distinguishing policy statements from legislative rules, 114–15
interpretive rules, 111–12
interim—final rules, 111
legislative/nonlegislative distinction, 99–101
legislative rules, 100
legislative rules (broad construction of rulemaking authority), 100
non-legislative rules (types), 100
policy statements, 114–15
procedural rules, 100, 109–10
retroactivity, 98

SEARCH AND SEIZURE
See Obtaining Information

SCHECHTER POULTRY
See Nondelegation Doctrine (Legislative Power)

***SCHOR* FRAMEWORK**
See Nondelegation Doctrine (Judicial Power)

SECTION 1983
See Judicial Review—Tort Liability of Government and Officials

SEPARATION OF FUNCTIONS
See Adjudicative Integrity

SEPARATION OF POWERS
formalism versus functionalism, 3
in general, 3

SOVEREIGN IMMUNITY
See Judicial Review—Sovereign Immunity

STANDING
See Judicial Review—Standing

STARE DECISIS
See Adjudicative Integrity, Judicial Review—Scope
    (*Chevron* deference)

STATE ACTION
    See also Due Process—Right to a Hearing
distinguishing state and non-state action, 42–43
requirement for triggering due process, 42

STATUTORY STANDING
See Judicial Review—Standing

STAYS PENDING JUDICIAL REVIEW
See Judicial Review—Timing

SUBPOENA POWER
See Obtaining Information

SUBSTANTIAL EVIDENCE REVIEW
See Judicial Review—Scope

TAXPAYER STANDING
See Judicial Review—Standing

THIRD PARTY STANDING
See Judicial Review—Standing

UNITARY EXECUTIVE
See Removal Power

***VERMONT YANKEE* PRINCIPLE**
See Rulemaking Procedures

ZONE OF INTERESTS
See Judicial Review—Standing